STENA

A GROUP FLEET HISTORY

W. J. Harvey

http://worldshipsociety.org

Other Titles by the same author: -

GLEN AND SHIRE LINES **In association with Malcolm Cooper and William Laxon.**
The history of the London based Glen & Shire Lines, having their origins in Scotland and Wales.
(Published by Ships In Focus Publications, Longton, 2005 – ISBN 1 - 901703 – 65 - 7)

BP TANKERS: A Group Fleet History. **In association with Dr. Ray Solly.**
A profusely illustrated history of this multi-faceted fleet of over 1,000 vessels, be they owned outright, or through subsidiary or associate companies. The work also details the development of the tanker in parallel with the growth of the group since its inception as the Anglo-Persian Oil Company.
(Published by Chatham Publishing Ltd., London, 2005 - ISBN 1 – 86176 – 251 - 6)

JEBSENS - A Group History.
The history of Norway's Kristian Jebsen Rederi AS, (KJR), and their multi-national group of companies.
(Published by The World Ship Society Ltd., Windsor, 2005 - ISBN 0 - 9543310 - 6 - 0)

ARKLOW SHIPPING
A profusely colour-illustrated fleet history of the ever-expanding, Arklow based shipping group, from 1966, including their formative companies and now also, a Netherlands based subsidiary.
(Published by Bernard McCall, Portishead, 2004 - ISBN 1-902953-15-0)

SHAMROCK SHIPPING – Incorporating the David Dorman Group.
The history of these Irish based companys from 1888 and 1863 respectively through unification to today's much diminished shipping activity.
(Published by The World Ship Society Ltd., Windsor, 2004 - ISBN 0 9543310 - 3 - 6)

SAFMARINE - The South African Marine Corporation Ltd – A Group History.
In association with C. R. Mackenzie.
The history of the Cape Town based company from 1946 until its 1999 break up and sale.
(Published by The World Ship Society, Gravesend, 2002 - ISBN 0 905617-98-3)

THE CLYDE SHIPPING COMPANY. **In association with P. J. Telford.**
The history of the Glasgow based Company from 1815 until its 2000 acquisition by Cory Towage Ltd.
(Published by P. J. Telford, Canterbury, 2002 - ISBN 0 9542527-0-5)

CORY TOWAGE LTD – A Group History
The history of the company and their owned, managed, and chartered vessels, together with the fleets of their subsidiary and associated companies.
(Published by The World Ship Society, Gravesend, 2000 - ISBN 0 905617-93-2)

SHIPS IN FOCUS – BLUE FUNNEL LINE **In association with John Clarkson and Roy Fenton.**
A pictorial fleet history of the Liverpool based shipping group.
(Published by Ships in Focus Publications, Longton, 1998 - ISBN 1 901703-00-2)

HADLEY
The history of the Hadley Shipping Company Ltd., and their associate companies.
(Published by The World Ship Society, Gravesend, 1997 - ISBN 0 905617-83-5)

HEAD LINE (G. Heyn & Sons Ltd.)
The history of the Ulster Steamship Company Ltd., and their associate companies.
(Published by The World Ship Society, Kendal, 1990 - ISBN 0 905617-53-3)

STENA (1939 – 1989)
The first fifty years of the Swedish controlled multi-national shipping and trading group.
(Published by Stena Ab, Gothenburg, 1990 - ISBN 91 85786-411)

EMPIRE TUGS **In association with Ken Turrell.**
The history of the EMPIRE prefixed, British Government tugs, introduced during World War 2.
(Published by The World Ship Society, Kendal, 1988 - ISBN 0 905617-47-9)

Contents

Published in the United Kingdom by The World Ship Society Ltd, Mayes House, Vansittart Estate, Arthur Road, Windsor. SL4 1SE.

ISBN 0 – 9543310 – 7 - 9

Printed by The Amadeus Press, Ezra House, West 26 Business Park, Cleckheaton, BD19 4TQ.

The World Ship Society Ltd.

What is now known as the World Ship Society Ltd., was originally the "brain child" of Michael Crowdy, and was brought about more or less by chance.

In 1946, Michael was corresponding with various people interested in ships, and as the number of correspondents grew, it became necessary to duplicate the information he received in order to circulate it. As young as he was, Michael realized the potential existing for an organization such as the Ship News Club and with a great deal of encouragement and some financial support from his father, Michael launched the Ship News Club.

His first publications in early 1947 were duplicated sheets containing news of ships, merchant and naval, whose names began with the letters A-L, followed a couple of months later with further lists containing the M-Z ships, thus sowing the seed for today's monthly Society journal "Marine News".

As news of the organization spread, membership increased - 50 in January 1947, 200 by December and 330 by July 1948. The first Annual General Meeting of the Ship News Club was held in London in 1949 and a decision was taken to rename the organization as The World Ship Society, and since then a steady growth has taken place and a healthy archive of specialist reference material, including one of the largest collections of Lloyd's Registers, is now held by volunteer custodians to answer member queries. Also from one of the world's largest collections of ship photographs, negatives and slides, monthly photograph offers are made in Marine News.

All the tasks carried out within the organization since its formation, have been at the hands of volunteers from the within the membership. There are no full-time, paid staff, and only since recent incorporation as a Limited liability concern, has there been a registered office.

Apart from boasting some 4,000 members, and many local branches worldwide, the Society prides itself on the knowledge and enthusiasm of its members, and their willingness to help others in their interest in shipping. In the 1950's, with the production of early versions of fleet histories, the chrysalis was formed for what is now a prolific list of publications produced over the years by the Society on behalf of member authors. Those books, renowned for their high quality, authoritative and comprehensive content, cover primarily shipping company histories, but in parallel also cover naval topics such as classes of warship, war subjects such as convoys, invasion fleets etc to name but a few.

For an annual subscription, you can become a member of this highly respected organization and obtain access to all the facilities available, including discounts of our publications, and receive our 64-page monthly journal Marine News that contains a wealth of information on naval vessels, maritime events, ships sales, transfers and renamings, casualties, demolitions and new vessels, together with features, and many photograph offers. If you are interested in becoming a member of this worldwide family, and would like further information, please visit our website **http://worldshipsociety.org**; or send either a stamped addressed envelope (UK only), or two International Reply Coupons (outside UK) to:

The Honorary General Secretary, The World Ship Society Ltd., 101, The Everglades, Dukes Meadow Drive, HEMPSTEAD, GILLINGHAM, Kent ME7 3PZ UK.

Foreword

In 1989 Stena became involved with the Society through collaboration to produce a book to commemorate their first fifty years of trading. That original work was published by the Company in 1990, and was much in their own style.

Since that time the Stena Group has prospered and grown to much more than could have been envisaged at that time.

As a result of that growth, the company representative, with whom I had worked on the earlier book, approached both the Society and myself as author during the summer of 2005. The question was simple. "Is there any possibility of producing an updated version of the earlier work to better reflect the current company operations, and to also coincide with our achieving sixty years in ship owning"?

Fortunately I had been keeping fairly much abreast of the fleet changes, so the task was not too arduous. Following discussions with all the relevant parties, it was agreed that this edition would be produced and published by the Society, in keeping with their house style, and be on behalf of the company.

W. J. Harvey

Company Overview

STEN ALLAN OLSSON
(Courtesy Stena Ab.)

1939

During September, overshadowed by the opening hostilities of the Second World War, Sten Allan Olsson established a trading company, and in doing so laid the foundations for today's extensive field of operations. The primary areas of operation for his enterprise were metals and materials recovery in the engineering industry, an area still greatly served by the present organisation.

1941

Maskinaffaren Generator Ab., a manufacturer of high pressure and hot water boilers, acquired.

During the remainder of Second World War, with Sweden remaining neutral, the company did little in the way of expansion, concentrating on consolidating its market position and reputation. Following the ravages of war most countries were trying to re-establish their transport networks that had fallen victim to the war machine. With road and rail communications in disarray there was a strong reliance on sea transport for the movement of materials.

1946

Sten Olsson took a step, which on retrospect neither he nor his family have ever regretted. That was his entry into the cargo ship owning fraternity, embarking along the same path as his father, Gustaf Olsson, who had purchased his first ship as far back as 1903.

(For dry-cargo operations and that fleet - see Part One)

1951

Sten A. Olsson Metallprodukter was founded.

1953

Sten A. Olsson Handels Ab., created as the controlling body for the shipping activity, either through direct ownership, or by management of vessels owned elsewhere in the group.

1954

Sten A. Olsson Handels Ab., placed orders for the first new cargo vessels to be constructed for the company.

1955

Sten A. Olsson Handels Ab., purchased a small oil-bunkering tank-barge and in doing so created another facet to their business. The tanker activity was temporarily halted upon sale of the vessel in 1960.

(For tanker operations and that fleet - see Part Two)

1962

Skagenlinjen Ab., the remnants of this failed concern were acquired to operate passenger services from Gothenburg.

(For passenger and RoRo operations and that fleet - see Part Three)

1963

Stena Ab, created as part of a restructuring of the company. With the new name style also came a new funnel design. It was a black funnel with a broad red band, separated by a narrow white band, top and bottom. On the red band is a large "S" the tail of which carries a small ship poised on a wave, in a head on view. At this time, with few exceptions, their ship hulls became painted in white with the company logo on their prow.

1964

Rederi Ab. Concordia was acquired from other Swedish owners, together with three small coastal tankers. This acquisition was to give further brief experience of tanker operations, all three vessels being quickly sold.

1965

Skagenlinjen Ab., was rebranded as ***Stena Line Ab***., and with the introduction of RoRo car ferries, **STENA** was introduced as a prefix name. That prefix has since become almost a household name in the shipping fraternity. The formation of the prefix is fairly self-explanatory, in so much that it is the first name, and second initial of the founding owner, **STEN A.** Olsson.

1966

STENA NORDICA was chartered-out to British operators. This was the first such charter undertaken and set the template for a future successful area of operations for the company.

1970

Two of four freight ferries under construction were taken on external charter and two were subsequently purchased by their charterer.

(For freight ferry operations and that fleet - see Part Three)

1972

A major restructuring of the company saw a three way split. From that division emerged,
Stena Line Ab., to control the shipping operations.
Stena Metall Ab., to look after the metals recovery activities.
Rederi Ab., Concordia to act as the parent company.
The three divisions were effectively, metals, shipping and passengers.

1975

Northern Coasters Ltd., London, created.

1976

An opportune purchase saw the company enter into the lucrative and expanding support business for the offshore oil industry.

(For offshore operations and that fleet – see Part Four)

1978

Greek company, ***Soutos - Hellas Ferry Services***, commenced operations between Volos in Greece, and Lattakia in Syria, on 2 November, offering seven round trips per month. For this service STENA NORDICA was chartered and renamed HELLAS. The object of the operation was to offer long distance European lorry drivers a safer alternative to driving through Turkey. Subsequently as this service became stronger, Stena bought into the company through two sources, ***Polyzena Maritime Company Ltd.,*** and ***Capulet Navigation Company Ltd.,*** their Cypriot based subsidiary owners of SYRIA and HELLAS - employed on the route during 1981. Those vessels were members of the Korean built series and were firstly jumboised at Bremerhaven, returning later to be lengthened to meet increased traffic demands on the route.

The group continued to expand and to further diversify, with the purchase of 50% of the share capital in ***Yngve Kullenberg Byggnads Ab.,*** and 100% of ***Plm Atervinning Ab.,*** by the Metals division.

Rederi Ab Concordia created the new subsidiaries - ***Stena Shipping Line; Stena Atlantic Line Ltd; Stena Container Line Ltd.,*** and ***Stena Cargo Line Ltd***.

In the financial year 1978/1979, the turnover of the group exceeded S.kr.1 billion for the first time.

1979

Northern Cold Storage (Transport) Ltd., created to own a newly acquired gas tanker.
Stena Caribbean Line created.

1980

Rederi Ab., Goteborg - Frederikshavn Linjen, (Sessan Line), hitherto associated with Tor Line Ab., henceforth decided to charter all of their ships to Stena. In connection with this Stena assumed responsibility for the greater part of the personnel, both ashore and afloat. The agreement, which involved and exchange of shares, was regarded by some as an unwritten take over by Stena, and by others as a merger of companies but either way, as an essential pre-requisite to enable the ferry business to continue with satisfactory earnings. From the pooling agreement emerged ***Stena - Sessan Line Ab***.

Stena Ab entered the real estate business when ***J. Alfred Olsson & Soner Byggnads Ab***., was purchased and renamed ***Stena Fastighets-furvalting Ab.,*** which in turn, bought shares in other minor companies in that business.

Rederi Ab., Concordia, created further new multi-national subsidiaries:
Snowdrop Shipping Ltd; Stena Ocean Line Ltd.; Stena Fastighets Ab; Fastighets Ab., Josephina: Stena Freight Ab.; Stena Shipping Ab.; Stena Atlas Line Ltd.; Stena RoRo Line Ltd.; Stena Gulf Line Ltd.; Stena Caribbean Line Ltd.; Stena (UK) Ltd.; Placida Maritime Inc, and ***Pacific Offshore Services Ltd.,***

Stena Metall Ab., ceased ship breaking at their Gothenburg yard.

1981

The Metal division saw many changes through restyling of company titles and the purchase of further subsidiaries.
Stena Metal Ltd., was restyled as ***Park Sea Metal Ltd***.,
Stena Metal, Stockholm Ab., was restyled as ***Stena Altervinning Ab***.
Bennoferrum Ab., was purchased and restyled as ***Stena Kemi Ab.,***
Ing. Gunnar Nilsson Ab., was purchased and restyled as ***Stena Metal Oster - Gotland Ab.***
Stena Stal was restyled as ***Stena Pulp Ab***.

Rederi Ab., Concordia *created the subsidiaries* ***Stena Finance (Holland) BV.; Nautica (Belgium) NV.; Marine Management Ltd.;*** and ***Contrast Maritime Inc.***

Stena Line Ab., created the subsidiaries ***Varberg - Grenaa Linjen Ab.; Polyzena Maritime Company Ltd.,*** and ***Capulet Navigation Company Ltd***.

At the outbreak of hostilities between Britain and Argentina over the Falkland Islands, Stena vessels featured prominently in the support role being both chartered and requisitioned by the British Government. The vessels concerned were STENA SEASPREAD and STENA INSPECTOR chartered as heavy forward repair ships, the latter being transferred to the British registry and ELK: BALTIC FERRY and NORDIC FERRY, requisitioned as transport vessels. HELLAS and SYRIA were transferred from the Mediterranean to replace BALTIC FERRY and NORDIC FERRY.

1982

Brought another major restructuring of the group.
Stena Line Ab. was restyled as ***Stena Ab***. and henceforth assumed the role of parent company.
Stena - Sessan Linjen Ab., *was* restyled as ***Stena Line Ab***.,
Stena Pulp Ab., was restyled, as ***Stena Returpapper Ab***.
Industriavfall I Sundsvall was purchased and restyled as ***Stena Metall Handellstal Ab.***

Rederi Ab. Concordia was also reorganising and incorporated yet more subsidiaries - ***Stena Diagnostics Ab.; Stena Ferry Ab., Vikon Enterprises Ltd., Stena Challenger Ltd., Stena Tank Ab,*** and ***Stena Cervin Ab.***

Stena Ab., now acting as parent company also produced their share of new companies - ***Stena Holdings (UK) Ltd.; Stena Oceanics Ltd.,*** *and* ***Stena Subsea. Stena Bulk Ab.,*** was also created to co-ordinate the tanker and bulk dry cargo businesses.

1983

Stena Ab., *acquired the ailing* ***Lion Ferry Ab***., together with their one remaining ship, EUROPAFARJAN III.

Rederi Ab. Concordia, *with planned expansion into the bulk and oil markets,* set about further reorganization. *They created the subsidiaries -* ***Ewan Enterprises Ltd.; Fernwood Inc.; Hellas Ferries Company Ltd S. A., Samos Pearl Shipping Company Ltd.; Seaburg Inc.; Seafarer Maritime,*** and ***Concordia Maritime Ab.***
The newly created, and publicly listed ***Concordia Maritime Ab.,*** in turn, created numerous subsidiaries - ***Adriatic Line Ltd., Evelyn Ltd., Freeburg Inc., Frostburg Inc., Newburg Inc., Oldburg Inc.,*** and ***Tanker Finance Ltd.***

Stena Ab., created ***Sessanlinjen Denmark AS., Stena Portlink Ab., Stena Invest Ab.,*** and ***Stena Drilling Ab***., *and so it continued.*

The group began investing, either as part or sole owner, in all sizes of oil and chemical tankers and bulk carriers. Subsequently, several ship management companies were created in conjunction with other parties: ***Swedish Caledonian Marine Management: Three Crowns Marine Management: Northern Marine Management Ltd.,*** and ***Northern Marine Management (Cyprus) Ltd.***

The group further diversified when it acquired a small mail - order business and also entered the pharmaceutical business through the activities of ***Stena Diagnostics Ab.,*** undertaking research chemistry activities.

1984

Stena Portlink Ltd., was created to operate the newly inaugurated, UK end, of PORTLINK operations to Felixstowe, with calls at Immingham, on Humberside, as and when required.

STENA GRECIA
One of the vessels on the PORTLINK service

(Internet source)

Stena Ferries Ltd., was the second new company to be founded by ***Stena Holdings (UK) Ltd.***

1985

Arctic Line was created to own the bulk carrier STENA ARCTICA that was to undertake a charter as mothership for a Swedish scientific exploration.

1986

Having become apparent to many ship-owners, including Stena, that it was a much better proposition to lease vessels than to own them, Stena commenced to lease in a small way.

Stena Bulk Ab, and ***Texaco Inc,*** commenced a long-term partnership agreement with VLCC's

1987

On 1 July Stena Portlink acquired ***Danish Container Line*** *and 51% of* ***Marina Shipping Short Sea AS***., (including ***Marina Short Sea Shipping***, Hull). Coupled with these purchases, a new service was inaugurated between Hull – Esjberg whilst rationalisation of other Portlink schedules between Felixstowe and Esjberg was undertaken to allow greater flexibility, regarding the fleet.

A new innovation in ship management was initiated by the group when ***Liro Shipping Ab.,*** was appointed as managers of STENA GOTHICA. This new company consisted of two Captains and two Engineers employed by Stena. The company name LIRO is simply the first letter of all four first Christian name:- **L**ars Winck, (Capt.); **I**ngemaar Fallgren, (Capt.); **R**olf Littorin, (Eng.); and **O**lle Davidsson, (Eng.). They set themselves up with a small office ashore to handle the documentation etc., but the day-to-day management of the ship was carried out on board. This proved in itself, a more effective method of controlling costs, with the managers on board able to see were economies could be made and repairs undertaken, were necessary. The fact that all were experienced seafarers, as opposed to land based managers, also enhanced the overall performance.

A contract was signed with Blohm & Voss of Hamburg on 25 August, for the conversion of STENA SHIPPER into a 1,600 passenger ferry with 174 cabins, some for handicapped people. The vessel arrived at their yard on 4 September and work commenced. This was to cost DM 40,000,000 and was to be completed by the end of December. Upon completion of this work the vessel was to be demise chartered to Nordstrom & Thulin Ab., Stockholm, and was initially renamed N & T 700, but this was later altered to GRAIP, when the charterers purchased the vessel.

In the autumn, it was decided that ***Stena Line Ab*** would be entered on the Stockholm Stock Exchange O-List. This was undertaken in the spring of 1988 and provided approximately 16,500 shares for sale. With this transaction came a vast reshuffle within the fleet as vessels were sold or chartered by ***Stena Ab,*** to ***Stena Line Ab*** together with control of ***Lion Ferry Ab***.

1988

Having suffered continued delays at the shipyard since the placing of the order, coupled with the changes in the ferry market, the contract for the third of the ill-fated Polish ships, which had been launched, without a name or ceremony on the 28th October 1984, was sold for a reported $13 million to the London based Oceanic Finance Company for chartering to the Fred Olsen Group, Norway. It had been reported that the third and fourth ships of the series would be named STENA BALTICA and STENA POLONICA.

The cancelled STENA BALTICA (5) seen as BONANZA under tow enroute to Greece for completion.
(Hans Mornhout collection)

The Olsen purchase was to have been completed in Germany by Bremer Vulcan. To be named BONANZA, she was destined for use on their Kristiansand - Hirtshals, (Norway - Denmark) service. She was however, subsequently resold in her incomplete state, to Greek interests in Crete, for $15 million and was towed to Greece, with the name

BONANZA in blue, on the unpainted hull, and completed as a car ferry. The Olsen Group were reported to have made an undisclosed payment for the termination of the charter from the financiers but still to have made $1 million profit on the deal.
The fourth hull was also sold to Greek based operators for lengthening and completion as a cruise liner and was towed to Greece for the work to be undertaken, something that has yet to be achieved since the bankruptcy of the owners.

Stena Line Ab, was the successful contender from the 25 bidders for the purchase of the two ships and business interests of ***British Colombia Steamship Co.,*** Canada. Following the success a new company was formed as ***BC Stena Line Ltd.***

Stena Ab, during November, successfully purchased ***BUE Services***, including ***BUE Subsea Ltd.,*** and ***Subsea Surveys Ltd.,*** London. Their fleet of mainly chartered vessels was reportedly not included in the transaction.

1989

During the opening months the ***Stena Group*** acquired an 8% holding in ***Sea Containers International***, on the New York Stock Exchange. Sea Containers specialised in the bareboat and container chartering market and were the parent company for ***Sealink British Ferries Ltd.*** To strengthen the bid, Stena were joined by ***Tiphook*** the container chartering specialists. With the joint bid it was hoped that a successful acquisition of the shipping sector of Sea Containers that included Sealink British Ferries Ltd., could be achieved and taken into the Stena household, whilst the container fleet and business would be taken over by Tiphook. Within Sea Containers assets were several British ports that had been sold to James Sherwood by the British Government as part of the privatisation of Sealink. This would then give Stena several bases within the U.K. to start expanding the Sealink operations. The revised offer was submitted toward the end of 1989 and whilst under consideration by the Sea Containers shareholders, James Sherwood was hastily reshuffling finances to stave off the bid that was considered to be attractive enough to the shareholders.

A $4.7m profit was returned on the sale of STENA ARCTICA that had been employed with a Swedish scientific expedition in Antarctica.

Stena Ab., from the Netherlands Government, acquired Stoomvaart Maatschappij Zeeland. The Government referred to this line as Crown Line pending their disposal, indeed the logo was painted on the ship sides. With the company came one ship KONINGIN BEATRIX employed on their Harwich - Hook of Holland service, in conjunction with Sealink British Ferries. She operated opposite Sealink's ST. NICHOLAS, a vessel chartered from STENA until purchased by her charterers. Within a few months of acquiring Crown Line the KONINGIN BEATRIX was fully transformed into Stena livery and the required 18-months notice of intent issued to Sealink wherein it stated that when the notice period had elapsed, Stena would no longer operate within the pooling arrangements.

Houlder Offshore Ltd., was purchased for £12m., when offered by their parent, the C. Y. Tung organisation of Hong Kong.

1990

Negotiations had continued for control of the ***Sea Containers International Group*** until 14 January 1990, when it was announced that the acquisition of the Sherwood "Empire" would be concluded after due diligence. However, during the prolonged negotiations, Sea Containers had disposed of several Sealink vessels, either to other operators or to Leasing Companies on charter-back agreements in an attempt to revalue the Sea Container Group and keep it out of Stena hands. Amongst the vessels taken over within the Sealink operations were some of the vessels that Stena had sold to Sealink and to other owners over the years. Control was handed to ***Stena Ab*** on 31 May 1990. Written into the terms of sale was a clause requiring the retention of the Sealink brand name, funnel markings and hull colours for five years. Shortly after acquisition Sealink was transferred to ***Stena Line Ab,*** who in turn restyled the operation as ***Sealink Stena Line Ltd***., and subsequently ***Stena Sealink Line Ltd.*** Gradually the "Scandinavian concept" was introduced with plans drawn up for re-location of tonnage to better suit the needs of the various routes.

Supplementing the above transaction the company also acquired a percentage holding in some of the vessels operated by the French partners in the Sealink operation. Subsequently that involvement was to provide Stena with a small financial involvement in ***Seafrance S.A.,*** upon its creation.

1994

Stena Group provided the initial two vessels on demise charter to the new Turkish ferry operator ***Und RoRo Isletereli A.S.,*** and also further assisted with the acquisition of other vessels for their fleet.

1995

Coflexip Stena Offshore Services Ltd., created as a result of a merger with the French ***Comex S.A.***

StenTex Management (50:50 Stena and Texaco) created to operate and manage the fleets of both partners. ***Stena Tanker Management (Bermuda) Ltd***. also created

The funnel colours for the entire Stena Group fleet was amended slightly with the black top and base being changed to blue. The house flag also underwent change. A thin blue band was added to the top and bottom outer edge in similar proportion to the existing white band and the ship was removed from the tail of the "S", although it remains in place, both on the funnels and bow crest. However the wave that intertwined the "S" was removed. The scroll-lines were also removed from either side of the bow crest on the ferries, leaving the crest to stand-alone. (See rear cover)

The freight-only RoRo-ferries henceforth all had blue hulls with a white Stena Line logo on the side.

1996

Stena Sealink Line Ltd., restyled ***Stena Line Ltd.***, on 1 January, at the end of the statutory five-years retention of the SEALINK trading name, and henceforth adopted the full amended Stena Line livery of white hulls with a red line low down just above the blue boot topping. A Stena Line logo was introduced in blue, being positioned low on the hull about one third of the ship's length from the bow. Normally this is above the red line but some vessels have been seen with the logo breaking the line.

Universe Tankships (Delaware) L. L. C. (including subsidiary companies), was acquired by ***Concordia Maritime Ab***, in November. Around that time also, the tanker fleet all had a yellow, blue, yellow stripe arrangement (Swedish national colours) painted forward on their hulls, aft of name, running from main deck diagonal (about 45 degrees) aft, down to waterline. On some later vessels this appeared more of a pennant style rather then straight line.

Joint venture established with ***Ugland*** for the development of shuttle-tanker business.

The Atlantic Drilling co-operation with Ben Line Steamers of Leith was acquired together with the rig OCEAN BENLOYAL (now STENA DEE)

1997

Sweferry Ab acquired by ***Stena Ab.*** and restyled as ***Scandlines Ab.***

1998

Lion Ferries Ab, closed.

P&O Stena Line Ltd., created 60:40 with P & O Ferries Ltd., for English Channel services.
P&O Stena Line Ship Management Ltd., also created.

2000

Stena sold its shareholding in SEAFRANCE RENOIR and SEAFRANCE CEZANNE to Seafrance S.A., thus terminating involvement in that organisation.

Orders placed in China, Poland, Croatia and Korea for new tankers, and ferries.

Coflexip Stena Offshore Services Ltd., agreed in October, the acquisition of the Houston based Deepwater Division of Aker Maritime ASA, for \$513m and debt liability of \$112m equating to a 30% equity shareholding.

2001

Coflexip purchased the outstanding shareholding in ***Coflexip Stena Offshore Services Ltd.***, from Stena, and restyled as ***Technip Offshore Ltd.***.

Stena retained the fleet of drilling rigs and created ***Stena Drilling Ltd.***

StenTex taken over fully by Stena Bulk and their activities fully integrated into the latter.

Stena Line Ab, was taken 100% out of the Swedish Stock Exchange and returned to private ownership.

2002

P&O Stena Line Ltd., was dissolved with P&O acquiring Stena's 40% interest for £150 million. As part of the severance-package Stena acquired three of their former vessels (of the eleven late - 1970's built Korean sisters) that had been leased then sold to P&O for their Felixstowe service operated by North Sea Ferries. The Dover based vessels passed fully to P&O together with the Stena interests on the routes, excepting AQUITAINE, which was henceforth taken on charter.

StenOak was created 50:50 by Stena Bulk, utilizing the services of Gothenburg Chartering, and Hong Kong based Oak Bulk Carriers, to explore the Panamax dry-bulk markets by operating initially, YONG JIA (74,823dwt/2001) on charter until October 2005. She was replaced and supplemented by further vessels.

2003

Stena Line as a result of speed restrictions imposed on their HSS vessel at the extreme ends of the route, had formulated plans for the development a new port facility to seaward of Cairnryan. New berths and larger ships were planned with Stena relocating their Scottish terminal seaward from Stranraer. However, unforeseen events initially changed that plan. A "Memo Of Understanding" was agreed 50:50 with ***P&O (Irish Sea) Ltd.*** to develop Cairnryan, P&O's Scottish terminal at the mouth of Loch Ryan.

Within the deal P&O also agreed the sale to Stena of their Irish Sea services Larne – Fleetwood and Dublin – Liverpool including 6 vessels, EUROPEAN ENVOY, EUROPEAN LEADER, EUROPEAN PIONEER, EUROPEAN SEAFARER, NORBANK and NORBRAE, and the ports assets at Dublin, Fleetwood and Liverpool. The port of Larne was also included but the transaction was referred to the UK Competition Commission. That aside there were local residents raising objections against the planned development of the port at Cairnryan on, among others, environmental issues, and the plan was deferred for consultative review.

2004

The Competition Commission after deliberation agreed to only part transfer. In the end Stena acquired for 70.8 million Euros, Larne – Fleetwood and the port assets at Fleetwood and Larne. P&O retained the Dublin – Liverpool route, NORBANK, NORBRAE and facilities but closed their Mostyn service with both surplus vessels - EUROPEAN ENVOY and EUROPEAN AMBASSADOR being acquired by Stena, the latter being transferred to the Sweden-Poland route and renamed STENA NORDICA. The former EUROPEAN ENVOY, renamed ENVOY was quickly resold. The Cairnryan Port joint development remained stalled pending fuller assessment. Objectors argued that the port itself would not easily lend to construction of any additional berths. Stena Line meanwhile retained the option reverting to their original plan of developing a new port facility to seaward of Cairnryan.

Concordia Maritime Ab, (now only 52% Stena owned), and Stena Bulk, jointly created ***Arlington Tankers Ltd.,*** a Bermuda based concern that was successfully launched (14 times oversubscribed), onto the New York Stock Exchange during November. The new operation acquired six vessels from the parents together with a charter-back agreement. Following the shares offering Concordia Maritime retained 10% and Stena Bulk 5% in the new concern.

2005

PRIDE OF AQUITAINE was released from charter during the summer by P&O as part of their further rationalization of ferry routes. Part of that reformation saw their Portsmouth – Le Havre service scrapped with both vessels sent to the River Fal for lay-up. Meanwhile, French shipping group Louis Dreyfus et Cie. had stepped in and arranged the charter of PRIDE OF AQUITAINE which was sent to Dunkirk for overhaul and emerged as NORMAN SPIRIT to re-instate the service under the auspices of LD Lines from September / October. Louis Dreyfus however negotiated the outright purchase of the vessel upon completion of her overhaul.

Planning permission for the joint development of the Port of Cairnryan was, at the end of the year, finally given the green light by the Authorities, following the acceptance of recommendations within the consultative report. At the time of writing it was estimated that the development could be completed as early as 2007.

Fleet Notes.

Charter Types As Defined By The Company.

Basic Charter

Wherein the vessel remains in owner's colours and name for the duration and during which the owner is responsible for the day-to-day maintenance.

Bareboat Charter

Wherein the vessel is given the charterer's colours and choice of name, but remains registered under the owner's name. The charterer is responsible for day-to-day maintenance.

Demise Charter

Wherein the ship is registered under the charterer's name and is treated as one of their fleet with a lease fee paid to the owners.

Notes On The Ship Histories

The first section contains, above most vessels names, the "International Maritime Organisation Number" (IMO), which remains with the vessel throughout its life. This number must now be visibly displayed on the exterior of a vessel. The most common place that I have seen so far is on the stern near the name and port of registry.

On the next line is the fleet chronology number, ship name, the number of vessels that have carried the name in the fleet, the period in the fleet and below that the three tonnages – (**g.** = gross) (**n.** = net) (**d.** = deadweight), followed by the dimensions between perpendiculars for earlier vessels given in feet and tenths of feet. From 1956 dimensions were henceforth given in feet and inches. The new style dimension was accompanied by a different formula. The overall length, breadth extreme and summer draught were quoted giving a more realistic measurement, although giving the impression of a larger vessel. Lloyds Register changed to metric dimensions overall, in 1975. **(BB)** placed after the length figure indicates the vessel having a bulbous bow. Any changes to these details during the vessel's career are also recorded. Occasionally there are changes in formula for measuring tonnages (tonnage conventions) and the resultant figures often give the impression of a much larger ship without any physical alteration.

The second section contains the machinery details - number of engines (if more than one), followed by either steam turbines, or **C**.= compound; **T**.= Triple expansion, followed by the number of cylinders, for steam reciprocating machinery. For diesel machinery the number of cylinders is followed by **S. C.** = stroke cycle and **S. A**.= single acting or **D. A.** = double acting. Both types are succeeded by (cylinder sizes x stroke length) then by machinery type, (where known) and the manufacturer thereof, followed by the figure and whichever of the following denominators that is applicable - **HP** = horse power, **IHP** = indicated horse power, **RHP** = registered horse power, **NHP** = nominal horse power, **SHP**= shaft horse power, **BHP** = brake horse power. (E.g. 2,500 IHP), followed by the vessel speed (where known) and any supplementary propulsion units (on later vessels). Any changes of engines during the vessel's career are also recorded.

The final section contains the ship history commencing with a description of the vessel type, followed by the keel laying, launch and completion dates (whichever are known), the shipbuilder, (Yard No.) etc., followed by the vessel's career.

All ship histories have been corrected to February 2006.

Part One - Dry-Cargo Operations.

Post war a surplus of tonnage built by the Allies was being sold at reasonable prices to ship-owners of approved nations who wished to modernize their fleet. The end product of these transactions, in many cases was obsolescent tonnage being sent for demolition. Some of those vessels still had some useful life left and with the profits from his scrap metal business, Sten A. Olsson purchased the HAUG II, a whaler, which he sent for conversion into a cargo vessel. When the conversion work was completed the vessel was registered in the ownership of Maskfabrikinaffaren Generator Ab., and was renamed DAN, after Sten's son.

Sten's philosophy at the outset of this venture was "Give the customer what they want" and that is still true of company attitudes today. During the next few years several old naval vessels were purchased, of which one was the steam-engined trawler OLIVE. This was similarly sent for conversion into a cargo vessel including being refitted with an oil engine. To get this new engine Olsson had also purchased the wooden hulled minesweeper M.M.S.253, which was diesel powered. The engine was transferred to OLIVE, and the wooden hull subsequently broken up. The OLIVE was given the new name SAMBA, and was registered in the joint ownership of Sten A. Olsson and Helge Olofsson. This partnership was, quickly, to transform into Rederi Ab Samba.

Throughout the early 1950's the company's operations were concentrated on cargo traffic and, one new ship was completed during 1952 as CHRISTOFER, the contract having been purchased from fellow Swede, Rederi Rawall, whilst still under construction.

At this time the funnel design was buff, on which a blue disc contained a white, three legged device, similar to that used by the German Mercedes motor company, although without the outer ring. Between each leg were the white letters, S.A.O.

By 1955, having with one exception, purchased all second hand ships, the Company found itself in a position to have no less than four ships designed to meet their requirements. All of these vessels would be built with machinery and accommodation superstructure aft. Whilst they were being built, and for some time afterward, the Company continued to buy and sell second hand tonnage, some of which remained in the fleet for only a short period and which included two old tugs.

The scrap metal business was also expanded to include shipbreaking. Through this activity some of the old vessels purchased were traded for a short period before being broken up. The activity for these vessels was usually collecting cargoes of scrap metal for their owner's business, which by the end of 1960 had owned around twenty-five vessels and had chartered others, all of which, excepting the two tugs, were kept reasonably well employed on cargo operations. During the next four years ships continued to enter and leave the fleet as trade dictated.

With the view to a bargain, and quick profit, the company in 1966 purchased two small general cargo vessels, which were renamed ATHOS and RHODOS, before being sold to Cypriot buyers after only a few months.

In 1968-69 another pair of small coaster were purchased, but in their case they became the only sea-going cargo vessels, to carry the STENA prefix adopted in 1965. They were successfully traded for around two years being seen in both Irish and Mediterranean ports before being sold in 1970.

Over the next 11 years fewer cargo vessels passed through the company hands as they moved more and more into the RoRo freight and passenger ferry business, although the size of cargo vessel did increase dramatically in 1978 when two large cargo-liners were purchased. One was sold almost immediately whilst the other was loaded with scrap metal and sent eastward enroute for demolition. Because of machinery problems, she never reached her ultimate destination and ended her days in the hands of Gadani Beach shipbreakers.

That apart from ownership of a small auxiliary Galeas for a few months brought the old-style conventional general cargo operations aspect of the business to a close in 1982. By 1984 the company through the establishment of Stena Bulk Ab, moved into dry-bulk carrier operations in a limited scale. The vessels employed were all chartered or managed with the exception of STENA ARCTICA. Before I am challenged regarding my earlier statement, yes, this was a cargo vessel with a STENA prefixed name, but was actually employed as a mothership for a Polar expedition and was not commercially traded.

Although the company successfully operated the bulk carriers it soon became apparent that their market place was quite volatile, especially with an abundance of new tonnage entering service against a Worldwide slump in business. On the other hand quality tankers were always in demand as the worldwide thirst for oil and chemicals increased. Stena Bulk had also become heavily involved with tanker operations. It was therefore no surprise that bulkers were phased out in favour of further tanker expansion.

There was however, a revival in the late 1990's when through the Stena subsidiaries Universe Tankships (Delaware) LLC, and Northern Marine Management three bulk carriers and a containership were operated under management.

Stena Bulk in 2002 furthered the activity in dry-bulk trade with Hong Kong based Oak Bulk Carriers, through a 50:50 partnership StenOak, to explore the Panamax dry-bulk markets.

The General Cargo Fleet

DAN

(Courtesy Stena Ab.)

C.1. HAUG II / DAN (1947 - 1953)

As built: 239g. 107n. 113.4 x 23.1 x 13.8 feet.
Post 1948: 309g. 201n. 143.8 x 23.0 x 14.0 feet.
As built: T.3-cyl. (14", 22" & 37½" x 24") engine made by the shipbuilder.
Post 1948: 4-cyl. 2 S.C.S.A. oil engine made by Frederikshavn Jernstoberie & Maskfabrik, Frederikshavn.
Auxiliary, 3 masted schooner, converted from a Whaler.
1925: Completed as SCOTT by Akers Mekaniska Verksteder, Oslo (Yard No. 423), for AS Sydhavet, (J. Rasmussen, manager), Norway. 1930: Owners restyled as Hvalfanger AS Sydhavet, (J. Rasmussen, manager). 1936: Sold to Hvalfangstslsk Haugar AS, (O. A. Haluorsen, manager), Norway, and renamed HAUG II. 22.10.1947: Purchased by Sten Allan Olsson, Sweden, and sent for lengthening and conversion into a motor cargo ship. 21.10.1948: Renamed DAN and registered in the ownership of Maskinfabrikafferen Generator Ab, (Sten A. Olsson, manager), Sweden. 14.1.1953: Sailed from Gdynia, bound to Degerhamn with a cargo of coal, in company with DEOLUS. 18:00hrs. 14.1.1953: When about 10 miles North from Rixhoft, vessel altered course, steering toward the Oelands Southern Shoal. This was the last sighting of the vessel. 20.1.1953: Declared "Missing presumed lost".

C.2. M. M. S. 253 (1947 - 1948)

164g. 62n. 113.1 x 22.3 x 10.4 feet.
6-cyl. 2 S.C.S.A. (14" x 17") oil engine made by Fairbanks, Morse & Company, Beloit, Wisconsin, U.S.A.
Wooden hulled minesweeper.
4.3.1943: Launched by Le Blanc Shipbuilding Company Ltd., Mahone Bay, N. S. (Yard No. 2), for The Admiralty, London. 9.1943: Completed. 1947: Purchased by Sten A. Olsson, Sweden. 1948: Vessel demolished and the engine transferred to SAMBA (1), which see.

C.3. EJDERN (1947 - 1948)

164g. 72n. 96.7 x 21.5 x 8.7 feet.
C.2-cyl. (14-3/8" & 26¼" x 17½") engine made by the shipbuilder. 24 NHP.
1902: Completed as LINKOPING by W. Lindbergs Ab, Stockholm (Yard No. 249), for Linkopings Nya Rederi Ab., (C. Thorngren and subsequently Jac Svensen, manager), Sweden. 1935: Owners restyled Rederi Ab Linkoping-Nykoping, (Jac Svensen, manager). 1938: Sold to K. A. Johansson and Others, Sweden. 1941: Sold to Trafik Ab Ockero - Skargard, (J. W. Berg, manager), Sweden and renamed EJDERN. 1947: Purchased by Sten A. Olsson, Sweden. 1948: Believed demolished.

C.4. SAMBA (1) (1948 - 1956)

462g. 151n. 151.5 x 27.5 x 14.8 feet.
Post 1952: 573g. 327n. 180.0 x 27.5 x 14.8 feet.
As built: T.3-cyl. engine made by the shipbuilder.
Post 1948: 6-cyl. 2 S.C.S.A. (14" x 17") oil engine made by Fairbanks Morse & Company, Beloit, Wisconsin. (transferred from M.M.S.253, q.v.).
Motor cargo vessel, converted from a steam Naval type trawler.
26.2.1940: Launched as OLIVE by Hall, Russell & Company Ltd., Aberdeen (Yard No. 1075), for The Admiralty, London. 5.1940: Completed. 16.7.1948: Purchased by Sten A. Olsson and Helge Olofsson, Sweden, converted into a motor cargo vessel and renamed SAMBA. 1951: Purchased outright by Sten A. Olsson. 1952: Lengthened. 1955: Transferred to Rederi Ab Samba, (Sten A. Olsson, manager). 28.12.1956: Whilst on a ballast voyage from Rotterdam to Odda, suffered main engine failure and grounded at a position 2 miles South of Lerwick, becoming a total loss.

5185958

C.5. WALNUT (1948)

520 tons displacement 153.0 x 27.6 x 14.7 feet.
Post 1953: 456g. 368n. 610d. (49.99 x 8.41metres overall x 4.420 metres draught.)
As built: T.3-cyl. engine made by unlocated builder.
Post 1953: 12-cyl. 4 S.C.S.A. (125 x 140mm) oil engine made by General Motors Corporation, Detroit. 9kts.
Steam Naval type trawler.
12.8.1939: Launched by Smith's Dock Company Ltd., South Bank, Middlesbrough (Yard No. 1071), for The Admiralty, London. 16.7.1948: Purchased by Sten A. Olsson and quickly resold to Baltic refugees for use on a single voyage to Canada. c1953: Sold to Borromee Verreault, Halifax N.S., converted into a cargo vessel, and renamed KETA (O.N. 197577). 1960: Owners restyled as Verreault Navigation Inc. 12.1975: Demolished by Nittolo Metal Company, at Les Mechins, Port Quebec.

C.6. STEFAN (1) (1950 - 1952)

843g. 349n. 221.5 x 29.1 x 11.9 feet.
T.3-cyl. (15" 25" & 40" x 27") engine made by the North Eastern Marine Engineering Company Ltd., Newcastle. 93 NHP.
7.1898: Completed as HELIOS by Wood, Skinner and Company Ltd., Newcastle (Yard No. 74), for Dampschiffahrtges Neptun, Germany. 1925: Sold to J. A. Lilja, Sweden, and renamed PLATO. 1927: Sold to Rederi for Angaren Plato, (G. F. Persson, manager), Sweden. 1930: Sold to Rederi Ab Henckel, (H. Trolle Henckel, manager), Sweden. 1950: Purchased by Maskinfabrikafferen Generator Ab, (Sten A. Olsson, manager), and renamed STEFAN *. 30.7.1952: Sold to the British Iron & Steel Corporation for demolition, and allocated to P. & W. MacLellan Ltd., Bo'ness.

*N.B. Although Lloyd's Register quoted STEFFAN, the company insist STEFAN and have shown records accordingly.

5042508

C.7. MAGDA (1951 - 1958)

As built: 159g. 111n. 88.1 x 22.6 x 8.9 feet.
Post 1928: 210g. 127n. 108.1 x 22.6 x 8.7 feet.
As built: 4-cyl. 4 S.C.S.A. (12½" x 16") oil engine made by Frederikshavn Jernstoberie & Maskfabrik, Frederikshavn. 34 NHP.
Post 1923: 4-cyl. 4 S.C.S.A. (12-3/8" x 16") oil engine made by Brodr Houmoller, Frederikshavn. 34 NHP.
Post 1927: 3-cyl. 4 S.C.S.A. (11" x 17¾") oil engine made by Motorenfabrik 'Deutz' A.G., Koln-Deutz. 28 NHP.
Post 1932: 6-cyl. 4 S.C.S.A. (8-11/16" x 13") oil engine made by Soc.de Const. Mec., La Corneuve.
Post 1953: 3-cyl. 2 S.C.S.A. (230 x 400mm) oil engine made by Frederikshavn Jernstoberie & Maskfabrik, Frederikshavn. 150 BHP.
Steel auxiliary 3 masted schooner.
1920: Completed as NORIS by Marstal Staalskibsverf, Marstal (Yard No.28), for H.A. Lorentzen, Denmark. 1923: Sold to H. C. Carlsen, Denmark, re-engined, and renamed DUEN. 1926: Sold to Johs Thode, Germany, and renamed GUNTHER. 1927: Re-engined. 1928: Lengthened, and renamed ERNO. 1932: Sold to Soc. d'Arm. Ch. Balier, Fecamp, re-engined, and renamed MARCEL JEAN. 1951: Purchased by Sten A. Olsson, and renamed MAGDA. 1953: Re-engined, and transferred to Sten A. Olsson Metallprodukter. 29.9.1958: Sold to MS Berna PR, (Bertil W. Hedding 10% and Holger Rummback 90%), Sweden, and renamed BERNA. 1959: Purchased outright by Bertil W. Hedding. 17.11.1966: Sold to Eurosa Ltd., Panama. 1984: Flag and port of registry deleted from Lloyd's Register, because her continued existence was in doubt.

5411802

C.8. CHRISTOFER (1) (1952 - 1954)

477g. 277n. 161.1 x 27.8 x 9.6 feet.
6-cyl. 2 S.C.S.A. (230 x 400mm) oil engine made by Frederikshavns Jernstoberie & Maschinenfabrik, Frederikshavn, geared to a controllable pitch propeller. 270 BHP.
General cargo vessel.
1952: Ordered from Orenstein - Koppel & Lubecker Maschinenbau A.G., Lubeck (Yard No. 473) by Rederi Rawall, Sweden. 24.5.1952: Launched for Sten A. Olsson, Sweden. 25.8.1952: Completed. 28.10.1954: Sold to Blekinge Angbats Ab, (W. Lundstrom, manager), Sweden, and renamed BERGELIOT. 1963: Sold to Knud Valdemar Kriger Nordendorph, Sweden, and renamed INGRID MARIANNE. 1964: Owners restyled as Ab Skeppsservice, (Knud Nordendorph, manager). 30.10.1968: Sold to N. W. Sorensen PR, (Fru Eva Sorensen, manager), Denmark, and renamed GRETHE PETER. 1973: Transferred to Eva Sorensen Partrederei, Denmark, and converted into a dredger / sand carrier. 6.1985: John Schmidt commenced demolition at Vejle.

C.9. VINTERHAMN (1952 - 1956) Iron steamship.

152g. 93n. 83.2 x 18.7 x 7.5 feet.
C.2-cyl. (10¾" & 21-7/8" x 17½") engine made by the shipbuilder. 17 NHP.
1878: Completed as GUSTAVSBERG II by Motala Company, Motala, for Aktiebolag Gustavsberg Fabriks Interessenter, (O. W. Odelsberg, later A. S. W. Odelsberg, managers), Sweden. 1943: Sold to Stockholm - Sandhamns Rederi Ab, (J. G. Ohlin, manager), Sweden, and renamed VINTERHAMN. 1950: Sold to Waxholms Nya Angf. Ab, (W. Rosendahl, manager), Sweden. 1952: Purchased by Sten A. Olsson, Sweden. 1953: Transferred to Sten A. Olsson Metallprodukter. 1955: Demolished.

C.10. GUSTAF LAGERBJELKE (1953 - 1954) Sloop.

179g. 124n. 96.4 x 19.7 x 7.4 feet.
C. 2-cyl. (13¼" & 23½" x 17½") engine made by the shipbuilder. 19 NHP.
1890: Completed by Bergsunds Mek. Verksted, Stockholm (Yard No.207), for Orebro Nya Rederi Aktiebolag, (G. A. Flodman, later G. Tidholm and 1924 G. Thermoenivs, managers), Sweden. 1925: Sold to Trafik Ab Malaren-Hjelmaren, (J. W. Rickander, manager), Sweden. 1930: H. A. Bertheau, appointed manager. 1933: Removed from management. 1935: Sold to Orebro Rederi Ab (Arvid Andersson, manager), Sweden. 1953: Purchased by Sten A. Olsson. 1954: Sold and converted into a barge. No further details known.

C.11. GUNNY (1954 - 1955)

2,478g. 1,437n. 250.5 x 43.8 x 22.2 feet.
As built: T.3-cyl. (20" 33" & 54" x 40") engine made by the shipbuilder. 328 NHP.
Post 1947: 6-cyl. 2 S.C.S.A. (17" x 27") oil engine made by Busch - Sulzer Bros. Diesel Engine Company, St. Louis, U.S.A.
Post 1957: 6-cyl. 4 S.C.S.A. (432 x 686mm) oil engine made by Kloeckner Humboldt-Duetz, Koeln.
General cargo vessel.
8.1918: Completed as LAKE ORMOC by Detroit Shipbuilding Company, Wyandotte (Yard No.228), for the United States Shipping Board, U.S.A. 1927: Sold to Ford Motor Company, U.S.A. 1947: Sold to Rederi Ab Ragne, (Ragnar Nilsson, manager), Sweden, re-engined and renamed SIGNEFJORD. 1949: Sold to Rederi Ab Skansholmen, (K. E. Hermansson, manager), Sweden, and renamed GUNNY. 1954: Purchased by Sten A. Olsson, Sweden. 1955: Sold to Michele Assanto di Cupillo, Italy. 1957: Re-engined. 1962: Sold to Maddalena Mabzella, Italy. 22.12.1962: Whilst on a voyage from Casablanca to Venice, with a cargo of phosphates, stranded in heavy weather, and sank at a position 38.54.40N., 17.8.20E.

5339834

C.12. STEFAN (2) (1955 - 1966)

498g. 303n. 940d. 185' 2" x 33' 2" x 12' O".
As built: 6-cyl. 2 S.C.S.A. (290 x 490mm) oil engine made by Alpha Diesel AS., Frederikshavn. 720 BHP. 11 kts.
Post 1.1974: 6-cyl. 4 S.C.S.A. (350 x 500mm) oil engine manufactured in 1971, by G. K. D. Praha, Praha. 550 BHP.
Ice strengthened general cargo vessel.
2.3.1955: Launched by Solvesborgs Varv Ab, Solvesborg (Yard No.40), for Maskfabrikinaffaren Generator Ab, (Sten A. Olsson, manager), Sweden. 19.4.1955: Completed. 1959: Transferred to Sten A. Olsson Handels Ab, Sweden. 1963: Owners restyled as Stena Ab. 1966: Sold to S. A. G. Beck, Denmark, and renamed GIMLE. 1970: Sold to Marcus Kioseglou, Greece, and renamed MARINA. 1971: Sold to Stavros Skordalakis and G. Tsironis and Company, Greece, re-engined, and renamed GEORGIOS II. 1.1974: Re-

engined. 1979: Sold to Skordalakis Bros. Shipping Enterprises, Greece. 1991: Sold to Georgios II Naftiki Eteria, (Skordalakis Bros. Shipping Enterprises, managers), Greece. 1997: Renamed GEORGIOS 2, and removed from management. 1998: Renamed GEORGIOS. 2000: Reported as having been demolished.

STEFAN

(The World Ship Society Ltd.)

C.13. KONGA (1956 - 1960)

1,546g. 845n. 2,400d. 246.6 x 37.4 x 15.8 feet.
T.3-cyl. (19", 32" & 53" x 36") engine made by the shipbuilder. 169 NHP.
General cargo vessel.
1905: Completed as T. M. WERNER by Helsingors Jernsk & Msk., Elsinor (Yard No. 105), for Dampskselskibs, Vendila, (Svendsen and Christensen, managers), Denmark. 1929: Sold to Rederi AB Sundsborg, (Henning Edling, manager), Sweden, and renamed SUNDSBORG. 1936: Sold to Rederi Ab Hasting, (Erik Hakanson, manager), Sweden, and renamed HOVDING. 1956: Purchased by Sten A. Olsson Handels Ab, Sweden, and renamed KONGA. 28.9.1960: Glucksmans Metallaffar commenced demolition, at Goteborg.

CHRISTOPHER **as SAVONIA**

(W. J. Harvey)

C.14. CHRISTOFER (2) (1956 - 1964)

499g. 289n. 980d. 198' 9" x 33' 0" x 12' 0½".
4-cyl. 2 S.C.S.A. (340 x 570mm) oil engine made by Nydqvist & Holm Ab, Trollhattan. 760 BHP. 11.5 kts.
General cargo vessel.
22.10.1955: Launched by Lidingoverken KS Ab, Live, Lidingo (Yard No. 22), for Sten A. Olsson Handels Ab, Sweden. 14.4.1956: Completed. 1964: Sold to Ab Skeppsservice, (Knud Nordendorph, manager), Sweden and renamed SAVONIA. 18.12.1969: During a voyage from Storugns to Hernosand, with a cargo of limestone, capsized and sank at a position 10 miles South West from Gotska Sandon.

PORTOS

(The World Ship Society Ltd.)

C.15. PORTOS (1956 - 1964)

899g. 568n. 1,500d. 186.0 x 34.1 x 14.2 feet.
As built: 6-cyl. 4 S.C.S.A. oil engine made by Motorenfabrik-Werke- Mannheim, Mannheim.
Post 1951: 6-cyl. 4 S.C.S.A. (400 x 460mm) oil engine manufactured in 1941, by Motorenwerke Mannheim, Mannheim.
Post 1966: 8-cyl. 4 S.C.S.A. (320 x 420mm) oil engine made by Ansaldo Stab. Mecc., Genoa. 1,300 BHP.
General cargo vessel.
1943: Completed as OTTER by Deutsche Werke A. G., Kiel. [N.B. No details for this period have been located at Lloyds Register of Shipping or their suggested sources]. 1951: Purchased by Jakobstad Rederi Ab, Finland, and renamed ANITA. 1951: Re-engined. 1956: Purchased by Sten A. Olsson Handels Ab, Sweden, and renamed PORTOS. 1964: Sold to Speditione Lucchi, Italy, and renamed PUPI. 1965: Sold to Ferdinand Tessarin, Italy and renamed LILION. 1966: Re-engined. 1973: Sold to Italian shipbreakers.

C.16. RHODOS (1) (1956 - 1957)

1,389g. 829n. 2,250d. 240.3 x 37.2 x 16.6 feet.
T.3-cyl. (18-5/16", 29-15/16" & 49¼" x 33-7/16") engine made by the shipbuilder.
General cargo vessel.
8.1904: Completed as BRYSSEL by Soc. Anon le Vulcain Belge, Hoboken for Dampskselsk Vulcan, (C. P. Jensen, manager), Denmark. 1908: N. P. Neilsen and J. H. Just, appointed as managers. 1914: N. P. Neilsen appointed as manager. 1916: Sold to Dampskselsk Trafic, (P. L. Fisher, manager), Denmark. 1923: Sold to Rederi Ab Sirius, (E. R. Killman, manager), Sweden, and renamed VERA. 1928: O. Hillerstrom appointed as manager. 1941: F. Hillerstrom appointed as manager. 1943: Sold to Rederi Ab Gotha, (G. A. Bratt, manager), Sweden, and renamed PATRIA. 1956: Purchased by Sten A. Olsson Handels Ab, Sweden, and renamed RHODOS. 16.3.1957: Whilst on a voyage from Ventspils to France with a cargo of ore, grounded outside Ventspils. 2.4.1957: Refloated, but declared a constructive total loss, and was subsequently sold for demolition. 28.2.1958: Robert Bornhofen K. G., Hamburg, commenced work.

ATOS being stripped at Gothenburg

(The World Ship Society Ltd.)

C.17. ATOS (1956 - 1965)

1,230g. 677n. 1,968d. 230.0 x 36.5 x 16.0 feet.

T.3-cyl. (17" 28" & 46" x 33") engine made by the North Eastern Marine Engineering Company Ltd., Newcastle.
General cargo vessel.
9.1909: Completed as QUERIDA by Swan, Hunter & Wigham Richardson, Newcastle (Yard No. 822), for the Donald Steamship Company Ltd., (T. L. Evans, manager), Bristol. 1914: Taken over by the Shipping Controller, London, (J. Cory & Sons Ltd., managers). 1920: Sold to West Glamorgan Steamers Ltd., Swansea. 1923: J. Pridmore appointed as manager. 1925: W. A. Jenkins appointed as manager. 1926: Sold to S. Banck, Sweden, and renamed ELLA. 1943: Sold to Rederi Ab Gotha, (G. A. Bratt, manager), Sweden, and renamed ARDENNIA. 1956: Purchased by Sten A. Olsson Handels Ab, Sweden, and renamed ATOS. 1963: Owners restyled Stena Ab, Sweden. 25.8.1965: Sold to Torsten Johannisson, Gothenburg, for conversion into a barge, but was completely demolished.

5216616

C.18. MADELEINE (1956 - 1970)

499g. 289n. 960d. 198' 9" x 33' 0" x 12' 0½".
4-cyl. 2 S.C.S.A. (340 x 570mm) oil engine made by Nydqvist & Holm Ab, Trollhattan. 760 BHP. 11.5 kts.
Ice strengthened general cargo vessel.
6.7.1956: Launched by Lidingoverken KS Ab Live, Lidingo (Yard No. 23), for Sten A. Olsson Handels Ab, (Sten A. Olsson, manager), Sweden. 26.10.1956: Completed. 1963: Transferred to Rederi Ab Samba, (Stena Ab, managers), Sweden. 1970: Sold to Stig T. A. Ivarsson, Sweden. 1974: Sold to Ingemar Gudmundsson, Sweden, and renamed ADELE. 1975: Sold to Koukoulis and Company, Greece, and renamed ARIS III. 1981: Sold to Nik and John Kairis and Company, Greece. 1983: Sold to Ourania Malamoutsi and Company, Greece. 1986: Sold to Neosalaminiaki Marine Company, Greece, and renamed AGIOS NIKOLAOS. 1988: Transferred to Neosalaminiaki Shipping Company, Greece. 1988: Sold to Demetrios, Stavros and George Valhalis, Greece, and renamed ANNA V. 1989: Sold to Stamatakis Stefanos and Company Ltd., Greece. 5.10.1989: Wrecked on Agion Oros during a voyage from Halkidiki to Piraeus.

C.19. FORSHAGA (1956 - 1957)

213g. 124n. 275d. 102' 4" x 22' 9" x 10' 10"
C.2-cyl. (12" & 24" x 15") engine made by the shipbuilder.
Iron cargo vessel.
1887: Completed by Eriksbergs M.V.., Gothenburg (Yard No. 94), for K. A. Ahlmark, Sweden.
1894: Sold to Forshaga Angb. Ab, (K. A. Ahlmark, manager), Sweden. 1902: A. Uppvall appointed as manager. 1909: J. Bergenendorff appointed as manager. 1917: Sold to Angb. Karlstad, (same manager), Sweden. 1918: Sold to Varmlands Rederi Ab, (same manager), Sweden. 1921: Removed from management. 1928: A. F. Olson appointed as manager. During W.W.2: Bror Petterson appointed as manager. 1952: Bengt Rejmer appointed as manager. 1956: Purchased by Sten A. Olsson Handels Ab, (Sten A. Olsson, manager), Sweden. 1957: Demolished by Leon Engelen at Willebroek.

C.20. SVAN (1956)

1,075g. 577n. 208.7 x 33.6 x 13.6 feet.
T.3-cyl. (16" 26½" & 44" x 30") engine made by the shipbuilder. 106 NHP.
General cargo vessel.
1907: Completed as DAHLIA by Lindholmens Varf, Ab., Gothenburg (Yard No. 397), for Nordiska Rederi Ab, (W. Lundkvist, and later, H. Metcalfe, manager), Gothenburg. 1919: Sold to Rederi Ab Svenska Lloyd, Sweden. 9.4.1940: Detained at Bergen by German invasion forces and seized as a war prize. 1940: Renamed MUHLHAUSEN, by the Deutsches Reich (Admiral de KMD, Hamburg). 1940: Renamed JOHANNES WILLI, Deutsches Reich (Bissmark Linie GmbH, Hamburg, managrs). 5.1947: Returned to Rederi Ab Svenska Lloyd, and renamed FRISIA. 1956: Sold to Rederi Ab Svan, (Lennart Petterson, manager), Bleket, and renamed SVAN. 1956: Sold to Sten A. Olssons Handels Ab., (Sten Allan Olsson, manager), Gothenburg. 1956: Sold to Nikos Kathreptis & Company, Piraeus, and renamed FRI. 30.11.1960: Arrived at St. George's Bay, Greece, for demolition.

C.21. ANKARSVIK (1957-) iron tug.

73g. 14n. x x feet.
Steam machinery.
1874: Completed as VIRGO by *NO FURTHER DETAILS KNOWN.*

C.22. SILLRE (1957-) iron tug.

88g. 19n. x x feet.
Steam machinery.
1875: Completed as ORNSKOLDVIK by. *NO FURTHER DETAILS KNOWN.*

MARGIT

(World Ship Society Ltd)

5221972

C.23. MARGIT (1957 - 1965)

As built: 842g. 293n. 216.1 x 35.6 x 12.1 feet.
Post 1957: 993g. 443n. 256.0 x 35.6 x 12.0 feet.
5-cyl. 2 S.C.S.A. (20½" x 27-9/16") oil engine made by Kockums M.V. Ab, Malmo. 900 BHP. 10 kts.
General cargo vessel.
5.1935: Completed as WARUN by Nya Varvs, Oresund, Landskrona (Yard No. 34), for Stockholms Rederi Svea, (Eman Hogborg, manager), Sweden. 1940: Converted into minelayer, by the German Navy. 1945: Returned to Stockholms Rederi Svea, Sweden, and converted back into a cargo vessel. 1956: Suffered grounding damage and was declared a constructive total loss and sold for demolition. 1957: Purchased in part by Sten A. Olsson Handels Ab, through Rederi for MS Margit, (Hjalmar Sjosten, manager), Sweden, repaired, lengthened, and renamed MARGIT. 1964: Purchased outright by Stena Ab, Sweden. 1965: Sold to Levante Shipping Company Ltd., Cyprus, and renamed ARISTIDES. 1979: Sold to Astritis Maritime Inc., Panama, and renamed RIVERSIDE. 1998: Entry removed from Lloyd's Register – continued existence in doubt.

5101366

C.24. ELISABETH (1957 - 1961)

499g. 288n. 960d. 198' 9" x 33' 0" x 12' 0½".
4-cyl. 2 S.C.S.A. (340 x 570mm) oil engine made by Nydqvist & Holm Ab, Trollhattan. 840 BHP. 11.5 kts.
Ice strengthened general cargo vessel.
21.1.1957: Launched by Lidingoverken Kb, Ab Live, Lidingo (Yard No. 24), for Sten A. Olsson Handels Ab, Sweden. 30.3.1957: Completed for Rederi Ab Samba, (Sten A. Olsson Handels AB, managers), Sweden. 1961: Sold to N. V. Rederij "Skandia", (Vereenigd Cargodoorskantoor, managers), Holland. 1966: Sold to Daniel Johansson, Sweden. 17.5.1974: Whilst lying at Waalhaven, Rotterdam, undergoing repairs, fire broke out heavily damaging the crew accommodation and engine room aft. 1974: Sold to Beirut Trading Company, Lebanon, repaired, and renamed BEIRUT TRADER. 1976: Sold to Agence Generale Maritime S.a.r.l. (Agemar), Lebanon and renamed LA PROVIDENCE. 1985: Renamed ELIZABETH. 1990: Reported as having been demolished at an unspecified location.

C.25. ENOS (1) (1957 - 1960)

1,383g. 734n. 2,060d. 226.5 x 42.2 x 17.6 feet.
Two, C.2-cyl. (20½" & 32" x 21¼") engines made by Jonkopings M.V., Jonkoping.
General cargo vessel.
1901: Completed as TYR by O. A. Brodin, Gefle (Yard No. 42), for Angf. Ab Kjell, Sweden. 1938: Sold to Rederi Ab Nord Sverige, (Axel F. Andersson, manager), Sweden and renamed HEMSO. 1957: Purchased by Sten A. Olsson Handels Ab, Sweden and renamed ENOS. 11.1960: Demolition commenced by Van Den Bosche, at Boom, Belgium.

C.26. SAMBA (2) (1959 - 1961)

910g. 387n. 1,100d. 203.6 x 32.7 x 13.7 feet.
5-cyl. 2 S.C.S.A. (13-9/16" x 22-13/16") oil engine made by Nydqvist & Holm Ab, Trollhattan.
General cargo vessel.
13.6.1949: Launched as MUNKFORS by the Goole Shipbuilding & Repairing Company Ltd., Goole (Yard No. 469), for Uddeholms Ab, Sweden. 9.1949: Completed. 1959: Purchased by Rederi Ab Samba, (Sten A. lsson Handels Ab, managers), Sweden, and renamed SAMBA. 1961: Sold to P. V. Christensen, Denmark,

and renamed KIM. 1965: Sold to Emm Pelekanos & Company, Greece and renamed SINERGASIA. 18.12.1966: Whilst on a voyage from Cagliari to Ronskar, during a storm, suffered main engine failure near Ulmea, and subsequently grounded. All of her 13 crew perished.

SAMBA

(The World Ship Society Ltd.)

C.27. KORSHAMN (1960 - 1961)

As built: 253g. 130n. 102.3 x 23.3 x 10.7 feet.
Post 1951: 323g. 224n. 500d. 144.6 x 23.3 x 10.2 feet.
Post 1960: 314g. 200n. 500d. 144' 7" x 23' 4" x 9' 8".
As built: Steam powered machinery, type and manufacturers therof unlocated.
Post 1951: 6-cyl. 4 S.C.S.A. (275 x 310mm) oil engine manufactured, in 1933, by Motorenwerke Mannheim A.G., Mannheim.
General cargo vessel.
1945: Completed as WILHO by Oulun Konepaja OY, Oulu, for OY Wilho, (C. J. S. Mattsson, manager), Finland. 1950: Owners restyled Ab Wilho OY, (Altons Hakans, manager), Finland. 1951: Sold to OY Korshamn Ab, Finland, lengthened and converted into a motorship. 1955: Sold to Rederi Ab Kvarken, (Johannes Nymark, manager), Finland. 1960: Purchased by Sten A. Olsson Handels Ab, Sweden. 1961: Sold to Paola Caruso, Italy, and renamed CLIZIA. 6.2.1969: Whilst on a voyage from Porticello to Algiers, with a cargo of chicken feed, stranded in heavy seas off Marethimo, near Trapani, and subsequently sank.

5077163

C.28. COLOMBIA (1960 - 1964)

1,759g. 1,079n. 2,235d. 274.8 x 38.2 x 20.5.feet.
7-cyl. 2 S.C.S.A. (500 x 690mm) Polar type, oil engine made by Atlas Diesel Ab, Stockholm. 2,050 BHP.
General cargo vessel.
1946: Launched by Ab Ekensbergs Varv, Stockholm (Yard No. 188), for Compania Colombiana de Navigacione Maritima S.A., (COLDEMAR), Colombia. 4.1947: Completed. 1960: Purchased by Rederi Ab Samba, (Sten A. Olsson Handels Ab, managers), Sweden. 1963: Managers restyled Stena Ab. 1964: Sold to Carlos A. Gothong Line, Philippines, and renamed DON SULPICIO. 1969: Renamed DONA GLORIA. 1974: Sold to Sulpicio Lines, Philippines. 6.1984: Sold to L. Acuario Marketing Corp., Caloocan, Manila, for demolition.

C.29. SARABANDE (1961)

1,722g. 626n. 2,250d. 295.6 x 45.0 x 13.9 feet.
5-cyl. 2 S.C.S.A. (560 x 1680mm) oil engine made by the shipbuilder.
General cargo vessel.
20.10.1937: Launched as PALOMARES by Wm. Doxford & Sons Ltd., Sunderland (Yard No. 635), for McAndrew & Company Ltd., London. 2.1938: Completed. 1959: Sold to Oluf Svendsen, Denmark, and renamed MARY SVEN. 1961: Purchased by Sten A. Olsson Handels Ab, Sweden, and renamed SARABANDE. 5.10.1961: Whilst on a voyage from Oslo to Basrah, with a cargo of timber, vessel caught fire at a position 23.6N., 59.20E. When vessel began to acquire a list during the attempts to control the fire the crew abandoned ship. 9.10.1961: Sighted still afloat at a position 23.3N., 59.16E., with light smoke still visible. 17.10.1961: A search was initiated off Ras Ash Shajar but found no trace. 19.10.1961: Vessel was sighted by search aircraft, aground at a position 20 miles N. W. from Sur, near Kalhat. 12.12.1961: Deleted from the Swedish register as a total loss.

5260837
C.30. RHODOS (2) (1966 - 1967)
499g. 242n. 1,055d. 217' 8" x 32' 11" x 12' 4½".
8-cyl. 2 S.C.S.A. (290 x 490mm) oil engine made by Alpha Diesel AS, Frederikshavn, geared to a controllable pitch propeller. 960 BHP. 12 kts.
General cargo vessel.
16.4.1958: Launched as OCTAVIA by Solvesborgs Varv Ab, Solvesborg (Yard No. 51), for Rederi Ab Svenska Lloyd, (K. R. Bokman, manager), Sweden. 28.8.1958: Completed. 1961: Kjell Andersen appointed as manager. 1966: Purchased by Stena Ab, Sweden, for £70,000, and renamed RHODOS. 1967: Sold to Island Shipping Company Ltd., Cyprus, and renamed ISLAND SEA. 17.8.1968: Whilst on a voyage from Iquitos to Manaus, was seriously damaged in a collision with a floating log at a position approximately 120 miles from her destination. 1974: Sold to Kastalia Compania Naviera Ltd., Cyprus, and renamed SKYROCKET. 18.2.1975: Whilst on a voyage from Plymouth to Thessalonika, developed engine trouble and leaks and sank at a position 36.30N., 20.00E., approximately 70 miles off Rylos.

C.31. ATHOS (1966 - 1967)
498g. 236n. 1,055d. 217' 8" x 32' 11" x 12' 4".
8-cyl. 2 S.C.S.A. (290 x 490mm) oil engine made by Alpha Diesel AS, Frederikshavn, geared to a controllable pitch propeller. 960 BHP. 12.5 kts.
General cargo vessel.
9.1.1958: Launched as VALERIA by Solvesborgs Varv Ab, Solvesborg (Yard No. 50), for Rederi Ab Svenska Lloyd, (K. R. Bokman, manager), Sweden. 5.5.1958: Completed. 1961: Kjell Andersen appointed as manager. 1966: Purchased by Stena Ab, Sweden, for £70,000, and renamed ATHOS. 1967: Sold to Island Shipping Company Ltd., Cyprus and renamed ISLAND SUN. 3.10.1968: Whilst on a voyage from Belim to Savannah, grounded on Cat Island, at a position 24.28 N., 75.31 W, in the Bahamas, and appointed as a total loss.

STENA PAPER loading seed potatoes destined for the Canary Islands at Londonderry.

(W. J. Harvey)

5301368
C.32. STENA PAPER (1968 - 1970)
499g. 291n. 1,145d. 244' 2" x 35' 6" x 12' 0½".
12-cyl. 4 S.C.S.A. (9¾" x 10½") vee type oil engine made by Davey, Paxman & Company Ltd., Colchester. 1,350 BHP. 12.5 kts
Ice Strengthened, general cargo vessel.
19.8.1957: Launched as ROYAL PAPER by Ab Gavle Varv, Gavle (Yard No. 97), for Ab Statens Skogsindustrier, Sweden. 28.10.1957: Completed. 1968: Purchased by Stena Ab, (Sten A. Olsson, manager), Sweden, and renamed STENA PAPER. 1970: Sold to Saimaan Kanavalaivat Oy., Finland, and renamed PALLI. 1974: Sold to Horseshoe Bay Shipping Company Ltd., Panama, and renamed COSTIS TAF. 1979: Renamed DOVER. 27.6.1979: Whilst on a voyage from Iraklion to Marseilles, vessel suffered an engine room explosion off Canea, Crete and was gutted by the resultant fire.

STENA WOOD at Malta

(The World Ship Society Ltd.)

5301435

C.33. STENA WOOD (1969 - 1970)

499g. 289n. 1,163d. 244' 2" x 35' 6" x 12' 0½".
12-cyl. 4 S.C.S.A. (9¾" x 10½") vee type oil engine made by Davey, Paxman & Company Ltd., Colchester. 1,350 BHP. 12.5 kts.
Ice strengthened, general cargo vessel.
20.10.1956: Launched as ROYAL WOOD by Ab Gavle Varv, Gavle (Yard No. 94), for Ab Statens Skogsindustrier, Sweden. 17.1.1957: Completed. 1969: Purchased by Stena Ab, (Sten A. Olsson, manager), Sweden, and renamed STENA WOOD. 1970: Sold to Saimaan Kanavalaivat Oy., Finland, and renamed SOSKUA. 1974: Sold to Capricorn Bay Shipping Company Ltd., Panama, and renamed ALEXIS TAF. 22.2.1977: Dragged her anchor whilst undergoing engine repairs and grounded at Cabo de Gata. 27.2.1977: Refloated and subsequently arrived at Gibraltar for discharge after which she sailed as SFAKIA under Cypriot registry. 4.6.1977: Arrived at Pireaus, and laid up. 1.1978: Sold to Seabell Company, Cyprus, and renamed BRISTOL. 28.1.1978: Whilst a voyage from Novorossisk to Italy, vessel caught fire. 30.1.1978: Beached at Saraylar, Marmara Island and subsequently foundered in shallow water.

5137107

C.34. RHODOS (3) (1971 - 1972)

7,065g. 4,120n. 8,179d. 437.4 x 56.6 x 23.9 feet.
Two, 6-cyl. 2 S.C.S.A. (630 x 1300mm) oil engines made by the shipbuilder. 3,500 BHP.
Ice strengthened, general cargo vessel.
2.9.1947: Launched as GUAYANA by Ab Gotaverken, Goteborg (Yard No. 619), for Rederi Ab Nordstjernen, (A. A. Johnson, manager), Sweden. 5.1948: Completed. 1971: Purchased by Stena Ab (Sten A. Olsson, manager), Sweden, and renamed RHODOS. 1972: Sold to Golden Crown Shipping Company (Liberia) Ltd., Panama, and renamed GOLDEN CROWN. 23.3.1977: Arrived at Kaohsiung for demolition.

C.35. MONARDA / ENOS (2) / STENA METALLICA (1971 - 1977)

1,536g. 801n. 2,970d. 269.2 x 40.4 x 16.0 feet.
T.3-cyl. (18½", 29-15/16" & 48-7/16" x 33½") engine made by the shipbuilder. 10 kts.
Ice strengthened, general cargo vessel.
8.1935: Completed as HERA by Nya Varvs, Oresund, Landskrona (Yard No. 36), for Ab Transmarin, (B. Ingelsson, manager), Sweden. 1938: S. Redig, appointed as manager. 1959: Sold to Monark Line Ab, (Arnold de Champs, manager), Sweden, and renamed MONARDA. 1971: Purchased by Stena Ab, (Sten A. Olsson, manager), renamed ENOS, but vessel was not registered as such being transferred to Stena Metall Ab, (Sten A. Olsson, manager), converted into a dumb barge, at their Gothenburg shipbreaking yard, and renamed STENA METALLICA. 2.7.1977: Demolition commenced.

5031224

C.36. HUMBER (1978 – 1979)

8,627g. 4,707n. 12,145d. 488' 8" x 62' 3" x 39' 7"
6-cyl. 2 S.C.S.A. (670 x 2,320mm) oil engine made by Wm. Doxford & Sons (Engineers) Ltd., Sunderland. 6,800 BHP. 15.5 kts.
General cargo vessel.
4.6.1958: Launched as AUTHOR by Wm.Doxford & Sons (Shipbuilders) Ltd., Sunderland (Yard No. 827), for the Ruthin Steamship Company Ltd., Bermuda. 24.9.1958: Completed. 1966: Transferred to the

Charente Steamship Company Ltd., (T. & J. Harrison Ltd., managers), Liverpool. 21.7.1978: Purchased by Stena Atlantic Line Ltd., Bermuda, and renamed HUMBER and registered at London. 30.7.1978: Arrived at Falmouth with engine trouble. 5.8.1978: Departed Falmouth bound to Kiel. 13.8.1978: Suffered an engine-room fire and towed to Rendsburg for repair. 11.10.1978: Reported as stopped with engine failure in the Red Sea. 18.10.1978: Arrived at Karachi with engine trouble. 9.11.1978: Berthed for discharge then placed in lay-up and subsequently sold to Muslim Rolling Mills, 25.2.1979: Arrived at Gadani Beach, for demolition. 18.6.1979: Work commenced.

HUMBER transiting the Kiel Canal

(W. J. Harvey)

ADMINISTRATOR negotiating the Birkenhead Dock system

(W. J. Harvey)

5002871

C.37. ADMINISTRATOR / TYNE (1978)

8,627g. 4,707n. 12,145d. 488' 8" x 62' 3" x 39' 7"
6-cyl. 2 S.C.S.A. (670 x 2,320mm) oil engine made by Wm. Doxford & Sons (Engineers) Ltd., Sunderland. 6,800 BHP. 15.5 kts.
General cargo vessel.
20.3.1958: Launched as ADMINISTRATOR by Wm. Doxford & Sons (Shipbuilders) Ltd., Sunderland (Yard No. 826), for the Ruthin Steamship Company Ltd., Bermuda. 23.7.1958: Completed. 1966: Transferred to the Charente Steamship Company Ltd., (T. & J. Harrison Ltd., managers), Liverpool. 31.7.1978: Purchased by Stena Atlantic Line Ltd., Bermuda, and renamed TYNE but before being registered or traded as such, was immediately resold to Oriental Maritime (Pte) Ltd., Singapore, and renamed ORIENTAL SEA. 29.12.1978: Arrived at Chittagong for demolition by Trans Overseas Ltd.

5372460

C.38. MARIA CELESTE (1981 - 1982)

For details pre 1943 see footnote.
Post 1943: 128g. 75n. 163d. 101.8 x 18.1 x 6.8 feet.
Post 1963: 122g. 36n. 163d. 101.8 x 18.1 x 6.8 feet.
Post 1963: 2-cyl. 2 S.C.S.A. (330 x 370mm) oil engine made by AS. Hundested Motorfabrik, Hundested. 120 bhp.

Auxiliary sailing Galeas.
1905: Completed as MARGRIETHA by B. Niestern & Zonen, Delfzijl, Holland. 1943: Sold to Hans Schroder, Denmark, lengthened, motorised, and renamed ELSE. 1960: Sold to P. E. Hansen, Denmark, and renamed ULLER. 1963: Re-engined. 1971: Sold to Henri Kristensen, Denmark, and renamed HERI. 1979: Sold to Rederi Celeste I, (Leif Martin Christensen, manager), Denmark, and renamed MARIA CELESTE. 1981: Purchased by Stena Metall Ab, Sweden. 1982: Sold to Arni Avelin Bogserbats Ab, Sweden. 1983: Sold to Fred Stafrin, Sweden. 1988: Sold to Partrederiet for m.s. Heri, Sweden, and renamed HERI. 2005: Sold to R. Molin, Sweden.

N.B. Believed to have been under 100 tons between 1905-1943 resulting in no details being found at Lloyd's Register, nor their recommended sources.

The Bulk Carrier Fleet

Under the operational control of
Stena Bulk Ab
Concordia Maritime Ab
Northern Marine Management Ltd.

STENA ARCTICA (1)

(Courtesy Stena Ab)

7519282

B.1. STENA ARCTICA (1) (1985 - 1989)

As built: 21,110g. 13,323n. 31,900d. 185.83 x 26.50 x 11.443 metres.
Post 1994: 21,892g. 10,502n. 31,900d.
7-cyl. 2 S.C.S.A. (740 x 1,600mm) B&W 7K74EF type oil engine made by the shipbuilder. 15,140 BHP. 16 kts. Thwartship thrust controllable pitch propeller forward.
Ice strengthened, bulk carrier with a container capacity of 832 TEU.
1975: Ordered as COLUMBIALAND from Eriksbergs MV Ab (Lindholmen Division), Goteborg (Yard No. 705), by Angf.Tirfing Ab, Sweden. 25.11.1977: Launched for Brostroms Rederi Ab, (Brostroms Shipping Company Ltd., managers), Sweden. 22.3.1978: Completed. 1979: Renamed SEATRAIN LONDON. 1979: Renamed COLUMBIALAND. 1985: Purchased by Concordia Maritime Ab, transferred to Stena Bulk Ab, and renamed STENA ARCTICA. 1985: Transferred to Arctic Line Ab, and Bahamas flag. 1986: Northern Marine Management Ltd., appointed as managers. 1987: Transferred to Concordia Maritime Ab, Sweden, and removed from management. 1988: Shardik Ab, appointed as managers. 4.1989: Sold to Brostroms Rederi Ab, (Brostroms Shipping Company Ltd., managers), Sweden, and renamed COLUMBIALAND, at Blohm & Voss's shipyard, Hamburg. 1990: Sold to United Cruising Company Ltd., (Brostroms Rederei Ab (Brostroms Shipping Company Ltd.), managers). 1992: Sold to Columbialand Shipping Pte. Ltd., (Kontiki Shipping Pte. Ltd., managers), Singapore. 1993: Ferm International Ship Management AS, appointed as managers. 2000: Sold to Donnington Shipping Pte Ltd., (ASP Shipmanagement Singapore Ltd., managers), Singapore. 2003: Sold to Senior Shipping Ltd., Glasgow, (ASP Seascot Shipmanagement Ltd., Glasgow, managers), and transferred to the British flag.

Chartered Or Managed Dry-Bulk Carriers / Container Ships

operated by

Stena Bulk Ab
Minority- Part Owned,
or
Commercially / Technically Managed by Northern Marine Management Ltd., For Non-Stena Group Owners

FEDERAL HURON

(Internet source / David Kohl)

7803803

BC.1. FEDERAL HURON (1984 - 1986)

As built: 15,977g. 9,672n. 23,323d. 176.51(BB) x 23.09 x 10.41 metres.
Post 1980: 18,461g. 13,708n. 28,676d. 199.80(BB) x 23.09 x metres.
Post 1995: 14,843g. 10,413n. 28,676d.
8-cyl. 2 S.C.S.A. (700 x 1,200mm) MAN K8Z70/120E type oil engine made by VEB Diesel Motorenwerke Rostock, Rostock, geared to shaft with a controllable pitch propeller. 11,200 BHP. 16.25 kts. Thwartship thrust controllable pitch propeller forward.
Ice strengthened, bulk carrier / 1,010 TEU container carrier.
13.3.1978: Keel laid as FONTENOY by VEB Mathias-Thesen-Werft, Wismar (Yard No. 114) for Societe de Courtage et Transports S.A., France. 17.6.1978: Launched. 30.9.1978: Completed for Societe Courtage & Transport, France. 1979: Sold to Federal Pacific, (Liberia), Ltd., Liberia, and renamed FEDERAL HURON. 1980: Sold to Belcan N.V., (N.V., UBEM S.A., managers), Belgium. 1980: Lengthened. 1984 - 1986: Chartered by Stena Bulk Ab. / Concordia Maritime Ab. 1986: Sold to North River Overseas S.A., Panama. 4.6.1988: Grounded three miles off Masinloc during the passage of Typhoon Susan. 11.6.1988: Refloated with minimal damage. 1989: Renamed HURON 1991: Sold to Alexander's Unity Shipping Company Ltd., (Alexco Shipmanagement (Hellas) Ltd., managers), and renamed ALEXANDER'S UNITY, under the Maltese flag. 1992: Sold to Explorer Maritime S.A., (Rokoship Inc., managers), Panama, and renamed LAS BOLINAS. 1997: Sold to Serenity Navigation Ltd., (Seastar Chartering Ltd., managers), under the Panamanian flag. 2000: Sold to Lito Shipping Company Ltd., (DST Shipping Inc., managers), and renamed STAVROS, under the Maltese flag. 2001: Sold to Sea Priority S.A., (same managers). 16.2.2002: Beached at Alang for demolition by Hatim Steel.

7045607

BC.2. PASITHEA (1984 - 1986)

80,225g. 68.442n. 155,407d. 300.52(BB) x 44.23 x 17.139 metres
10-cyl. 2 S.C.S.A. (840 x 1,800mm) B&W 10K84EF type, oil engine made by Hitachi Zosen, Sakurajima Works, Osaka. 22,700 BHP. 16 kts.
Ore / oil carrier.
1.9.1970: Launched by Hitachi Zosen, Innoshima (Yard No. 4263), for Metis Shipping Company, (Andreadis organisation), Greece. 29.1.1971: Completed. 1984: Sold to SAO Financing & Trading S. A., Greece, and chartered by Stena Bulk Ab., / Concordia Maritime Ab. 1986: Released from charter. 4.8.1990: Departed from Kashima to avoid the approaching typhoon "Vernon" and subsequently disappeared with her crew of 31. A lifeboat from her was found drifting in a position 36.09N., 141.52E. together with an oil slick and other articles in the area.

7127170

BC.3. PONTOPORIA (1984 - 1986)

80,194g. 67,815n. 155,375d. 301.02(BB) x 44.25 x 17.160 metres
10-cyl. 2 S.C.S.A. (840 x 1,800mm) B&W 10K84EF type, oil engine made by Hitachi Zosen, Sakurajima Works, Osaka. 22,700 BHP. 16 kts.
Ore / oil carrier.
7.9.1971: Launched by Hitachi Zosen, Innoshima (Yard No. 4264), for Pax Steamship Company S.A., (Andreadis organisation), Greece. 22.12.1971: Completed. 1984 until 1986: Chartered by Stena Bulk Ab., / Concordia Maritime Ab. 1990: Sold to Jacamar Inc., (Societe Anonyme Monegasque d'Administration Maritime et Aeriene (S.A.M.A.M.A.), managers), and renamed CORNELIAN. 1995: Sold for demolition.

8000331

BC.4. RAYNA (1984 - 1986)

32,293g. 25,553n. 59,400d. 224.52(BB) x 32.0 x 12.401 metres.
6-cyl. 2 S.C.S.A. (760 x 1,550mm) Sulzer 6RND76M type, oil engine made by Hitachi Zosen, Sakurajima Works, Osaka. 13,500 BHP. 14.75 kts.
Bulk Carrier, strengthened for heavy cargoes.
1980: Ordered from Hitachi Zosen, Hiroshima Works, Innoshima (Yard No. 4672), by Anders Jahre, Norway. 27.12.1980: Keel laid. 10.3.1981: Launched as RAYNA for Epos Marine Corporation, Greece. 19.6.1981: Completed. 11.1984: Taken on charter by Stena Bulk Ab. 1986: Renamed STENA TRUST. 1988: Transferred to Australica Shipping (Pte.), Ltd., (Northern Marine Management Ltd., managers), Singapore, and renamed STENA AUSTRALICA. 1988: Sold to P.C.-Tan Investments Pte. Ltd., (International United Shipping Agency Ltd., managers), Singapore, and renamed UNITED AMBITION. 1995: Sold to the Great Eastern Shipping Company Ltd., (Five Stars Shipping Company Pvt Ltd., managers), India, and renamed JAG MANEK. 2000: Sold to Ohkoshi Maritime S. A., (Dong Luk Marine Company Ltd., managers), Panama, and renamed KOURYU. 2002: Sold to Ohkosho Maritime S.A., (TMT Company Ltd., Taipai, managers), and renamed LUCKY DUCKLING, under the Panamanian flag 2003: Sold to Estimar Marine, Taipai, China, (same managers), and renamed LUSTRE DUCKLING, retaining the Panamanian flag.

8105636

BC.5. STENA FORTUNA (1986 - 1989)

32,241g. 25,626n. 60,005d. 224.52(BB) x 32.26 x 12.458 metres.
6-cyl. 2 S.C.S.A. (760 x 1,550mm) Sulzer 6RND76M type, oil engine made by the shipbuilders Sakurajima Works, Osaka. 13,500 BHP. 14.75 kts.
Bulk carrier, strengthened for heavy cargoes.
1981: Ordered from Hitachi Zosen, Hiroshima Works, Innoshima (Yard No. 4702), by Anders Jahre, Norway. 3.12.1982: Keel laid. 10.02.1983: Launched as CAPTAIN STAMATIS for Sotiras Maritime Corp., (Phoenix Maritime Agencies Inc., managers), Greece. 27.4.1983: Completed. 1986: Sold to Yulie Glory Shipping Corp., Philippines, chartered by Stena Bulk Ab., / Concordia Maritime Ab., and renamed STENA FORTUNA. 1987: Sold to the San Lorenzo Shipping Corporation. 1989: Released from charter, sold to Drystone Shipping Ltd., (V Ships (U.K.) Ltd., managers), Bahamas, and renamed FORTUNA. 1994: Sold to Blue Cove Marine Ltd., (Marine Managers Ltd., managers), and renamed TRIDENT FORTUNE. under the Greek Flag. 2002: Sold to Brass Shipping Company Ltd., Dubai, (Emirates Trading Agency LLC, Dubai, managers), and renamed PEARL OF SHARJAH, under the Cypriot flag.

BC.6. STENA TRUST (1986 - 1988) see ship No. BC.4 above.

BC.7. STENA AUSTRALICA (1988) see ship No. BC.4. above.

8102256

BC.8. STENA AFRICA (1988)

36,341g. 26,372n. 64,584d. 224.37 x 32.24 x 13.023 metres.
7-cyl. 2 S.C.S.A. (670 x 1,700mm) B&W 7L67GFCA type oil engine made by Hyundai Shipbuilding & Heavy Industries, Ulsan. 15,200 BHP. 14.5 kts.
Bulk carrier.
20.1.1982: Keel laid as FORT PROVIDENCE by Hyundai Heavy Industries Company Ltd., Ulsan (Yard No. 188), for Canadian Pacific (Bermuda) Ltd., (Canadian Pacific Steamships Ltd., managers), London. 2.4.1982: Launched. 26.7.1982: Completed. 1985: Canadian Pacific Bulkship Services Ltd., became managers. 1986: Transferred to the Hong Kong flag. 1988: Chartered to Stena Bulk Ab., (BCP Ship Management Ltd., managers), and renamed STENA AFRICA. 1988: Sold to El Seguro Inc., Greece, and renamed CAPTAIN GEORGE L. 2003: Sold to Sportif Maritime S.A., Greece, (Stamford Navigation S.A, Piraeus, managers), and renamed CAPTAIN GEORGE I. 4.2005: Sold to Godiva Ship Management SA, Piraeus, (same managers), under the Panamanian flag.

6809563

BC.9. CONVEYOR (1996 - 2001)

As built: 39,503g. 29,595n. 75,608d. 799' 2"(BB) x 106' 2" x 47' 8¾"
Post 1994: 44,099g. 22,585n. 75,608d. 243.59(BB) x 32.36 x 14.548 metres.
Two steam turbines made by General Electric Corp, Lynn, Mass., double reduction geared to screw shaft. 16,500 SHP. 15.5 kts.
Self-discharging bulk carrier.
25.11.1967: Launched as UNIVERSE CONVEYOR by Kure Zosensho K. K., Kure (Yard No. 152), for Seatankers Inc., Liberia. (O.N. 2933). (Ludwig's National Bulk Carrier Group). 1968: Completed. 1980: Sold to N. D. S. Shipping Inc., Liberia, and renamed CONVEYOR. 1996: Universe Tankships (Delaware) L. L. C., (Stena Group) appointed as managers. 2001: Northern Marine Management USA L.L.C, appointed as managers. 14.11.2001: Arrived at Alang for demolition.

7035951

BC.10. KURE (1996 - 2002)

As built: 76,003g. 61,128n. 159,162d. 996' 9"(BB) x 142' 2" x 57' 2½"
Post 1994: 89,623g. 47,667n. 159,162d. 303.82(BB) x 43.34 x 17.477 metres.
Two steam turbines made by the shipbuilder at their Tokyo Works, double reduction geared to screw shaft. 27,500 SHP. 15.5 kts.
Self discharging bulk Carrier.
15.10.1970: Launched as CEDROS PACIFIC by Ishikawajima Harima Heavy Industries (IHI), Kure (Yard No. 2118), for Seatankers Inc., Liberia. (O.N. 3764). (Ludwig's National Bulk Carrier Group). 1971: Completed as UNIVERSE KURE for Universe Tankships Inc., Liberia. 1980: Sold to N. D. S. Shipping Inc., Liberia, and renamed KURE. 1996: Universe Tankships (Delaware) L. L. C., (Stena Group) appointed as managers. 2001: Northern Marine Management USA L.L.C, appointed as managers. 21.11.2002: Departed from Mitsukoshima enroute to Xinhui for demolition.

LOCUST (Courtesy Fotoflite)

7001027

BC.11. LOCUST (1996 - 2001)

As built: 75,392g. 61,642n. 162,813d. 990' 10"(BB) x 142' 3" x 57' 3"
Post 1994: 88,826g. 46,845n. 162,813d. 302.01(BB) x 43.36 x 17.450 metres.
Two steam turbines made by the General Electric Corp, Lynn, Mass., double reduction geared to screw shaft. 23,000 SHP. 16 kts.
Bulk Carrier.
31.10.1969: Completed as UNIVERSE AZTEC by Ishikawajima Harima Heavy Industries (IHI), Kure (Yard No. 2116), for Seatankers Inc., Liberia, (O.N. 3357). (Ludwig's National Bulk Carrier Group). 1975: Transferred to Universe Tankships Inc., Liberia. 1988: Transferred to Valeswood Company Inc., Liberia, and renamed LOCUST. 1996: Universe Tankships (Delaware) L. L. C., appointed as managers. 2001: Northern Marine Management USA L.L.C, appointed as managers. 24.9.2001: Departed from Tubarao enroute to Xinhui for demolition. 15.11.2001: Reported as demolished.

8030130

BC.12. KITT (1998 - 2003)

As completed: 19,579g. 5,873n. 11,434d. 193.91 x 30.00 x 5.001 metres.
As commissioned: 12,480g. 3,744n. - d.

Post 1994: 19,579g. 5,873n. 11,434d.
Two 6-cyl. 4 S.C.S.A. (400 x 460mm) Pielstick 6PC2-5L-400 type engines made by Astilleros Espanoles S. A., Olaveaga Works, Bilbao, reverse reduction geared to twin screw shafts. 7,800 BHP. 13 kts. Twin thwartship thrust propellers forward. (800 BHP)
Fixed Guide 924 TEU containership.
15.12.1981: Keel laid as (Semi-submersible Barge Carrier Dock Ship) JOSEFA TORRES by Astilleros Espanolles S.A., (AESA) Factoria de Sestao, Bilbao (Yard No. 253), unspecified owners. 25.6.1982: Launched. 1983: Completed and placed in lay-up for sale. Subsequently sold to Eastgate Shipping Corp, (Shipping Management S.A.M. (V. Ships), managers), and sent for conversion into a 616 TEU fixed guide, containership under the Liberian flag. 1988: Commissioned as WESTPHALIA. (O.N. 8344). 1993: Renamed EASTGATE. 1996: Sold to unspecified owners, (Cathcart Shipping Ltd., managers), and renamed KITTY under the Bahamas flag. (O.N. 728092). 1998: Sold to Flexone N. V. (Northern Marine Management Ltd., managers), and renamed KITT, under the Bahamas flag. 2003: Sold to Eide Marine Services AS, Hoylandsbygd, Norway, further converted into a dock / heavy lift ship, and renamed EIDE TRANSPORTER, (Karmoy Skipsconsult Management AS), retaining the Bahamas flag. 6.2004: Removed from management.

Dry-Bulk Carriers Chartered By StenOak

YONG JIA

(Internet source)

9236183

YONG JIA (2002 - 2005)

40,437g 25,855n. 74,500d. 225.00 x x 14,250 metres
5-cyl. 2 S.C.S.A. (600 x 2,292m) B&W 5S60MC type engine made by the shipbuilder. 11,624 BHP. 14.5 kts.
Panamax gearless dry-bulk carrier
18.10.2000: Keel laid by Hudong Shipyard, Shanghai (Yard No. H1283A), for Silvercord Shipping Company Ltd., Shenzhen, Republic of China (COSCO-Dalian Shipping Company, managers) under the Hong Kong flag. 28.12.2000: Launched. 30.3.2001: Completed, under Hong Kong flag. 10.2004: COSCO-Shenzhen Shipping Company, appointed as managers.

9278430

PACIFIC BREEZE (2005 -)

39,802g. 25,830n. 76,343d. 217.3 BP 32.26 moulded 19.3 moulded Bulb 4.6 from PP
7-cyl. 2 S.C.S.A. (500 x 2000mm) Mitsui-MAN-B&W 7S50MC-C engine (No.4327) made by Mitsui Engineering & Shipbuilding, 8210kw 14.5 kts.
Panamax gearless dry-bulk carrier

3.10.2003: Keel laid by Sumitoma Heavy Industries (Yard No. 1302). 27.2.2004: Launched. 2.8.2002 until 15.4.2003: Intended for Panamanian flag. 15.4.2003 until 3.2.2004: Intended for Liberian flag. 28.4.2004: Completed for Alba Shipping (UK) Ltd., London, (Scinicariello Ship Management Srl, Naples, managers), under the Isle of Man register.

9080649

EVER YOUNG (2005 -)

38,632g. 24,570n. 73,081d. 225.00(BB) x 32.28 x 13.913 metres

6-cyl. 2 S.C.S.A. (600 x 2,292mm) B&W 6S60MC type engine manufactured by Hyundai Heavy Industries Company Ltd., Ulsan. 11,791 BHP. 14.5 kts.

Panamax gearless dry-bulk carrier

20.3.1995: Keel laid as DARYA PREETH by Samsung Heavy Industries Company Ltd., Geoje (Yard No. 1125), for Preeth Shipping Ltd., (Chellaram Shipping (Hong Kong) Ltd., managers), Hong Kong. 1.08.1995: Launched. 17.8.1995: Completed. 2005: Sold to Shinan Capital Company Ltd, Ansan, S. Korea, (Joong Ang Shipping Company Ltd, Seoul, managers), and renamed EVER YOUNG.

Part Two - Tanker Operations.

Later under the operational control / commercial or technical management of
Stena Bulk Ab
Concordia Maritime Ab
Northern Marine Management Ltd., Clydebank, UK.
Universe Tankships (Delaware) LLC, later restyled as Northern Marine Management USA, LLC, Houston, Texas.
Northern Marine Management (Deutschland) GmbH, Hamburg.
Stentex Management Inc. later restyled as Stena Tanker Management (Bermuda) Ltd

A natural progression from dry-cargo operations was wet-cargo or tankers. A small tanker KANALTANK, was acquired in 1955 and experience gained during her 5-years in the fleet was put to good use a few years later when in 1964, an unexpected opportunity for further tanker experience presented itself. Rederi Ab Concordia was acquired together with their three almost new coastal tankers. These were however disposed of after only a short period in Stena employment, thus placing tanker operations in dormancy until some 14 years later when with the acquisition of MALMROS MULTINA the group entered the gas transport business. This vessel was virtually new and after 3-years successful trading she provided the impetus for developing the tanker trades. *Stena Bulk Ab.*, was incorporated during 1983 to co-ordinate the tanker and dry bulk-cargo trades business which expanded rapidly with several ships being either time or voyage chartered. Some of these vessels were renamed into the STENA style whereas others remained unchanged. All of those vessels renamed with the STENA prefix were chartered with an option to purchase. On the other hand some of the chartered vessels were invested in by the group during their charter period, but only in a small way, remaining registered in their original owner's name, thus by 1986 Stena Bulk were operating 15 vessels totalling some 1.75 million tons deadweight.

Although the company successfully operated some chartered bulk carriers during the 1980's it soon became apparent that the future lay with quality tankers and bulker operations were phased out.

The range of tankers was quite wide, from small chemical through medium size product carriers to "Very Large Crude Carriers (VLCC's)". The latter type was in use during the Iraq/ Iran war and indeed one fell victim to the conflict in 1986 when attacked by Iraqi forces. ACHILLES ex STENA ATLANTICA was subsequently declared a total loss and demolished.

Toward the end of 1988, with the Iraq/ Iran war over to all intents and purposes, the need for Ultra Large Crude Carriers (U.L.C.C.) to act as floating storage tanks rapidly diminished, resulting in the Concordia Maritime activity with the four chartered vessels STENA KING, STENA QUEEN, STENA CONCORDIA, and STENA EXPLORER being decreased in parallel. The STENA KING and STENA QUEEN, two of the worlds top six largest ships had been chartered at $9,000 per day for seven years with the option to purchase after either three or seven years and were employed at Sirri Island on a series of short 3 or 6-month charters. The other pair were among several VLCC's used by Concordia Maritime to either run the gauntlet ferrying the oil from ports like Kharg Island to the giant "Motherships" at Sirri Island, or to export the Iranian oil from them to destinations around the world. With the cessation of hostilities STENA decided to charter the STENA KING and STENA QUEEN on the spot market and secured lucrative charters for them. On 24 April 1989, STENA QUEEN was delivered at $16,500 per day to the Kuwait Petroleum Organization following dry-docking at Dubai. On 5

May STENA KING was delivered at $17,250 per day to VELA the Saudi chartering organization, whilst off Portugal.

Following company success in the large tanker market since the mid-80's, utilizing amongst others, STENA CONCORDIA and STENA EXPLORER both on a 10-year charter to Concordia Maritime coupled with an option to purchase from Daniel K. Ludwig's - Universe Tankships organization, a another six sister ships were purchased from Ludwig during 1989, enbloc for US$200 million, the class operated to 6 owned and 2 chartered. In that year the operational fleet weighed-in at 4.3 million tons deadweight. Ludwig had long believed in his policy of building vessels to higher than normal specification especially in hull plate thickness. It was therefore a set of high quality and well maintained vessels that Stena acquired each with high life expectancy. Although each averaged 17-years, they were in much better condition than similar aged, but lower specification vessels that had already found their way to the scrap yard.

STENA CONDUCTOR (1) was one of the former Ludwig VLCC sister ships. (Courtesy Stena Ab)

As the 1990's progressed so too did company involvement with tankers. In 1993 Stena Bulk were a driving force in VLCC chartering from West Africa, bringing together BP and Shell (USA) thus creating the first space share of tankers. The size and types of tanker were varied with a continual turnover of vessels on charter or under the management of group companies. Having been associated with Texaco for some time it came as no surprise that both partners in 1994, announced the Strategic Marine Alliance involving 50 million tons of international oil cargo shipments per year. Modernisation was also the name of the game with double-skin hull vessels replacing obsolescent single hulls. Coupled with this came the twin engined, twin-ruddered "Max" series of vessels. C-max, V-max and the P-max currently under construction and the E-max emerging from the drawing board.

As the new vessels were entering service the old 1970's built Ludwig vessels, although still performing valuable service were becoming out-moded, although they still had new potential. Several found new owners and employment, the first, in 1994, being sold to ELF, and converted into offshore production/storage vessel, because of the soundness of her hull. Several others subsequently followed a similar path for other operators. Unfortunately there was limited opportunity for this type of work and others found their way to the shipbreakers after thirty or so years service. 1994 also saw the signing of a 5-year, long-term Contract Of Agreement with Petrofina for VLCC transportation of crude from the Middle East to Europe. This was a pioneering "market-related" contract that subsequently became the industry standard.

Stena Bulk's reputation was growing, as was their clientele. 1995 saw an 8-year agreement signed with Engen Petroleum for VLCC shipment of crude oil, at a fixed-rate, from Middle East to South Africa This was the same year that the previous association between Stena Bulk and Texaco was made official with the launch of (50:50) StenTex, with offices world-wide to handle around 600 cargo movements per annum.

The offshore oil industry had long been a source of revenue for the Stena group through their support craft and drilling rig operation (see section 4), but was henceforth to provide further earnings from the transportation of oil. A 50:50 partnership was established in 1996, with the Ugland Group of Norway. Stena Ugland was the vehicle for the investment in shuttle-tankers on 10-15 year contracts with Esso Norway. Concordia Maritime acquired universe Tankships.

The successful operations undertaken by Stena Bulk and its high reputation had attracted the attention of Russian tanker operator Novoship that in the mid 1990's placed several of their fleet under the control of Stena Bulk. Apart from new vessels being added with Stena names, further new business was to spawn from within Russia's oil industry. Progreta S.A., operator of oil terminals and distribution routes, early in 2002, engaged a Finnish Consultancy to study and report on methods of improving their operation. Within that report's recommendations was the introduction of dedicated tonnage and competent experienced operators thereof. By mid-year Stena Bulk had been selected and the first of a series of new purpose-built vessels were ordered to service a ten-year contract to export Russian oil from Baltic ports.

Two VLCC type tankers STENA ARCTICA and STENA ANTARCTICA and an option (STENA ATLANTICA) were ordered in Korea for 2005 delivery whilst contracts for four of the "Stena P-max" products carriers on order by Concordia Maritime / Stena Bulk in Croatia, were sold to Novoship for back-charter to Stena Bulk. Other vessels under construction for Stena would also be utilized. STENA CONTENDER, completed in December 2003, lifted, on behalf of Sibneft, her first cargo from Primorsk on 1 February 2004, whilst Stena Bulk also took her sister LIGOVSKIY PROSPECT for operation.

China Ocean Shipping Company (COSCO) also entered the scene and provided two newly constructed vessels for Stena Bulk operation. DA MING HU and DA YUAN HU were originally intended to carry the names STENA COSMOPOLITAN and STENA COSMOGRAPHIC respectively, the "COS" rather than the usual "CON" or "COM", reflecting their Chinese ownership, but in the end this did not happen.

In the autumn of 2004, in an unexpected move, STENA VISION and STENA VICTORY, from Concordia Maritime subsidiaries, together with STENA COMPANION, STENA COMPATRIOT, STENA CONCORD and STENA CONSUL from Stena subsidiaries, were sold in a package deal to the newly incorporated Arlington Tankers Ltd., Bermuda, which was successfully launched onto the New York Stock Exchange. All six vessels, as part of the transaction were arranged with charter back agreements. Arlington Tankers therefore acquired a very young fleet averaging 1.5 years, and consisting of three pairs of sisters - VLCC, Panamax and Clean Products.

With the coming of the New Year, so to came several interesting transactions. Arlington Tankers acquired a further pair of clean products tankers from Stena. STENA CONTEST and STENA CONCEPT were acquired more or less from the shipyard for US$ 46.5 million each.

In the St Petersburg Times of 3 May 2005, an article discussed the establishment of a co-operative between Stena Bulk / Concordia Maritime and the Russian OAO Sovcomflot, with a stated value of $ 1 billion, that could potentially see the construction of up to ten very large crude carriers (VLCC) of around 200,000 dwt each.

During the summer two further co-operations was announced by Stena Bulk, one with Sonangol, the Angolan oil producer, to operate a pooled fleet, and the second with new Russian partners. The Russian partnership however was to take a different route to previous in that it was for the construction of a series of 15,000 dwt chemical / refined products tankers. To be built at the Vyborg shipyard, the six vessels (and two options) are destined to develop trade in the both the Northern European and Caspian Sea areas and were reported as in conjunction with Transpetrol of Moscow.

During September 2005, the contracts for two tankers were sold for US$112 million to the Greek shipping concern, Aries Maritime Transport coupled with a 2.5 year bareboat-charter agreement, thus STENA COMPASS and STENA COMPASSION would enter company service. The deal reportedly returned some US$ 46 million net-profit to Stena and was also a profit sharing deal with the new owners who would receive 30%.

An article carried in "Lloyd's List" on the 11 October 2005 expanded the information released earlier in the St Petersburg Times of 3 May 2005. The article detailed the size of the fleet and timescales for establishment of the fleet of ice-class 1A vessels to comply with the impositions of the Primorsk Terminal operators. The Sovcomflot - Stena Bulk joint venture due to commence in January 2006, in its first year, is expected to handle approximately 33% (23 million tons) of exports from the terminal. The pool of 10 - 15 high ice-class vessels is expected to expand over the next few years with operators Neste Oil of Finland, Teekay of Norway and Stena's Russian partner Progreta expected to join. Stena has as part of the deal allocated the two ice-class vessels under construction or on order to the pool. STENA ANTARCTICA had her name changed to SCF BALTICA whilst STENA ARCTICA retained her name. Further vessels under construction were chartered from Italian owners and allocated the names STENA ANTARCTICA and STENA ATLANTICA.

In separate negotiations at year end, the Sovcomflot Stena partnership were competing for a $300million project for up to five 75,000 tons ice-class 1A shuttle tankers to operate from the Varandei Terminal in the Arctic to Murmansk on behalf of Lukoil.

The Tanker Fleet

OWNED VESSELS

5180960
T.1. KANALTANK (1955 - 1960)
As built: 125g. 71n. 82.7 x 19.1 x 9.2 feet.
Post 1957: 149g. 71n. 94' 4"x 19' 1"x 6' 0".
Post 1948: 3-cyl. 4 S.C.S.A. (8¾" x 11½") oil engine made by R. A. Lister Ltd., Dursley.
Post 1958: 4-cyl. 2 S.C.S.A. (230 x 400mm) Alpha type oil engine manufactured in 1953 by Frederikshavns Jernstoberie & Maschinfabrik, Frederikshavn. 940 BHP.
Motorised tankbarge, converted from a dumb tankbarge.
1916: Completed as OLJELAETGER No.3 by Kaldnes M.V., Tonsberg (Yard No. 37), for Oslo Oljebunkring AS, (Olav Evensen, manager), Norway. 1948: Motorised and renamed KRISTIAN. 1951: Sold to Nor and Vacuum AS, Norway, and renamed VACUUM 51. 1955: Purchased by Sten A. Olsson Handels Ab, (Sten A. Olsson, manager), Sweden, and renamed KANALTANK. 1957: Lengthened. 1958: Re-engined. 1960: Sold to Ab Donsotank, (Kristen Kristensen, manager), Sweden. 1968: Sold to Sven Emil Gustafsson, Sweden, and renamed NORRTANK. 1972: Sold to Sven Lindberg, Sweden. 1973: Sold to Inge Sanden, Sweden, and renamed RONE. 1978: Owners restyled PR MT Rone, (Bunkerservice I Stockholm Ab, managers). 1980: Owners restyled PR Rone, and removed from management. 19.2.1981: Foundered in heavy seas, having taken on water in the engine room, at a position 15 miles N. W. from Visby.

6407274
T.3. POLANA (1964 - 1966)
As built: 500g. 307n. 1,043d. 206' 9" x 31' 8" x 12' 4".
Post 1995: 694g. 372n. 1,077d.
6-cyl. 4 S.C.S.A. (320 x 480mm) MWM TBRH348SU type oil engine made by Motorenwerke Mannheim A.G. (MWM), Mannheim. 900 BHP. 11.5 kts.
Ice strengthened, motor tanker.
28.1.1964: Launched by Krogerwerft GmbH & Company KG, Schnacht-Audorf, (Yard No. 1196), for Rederi Ab Concordia, (Bertil Magnusson, manager), Sweden. 14.3.1964: Completed. 1964: Owners purchased by Stena Ab, Sweden. 1966: Sold to Rederiet for m.t. Sirion, (Ingmar Matsgaard, manager), Sweden, and renamed SIRION. 1971: Sold to S. Sason and Spirit Shipping and Transport Company, Greece, converted into a wine / vegetable oil tanker, and renamed ELPIDA II. 1976: Sold to 'Pibiemme' Compagnia di Navigazione S.p.A., Italy, and renamed UNIONE SECONDA. 2001: Sold to Hydromar S.p.a., Livorno, Italy.

6411196
T.2. SIRONA (1964 - 1965)
500g. 307n. 1,043d. 206' 9" x 31' 8" x 12' 4".
6-cyl. 4 S.C.S.A. (320 x 480mm) MWM TBRH348SU type oil engine made by Motorenwerke Mannheim A.G. (MWM), Mannheim. 900 BHP. 11.5 kts.
Ice strengthened, motor tanker.
2.4.1964: Launched by Krogerwerft GmbH & Company KG, Schnacht-Audorf, (Yard No. 1197), for Rederi Ab Concordia, (Bertil Magnusson, manager), Sweden. 21.5.1964: Completed. 1964: Owners purchased by Stena Ab, Sweden. 1965: Sold to Rederi I/S Terkol, Denmark, and renamed KAREN TERKOL. 1972: Sold to M. A. P. Tankers Inc., Liberia, and renamed MAKUMBA. 1974: Sold to Petrostar Company Ltd., Saudi Arabia. 1975: Renamed PETROSTAR II. 1993: Sold to Abushal Shipping and Trading Establishment, Saudi Arabia, and renamed AL MA'A 1.

6501355
T.4. ROLLO (1964 - 1965)
As built: 500g. 307n. 1,043d. 206' 9" x 31' 8" x 12' 4".
Post 1990: 497g. 300n. 1,055d.
Post 1998: 897g. 0n. 1,055d.
6-cyl. 4 S.C.S.A. (320 x 480mm) MWM TBRH348SU type oil engine made by Motorenwerke Mannheim A.G. (MWM), Mannheim. 900 BHP. 11.5 kts.
Ice strengthened, motor tanker.
20.10.1964: Launched by Krogerwerft GmbH & Company KG, Rendsburg, (Yard No. 1302), for Rederi Ab Concordia, (Bertil Magnusson, manager), Sweden. 10.12.1964: Completed and sold to Rederiet B. Tornvall Ab, (Rederi Ab Concordia, managers), Sweden. 2.1965: Removed from management. 1970: Sold to de Haas Scheepvaart Maatschappij N. V., Netherlands, and renamed MARE ALTUM. 1977: Owners taken over by

Nedlloyd N. V., Netherlands. 1978: Owners restyled Nedlloyd Bulkchem B. V. 1983: Sold to Effluents Services Ltd., Liverpool, and renamed KINDER. 1988: Sold to Star Tsilairas Maritime and Commercial Company, Greece, and renamed ALEX. 1989: Sold to Star Commercial Shipping Company, Greece. 1993: Lloyd's Register Supplement No.10-May, erroneously stated delete owners – add broken up. 1998: Sold to Star Maritime Commercial Company, Greece. 1.2005: Sold to unspecified Greek buyers, and renamed AGIOS STEFANOS.

ROLLO **as MARE ALTUM** with Panocean funnel during charter

(W. J. Harvey)

7321544

T.5. MANDRILL (1979 - 1980)

34,230g. 20,406n. 41,256d. 216.42(BB) x 32.29 x 11.06 metres.
7-cyl. 2 S.C.S.A. (900 x 1,550mm) Sulzer 7RND90 type oil engine made by Compagnie de Const. Mec. Sulzer, (CCM Sulzer), Mantes. 20,300 BHP. 17.75 kts. Subsequently amended to 18,000 BHP.
Ice strengthened, liquified petroleum gas carrier. (LPG)
1972: Ordered as DOVERTOWN from Cons. Nav. & Ind. De la Mediterranee (C.N.I.M.), La Seyne (Yard No. 1398), by Lofoten Maritime Enterprises, Liberia. 21.6.1973: Launched for the Universal Gas and Oil Company Ltd., London. 5.6.1974: Completed as MALMROS MULTINA for Malmros RA, Sweden. 1979: Purchased by Northern Cold Storage (Transport) Ltd., London, and renamed MANDRILL. 1980: Renamed STENA OCEANICA. 1982: Triport Ferries (Management) Ltd., London, appointed as managers. 1983: Swedish Caledonian Marine Management Ltd., Edinburgh, appointed as managers. 1987: Transferred to Oceanica Shipping Private Ltd., (Austen Maritime Services Pte. Ltd., managers), Singapore. 1988: Northern Marine Management Ltd., appointed as managers. 1988: Sold to Partenrederi Gasstransport, (AS Havtor Management, managers), Norway, and renamed HAVPRINS. 1996: Bergesen d.y. ASA, appointed as managers. 27.4.2004: Demolition commenced at Jiangyin, China.

T.6. STENA OCEANICA (2) (1980 - 1988) see ship No. T.5 above.

7923562

T.7. PRODUCER (1983 - 1986)

22,587g. 13,743n. 39,742d. 173.79(BB) x 32.31 x 11.215 metres
5-cyl. 2 S.C.S.A. (760 x 1,550mm) Sulzer 5RND76M type oil engine made by R.O. Tvornica Dizel Motora, "3 Maj", Rijeka. 11,400 BHP. Thwartship thrust controllable pitch propeller forward.
Ice strengthened, oil / chemical tanker.
1979: Ordered as ATLAS PRODUCER from R.O. Brodogradaliste "3 Maj", Rijeka (Yard No. 609), by Atlas Chemical Carriers Corp., Liberia. 15.12.1981: Keel laid. 10.6.1982: Launched for Tiger Maritime Company S.A., Liberia. 24.12.1982: Completed. 1983: Renamed PRODUCER. 1986: Sold to Vroon B. V., Holland, and renamed FORT PRODUCER. 1987: Sold to Portlea Inc., (Hanseatic Shipping Company Ltd., managers), Liberia. 1990: Sold to KS Producer AS, (Troms Fylkes Dampskipsselskap, managers), Norway, and renamed OWL PRODUCER. 1993: Renamed TROMS PRODUCER. 1997: Sold to Chemical Trader Ltd., (Rederi Ab Sunship, managers), Liberia, and renamed MOON SAPPHIRE. 2002: Sold to Grove Marine Ltd., Singapore, (Thome Ship Management Ltd., Singapore managers), and renamed MONTE LUNA.

STENA ADRIATICA

(Courtesy Fotoflite)

7313676

T.8. STENA ADRIATICA (1983 - 1987)

As built: 12,805g. 7,578n. 22,705d. 159.49(BB) x 23.55 x 9.754 metres.
Post 1986: 12,805g. 7,578n. 22,705d. 161.19(BB) x 23.55 x 9.813 metres
Post 1989: 12,491g. 7,959n. 22,705d.
7-cyl. 2 S.C.S.A. (620 x 1,440mm) B&W 7K62EF type, oil engine made by Hitachi Zosen, Osaka. 9,400 BHP. 15 kts. Thwartship thrust controllable pitch propeller forward.
Clean products tanker.
31.3.1973: Launched as ESSO NAGOYA by Hitachi Zosen, Mukaishima (Yard No. 4363), for Esso Tankers Inc., Liberia. 11.7.1973: Completed. 1983: Purchased by Fernwood Inc., (Swedish Caledonian Marine Management Ltd., managers), Liberia, and renamed STENA ADRIATICA. 1983: Transferred to Adriatic Line Ltd., (same managers), Cayman Islands. 1987: Sold to Fal Bunkering Company Ltd., United Arab Emirates, and renamed FAL XII. 1988: Sold to National Marine Services, United Arab Emirates, and renamed SAJAA. 1989: Sold to Batan Shipping Ltd., (Transmarine Management ApS, managers), Panama, and renamed HELGA COB. 1990: Renamed AMPHION. 1993: Sold to Samta Maritime (Pte) Ltd., (Glory Ship Management Private Ltd., managers), Singapore, and renamed ASEAN PRESTIGE. 4.9.2000: Officially reported as having been demolished.

STENA PHOSPHORUS

(Courtesy Fotoflite)

8023773

T.9. STENA PHOSPHORUS (1983 - 1985)

As built: 5,712g. 3,159n. 8,661d. 129.65 x 19.41 x 6.970 metres.
Post 1994: 5,973g. 3,160n. 8,661d.
8-cyl. 4 S.C.S.A. (400 x 480mm) Sulzer 8ZL40/48 type, oil engine made by "Zgoda" Zaklady Urzadzen Technicznych, Swietochlowice, geared to a controllable pitch propeller. 5,800 BHP. 14.25 kts. Thwartship thrust propeller forward.
Ice strengthened, chemical tanker.
12.2.1981: Keel laid as OT PHOSPHORUS by Ab Oskarshamns Varv, Oskarshamn (Yard No. 439), for OT Rederi, Sweden. 12.6.1981: Launched. 13.10.1981: Completed. 7.1983: Purchased by Stena Bulk Ab (OT Shipping Ab, managers), and renamed STENA PHOSPHORUS. 1984: Transferred to Stena Ab. 1985: Sold to USSR - Latvian Shipping Company, Russia, and renamed ALEKSANDR KAVERZNEV. 1988: Sold to Cargo Chem Ltd., (Milton Marine Management Ltd., managers), Bahamas, and renamed ALPINE FINN. 1989: Mermaid Marine Management Ltd., appointed as managers). 1990: Sold Delship Trading Corp., (same managers), and renamed ALPINE ROSE. 1994: Sold to Mostraum KS, (Anders Utkilens Rederi AS, managers), Bergen, Norway, and renamed MOSTRAUM.

7917575

T.10. STENA SULPHUR (1983 - 1987)

As built: 5,722g. 4,600n. 8,706d. 129.62 x 19.41 x 6.965 metres.
Post 1994: 6,060g. 3,120n. 8,706d.
8-cyl. 4 S.C.S.A. (400 x 480mm) Sulzer 8ZL40/48 type, oil engine made by "Zgoda" Zaklady Urzadzen Technicznych, Swietochlowice, geared to a controllable pitch propeller. 5,800 BHP. 14.25 kts. Thwartship thrust propeller forward.
Ice strengthened, chemical tanker.
20.8.1980: Keel laid as OT SULPHUR by Ab Oskarshamns Varv, Oskarshamn (Yard No. 431), for OT Rederi, Sweden. 16.1.1980: Launched. 23.4.1981: Completed. 7.1983: Purchased by Stena Bulk Ab, (OT Shipping Ab, managers), and renamed STENA SULPHUR. 1984: Transferred to Concordia Maritime Ab, (same managers). 1986: Northern Marine Management Ltd., appointed as managers. 1987: Transferred to Sulphur Shipping Pte. Ltd., Singapore, and renamed SULPHUR. 1987: Sold to S. B. K. Finans AS., Denmark, and renamed CT STAR. 1987: Transferred to S. B. K. Finance (Isle of Man) Ltd., (Brit - Ship (Isle of Man) Ltd., managers), Isle of Man. 1990: Campbell Maritime Ltd., appointed as managers. 1992: Sold to C. T. Shipmanagement Ltd., (same managers), Isle of Man. 1995: Ferm International Shipmanagement Ab appointed as managers, and transferred to Swedish flag. 2001: Sold to Chemtrans Ab., Skarhamn, Sweden, (Brostroms Ship Management Ab., managers). 2004: Vestland Marine, Gdynia, Poland, appointed as managers), and transferred to the Maltese flag.

STENA SULPHUR

(Courtesy Fotoflite)

7386465

T.11. STENA ATLANTICA (2) (1983 - 1986)

As built: 138,821g. 104,301n. 269,195d. 334.02 x 55.07 x 20.432 metres.
Post 1984: 123,660g. 104,301n. 269,195d.
Two, General Electric type, steam turbines made by Astilleros Espanoles S.A., Sestao Works, Bilbao, double reduction geared to single screw shaft. 36,000 SHP. 15.75 kts.
Very Large Crude Carrier. (V.L.C.C.)
12.3.1976: Keel laid as SANTILLANA by Astilleros Espanoles S.A., Factoria du Puerto Real, Cadiz (Yard No.3), for Naviera de Castilla S.A., Spain. 13.1.1977: Launched. 20.9.1977: Completed. 31.7.1982: Arrived at Stavanger for lay up. 1983: Purchased by Sten A. Olsson, Sweden, and renamed STENA ATLANTICA. 1983: Transferred to Vikon Enterprises Ltd., (Three Crowns Marine Management Ltd., managers), Liberia. 1984: Transferred to Freeburg Inc., (same managers). 1986: Renamed ACHILLES. 13.7.1986: Whilst South of Kharg Island, during a ballast voyage, was struck by an Iraqi missile in the aftpeak and set on fire, at a position 28.07N., 51.04E. The fire was subsequently extinguished. 22.7.1986: Arrived in tow at Dubai and was subsequently repaired. 20.12.1986: Whilst anchored at a position 60 miles South from Kharg Island, effecting minor engine repairs, during a loaded voyage from Kharg Island to the Straits of Hormuz, was struck by an Iraqi missile in No.3 tank on the starboard side. The explosion ripped into the tank, toward the deck and ballast tank, igniting surface oil blown on deck, from six adjoining tanks. The ensuing fire destroyed all the lifeboats, and caused a large bubble between the deck and framework. When the fire was eventually extinguished the vessel proceeded to off Dubai, via Larak Island. 26.9.1987: Sold for demolition in Taiwan.

7381568

T.12. STENA CARIBICA (1984 - 1986)

19,459g. 14,482n. 31,185d. 183.62(BB) x 25.96 x 10.980 metres
6-cyl. 2 S.C.S.A. (740 x 1,600mm) B&W 6K74EF type, oil engine made by Hitachi Zosen, Japan. 12,000 BHP. 16 kts.

Oil / chemical tanker.
1973: Ordered from Korea Shipbuilding & Engineering Corp., Busan (Yard No.161), by the Gulf Oil Corp. 15.3.1974: Keel laid. 20.9.1974: Launched as AFRAN NEPTUNE for Afran Transport Corporation, (Gulf Oil), Liberia. 24.3.1975: Completed. 1984: Purchased by Oldburg Inc., (Stena Ab, managers), Liberia, and renamed STENA CARIBICA. 1986: Renamed PETROBULK STENA. 1987: Renamed CARIBICA and removed from management. 1988: Transferred to Sea Pride Inc., Panama. 7.9.1990: Whilst on a voyage from Taiwan to Singapore, suffered explosions and fire at a position 05.30N. 107.11E. Water entered her hull and she sank the following day at a position 05.26N. 107.35E. One member of her crew was killed.

STENA CARIBICA (Courtesy Fotoflite)

THORHAVEN / STENA CHEMICA whilst renaming (W. J. Harvey)

7383463

T.13. STENA CHEMICA (1984)

As built: 4,859g. 2,871n. 7,460d. 135.01(BB) x 17.51 x 6.986 metres
Post 1984: 4,462g. 2,785n. 8,178d.
Post 1995: 5,119g. 2,350n. 8,178d.
As built: 12-cyl. 4 S.C.S.A. (300 x 450mm)(centre), and two, 6-cyl. 4 S.C.S.A. (300 x 45mm) (wings), oil engines made by Grandi Motori Trieste, Trieste, geared to a single screw shaft with a controllable pitch propeller. 6,000 BHP. 16 kts. Thwartship thrust propeller forward.

Post 1984: Two, 6-cyl. 4 S.C.S.A. (320 x 420mm) MaK 9M453AK type oil engines manufactured in 1981 by MaK Maschinenbau GmbH, kiel. 6,000 BHP.
Ice strengthened, oil / chemical tanker.
1.11.1973: Keel laid as THORHAVEN by M.V. Sarpsborg AS KS, Sarpsborg (Yard No. 97), for 'Thorhaven' Schiffahrtsges de Vries & Co. GmbH K.G., (Tankreederei de Vries & Company K.G., managers), W. Germany. 13.7.1974: Launched. 28.11.1974: Completed. 1977: Transferred to Panamanian flag. 1984: Purchased by Evelyn Ltd., (Three Crowns Marine Management Ltd., managers), Liberia, and renamed STENA CHEMICA. 1984: Re engined, and renamed TOL EXPRESS. 1985: Transferred to Panamanian flag, (Northern Marine Management (Cyprus) Ltd., managers). 1988: Removed from management. 1989: Sold to Dayton International Inc., Liberia, and renamed DAYTON. 1991: Sold to Bakri Navigation Company Ltd., Panama, and renamed BAKRI ADVENTURER. 1992: Sold to Marshall Marine Corp., (Barber Ship Management Ltd., managers), Panama, and renamed HATAN. 1995: Red Sea Marine Services, appointed as managers. 1997: Sold to Trans Sea World Shipping Inc., Panama. 27.10.2001: Beached at Alang for demolition by Hussein Sheth Ship Breakers (P) Ltd., India.

THORALBE became STENA GOTHICA (Author's collection / Airfoto, Malacca)

7304883

T.14. STENA GOTHICA (1) (1984)

As built: 4,773g. 2,310n. 7,889d. 129.85(BB) x 17.53 x 7.011 metres.
Post 1984: 4,462g. 2,785n. 8,178d.
As built: 12-cyl. 4 S.C.S.A. (300 x 450mm)(centre), and two, 6-cyl. 4 S.C.S.A. (300 x 45mm) (wings), oil engines made by Grandi Motori Trieste, Trieste, geared to a single screw shaft with a controllable pitch propeller. 6,000 BHP. 16 kts. Thwartship thrust propeller forward.
Post 1984: Two, 7-cyl. 4 S.C.S.A. (300 x 450mm) reconditioned Wichmann 7AXA type oil engines manufactured in 1973 by AS Wichmann, Rubbestadneset. 6,000 BHP.
Ice strengthened, oil / chemical tanker.
2.4.1972: Keel laid as THORALBE, by Langvik, Sarpsborg M.V., Sarpsborg (Yard No. 93), for'Thoralbe' Schiffahrtsges de Vries & Co. GmbH K.G. (Reederei de Vries & Co. K.G., managers), W. Germany. 27.1.1973: Launched. 21.6.1973: Completed. 1977: Transferred to Panamanian flag. 1983: Renamed ALCHEMIST BREMEN. 1984: Purchased by Seaburg Inc., (Three Crowns Marine Management Ltd., managers), Liberia, and renamed STENA GOTHICA. 1984: Renamed STENA CARBOLICA. 1984: Re-engined. 1984: Renamed MARTA Z. 1986: Transferred to Seaburg (No.2) Inc., (Three Crowns Marine Management Ltd., managers), Liberia. 1987: Renamed CHEMICA. 1987: Renamed TOL PACER. 1989: Sold to Marlin Seatrade Inc., Liberia. 1990: To Forchemica di Fabrizio Foresi & Ci S.a.S., Italy, and renamed ROBERTA FORESI. 1992: Sold to Centro Leasing S.p.A., (Interchem S.r.l., managers), Italy, and renamed BETACRUX. 1997: Sold to Peachitree Management S.A., (Pan Nautic S.A., managers), Panama, and renamed ETA BETA. 1998: Sold to Durham Shipping Ltd., Panama. 1999: Sold to Green Ocean Shipping Inc., (Caroil Transport Marine, managers), Panama. 2004: Sold to Walfi Navegacion, (Petrocost, managers), Havana Cuba.

STENA PACIFICA (The World Ship Society Ltd.)

7525425

T.15. STENA PACIFICA (1984 - 1985)

As built: 70,475g. 53,566n. 132,478d. 276.51 x 40.06 x 16.911 metres.
Post 1984: 66,942g. 50,267n. 132,478d.
8-cyl. 2 S.C.S.A. (900 x 1,800mm) B&W 8K90GF type oil engine made by Astilleros Espanoles S.A., Manises Works, Valencia. 27,300 BHP. 15.25 kts.
Motor tanker.
28.11.1975: Keel laid as BEATRIZ MARIA by Astilleros Espanoles S.A., Factoria de Sestao, Bilbao (Yard No. 208), for Naviera Letasa S. A., Spain. 7.9.1976: Launched. 10.2.1977: Completed as ELVIRA C for Compania Vasco Contabrica de Navegacion S.A., Spain. 1984: Purchased by Frostburg Inc., (Three Crowns Marine Management Ltd., managers), Liberia, and renamed STENA PACIFICA. 1985: Transferred to First Maritime S.A., (First Leader Shipping S.A., managers), Greece, and renamed ELEONORA M. 1987: Transferred to Arctic Line Ltd., (Northern Marine Management Ltd., managers), Nassau, and renamed STENA PACIFICA. 1988: Sold to KS Osco Common, (Osco Shipping AS., managers), Norway, and renamed GULF ATLANTIC. 1989: Sold to KS Common Atlantic (Gleneagle Ship Management Company Inc., managers), Norway (NIS). 1992: Sold to Cloudesley Shipping Ltd., (Acomarit (U.K.) Ltd., managers), Cyprus, and renamed SUNRISE 1. 1993: Renamed SARABAND. 1995: Vancouver Shipmanagement Ltd., appointed as managers. 1997: Sold to Monsoon Shipping Company Ltd., (Eurotankers Inc., managers), Cyprus, and renamed MICHAEL. 1998: Sold to Petalon Shipping Company Ltd., (same managers), Malta. 10.10.2000: Suffered main machinery damage and towed 170 miles and anchored 20.10.2000, off Colombo. 2001: Declared as beyond economical repair and sold for demolition. 28.11.2000: Arrived in tow of SALVIGOUR (1,799/90), at Chittagong, Bangladesh for demolition.

T.16. STENA CARBOLICA (1984) see ship No. T.14 above.

T.17. MARTA Z. (1984 - 1987) see ship No. T.14 above.

T.18. TOL EXPRESS **(1984 – 1989)** see ship No. T.13 above.

T.19. ELEANORA M **(1985 – 1987)** see ship No. T.15 above.

T.20. ACHILLES **(1986 – 1987)** see ship No. T.11 above.

T.21. PETROBULK STENA **(1986 – 1987)** see ship No. T.12 above.

T.22. SULPHUR **(1987)** see ship No. T.10 above.

T.23. CHEMICA **(1987)** see ship No. T.14 above.

T.24. CARIBICA **(1987 – 1988)** see ship No. T.12 above.

T.25. STENA PACIFICA **(1987 – 1988)** see ship No. T.15 above.

T.26. TOL PACER **(1987 – 1989)** see ship No. T.14 above.

7929322

T.27. STENA CONQUEST (1989 – 1990)

As built: 39,995g. 30,756n. 86,408d. 243.59 x 41.64 x 12.777 metres.
Post 1991: 53,944g. 34,141n. 86,408d.
Post 1994: 52,003g. 22,515n. 86,408d.
10-cyl 4 S.C.S.A. (570 x 620mm) Pielstick 10PC4-2V-570 vee type oil engine made by the shipbuilder's Aioi works. 15,000 BHP.
Motor tanker.
8.9.1980: Keel laid as NEPTUNE PEGASUS by Ishikawajima Harima Heavy Industry (I.H.I.), Kure (Yard No. 2747), for Neptune Eta Lines Pte. Ltd., Singapore. 27.12.1980: Launched. 28.4.1.1981: Completed. 1988: Chartered by Stena Bulk Ab, with an option to purchase. 1989: Option taken and transferred to Golf Shipping Pte Ltd., (Stena Bulk Ab, managers), Singapore, and renamed STENA CONQUEST. 1990: Sold to Wind Conquest AS, (Wind Management AS, managers), Norway, and renamed WIND CONQUEST. 1991: Sold to Malaysian International Shipping Corporation Berhad (MISC), Malaysia, and renamed BUNGA KERANJI. 1999: Sold to Sea Spray Shipping Ltd., Malta, and renamed LATO M. 2000: Sold to Beauty Holdings Ltd., (Fairdeal Group Management S.A., managers), and renamed SORENA, under the Panamanian flag. 7.2004: Reported as renamed RENA for final voyage to unspecified shipbreakers. 22.7.2004: Demolition commenced.

7383401

T.28. STENA CONSUL (1) (1989 – 1991)

33,134g. 19,091n. 59,650d. 211.16(BB) x 32.24 x 13.22 metres.
6-cyl. 2 S.C.S.A. (900 x 1,800mm) B&W 6K90GFCA type oil engine made by Nylands Verksted AS., Oslo. 20,500 BHP.
Motor tanker.
11.8.1974: Keel laid as JANE MAERSK by Kaldnes M.V. AS, Tonsberg (Yard No. 203), for A. P. Moller, Denmark. 18.4.1975: Launched. 19.9.1975: Completed. 1984: Sold to VEB Deutfracht, E. Germany, and renamed SCHWEDT. 1988: Chartered by Stena Bulk Ab., with an option to purchase. 1989: Option taken and transferred to Ewan Enterprise Ltd., (Stena Bulk Ab., managers), Liberia, and renamed STENA CONSUL. 1990: Transferred to Consul Vessel Inc., (Wallem Shipmanagement Ltd., managers), Liberia. 1991: Renamed CONSUL, V.Ships (USA) Inc., appointed as managers. 1995: Renamed RED TEAL, (SOSEMA S. A., (Societe de Services Maritimes S. A.) appointed managers). 1995: Sold to Haworth Shipping Company Ltd., and removed from management. St. Vincent & The Grenadines flag.1996: Sold to Red Teal Shipping Corp. & Bumi Armada Navigation Sendirian Berhad, (SOSEMA S. A., (Societe de Services Maritimes) managers). 1997: Sold to Bumi Armada Navigation Sendirian Berhad, Kuala Lumpur, Malaysia, converted into a processing tanker storage vessel for offshore installations, and renamed ARMADA PERKASA.

7358133

T.29. STENA KING (1990 – 2002)

231,629g. 183,336n. 457,927d. 378.42(BB) x 68.05 x 25.04 mtrs.
Two, steam turbines made by Ishikawajima Harima Heavy Industries, (I.H.I.), Tokyo, double reduction geared to screw shaft. 45,000 SHP. 15.25 kts.
Ultra large crude carrier (U.L.C.C.).
1973: Ordered as BURMAH ENTERPRISE from China Shipbuilding Corp., Kaohsiung (Yard No. 2), by Marine Transport Lines (Oswego), Liberia. 10.3.1977: Keel laid. 31.1.1978: Launched for Burmah Enterprise Ltd., (Denholm Ship Management Ltd., managers), London. 1978: Completed. 1983: Burmah

Oil Tankers Ltd., appointed as managers. 1986: Transferred to Bermudan flag. 22.12.1987: Whilst berthed at Larak Island suffered minor damage, inflicted by Iraqi aircraft. 1988: Chartered with option to purchase by Stena Bulk Ab, and renamed STENA KING. 1990: Option taken and transferred to Royal Blue Shipping Ltd., (Northern Marine Management Ltd., managers). 2002: Sold to Oceanic Trans Shipping, Saudi Arabia, (same managers), and renamed FOLK II. 1.6.2003: Reported departing Barbados bound to mainland China shipbreakers.

STENA KING

(Courtesy Stena Ab)

STENA QUEEN (Courtesy Stena Ab)

7358121

T.30. STENA QUEEN (1990 - 2002)

231,629g. 183,336n. 457,927d. 378.42(BB) x 68.05 x 25.04 mtrs.
Two, steam turbines made by Ishikawajima Harima Heavy Industries, (I.H.I.) Tokyo, double reduction geared to screw shaft. 45,000 SHP. 15.25 kts.
Ultra large crude carrier (U.L.C.C.).
1973: Ordered as BURMAH ENDEAVOUR from China Shipbuilding Corp., Kaohsiung (Yard No. 1), by Marine Transport Lines (Oswego), Liberia. 18.11.1975: Keel laid. 3.6.1977: Launched for Burmah Endeavour Ltd., (Denholm Ship Management Ltd., managers), London. 1977: Completed. 1983: Burmah Oil Tankers Ltd., appointed as managers. 1986: Transferred to Bermudan flag. 14.5.1988: Whilst being used as a storage vessel at Hormuz Terminal, Larak Island, was attacked by Iraqi aircraft and set on fire. Fire was quickly extinguished and vessel sustained only minor damage. 1988: Chartered with option to purchase by Stena Bulk Ab, and renamed STENA QUEEN. 1990: Option taken and transferred to Royal Sky Shipping Ltd., (Northern Marine Management Ltd., managers). 2002: Sold to Oceanic Trans Shipping, Saudi Arabia, (same managers), and renamed FOLK I. 9.4.2003: Reported departing Kakinada bound to mainland China shipbreakers.

STENA CONCORDIA (The World Ship Society Ltd.)

7326908

T.31. STENA CONCORDIA (1990 - 2001)

As built: 122,199g. 101,698n. 273,408d. 337.07(BB) x 54.56 x 21.067 mtrs.
Post 1994: 132,206g. 101,322n. 273,616d.
Two, steam turbines, made by the shipbuilders Tokyo works, double reduction geared to screw shaft. 40,000 SHP. 16 kts.
Very Large Crude Carrier, (V.L.C.C.).
1973: Ordered as UNIVERSE BURMAH from Ishikawajima Harima Heavy Industries, (I.H.I.), Kure (Yard No. 2283), by National Bulk Carriers, Liberia. 5.2.1973: Keel laid. 24.5.1973: Launched. 20.9.1973: Completed for Universe Tankships Inc., Liberia. 1980: Sold to Gray Shipping Inc., Liberia. 1986: Chartered by Stena Bulk Ab / Concordia Maritime Ab, with an option to purchase, and renamed STENA CONCORDIA. 22:50hrs. 26.6.1987: Whilst on a ballast voyage at a position 27.58N., 49.29E. was struck in the engine room aft, by a missile which started a fire which was subsequently extinguished by her crew. 28.6.1987: Arrived in tow off Bahrain for repair. 21.7.1987: Returned to service. 22.12.1987: Attacked with shellfire by an Iranian Frigate, whilst off Dubai, suffering engine room damage. 24.12.1987: Reached Bahrain under her own power for repair. 1991: Option taken and transferred to Shining Seaways Ltd. 1993: Transferred to AFG Concordia Ltd., Partnership. 1997: Sold to Freehaven Ltd. (Universe Tankships (Delaware) L. L. C., managers). 2000: Transferred to Bermudan flag (O.N. 731281). 2001: Sold to Halliburton Produtos Ltda, Rio De Janiero, converted into an FPSO and renamed PETROBRAS 48, for charter - employment off the Brazilian coast. 8.2005: Sold to Baracuda & Caratinga Leasing B.V., Amsterdam, (Petrobras, managers).

7351812

T.32. STENA CONDUCTOR (1) (1990 - 2003)

As built: 122,199g. 101,698n. 273,409d. 337.07(BB) x 54.56 x 21.07 mtrs.
Post 1994: 132,206g. 101,322n. 273,409d.
Two, steam turbines made by the shipbuilders Tokyo Works, double reduction geared to screw shaft. 40,000 SHP. 16 kts.
Very Large Crude Carrier, (V.L.C.C.).
1973: Ordered as UNIVERSE EXPLORER from Ishikawajima Harima Heavy Industries, (I.H.I.), Kure (Yard No. 2284), by National Bulk Carriers, Liberia. 11.9.1973: Keel laid. 10.12.1973: Launched. 3.4.1974: Completed for Universe Tankships Inc., Liberia. 1980: Sold to Gray Shipping Inc., Liberia. 1986: Chartered by Stena Bulk Ab / Concordia Maritime Ab, with option to purchase, and renamed STENA EXPLORER. 18.6.1987: Struck a mine at a position 28.57N., 48.47E., whilst on a loaded voyage. 24.6.1987: Arrived Khor Fakkan Anchorage, from Mina al Ahmadhi to iquefied cargo. Subsequently repaired. 27.7.1987: Sailed for Singapore after reloading. 1990: Option taken and renamed STENA CONDUCTOR, registered owner remaining Gray Shipping Inc. 1997: Sold to Seahaven Ltd. (Universe Tankships (Delaware) L. L. C., managers). 2003: Sold to Single Buoy Moorings S.A., Marly Switzerland, converted into an offshore processing vessel, and renamed FPSO ATLAS, under the Bermudan flag.

STENA CONSTELLATION (The World Ship Society Ltd)

7370246

T.33. STENA CONSTELLATION (1990 - 2005)

As built: 122,199g. 101,698n. 273,410d. 337.96(BB) x 54.51 x 21.07 mtrs
Post 1994: 132,206g. 101,322n. 273,410d.
Two steam turbines made by the shipbuilders Tokyo works, double reduction geared to screw shaft. 40,000 SHP. 14 kts.
Very Large Crude Carrier, (V.L.C.C.).
1972: Ordered as UNIVERSE SENTINEL from Ishikawajima Harima Heavy Industries, (I.H.I.), Kure (Yard No 2346), by National Bulk Carriers, Liberia. 24.2.1975: Keel laid. 30.5.1975: Launched. 23.12.1975: Completed for Universe Tankships Inc., Liberia. 1980: Sold to Gray Shipping Inc., Liberia, and renamed HAMLET. 1988: Chartered by Stena Bulk Ab, with an option to purchase. 1990: Option taken and transferred to Hickory Maritime Ltd., (Stena Bulk Ab, managers), Liberia, and renamed STENA CONSTELLATION. 1992: Transferred to Stena Constellation Shipping Ltd., Houston, Texas. 1996: Universe Tankships (Delaware) L. L. C., appointed as managers. 2005: Sold to unspecified Bermudan flag operators, (SBM Production Contractors S. A., Monte Carlo, Monaco, managers), and renamed CAPELLA.

7370181

T.34. STENA CONTENDER (1) (1990 - 1995)

As built: 122,199g. 101,698n. 273,268d. 337.04(BB) x 54.56 x 20.981 metres
Post 1994: 132,206g. 101,322n. 273,268d.
Two steam turbines made by the shipbuilders Tokyo works, double reduction geared to screw shaft. 40,000 SHP. 16.75 kts.
Very Large Crude Carrier, (V.L.C.C.).
1973: Ordered as UNIVERSE RANGER from Ishikawajima Harima Heavy Industries, (I.H.I.), Kure (Yard No. 2293), by National Bulk Carriers, Liberia. 14.12.1973: Keel laid. 19.4.1974: Launched. 12.8.1974: Completed for Universe Tankships Inc., Liberia. 1980: Sold to Gray Shipping Inc., Liberia, and renamed MENANIC. 1988: Chartered by Stena Bulk Ab., with an option to purchase. 1990: Option taken and

transferred to Noah Navigation Ltd., (Stena Bulk Ab., managers), Liberia, and renamed STENA CONTENDER. 1992: Transferred to Stena Contender Shipping Ltd. 1995: Sold to B. E. Storage Ltd., (Single Buoy Moorings Inc., managers), Bahamas, and renamed NKOSSA 1. 1996: Converted into an FPSO. 1998: Managers restyled as SBM Production Contractors Inc. 12.2.2004: Sold to SBM-Imodco, Houston, Texas, and renamed YOHO. 9.2005: Sold to Mobil Producing Nigeria Unlimited, Houston, Texas. (SBM-Imodco, Houston, Texas, managers).

STENA CONTENDER (Courtesy Stena Ab)

STENA CONCEPT (The World Ship Society Ltd.)

7370234

T.35. STENA CONCEPT (1) (1990 - 2003)

As built: 122,199g. 101,698n. 253,998d. 337.04(BB) x 54.51 x 20.116 mtrs.
Post 1994: 132,206g. 101,322n. 253,998d.
Post 2000: 132,206g. 103,147n. 264,653d.
Two steam turbines made by the shipbuilders Tokyo works, double reduction geared to screw shaft. 40,000 SHP. 16 kts.
Very Large Crude Carrier, (V.L.C.C.)
1973: Ordered as UNIVERSE MONITOR from Ishikawajima Harima Heavy Industries, (I.H.I.), Kure (Yard No.2345), by National Bulk Carriers, Liberia. 15.11.1974: Keel laid. 18.2.1975: Launched. 7.11.1975 Completed for Universe Tankships Inc., Liberia. 1980: Sold to Gray Shipping Inc., Liberia, and renamed MOSELLE. 1988: Chartered by Stena Bulk Ab., with option to purchase. 1990: Option taken and transferred to Hillsbrook Shipping Inc., (Stena Bulk Ab., managers), Liberia, and renamed STENA CONCEPT. 1992: Transferred to Stena Concept Shipping Ltd., Houston, Texas. 1997: Universe Tankships

(Delaware) L. L. C., appointed as managers. 2000: Transferred to Bermudan flag (O.N. 731282). 5.8.2003: Reported at Singapore enroute to Chinese shipbreakers.

7370193

T.36. STENA CONGRESS (1990 - 2005)

As built: 122,199g. 101,698n. 273,206d. 337.04(BB) x 54.54 x 21.070 mtrs.
Post 1994: 132,206g. 101,322n. 273,206d.
Two steam turbines made by the shipbuilders Tokyo works, double reduction geared to screw shaft. 40,000 SHP. 16 kts.
Very Large Crude Carrier, (V.L.C.C.)
1973: Ordered as UNIVERSE MARINER from Ishikawajima Harima Heavy Industries, (I.H.I.), Kure (Yard No. 2294), by National Bulk Carriers, Liberia. 24.4.1974: Keel laid. 24.7.1974: Launched. 13.11.1974: Completed for Universe Tankships Inc., Liberia. 1980: Sold to Gray Shipping Inc., Liberia, and renamed PECONIC. 9.7.1987: Whilst on a ballast voyage from Loop Terminal to Mena Saud was struck in a bunker tank by an Iranian missile at a position 28.15N., 49.23E., 8 miles from the Zulof Oilfields. The fire was extinguished with the assistance of SMIT MATSAS 2. 10.7.1987: Arrived at Bahrain for repairs. 20.7.1987: Departed for Ran Tanura. 1988: Chartered by Stena Bulk Ab., with option to purchase. 1990: Option taken and transferred to Herndon Maritime Corp., (Stena Bulk Ab., managers), Liberia, and renamed STENA CONGRESS. 1992: Transferred to Stena Congress Shipping Ltd. 1997: Universe Tankships (Delaware) L. L. C., appointed as managers. 2000: Transferred to the Bermudan flag. 2.2005: Sold to SBM Production Contractors Inc., Monte Carlo, Monaco, for conversion into an FPSO, and renamed FPSO CAPIXABA, under the Maltese flag.

STENA CONTINENT (Courtesy Stena Ab)

7370208

T.37. STENA CONTINENT (1990 - 2001)

As built: 122,199g. 101,698n. 273,187d. 337.04(BB) x 54.54 x 21.067 mtrs.
Post 1994: 132,206g. 101,322n. 273,187d.
Two steam turbines made by the shipbuilders Tokyo works, double reduction geared to screw shaft. 40,000 SHP. 16 kts.
Very Large Crude Carrier, (V.L.C.C.)
1973: Ordered as UNIVERSE GUARDIAN, from Ishikawajima Harima Heavy Industries, (I.H.I.), Kure (Yard No. 2336), by National Bulk Carriers, Liberia. 31.7.1974: Keel laid. 8.11.1974: Launched. 10.4.1975: Completed for Universe Tankships Inc., Liberia. 1980: Sold to Gray Shipping Inc., Liberia, and renamed ARCADIA. 1988: Chartered by Stena Bulk Ab., with option to purchase. 1990: Option taken and

transferred to Hillcrest Maritime Inc., (Stena Bulk Ab., managers), Liberia, and renamed STENA CONTINENT. 1992: Transferred to Stena Continent Shipping Ltd.1997: Universe Tankships (Delaware) L. L. C., appointed as managers. 2000: Transferred to Bermudan flag (O.N. 731283). 2001. Sold to Kellogg, Brown & Root, Houston, (Brown & Root, managers), converted into an FPSO at Jurong, Singapore, and renamed PETROBRAS 43, for charter – employment off the Brazilian coast. 8.2005: Sold to Baracuda & Caratinga Leasing B.V., Amsterdam, (Petrobras, managers).

STENA CONVOY (Courtesy Stena Ab)

7226885

T.38. STENA CONVOY (1990 – 2003)

As built: 117,246g. 97,576n. 262,631d. 336.00(BB) x 54.56 x 20.289 metres
Post 1994: 127,535g. 97,318n. 262,631d.
Two steam turbines made by the shipbuilders Tokyo works, double reduction geared to screw shaft. 40,000 SHP. 16.75 kts.
Very Large Crude Carrier, (V.L.C.C.)
1972: Ordered as UNIVERSE PIONEER from Ishikawajima Harima Heavy Industries, (I.H.I.), Kure (Yard No. 2268), by National Bulk Carriers, Liberia. 6.6.1972: Keel laid. 12.8.1972: Launched. 2.12.1972: Completed for Universe Tankships Inc., Liberia. 1980: Sold to Gray Shipping Inc., Liberia, and renamed LAUREL. 1988: Chartered by Stena Bulk Ab., with an option to purchase. 1990: Option taken and transferred to Nuevo Leon Maritima S. A., (Stena Bulk Ab., managers), Liberia, and renamed STENA CONVOY. 1992: Transferred to Stena Convoy Shipping Ltd. 1995: Transferred to C.M. Convoy Shipping Ltd. 1997: Universe Tankships (Delaware) L. L. C., appointed as managers. 2000: Transferred to Bermudan flag. 5.6.2003: Reported at Singapore enroute to Chinese shipbreakers.

9003081

T.39. STENA CONFIDENCE (1) (1990 – 1995)

As built: 52,450g. 28,000n. 97,113d. 246.84(BB) x 42.0 x 13.419 metres.
Post 1994: 52,500g. 28,137n. 97,113d.
6-cyl. 2 S.C.S.A. (720 x 2,500mm) Sulzer 6RTA72 type oil engine made by Mitsubishi Heavy Industries Ltd., Kobe. 12,240 BHP. 14 kts.
Double skinned tanker.
1990: Ordered 50:50 by Stena Ab & Mitsui O.S.K. from Imabari Zosen, Marugame (Yard No. 1177). 16.4.1990: Keel laid. 21.8.1990: Launched. 30.10.1990: Completed for Sona Maritime S. A., (Mitsui O.S.K. Lines Ltd., managers), Panama. 1995: Renamed SEA CONFIDENCE, and removed from management. 1997: Sold to Cypress Maritime (Panama) S. A., Panama. 1999: Sold to Top Spin Shipping Ltd., (Minerva

Marine Inc., managers), Malta, and renamed MINERVA HELEN. 2002: Sold to Sunflower Navigation, Athens, (Cardiff Marine S.A., Athens, managers), and renamed CORCOVADO, retaining Maltese flag. 2004: Sold to Big Ship Corp Inc., (Novoship (UK) Ltd., London, managers). 2.2005: Renamed ALMIRANTE BRION, under Venezuelan flag. 8.2005: Sold to Sudamerica De Transportes Petrolero, London, (same managers).

STENA CONFIDENCE (1) at New York (Courtesy Stena Ab.)

T.40. CONSUL (1991 - 1995) see ship No. T.28 above.

STENA BARBADOS (Courtesy Fotoflite)

8914192

T.41. STAR BARBADOS / STENA BARBADOS (1994 - 2003)

4,094g. 2,129n. 6,330d. 101.52 x 17. 60 x 6.071 metres.
8-cyl. 4 S.C.S.A. (320 x 360mm) Normo BRM-8 type oil engine made by BMV Bergen Diesel AS, Bergen, geared to a controllable pitch propeller. 4,000 BHP 10.2 kts. Thwartship thrust propeller forward.
Ice strengthened, oil, chemical, caustic soda tanker.
9.10.1989: Keel laid as KATARINA by Argos Engineering Company Pte. Ltd., Singapore (Yard No. 8630), for Mai Shipping KS, (H. E. Hansen-Tangen, managers), Bahamas. 12.7.1990: Launched. 4.3.1991: Completed. 1994: Sold to CM Barbados Shipping Ltd., Bahamas, (Stentex Shipmanagement Ltd., managers), and renamed STAR BARBADOS. 1995: Renamed STENA BARBADOS, (Northern Marine Management Company Ltd., appointed as managers). 1996: Transferred to Concordia Maritime Ab, (Fern

International Ship management Ab., appointed as managers). 2000: Sold to Wisby Tankers Ab., Visby, Sweden, (Wisby Shipmanagement Ab., Visby, managers). 2003: Renamed WISBY BARBADOS.

STENA SIRITA (Courtesy Fotoflite)

9188099

T.42. STENA SIRITA (1999 -)

76,836g. 34,036n. 127,466d 262.61(BB) x x 15.500 metres.
Two, 7-cyl. 2.S.C.S.A. (500 x 1,910mm) B&W 7S50MC type oil engines made by Mitsui Engineering & Shipbuilding Company Ltd., Tamano, geared to twin controllable pitch propellers. 22,280 BHP. 14.8 kts. Two Thwartship thrust propellers forward & aft.
Bow loading tanker for offshore installations.
1.11.1998: Keel laid by Hashihama Shipbuilding Company Ltd., Tadotsu (Yard No. 1157), for P/R Stena Ugland Shuttle Tanker, Grimstad, Norway, (Ugland Nordic Shipping ASA, managers), Norway. 30.3.1999: Launched. 10.8.1999: Completed. 2000: IUM Ship Management AS., Grimstad, appointed as managers. 2005: Ugland Nordic Shipping AS, Sandefjord, appointed as managers.

STENA VISION

(Courtesy Stena Ab)

9205081

T.43. STENA VISION (2001 -)

163,761g. 110,069n. 312,638d. 336.00 (BB) x 70.9 x 19.00 metres
Two, 7-cyl. 2 S.C.S.A. (600 x 2,292mm) B&W 7S60MC type engines made by the shipbuilder. 38,681 BHP. 17 kts.
V-max class double skinned, twin rudder, tanker

17.10.2000: Keel laid by Hyundai Heavy Industry Company Ltd., Ulsan (Yard No.1250), for Concordia Maritime Ab, Sweden, under Liberian flag. 2.1.2001: Launched. 24.4.2001: Completed for CM V-Max 2 Ltd., (Universe Tankships (Delaware) L.L.C., managers). 5.2005: Transferred to Vision Ltd., Houston, Texas, and to Bermudan flag, (Northern Marine Management USA L.L.C., Houston, appointed as managers.

9205093

T.44. STENA VICTORY (2001 -)

163,761g. 110,069n. 312,679d. 336.00 (BB) x 70.9 x 19.00 metres

Two, 7-cyl. 2 S.C.S.A. (600 x 2,292mm) B&W 7S60MC type engines made by the shipbuilder. 38,681 BHP. 17 kts.

V-max class double skinned, twin rudder, tanker

5.12.2000: Keel laid by Hyundai Heavy Industry Company Ltd., Ulsan (Yard No.1251), for CM V-Max 1 Ltd., (Universe Tankships (Delaware) L.L.C., managers). 22.3.2001: Launched. 29.6.2001: Completed. 5.2005: Transferred Victory Ltd., Houston Texas, and to Bermudan flag, (Northern Marine Management USA L.L.C., Houston, appointed as managers).

STENA NATALITA (Courtesy Fotoflite)

9206671

T.45. STENA NATALITA (2001 -)

62,393g. 30,304n. 108,073d. 246.30(BB) x43.00 x 15.019 metres.

Two, 6-cyl. 2.S.C.S.A. (600 x 2,292mm) B&W 6S60MC type oil engines made by Mitsui Engineering & Shipbuilding Company Ltd., Tamano, geared to twin controllable pitch propellers. 33,360 BHP. 15 kts. Two Thwartship thrust propellers forward & aft.

Bow loading tanker for offshore installations.

14.9.2000: Keel laid by Tsuneishi Shipbuilding Company Ltd., Numakuma (Yard No. 1166), for P/R Stena Ugland Tankers III DA, Grimstad, (IUM Shipmanagement, Grimstad, managers), under Cayman Islands flag. 27.12.2000: Launched. 27.5.2001: Completed. 2005: Transferred to Bahamas flag.

STENA SPIRIT (Internet source)

9208033

T.46. STENA SPIRIT (2002 -)

82,650g. 46,578n. 152,244d. 274.30 (BB) x x 16.4 metres
6-cyl. 2 S.C.S.A. (700 x 2,800mm) B&W 6S7-MC-C type engine made by the shipbuilder at Changwon, geared to a controllable pitch propeller. 22,799 BHP. 15.2 kts. Thwartship thrust propeller forward.
Double skinned, bow loading tanker for offshore installations.
4.9.2000: Keel laid as ERVIKEN by Samsung Heavy Industries Company Ltd., Koje (Yard No. 1305), for Viken Crude AS, (Vista Ship Management A/S, managers), Norway. 25.11.2000: Launched. 19.1.2001. Completed. 2002: Sold to P/R Stena Spirit Tankers, Grimstad, (IUM Shipmanagement, Grimstad, managers), and renamed STENA SPIRIT, under the Bahamas flag.

STENA CARIBBEAN (Internet source / L. Van Duivendijk)

9228875

T.47. STENA CARIBBEAN (2002 -)

8,613g. 3,308n. 10,400d. 120.65 (BB) x 23.8 x 6.500 metres.
Two, 6-cyl. 4 S.C.S.A. (320 x 350mm) Wartsila 6R32LND type oil engines each 3,018 BHP., made by Wartsila S. A. C. M. Diesel, driving a generator powering 2,200Kw 1RN4 506-6FM90-Z type electric motors made by Siemens AG, driving twin fixed pitch directional propellers. 12 kts. Fixed pitch thwartship thrust propeller forward.
Double hull, diesel-electric powered liquified gas and oil products tanker.
30.11.2001: Keel laid by Stockznia im "Komuny Paryskiej" Gdynia, Poland (Yard No. 8226-1), for Stena Maritime AG (Universe Tankships (Delaware) L.L.C., managers). 8.3.2002: Launched. 25.6.2002: Completed for Stena Ferries Ltd., Ashford, (same managers). 2004: Northern Marine Management USA L.L.C., Houston, appointed as managers, remaining under British flag.

9228887

T.48. STENA CALYPSO (2002 -)

8,624g. 3,288n. 9,996d. 120.65 (BB) x 23.8 x 6.500 metres.
Two, 6-cyl. 4 S.C.S.A. (320 x 350mm) Wartsila 6R32LND type oil engines each 3,018 BHP., made by Wartsila S. A. C. M. Diesel, driving a generator powering 2,200Kw 1RN4 506-6FM90-Z type electric motors made by Siemens AG, driving twin fixed pitch directional propellers. 12 kts. Fixed pitch thwartship thrust propeller forward.
Double hull, diesel-electric powered liquified gas and oil products tanker.
18.3.2002: Keel laid by Stockznia im "Komuny Paryskiej" Gdynia, Poland (Yard No. 8226-2), for Stena Maritime AG. (Universe Tankships (Delaware) L.L.C., managers). 18.5.2002: Launched. 21.10.2002: Completed under British flag. 2003: Transferred to Stena Ferries Ltd., Ashford, (Northern Marine Management USA L.L.C., Houston, managers), retaining British registry.

STENA CALYPSO (Internet source / L. Van Duivendijk)

STENA VENTURE (Internet source / L. Van Duivendijk)

9252187

T.49. STENA VENTURE (2003 -)

39,272g. 20,743n. 72,000dwt 228.5 x 32.2 x 19.6 metres.
7-cyl. 2 S.C.S.A (500 x 1,910mm) B&W 7S50MC type oil engine made by Hitachi Zosen Corporation, Nagasu Kumamota. 13,601 BHP. 15 kts.
5.4.2002: Keel laid as SANKO VENTURE by Hitachi Zosen Corporation, Maizuru (Yard No. 4990), for Glory Transportation Inc., Hong Kong. 31.7.2002: Launched. 20.11.2002: Completed. 2003: Sold to Stena Venture (Hong Kong) Shipping Ltd., (V-Ships Germany, Hamburg, managers), Germany, and renamed STENA VENTURE, under Hong Kong flag. 2005: Transferred to Stena Venture Shipping GmbH, Hamburg, (same managers), under Marshall Islands flag.

9255933

TC.50. STENA COMPANION (2) (2003 -)

41,593g. 20,919n. 72,735d. 228.6 x 32.23 x 12.5 metres.
6-cyl 2S.C.S.A. (600 x 2,292mm) MAN B&W 6S60MC type oil engine made by Mitsui Engineering & Shipbuilding Company Ltd., Tamano. 16,680 BHP. 14.8 kts.
Double skinned tanker.
11.2.2003: Keel laid by Dalian Shipyard, Dalian, Peoples Republic of China (Yard No. PC720-1), for Panisland Ltd., Bermuda (Northern Marine Management USA. L.L.C., Houston, managers) 3.7.2003: Launched. 8.1.2004: Completed. 2005: Transferred to Companion Ltd., Houston, USA, (same managers).

STENA COMPANION (2)

(Courtesy Stena Ab)

T.51. WISBY BARBADOS (2003 -) see ship No. T.41 above.

STENA CONCORD

(Internet source / John Gorton)

9258600

T.52. STENA CONCORD (2004 -)

27,357g. 13,866n. 47,171d. 182.5 (BB) x 32.23 x 12.200 metres.
6-cyl. 2 S.C.S.A. (500 x 2,000mm) MAN B&W 6S50MC-C type oil engine made by Strojogradnja "Uljanik" d.d., Pula, Croatia. 11,665 BHP. 14.5 kts.
Double skinned chemical / oil products tanker.
26.4.2003: Keel laid by Uljanik Brodogradiliste dd, Pula (Yard No. 448), for Oceanspirit Ltd., Houston, (Northern Marine Management USA L.L.C., Houston, managers). 13.9.2003: Launched. 26.2.2004: Completed for Concord Ltd., Houston, (same managers), under the Bermudan flag.

STENA COMPATRIOT (Internet source / Marcelo Lopes)

9255945
T.53. STENA COMPATRIOT (2004 -   )
41,593g. 20,919n. 72,735d. 228.6 x 32.23 x 12.5 metres.
6-cyl 2S.C.S.A. (600 x 2,292mm) MAN B&W 6S60MC type oil engine made by Mitsui Engineering & Shipbuilding Company Ltd., Tamano.
Double skinned tanker.
20.7.2003: Keel laid by Dalian Shipyard, Dalian (Yard No. PC720-2), for Panocean Ltd, Houston (Northern Marine Management USA. L.L.C., Houston, managers). 22.11.2003: Launched. 15.4.2004: Completed for Compatriot Ltd., Houston, (same managers), under the Bermudan flag.

9283459
T.54. WISBY VERITY (2004 -   )
4,295g. 2,150n. 7,479d. 116.30(BB) x x 7.1 metres.
8-cyl. 4 S.C.S.A. (320 x 480mm) MaK8M32 type oil engine made by Caterpillar Moteren GmbH & Company KG, Kiel, geared to a controllable pitch propeller. 5,221 BHP. 13 kts.
26.6.2002: Keel laid by Ferus Smit Leer GmbH, Leer (Yard No. 344), for Wisby Tankers Ab., Visby, Sweden, (Wisby Shipmanagement Ab., Visby, managers). 15.5.2004: Launched. 6.7.2004: Completed.

STENA ALEXITA (Courtesy Fotoflite)

T.55. STENA ALEXITA (1998 - 2004) see ship No. TC.42 in charter section

9299123
T.56. STENA PARIS (2005 -   )
36,000g. n. 65,200d 182.9 x x 13.0 metres.

Two, 6-cyl. 2 S.C.S.A. (460 x 1,932mm) B&W 6S46MC-C type oil engines made by the shipbuilder. 21,372 BHP.
P-max class double skinned, twin rudder, tanker
23.12.2004: Keel laid by Brodogradiliste, Split (Yard No. 441), for Concordia Maritime Ab. Sweden, planned for the Liberian flag. 4.6.2005: Launched. 14.12.2005: Completed for CM P-Max 1 Ltd., (Northern Marine Management Ltd., Clydebank, managers), under Swedish flag

STENA ARCTICA (2) at Gothenburg for christening ceremony (Courtesy Stena Ab)

9305556
T.57. STENA ATLANTICA (3) STENA ARCTICA (2) (2005 -)
65,293g. 35,715n. 117,099d. 249.79 x 44.07 x 15.422 metres
7-cyl. 2 S.C.S.A. (600 x 2,400mm) B&W 7S60ME-C type oil engine made by the shipbuilder. 21,490 BHP.
B-Max class - Ice strengthened, double skinned crude oil carrier.
23.12.2004: Keel laid by Hyundai Heavy Industries Company Ltd., Ulsan (Yard No. 1621), for Stena Rederi Ab, (Concordia Maritime Ab., managers), for Liberian flag. 9.9.2005: Launched as STENA ARCTICA. 1.11.2005: Completed, (Stena Bulk Ab, managers), under Swedish flag.

SCF BALTICA fitting out.

(Courtesy Sovcomflot)

9305568
T.58. STENA ANTARCTICA (1)/ SCF BALTICA (2005 -)
65,293g. 35,715n. 116,500d. 249.79 x 44.07 x 15.422 metres
7-cyl. 2 S.C.S.A. (600 x 2,400mm) B&W 7S60ME-C type oil engine made by the shipbuilder. 21,490 BHP.
B-Max - Ice strengthened, double skinned crude oil carrier.
23.12.2004: Keel laid by as STENA ANTARCTICA by Hyundai Heavy Industries Company Ltd., Ulsan (Yard No. 1622), for unspecified owners, (Concordia Maritime Ab., managers), for Liberian flag. 21.10.2005:

Launched. 6.12.2005: Completed as SCF BALTICA for Ashbourne Navigation Inc., (Concordia Maritime Ab, Gothenburg,) under Liberian flag.

9299135

T.59. STENA PROVENCE (2006 -)

36,000g. n. 65,200d 182.9 x x 13.0 metres.
Two, 6-cyl. 2 S.C.S.A. (460 x 1,932mm) B&W 6S46MC-C type oil engines made by the shipbuilder. 21,372 BHP.
P-max class double skinned, twin rudder, tanker
8.3.2005: Keel laid by Brodogradiliste, Split (Yard No. 442), for Concordia Maritime Ab, Sweden, under the Liberian flag. 4.8.2005: Launched for CM P-Max 1 Ltd., (Northern Marine Management Ltd., Clydebank, managers), under the Liberian flag

Tankers On Order Or Under Construction.

Stena P-Max Class.

Impression of the Stena P-max class of twin-engine, twin-rudder, double-skin hulled tanker. (Courtesy Stena Ab)

9299147

T. STENA PERFORMANCE (2006 -)

36,000g. n. 65,200d 182.9 x x 13.0 metres.
Two, 6-cyl. 2 S.C.S.A. (460 x 1,932mm) B&W 6S46MC-C type oil engines made by the shipbuilder. 21,372 BHP.
P-max class double skinned, twin rudder, tanker
4.6.2005: Keel laid by Brodogradiliste, Split (Yard No. 443), for Concordia Maritime Ab, Sweden. 5.11.2005: Launched for CM P-Max 2 Ltd., (Northern Marine Management Ltd., Clydebank, managers).

9299159

T. STENA PROGRESS (2006 -)

36,000g. n. 65,200d 182.9 x x 13.0 metres.
Two, 6-cyl. 2 S.C.S.A. (460 x 1,932mm) B&W 6S46MC-C type oil engines made by the shipbuilder. 21,372 BHP.
P-max class double skinned, twin rudder, tanker

4.8.2005: Keel laid by Brodogradiliste, Split (Yard No. 444), for CM P-Max 2 Ltd., (Northern Marine Management Ltd., Clydebank, managers).

9312444

T. STENA PRIMORSK (2006 -)

36,000g. n. 65,200d 182.9 x x 13.0 metres.

Two, 6-cyl. 2 S.C.S.A. (460 x 1,932mm) B&W 6S46MC-C type oil engines made by the shipbuilder. 21,372 BHP.

P-max class double skinned, twin rudder, tanker

2006: Brodogradiliste, Split (Yard No. 445), for CM P-Max 3 Ltd., (Concordia Maritime Ab)

9312456

T. STENA PROGRETA (2006 -)

36,000g. n. 65,200d 182.9 x x 13.0 metres.

Two, 6-cyl. 2 S.C.S.A. (460 x 1,932mm) B&W 6S46MC-C type oil engines made by the shipbuilder. 21,372 BHP.

P-max class double skinned, twin rudder, tanker

2006: Brodogradiliste, Split (Yard No. 446), for CM P-Max 3 Ltd., (Concordia Maritime Ab)

Other Types Of Tankers On Order.

9334698

T. STENA POLARIS (2006 -)

40,000g. 74,999dwt

Double skinned oil products tanker.

September 2004: Ordered from Brodospas Split (Yard No. 454) by Concordia Maritime Ab. for 10 year contract plying Finland to USA

9334703

T. STENA POSEIDON (2007 -)

40,000g. 74,999dwt

Double skinned oil products tanker.

September 2004: Ordered from Brodospas Split (Yard No. 455) by Concordia Maritime Ab. for 10 year contract plying Finland to USA

Chartered Or Managed Tankers

operated by

Stena Bulk Ab
Stentex Inc. (Stena & Texaco Management Inc)
Also
Minority- Part Owned, or Commercially / Technically Managed For Non-Stena Group Owners
by
Northern Marine Management Ltd., Clydebank, UK
Northern Marine Management USA, LLC, Houston, Texas.
(formerly Universe Tankships (Delaware) L.L.C.)
Northern Marine Management (Deutschland) GmbH, Hamburg.

(**N.B.** Northern Marine Management provide either Commercial or Technical management for those vessels quoted against their name. In the case of Technical management there will usually be another Commercial manager quoted)

TC.1. PASITHEA **(1984 - 1986)** see Ship No. BC.2 above.

TC.2. PONTOPORIA **(1984 - 1986)** see Ship No. BC.3 above.

TC.3. STENA EXPLORER (1) **(1986 - 1990)** see ship No. T.33 above.

TC.4. STENA CONCORDIA **(1986 - 1990)** see ship No. T.32 above.

TC.5. STENA KING **(1988 - 1990)** see ship No. T.29 above.

TC.6. STENA QUEEN **(1988 - 1990)** see ship No. T.30 above.

TC.7. NEPTUNE PEGASUS **(1988 - 1989)** see ship No. T.28 above.

TC.8. SCHWEDT **(1988 - 1989)** see ship No. T.29 above.

TC.9. HAMLET (1) **(1988 - 1990)** see ship No. T.34 above.

TC.10. MENANIC **(1988 - 1990)** see ship No. T.35 above.

TC.11. MOSELLE **(1988 - 1990)** see ship No. T.36 above.

TC.12. PECONIC **(1988 - 1990)** see ship No. T.37 above.

TC.13. ARCADIA **(1988 - 1990)** see ship No. T.38 above.

TC.14. LAUREL **(1988 - 1990)** see ship No. T.39 above.

STENA CONCERT (The World Ship Society Ltd)

8918265

TC.15. STENA CONCERT (1992 - 1999)

As built: 54,944g. 28,543n. 96,828d. 241.78(BB) x x 13.923 metres.
Post 1999: 56,855g. 28,453n. 96,828d.
7-cyl. 2 S.C.S.A. (620 x 2,150mm) Sulzer 7RTA62 type oil engine made by Mitsubishi Heavy Industries Ltd., Kobe. 12,260 BHP.
Double skinned tanker.
23.4.1991: Keel laid by Namura Ship Building Company Ltd., Imari (Yard No. 915), for Blue Exelsior Maritime Corp, Panama. 1.11.1991: Launched. 5.2.1992: Completed. 1995: Transferred to Robin Maritime S.A., (Thome Shipmanagement Private Ltd., managers), Panama. 1999: Sold to Andromeda Ltd., (Minerva Marine Inc., managers), Malta, and renamed MINERVA CONCERT. 2002: Sold to Polo Shipping, Athens, (Cardiff Marine S.A., Athens, managers), and renamed TSUNAMI, under the Maltese flag. 2005: Renamed SARATOSA.

STENA CONCERTINA (1) (The World Ship Society Ltd)

8917821

TC.16. STENA CONCERTINA (1) (1992 - 1999)

51,984g. 30,092n. 96,687d. 232.04(BB) x 42.03 x 14.217 mtrs.
6-cyl. 2 S.C.S.A. (620 x 2,150mm) Sulzer 6RTA62 type oil engine made by Diesel United Ltd., Aioi. 14,200 BHP.
Double skinned tanker.
17.7.1991: Keel laid by Sumitomo Heavy Industries Ltd., Oppama Shipyard, Yokosuka (Yard No. 1174), for Polaris Transport S.A., London (Mitsui O.S.K. Lines Ltd., managers), Panama. 10.12.1991: Launched. 24.2.1992: Completed. 1996: MOL Tankship Management Ltd., London, appointed as managers. 1999: Renamed ATLANTIC HERO.

7359307

TC.17. ENERGOS (1993 - 1996)

As built: 18,939g. 11,171n. 31,102d. 170.49(BB) x 25.96 x 11,056 metres
Post 1994: 18,235g. 11,046n. 31,102d.
6-cyl. 2 S.C.S.A. (760 x 1,550mm) Sulzer 6RND76 type oil engine made by H. Cegielski, Poznan. 12,000 BHP. 16.25 kts.
Tanker
20.4.1974: Keel laid as MOBIL REFINER by Rauma-Repola Oy, Rauma/Raumo (Yard No. 226), for Petroleum Transport International (Pty) Ltd., (Mobil Shipping Company Ltd., managers), S. Africa. 22.8.1974: Launched. 28.2.1975: Completed. 1989: Sold to Energos Transport Proprietary Ltd., and renamed ENERGOS (O.N. 2665), under St Vincent and The Grenadines flag. 1992: P&O Ship Management Ltd., London, appointed managers. 1993: Northern Marine Management Ltd., Glasgow, appointed as managers. 1996: Sold to New Boundary Shipping Company Inc., (Unicorn Marine Management Services, managers). 1998: Sold to Waterline Shipping Ltd., (Styga Compania Naviera SA, Piraeus, managers), and renamed LISSOS M, under the Maltese flag. 14.8.2002: Beached at Alang for demolition by Shree Saibaba Ship Breaking Company.

9012317

TC.18. STENA SAVONITA (1994 - 1997)

As built: 58,959g. 31,119n. 108,683d. 243.80(BB)x 42.03 x 15.02 metres.
Post 1994: 79,999d.
7-cyl. 2.S.C.S.A. (600 x 2,292mm) B&W 7S60MC type oil engine made by Mitsui Engineering and Shipbuilding Company Ltd., Tamano. 13,092 BHP. 14 kts.
Post 1994: Tanker for offshore installations.
21.1.1992: Keel laid as SAVONITA by Tsuneishi Zosen K.K., Numakuma (Yard No.662), for Savonita Shipping Ltd., (Ugland Maritime Services AS., managers), Norway. 25.5.1992: Launched. 9.11.1992: Completed. 1994: Converted and renamed STENA SAVONITA. 1997: Sold to Ugland Nordic Shipping AS, and renamed NORDIC SAVONITA. 2004: Sold to Nordic Savonita L.L.C., Grimstad, Norway, (IUM Shipmanagement, Grimstad, managers).

STENA SAVONITA
as NORDIC SAVONITA

(Internet source)

STAR CARIBBEAN (Courtesy Fotoflite)

7403366

TC.19. STAR CARIBBEAN (1994 - 1997)

131,303g. 104,286n. 273,775d. 337.04(BB) x 54.56 x 21.048 metres.
Two steam turbines made by the shipbuilder at their Tokyo Works, double reduction geared to screw shaft. 36,000 SHP. 16 kts.
Tanker.
31.8.1976: Keel laid as TEXACO CARIBBEAN by Ishikawajima Harima Heavy Industries Company Ltd., (IHI), Kure (Yard No. 2483), for Lexington Tankships Ltd., West Palm Beach, USA, (Texaco Marine Services Inc., managers), under the Panamanian flag. 14.1.1977: Launched. 15.4.1977: Completed. 1990: Renamed STAR CARIBBEAN. 1994: Stena Tanker Management (Bermuda) Ltd., appointed managers. 1997: Renamed MAGDELAINE, (Tankship Transport Ltd., West Palm Beach, managers), under the Bahamas flag

7403354

TC.20. STAR VERAGUAS (1994 - 1996)

As built: 125,856g. 104,496n. 274,165d. 337.02(BB) x 54.56 x 21.002 metres.
Post 1996: 131,303g. 104,286n. 274,165d.
Two steam turbines made by the shipbuilder at Tokyo Works, double reduction geared to screw shaft. 40,000 SHP. 16 kts.
Very large crude carrier (VLCC).
20.1.1976: Keel laid as TEXACO VERAGUAS by Ishikawajima Harime Heavy Industries Company Ltd., (IHI), Kure (Yard No. 2482), for Wellington Tankships Ltd., West Palm Beach, USA. 8.5.1976: Launched. 20.10.1976: Completed, under the Panamanian flag. 1990: Renamed STAR VERAGUAS. 1994: Stena

Tanker Management (Bermuda) Ltd., appointed managers. 1996: Renamed MARGAUX, (Tankship Transport Ltd., West Palm Beach, managers), under the Bahamas flag. 2006: Undergoing conversion to FPSO at Dubai, for service off Brazil.

STAR VERAGUAS (Courtesy Fotoflite)

STAR JAPAN (Courtesy Fotoflite)

7376812
TC.21. STAR JAPAN (1994 - 1999)

129,973g. 94,292n. 267,732d. 338.62(BB) x 53.62 x 20.551 metres.
Two steam turbines made by the shipbuilder, geared to screw shaft. 34,000 SHP. 16.5 kts.
Very large crude carrier (VLCC).
20.8.1974: Keel laid as TEXACO JAPAN by Mitsubishi Heavy Industries Ltd., Nagasaki (Yard No. 1733), for Texaco Panama Inc., Liberian flag. 14.12.1974: Launched. 24.4.1975: Completed. 1990: Renamed STAR JAPAN. 1994: Stena Tanker Management (Bermuda) Ltd., appointed managers. 1999: Sold to Dong Aheng Tankers Pte. Ltd., Hong Kong, and renamed JIU HUA SAN, under the Panamanian flag. 4.5.2003: Sailed from Kalbut bound for Chinese Shipbreakers.

7354890
TC.22. STAR AFRICA (1994 - 1997)

133,297g. 102,422n. 274,597d. 331.55(BB) x 56.06 x 20.700 metres.
Two steam turbines made by Kawasaki heavy industries Ltd., kobe, geared to screw shaft. 36,000 SHP. 16 kts.
Very large crude carrier (VLCC).
6.9.1973: Keel laid as TEXACO AFRICA by Mitsui Shipbuilding & engineering Company Ltd., Ichihara (Yard No. 980), for Texaco Panama Inc., Liberian flag. 29.3.1974: Launched. 4.7.1974: Completed. 1990: Renamed STAR AFRICA. 1994: Stena Tanker Management (Bermuda) Ltd., appointed as managers. 1997: Sold to Tanker Navigation ASA (Jahre-Wallem AS, managers), Bahamas, and renamed TN AFRICA. 22.10.2002: Reported as demolished.

STAR AFRICA (Courtesy Fotoflite)

STAR OHIO (Internet source)

9014846

TC.23. STAR OHIO (1994 -)

80,569g. 45,730n. 143,750d. 274.00(BB) x x 15.500 metres
6-cyl. 2 S.C.S.A. (600 x 2,674mm) B&W 6S70MC type engine made by Korea Heavy Industries & Construction Company Ltd., Changwon 20,941 BHP. 14.25 kts.
Tanker.
28.5.1992: Keel laid as CITADELLE by Samsung Shipbuilding & Heavy Industries Company Ltd., Koje (Yard No. 1089) for unspecified owners associated with LASMO. 9.8.1992: Launched. 9.10.1992: Completed as STAR OHIO for Texaco Panama Inc., Panama, under the Liberian flag. 1994: Stena Tanker Management (Bermuda) Ltd., managers. 2000: Northern Marine Management Ltd., Glasgow, appointed as managers.

7389510

TC.24. COMPANION / STENA COMPANION (1994 - 2002)

As built: 164,062g. 146,624n. 357,023d. 362.49 x 60.05 x 22.353 mtrs.
Post 1994: 169,593g. 149,369n. 357,023d.
Two steam turbines made by Stal-Laval - Kockums M.V. Ab, at Finspang, double reduction geared to screw shaft. 40,000 SHP. 15.5 kts.
Very large crude carrier (VLCC).
3.6.1976: Keel laid as SEA SONG by Kockums Varv (Shipyard) AB, Malmo (Yard No. 557) for Salenrederierna Ab, Stockholm. 24.1.1977: Launched. 10.3.1977: Completed. 1988: Sold to Acromar Shipping Ltd., Limassol, (Hanse Bereederungs-Gesellschaft mbH & Company K. G., managers), and renamed RADWAN G, under the Cypriot flag. 1990: Sold to Aquameander Corporation Inc., (Peder Smedvig AS, manager), Norway, and renamed HANSA VEGA. 1994: Renamed COMPANION, transferred to Bahamas flag, (Northern Marine Management Ltd., appointed as managers). 1995: Sold to Wheelhouse (Bermuda) Ltd., (same managers). 7.1997: Universe Tankships (Delaware) L. L. C., appointed as managers, and renamed STENA COMPANION. 2000: Transferred to Bermudan flag (O.N. 731279). 2002: Sold to Cotco Ltd., Leatherhead, Surrey, UK, (International Marine Ltd., Leatherhead, Surrey, managers), and renamed KOME KRIBI 1, under Cameroon flag.

ADYGEJA (Internet source / L. Van Duivendijk)

8014784

TC.25. ADYGEJA (1995 - 2004)

As built: 31,821g. 22,032n. 61,341d. 224.98 (BB) x x 12.521 metres
Post 1995: 36,782g. 18,166n. 61,341d.
6-cyl. 2 S.C.S.A. (760 x 1,550mm) Sulzer 6RND76M type engine made by Sumitomo Heavy Industries Ltd., Tamashima. 12,960 BHP. 15 kts.
Panamax type tanker.
1.7.1981: Keel laid as NORSE VENTURE by Oshima Shipbuilding Company Ltd., Oshima (Yard No.10054), for Aurora Carriers Inc., (Venture Shipping (Managers) Ltd., managers). 10.10.1981: Launched. 7.1.1982: Completed, under the Liberian flag. 1986: Sold to USSR-Novorrossiysk Shipping Company, (NOVOSHIP), Russia, and renamed ADYGEJA. 1995: Sold to Tuscany Maritime S. A., (Novoship U.K.) Ltd., London, managers), under the Liberian flag. 16.3.2004: Arrived at Chittagong for demolition.

9105061

TC.26. TAMAN (1996 -)

26,218g. 11,273n. 40,818d. 181.00(BB) x 32.03 x 11.00 metres
6-cyl. 2 S.C.S.A. (500 x 1,910mm) B&W 6S50MC type oil engine (No. 315) made by Strojogradnja "Uljanik" d.d., Pula, Croatia. 11,298 BHP. 15.1 kts.
Double-hulled oil / chemical tanker.
17.6.1994: Keel laid by Brodogradiliste "Uljanik"d.d., Pula (Yard No. 414), for Taman Shipping Inc., (Novoship (UK) Ltd., London, managers), under the Liberian flag. 24.6.1995: Launched. 2.2.1996: Completed.

9105097

TC.27. TEMRYUK (1996 -)

26;218g. 11,273n. 40,584d. 181.00(BB) x 32.03 x 10.980 metres
6-cyl. 2 S.C.S.A. (520 x 1,810mm) Sulzer 6RTA52U type oil engine made by "3 Maj" Motori I Dizalice d.d., Rijeka. 11,298 BHP. 15.1 kts.
Double-hulled oil / chemical tanker.
17.6.1994: Keel laid by Brodogradiliste "3 Maj", Rijeka (Yard No. 669), for Temryuk Shipping Inc., (Novoship (UK) Ltd., London, managers), under the Liberian flag. 28.7.1995: Launched. 6.3.1996: Completed.

9105102

TC.28. TIMASHEVSK (1996 -)

26;218g. 11,273n. 40,584d. 181.00(BB) x 32.03 x 10.980 metres
6-cyl. 2 S.C.S.A. (520 x 1,810mm) Sulzer 6RTA52U type oil engine made by "3 Maj" Motori I Dizalice d.d., Rijeka. 11,298 BHP. 15.1 kts.
Double-hulled oil / chemical tanker.
19.5.1995: Keel laid by Brodogradiliste "3 Maj", Rijeka (Yard No. 670), for Timashevsk Shipping Inc., (Novoship (UK) Ltd., London, managers), under the Liberian flag. 27.4.1996: Launched. 4.10.1996: Completed.

TIMASHEVSK

(Courtesy Fotoflite)

9105073

TC.29. TIKHORETSK (1996 -)

26;218g. 11,286n. 40,791d. 181.00(BB) x 32.03 x 11.00 metres
6-cyl. 2 S.C.S.A. (500 x 1,910mm) B&W 6S50MC type oil engine (No. 316) made by Strojogradnja "Uljanik" d.d., Pula, Croatia. 11,302 BHP. 15.1 kts.
Double-hulled oil / chemical tanker.
24.6.1995: Keel laid by Brodogradiliste "Uljanik"d.d., Pula (Yard No. 415), for Tikhoretsk Shipping Inc., (Novoship (UK) Ltd., London, managers), under the Liberian flag. 16.3.1996: Launched. 18.7.1996: Completed.

9105085

TC.30. TROITSK (1996 -)

26;218g. 11,286n. 40,816d. 181.00(BB) x 32.03 x 11.00 metres
6-cyl. 2 S.C.S.A. (500 x 1,910mm) B&W 6S50MC type oil engine (No. 317) made by Strojogradnja "Uljanik" d.d., Pula, Croatia. 11,298 BHP. 15.1 kts.
Double-hulled oil / chemical tanker.
4.6.1995: Keel laid by Brodogradiliste "Uljanik"d.d., Pula (Yard No. 416), for Troitsk Shipping Inc., (Novoship (UK) Ltd., London, managers), under the Liberian flag. 16.10.1995: Launched. 7.11.1996: Completed.

9112129

TC.31. TVER (1996 -)

26;218g. 11,286n. 40,743d. 181.00(BB) x 32.03 x 11.00 metres
6-cyl. 2 S.C.S.A. (500 x 1,910mm) B&W 6S50MC type oil engine made by by Tvornica Dizel Motora Split, Split. 11,302 BHP. 15.1 kts.
Double-hulled oil / chemical tanker.
23.5.1995: Keel laid by Brodogradiliste "Trogir", Trogir (Yard No. 219), for Tver Shipping Inc., (Novoship (UK) Ltd., London, managers), under the Liberian flag. 12.4.1996: Launched. 14.11.1996: Completed.

TAMBOV

(Courtesy Fotoflite)

9112753

TC.32. TAMBOV (1996 -)

26;218g. 11,299n. 40,727d. 181.00(BB) x 32.03 x 11.017 metres

6-cyl. 2 S.C.S.A. (500 x 1,910mm) B&W 6S50MC type oil engine made by Tvornica Dizel Motora Split, Split. 11,302 BHP. 15.1 kts.
Double-hulled oil / chemical tanker.
29.7.1995: Keel laid by Brodogradiliste "Split", Split (Yard No. 389), for Tambov Shipping Inc., (Novoship (UK) Ltd., London, managers), under the Liberian flag. 9.12.1995: Launched. 7.1996: Completed.

TIKHVIN

(Internet source / L. Van Duivendijk)

9112117

TC.33. TIKHVIN (1996 -)

26;218g. 11,299n. 40,727d. 181.00(BB) x 32.03 x 11.017 metres
6-cyl. 2 S.C.S.A. (500 x 1,910mm) B&W 6S50MC type oil engine made by Tvornica Dizel Motora Split, Split. 11,298 BHP. 15.1 kts.
Double-hulled oil / chemical tanker.
9.12.1995: Keel laid by Brodogradiliste "Split", Split (Yard No. 390), for Tikhvin Shipping Inc., (Novoship (UK) Ltd., London, managers), under the Liberian flag. 29.6.1996: Launched. 5.12.1996: Completed.

ABERDEEN

(Internet source / Boris Paulkin)

9125736

TC.34. ABERDEEN (1996 -)

47,274g. 26,719n. 87,055d. 221.84(BB) x x 15.50 metres
7-cyl. 2 S.C.S.A. (600 x 2,292mm) B&W 7S60MC type engine made by Manises Diesel Engine Company S.A., Valencia, geared to a controllable pitch propeller. 19,460 BHP. 14.5 kts. Two thwartship thrust controllable pitch propellers forward and one aft.
Bow loading shuttle tanker
9.2.1996: Keel laid by Astilleros Espanolles S.A., (AESA) Factoria de Sestao, Bilbao (Yard No. 306) 18.12.1996: Completed for Getty Maritime Inc., Clydebank, UK, (Northern Marine Management Ltd., Clydebank, managers), under the Bahamas flag.

STENA AKARITA

(Courtesy Fotoflite)

9000948

TC.35. STENA AKARITA (1996 - 2002)

As built: 58,959g. 31,119n. 108,735d. 243.80(BB) x 42.03 x 15.02 metres.
Post 1996: 58,928g. 31,088n 107,223d.
7-cyl. 2.S.C.S.A. (600 x 2,292mm) B&W 7S60MC type oil engine made by Mitsui Engineering and Shipbuilding Company Ltd., Tamano. 13,092 BHP. 15 kts.
Post 1994: Tanker for offshore installations.
1.5.1991: Keel laid as AKARITA by Tsuneishi Zosen K.K., Numakuma (Yard No.654), for Mayberry Shipping Ltd., (Ugland Maritime Services AS., managers), Norway. 11.9.1991: Launched. 26.12.1991: Completed. 1996: Converted and renamed STENA AKARITA. 1996: Transferred to Nordic Akarita KS, (Interocean Ugland Management AS, managers), Grimstad. 2002: Renamed NORDIC AKARITA. 4.2005: Renamed NAVION AKARITA.

9041186

TC.36. STENA COMPASS (1) (1996 - 2000)

52,552g. 28,137n. 97,078d. 246.80 x x 13.419 metres
6-cyl. 2 S.C.S.A. (720 x 2,500mm) Sulzer 6RTA72 type oil engine made by Mitsubishi Heavy Industries Ltd., Kobe. 13,800 BHP. 14 kts.
Tanker
6.12.1991: Keel laid as SETO BRIDGE by Imabari Zosen K.K., Marugame (Yard No. 1197) for Seto Bridge Shipping S.A., Panama. 16.3.1992: Launched. 29.7.1992: Completed as SETO BRIDE. 1993: Renamed HAWAIAN PRINCE. 1996: Renamed STENA COMPASS. 1997: Sold to San Lorenzo Shipping S.A., Panama. 2000: Renamed COMPASS I (OSG Ship Management Inc., Newcastle upon Tyne, appointed managers) 2002: Northam Carriers Ltd., Newcastle upon Tyne. 2003: Reverted to San Lorenzo Shipping S. A. 2004: Reverted to Northam Carriers Ltd., Newcastle upon Tyne, (same managers), and transferred to Marshall Islands flag. 2005: Sold to Otranto Shipping Company Ltd., Newcastle upon Tyne, (OSG Ship Management UK Ltd., Newcastle upon Tyne, managers), retaining Marshall Islands flag.

TOMSK

(Internet source / L. Van Duivendijk)

9112131

TC.37. TOMSK (1997 -)

26;218g. 11,273n. 40,703d. 181.00(BB) x 32.03 x 11.00 metres
6-cyl. 2 S.C.S.A. (500 x 1,910mm) B&W 6S50MC type oil engine (No. 318) made by Strojogradnja "Uljanik" d.d., Pula, Croatia. 11,298 BHP. 14.4 kts.
Double-hulled oil / chemical tanker.
12.4.1996: Keel laid by Brodogradiliste "Trogir", Trogir (Yard No. 220), for Tomsk Shipping Inc., (Novoship (UK) Ltd., London, managers), under the Liberian flag. 15.11.1996: Launched. 28.4.1997: Completed.

STENA COMMANDER arriving at Malta.

(The World Ship Society Ltd)

8802222
TC.38. STENA COMMANDER (1997 - 2001)
52,247g. 29,429n. 96,758d. 232.04(BB) x 42.03 x 14.029 metres
6-cyl. 2 S.C.S.A. (620 x 2,150mm) Sulzer 6RTA62 type engine made by the shipbuilder at Tamashima. 12,779 BHP. 14 kts.
Tanker.
26.12.1988: Keel laid as JAHRE PRESIDENT by Sumitomo Heavy industries Ltd., Oppama Shipyard, Yokosuka (Yard No. 1158), for KS AS Western Part, (Jorgen Jahre Shipping AS, managers), Norway. 4.4.1989: Launched. 30.6.1989: Completed. 1993: Renamed NORD-JAHRE PRESIDENT, (Jahre-Wallem Managemant AS, appointed as managers). 1997: Sold to Nord Ltd., (Universe Tankships (Delaware) L. L. C., managers), and renamed STENA COMMANDER. 2000: General Maritime Corporation appointed as managers. 2001: General Maritime Hellas, appointed as managers, and renamed GENMAR COMMANDER. 2003: Sold to GMR Commander Inc., New York, (General Maritime Management, New York, managers).

9000352
TC.39. STENA COMFORT (1997 - 2000)
145,403g. 98,440n. 258,096d. 338.00(BB) x 58.36 x 19.170 metres.
7-cyl. 2S.C.S.A. (800 x 3,056mm) B&W 7S80MC type oil engine made by Kawasaki Heavy Industries Ltd., Kobe. 25,200 BHP. 15.5 kts.
Ultra large crude carrier (ULCC).
23.4.1991: Keel laid as WISTERIA by Kawasaki Heavy Industries Ltd., Sakaide (Yard No. 1424) for Tsuru Maritime Corp., (Mitsubishi Logistics group) (Denholm Ship Management (U.K.) Ltd., managers), Liberia. 26.9.1991: Launched. 31.1.1992: Completed. 1997: Renamed STENA COMFORT, (Lino Marine Services Company Ltd., appointed as managers). 2000: Sold to Cassiopeia Line Shipping S.A., Seoul, S. Korea, (Hyundai Merchant Marine Company Ltd., Seoul, managers), and renamed PACIFIC COURAGE, under the Panamanian flag. 2005: Sold to High Sincerity Shipping Company SA, Seoul, S. Korea, (same managers), under the S. Korea flag.

9144770
TC.40. STENA COMMODORE (1) (1997 - 1998)
56,127g. 32,751n. 106,597d. 243.00 x 42.03 x 14.752 metres.
7-cyl 2 S.C.S.A. (580 x 2,416mm) Sulzer 7RTA58T type engine made by Diesels United Ltd., Aioi. 19,040 BHP. 14.75 kts.
Double skin tanker.
24.4.1997:Keel laid as NISSOS ANAFI by NKK Corp, Tsurumi (Yard No 166) for Royal Maritime Ltd., Piraeus. 28.6.1997: Launched. 27.10.1997: Completed for Sea Pearl Enterprises Ltd., Piraeus (Kyklades Maritime Corp (Kyklades Naftiki Eteria), Piraeus, managers), Greece. 1997: Renamed STENA COMMODORE. 1998: Renamed THERASSIA. 2005: Sold to Varun Shipping, Mumbai, and renamed AMBA BHAKTI.

9152507

TC.41. STENA ALEXITA (1998 - 2004)

76,836g. 34,036n. 126,466d 262.60(BB) x x 15.728 metres.
Two, 7-cyl. 2.S.C.S.A. (500 x 1,910mm) B&W 7S50MC type oil engines made by Mitsui Engineering and Shipbuilding Company Ltd., Tamano, geared to twin controllable pitch propellers. 22,280 BHP. 15 kts. Two Thwartship thrust propellers forward & aft.
Bow loading crude oil tanker for offshore installations.
5.11.1997: Keel laid by Hashihama Shipbuilding Company Ltd., Tadotsu (Yard No. 1129), for P/R Nordshuttle III DA, (Ugland Nordic Shipping ASA, managers), Norway. 30.3.1998: Launched. 26.8.1998: Completed. 2004: Sold to Stena Ugland Shuttle Tanker 1, Grimstad, (IUM Shipmanagement KS, Grimstad, managers). 2005: Ugland Nordic Shipping AS, Sandefjord, Norway, appointed as managers.

9165932

TC.42. SATURN GLORY (1998 -)

156,397g. 108,180n. 272,700d. 332.00 (BB) x 58.05 x 22.00 metres.
7-cyl. 2 S.C.S.A. (840 x 3,150mm) Sulzer 7RTA84T type engine made by Korea Heavy Industries & Construction Company Ltd., Changwon. 36,960 BHP. 15.75 kts.
Very large crude carrier (VLCC).
12.8.1997: Keel laid by Daewoo Heavy Industries Ltd., Okpo (Yard No. 5107), for Saturn International Maritime S.A., Athens, (Northern Marine Management Ltd., Clydebank, UK, managers), under the Panamanian flag. 15.11.1997: Launched. 6.2.1998: Completed. 2000: Gulf Marine Management S. A., Athens, Greece, appointed as technical managers. 2005: Transferred to Saturn Glory GmbH & Company K.G., Hamburg, (Northern Marine Management (Deutschland) GmbH, Hamburg, technical managers), retaining Panamanian flag.

9165346

TC.43. NEPTUNE GLORY (1998 -)

156,716g. 108,175n. 299,127d. 332.00 (BB) x 58.05 x 22.00 metres.
7-cyl. 2 S.C.S.A. (840 x 3,150mm) Sulzer 7RTA84T type engine made by Korea Heavy Industries & Construction Company Ltd., Changwon. 36,932 BHP. 15.75 kts.
Very large crude carrier (VLCC).
6.10.1997: Keel laid by Daewoo Heavy Industries Ltd., Okpo (Yard No. 5108) for Neptune International Maritime S. A., Athens, Greece, (Oriental Shipping, managers), under the Panamanian flag. 31.12.1997: Launched. 7.4.1998: Completed. 1998: Northern Marine Management Ltd., Clydebank, UK, appointed as managers. 2000: Gulf Marine Management S. A., Athens, Greece, appointed as technical managers. 2005: Transferred to DS-Rendite Fonds Nr 110 VLCC Neptune Glory GmbH & Company K.G., Hamburg, (Northern Marine Management (Deutschland) GmbH, Hamburg, technical managers), retaining Panamanian flag.

JUPITER GLORY arriving at Belfast 15/11/2003 for repairs, under control of six tugs.

(Courtesy Alan Geddes)

9085364

TC.44. JUPITER GLORY (1998 -)

156,752g. 107,517n. 298,816d. 332.00 x x 22.00 metres.
7-cyl. 2 S.C.S.A. (840 x 3,150mm) Sulzer 7RTA84T type engine made by Korea Heavy Industries & Construction Company Ltd., Changwon. 36,960 BHP. 15.75 kts.
Very large crude carrier (VLCC).
24.5.1994: Keel laid as ERICA by Daewoo Heavy Industries Ltd., Okpo (Yard No. 5090), for Erica Shipping Company S.A., Monrovia, (Gotaas-Larsen International Ltd., Monte Carlo, managers). 17.9.1994: Launched. 24.8.1995: Completed, under the Liberian flag. 1998: Sold to Jupiter Shipping S. A., Athens, (Northern Marine Management Ltd., Clydebank, managers), and renamed JUPITER GLORY, under the Panamanian flag. 2000: Gulf Marine Management SA, Athens, Greece appointed as managers. 2004: Sold to Mitsura Company SA, Athens, (same managers). 2005: Northern Marine Management (Deutschland) GmbH, Hamburg, appointed as technical managers, retaining Panamanian flag.

8705761

TC.45. REDINA (1999 –)

35,375g. 17,107n. 60,959d. 214.78(BB) x 32.23 x 12.939 metres
6-cyl. 2 S.C.S.A. (620 x 2,150mm) Sulzer 6RTA62 type engine made by Mitsubishi Heavy Industries Ltd. 11,610 BHP. 15 kts.
Crude oil tanker
28.7.1987: Keel laid as BUNGA ANGGEREK by Namura Shipping Company Ltd., Imari (Yard No. 891), for Malaysia International Shipping Company, Malaysia. 6.11.1987: Launched. 29.3.1988: Completed. 1999: Sold to Redina Maritime Ltd., (Paradise Navigation S.A., managers), and renamed REDINA under the Bahamas flag. (O.N. 8000303).

9009140

TC.46. BRAVEHEART (1999 -)

52,531g. 27,198n. 94,998d. 246.80(BB) x 42.00 x 13,187 metres.
6-cyl. 2 S.C.S.A. (720 x 2,500mm) Sulzer 6RTA72 type engine made by Mitsubishi Heavy Industries Ltd., Kobe. 13,800 BHP. 14 kts.
Crude oil tanker.
25.4.1991: Keel laid as PACIFIC PLUTO by Imabari Zosen KK, Marugame (Yard No. 1191), for Pacific Pluto S.A., (Iino Marine Service Company Ltd., managers), under the Panamanian flag. 26.9.1991: Launched. 10.1.1992: Completed. 1996: Sold to JP Tankers S. A. and removed from management. 1997: Sold to Rachel Lines S.A., (Iino Marine Service Company Ltd., managers). 1999: Sold to Braveheart Holding Corp., Hong Kong, (Wallem Ship Management Ltd, Hong Kong, managers), and renamed BRAVEHEART, under the Liberian flag. (O.N. 11157).

8907553

TC.47. MAGNITUDE (1999 – 2004)

54,962g. 27,471n. 96,136d. 241.78 x 42.00 x 13,624 metres.
7-cyl. 2 S.C.S.A. (600 x 2,292mm) B&W 7S60MC type engine made by Hitachi Zosen K.K., Osaka. 11,030 BHP. 14 kts.
Crude oil tanker.
25.12.1990: Keel laid as SANKO PARAGON by Namura Shipbuilding Company Ltd., Imari (Yard No. 909), for Brilliant Tankships Ltd., Liberia. 27.3.1992: Completed. 23.11.1999: Sold to Magnitude Holding Corporation, Oslo, (C. H. Sorensen Management AS, managers), Norway, and renamed MAGNITUDE, under Norway (NIS) flag. 2004: Polyar Tankers AS, Oslo appointed as managers.

9173654

TC.48. JAG LEELA (1999 -)

58,374g. 30,037n. 105,148d. 242.98(BB) x x 14.771 metres.
6-cyl. 2 S.C.S.A. (600 x 2,292mm) B&W 6S60MC type engine made by the shipbuilder. 16,680 BHP. 14 kts.
21.12.1998: Keel laid by Samsung Heavy Industries Company Ltd., Koje (Yard No.1233), for The Great Eastern Shipping Company Ltd., Mumbai, India. 14.2.1999: Launched. 1.3.1999: Completed.

9166417

TC.49. MOSCOW UNIVERSITY (1999 -)

56,076g. 32,748n. 106,521d. 243.00(BB) 42.03 x 14.752 metres.
6-cyl. 2 S.C.S.A. (580 x 2,416mm) Sulzer 6RTA58T type engine made by Diesels United Ltd. 16,314 BHP. 15.1 kts.

Double hulled crude oil tanker.
7.10.1998: Keel laid by NKK Corporation, Tsu (Yard No. 185), for Fancy Maritime Ltd., London, (Novoship (UK) Ltd., London, managers), under the Liberian flag. 15.12.1998: Launched. 26.3.1999: Completed.

MOSCOW UNIVERSITY

(Courtesy Fotoflite)

8308630

TC.50. LION (1999 -)

26,113g. 14,177n. 46,100d. 171.81(BB) x 32.26 x 13.398 metres.
4-cyl. 2 S.C.S.A. (760 x 2,200mm) Sulzer 4RTA76 type engine made by Cockerill-Sambre S.A. 11,150 BHP. 14 kts.
Double hulled, chemical / refined products tanker.
28.10.1983: Keel laid as JAHRE LION by N.V. Boelwerf S.A.-Temse (Yard No. 1515), for Petrobulk Carriers N.V., Exmar N.V., Esdam N.V. & Boelwerf N.V., (Exmar N.V., managers), Belgium. 7.11.1984: Launched. 6.5.1985: Completed. 1986: Renamed PETROBULK LION. 1996: Sold to Cortes Vessel Ltd., Partnership, Miami, USA, (V. Ships Florida LLC, Miami, managers), and renamed LION under the Liberian flag.

8309799

TC.51. BRALI (1999 -)

As built: 26,000g. n. 45,000d. 182.81(BB) x 31.95 x 13.094 metres.
Post 1986: 31,248g. 14,801n. 36,500d.
4-cyl. 2 S.C.S.A. (800 x 2,592mm) B&W 4L80MCE type engine made by Hyundai Engine & Machinery Company Ltd. 9,976 BHP. 14 kts.
Double hulled crude oil tanker.
1.11.1984: Keel laid as PROBO BRALI by Hyundai Heavy Industries Company Ltd., Ulsan (Yard No. 304), as a caustic soda ore / bulk / oil (OBO) carrier, for KS AS Bill Brali, (AS Bill, managers), Norway. 14.3.1985: Launched. 1.12.1985: Completed. 1986: Converted into a tanker, and renamed BRALI. Subsequently V. Ships Norway, appointed as managers). 1998: Transferred to Cordova Vessel Ltd., Partnership, Miami, (V.Ships Florida LLC, Miami, managers), under the Bahamas flag.

STENA COMMERCE (The World Ship Society Ltd)

9158264

TC.52. STENA COMMERCE (1999 - 2001)

159423g. 95,710n. 300,144d. 333.0 x x 21.13 metres.
7-cyl. 2 S.C.S.A. (800 x 3,056mm) B&W 7S80MC type engine made by the shipbuilder's Sakurajima Works Osaka. 34,650 BHP. 16 kts.

Double skinned tanker
1.3.1999: Keel laid by Hitachi Zosen, Nagasaki (Yard No. 5788) for Golden Ocean Services Ltd., Panama. 15.7.1999: Launched. 15.12.1999: Completed for Heatherfield Maritime Ltd., Isle of Man, (Stena Bulk Ab., managers), under the Panamanian flag. 2001: Sold to Golden Fjord Ltd., Glasgow, (V Ships (UK) Ltd, managers), and renamed FRONT COMMERCE, under the Liberian flag. 2004: Sold to Golden Fjord Shipping Ltd., Glasgow, (V. Ships UK Ltd., Glasgow, managers), and renamed OCANA, under Isle of Man flag.

STENA COMANCHE (1) (The World Ship Society Ltd)

9172674

TC.53. STENA COMANCHE (1) (1999 - 2001)

159423g. 95,710n. 300,133d. 332.94 x x 21.13 metres.
7-cyl. 2 S.C.S.A. (800 x 3,056mm) B&W 7S80MC type engine made by the shipbuilder's Sakurajima Works Osaka. 34,650 BHP. 15.5 kts.
Double skinned tanker
25.12.1998: Keel laid by Hitachi Zosen, Nagasaki (Yard No. 5888) for Golden Ocean Services Ltd., Panama. 14.5.1999: Launched. 15.12.1999: Completed for Aster Marine Ltd., Isle of Man, (Stena Bulk Ab, managers), under the Panamanian flag. 2001: Sold to Golden Estuary Inc., Dubai, (International Tanker Management Holding, Dubai, managers), and renamed FRONT COMANCHE, under the Liberian flag. 2003: Transferred to French flag. 2005: SOCATRA, Bordeaux, appointed as managers.

STENA COMMODORE (2) (The World Ship Society Ltd)

9176993

TC.54. STENA COMMODORE (2) (2000 - 2001)

159,397g. 95,799n. 298,620d. 332.95 x x 21.13 metres.
7-cyl. 2 S.C.S.A. (800 x 3,056mm) B&W 7S80MC type engine made by the shipbuilder's Sakurajima Works Osaka. 34,650 BHP. 16 kts.
Double skinned tanker
8.6.1999: Keel laid by Hitachi Zosen KK, Nagasaki (Yard No. 5988) for Golden Ocean Services Ltd., Panama. 13.10.1999: Launched. 16.2.2000: Completed for Eskdale Maritime Ltd., Bermuda (Borthern Marine Management Ltd., managers). 6.8.2001: Sold to Golden Channel Inc., Dubai, (International Tankers, managers), and renamed FRONT COMMODORE, under the Liberian flag. 2003: Sold to DS-Rendite-Fonds GmbH & Company, Hamburg, (International Tanker Management Holding, Dubai, managers)., retaining Liberian flag.

9196620

TC.55. SARAH GLORY (2001 -)

159,397g. 95,799n. 298,628d. 332.95)BB) x x 21.130 metres
7-cyl. 2 S.C.S.A. (800 x 3,056mm) B&W 7S80MC type engine made by the shipbuilder. 31,190 BHP. 15.5 kts.

Double hulled crude oil tanker.
18.12.2000: Keel laid as BERGE KYOTO by Hitachi Zosen, Ariaki Works, Nagasu (Yard No. 4970), for Igloo Shipping AS, (Bergesen d.y. ASA, Norway, managers). 31.5.2001: Completed. 2001: Sold to Sarah Maritime Ltd., (Gulf Marine Management S.A., commercial managers, Northern Marine Management Ltd, technical managers), and renamed SARAH GLORY, under the Panamanian flag.

9203277

TC.56. PLUTO GLORY (2001 -)

157,831g. 108,670n. 298,990d. 332.00 (BB) x 58.05 x 22.00 metres.
7-cyl. 2 S.C.S.A. (840 x 3,150mm) Sulzer 7RTA84T type engine made by the shipbuilder. 31,420 BHP. 15.1 kts.
Very large crude carrier (VLCC).
26.6.2000: Keel laid by Daewoo Shipbuilding & Marine Engineering Company Ltd., Okpo (Yard No. 5164) for Pluto Maritime Ltd., under the Panamanian flag. 3.10.2001: Launched. 26.1.2001: Northern Marine Management Ltd., Clydebank, UK, appointed as technical managers. 14.2.2001: Completed. 2001: Gulf Marine Management S. A., Athens, Greece, appointed as commercial managers. 9.2005: Sold to DS-Rendite-Fonds Nr.113 VLCC Pluto Glory GmbH & Company Tankschiff K.G., Hamburg, (Northern Marine Management (Deutschland) GmbH, Hamburg, technical managers).

MERCURY GLORY

(Internet source)

9203289

TC.57. MERCURY GLORY (2001 -)

157,831g. 108,670n. 298,990d. 332.00 (BB) x 58.05 x 22.00 metres.
7-cyl. 2 S.C.S.A. (840 x 3150mm) Sulzer 7RTA84T type engine made by the shipbuilder. 31,420 BHP. 15.1 kts.
Very large crude carrier (VLCC).
4.10.2000: Keel laid by Daewoo Shipbuilding & Marine Engineering Company Ltd., Okpo (Yard No. 5165) for Mercury Maritime Ltd., under the Panamanian flag. 23.12.2000: Launched. 26.1.2001: Northern Marine Management Ltd., Clydebank, UK, appointed as technical managers. 7.3.2001: Completed. 2001: Gulf Marine Management S. A., Athens, Greece, appointed as commercial managers. 9.2005: Sold to DS-Rendite-Fonds Nr. 112 VLCC Mercury Glory GmbH & Company Tankschiff K.G., Hamburg, (Northern Marine Management (Deutschland) GmbH, Hamburg, technical managers).

8618217

TC.58. STENA EPISKOPI (2001 - 2004)

142,639g. 82,042n. 265,316d. 322.07 x 56.04 x 19.802 metres
6-cyl. 2 S.C.S.A. (800 x 3,056mm) B&W 6S80MC type oil engine made by Hyundai Engine & Machinery Company Ltd., Ulsan. 24,279 BHP. 14.75 kts.
Very large crude carrier (VLCC).
3.4.1989: Keel laid as WORLD PENDANT by Hyundai Heavy Industries Company Ltd., Ulsan (Yard No. 499), for Colindale Company S. A., (World-Wide Shipping Agency Ltd., managers), Panama. 26.7.1989: Launched. 6.12.1989: Completed. 10.2001: Sold to Sola Shipping S.A., Norway, (Greenwich Ship Management & Brokerage S.A., Greece, managers), and renamed STENA EPISKOPI, under the

Panamanian flag. 21.7.2003: Polyar Tankers, Oslo, Norway, appointed as managers. 3.8.2004: Renamed EPISKOPI.

TC.59. FOLK I **(2002 - 2003)** see ship No T.29 above.

TC.60. FOLK II **(2002 - 2003)** see ship No T.30 above.

9086708
TC.61. GEMINI I (2002 - 2005)
21,142g. 11,177g. 28,840d. 178.96 x x 12.300 metres.
6-cyl. 2 S.C.S.A. (600 x 1,950mm) B&W 6DKRN60/195 type engine made by AO Bryanskiy Mashinostroitelnyy Zavod (BMZ), Bryansk. 10,937 BHP. 14.8 kts.
Ice strengthened, double hulled refined products tanker.
27.8.1991: Keel laid as GEMINI by Khersonskyi Sudnobudivnyi Zavod, Kherson (Yard No. 1424), for Diamond International Navigation Inc (Milbros Shipping AS, managers), under St Vincent & The Grenadines flag. 14.7.1992: Launched. 14.1.1994: Completed. 1994: Renamed IVER GEMINI. . 1995: Sold to I.G.T. Navigation Ltd., (same managers), Russia. 1998: PRISCO UK Ltd., appointed as managers, and transferred to Cypriot flag. 2002: Renamed GEMINI I, and PRISCO (Singapore) Pte Ltd., appointed as managers. 2005: Sold to Breeze A Marine Ltd, Monte Carlo, (V. Ships, Monaco, managers), and renamed BREEZE A, under the Maltese flag.

9112052
TC.62. CAPELLA (2002 - 2005)
21,142g. 11,177g. 28,840d. 178.96 x x 11.350 metres.
6-cyl. 2 S.C.S.A. (600 x 1,944mm) B&W 6L60MC type engine made by AO Bryanskiy Mashinostroitelnyy Zavod (BMZ), Bryansk. 10,794 BHP. 14.5 kts.
Ice strengthened, double hulled refined products tanker.
19.8.1995: Completed by Khersonskyi Sudnobudivnyi Zavod, Kherson (Yard No. 1427), for C.T. Navigation Ltd., (Milbros Shipping AS, managers), Russia. 1998: PRISCO (Singapore) Pte Ltd., appointed as managers, and transferred to Cypriot flag. 2005: Sold to Wave A Marine Ltd, Monte Carlo, (V. Ships, Monaco, managers), and renamed WAVE A, under the Maltese flag.

STENA CONFIDENCE (2)

(The World Ship Society Ltd.)

9270555
TC.63. STENA CONFIDENCE (2) (2003 -)
58,111g. 31,909n 107,060d. 235.0 x 42.0 x 21.3 metres.
6-cyl. 2 S.C.S.A. (600 x 2,400mm) MAN B&W 6S60MC-C type oil engine (No.4270) made by Mitsui Engineering & Shipbuilding Company Ltd, Tamano. 15,635 BHP. 14.8 kts.
Double skinned crude oil tanker.
17.6.2002: Keel laid as ISLAND COURAGE by Imabari Shipbuilding Company Ltd., Saijo (Yard No. 8013) for Danseco Ltd., Singapore, (Northern Marine Management Ltd., Glasgow, managers). 27.2.2003: Launched. 9.5.2003: Renamed STENA CONFIDENCE, under the Bahamas flag. 13.5.2003: Delivered.

9281891
TC.64. STENA CONDUCTOR (2) (2003 -)
58,111g. 31,909n 107,060d. 235.0 x 42.0 x 21.30 metres
6-cyl. 2 S.C.S.A. (600 x 2,400mm) MAN B&W 6S60MC-C type oil engine made by Mitsui Engineering & Shipbuilding Company Ltd, Tamano. 18,395 BHP. 14.8 kts.

Double skinned crude oil tanker.
19.6.2002: Keel laid by Imabari Shipbuilding Company Ltd., Saijo (Yard No. 8023), for Friend Shine Shipping S.A., Imabari, (Iino Marine Service, Minatoku, Tokyo, managers), Japan, under the Panamanian flag. 16.6.2003: Launched. 9.9.2003: Completed.

STENA CONDUCTOR (2)

(Internet source)

STENA CONQUEST

(Courtesy Fotoflite)

9252436

TC.65. STENA CONQUEST (2) (2003 -)

27,335g. 14,244n. 47,136d. 182.43(BB) x 32.22 x 12.197 metres.
6-cyl. 2 S.C.S.A. (500 x 1,910mm) B&W 6S50MC type oil engine (No. 343) made by Strojogradnja "Uljanik" d.d., Pula, Croatia. 11,665 BHP. 14.5 kts.
Double skinned chemical / oil products tanker.
22.5.2001: Ordered as HISPANICA by Uljanik Brodogradiliste dd, Pula (Yard No. 443) for Lancaster Shipping Company Ltd., Limassol. 24.8.2002: Keel laid. 8.2.2003: Launched. 24.6.2003: Completed, for Gestioni Armatoriali, Naples, (Fulltankers SrL, managers), Naples, Italy. 27.6.2003: Renamed STENA CONQUEST.

IBLEA (Internet source)

9271327

TC.66. IBLEA (2003 -)

56,477g. 32,300n. 104,854d. 294.10 (BB) x x 13.5 metres.
7-cyl. 2 S.C.S.A. (580 x 2,416mm) Sulzer 7RTA58T type engine (No.3832) made by Mitsubishi Heavy Industries Company Ltd., Japan. 20,223 BHP. 24.3 kts.
Double hulled crude oil tanker.

30.5.2002: Keel laid by Namura Shipbuilding Company Ltd., Imari (Yard No. 226), for V Ships (Germany) GmbH & Company, Hamburg. 27.12.2002: Launched for Scinicariello Ship Management SpA., Naples 27.3.2003: Completed for Iblea Shipping Ltd., Naples (Augustea Ship Management, managers), Naples, under Liberian flag.

9243021

TC.67. DESH RAKSHAK (2003 -)

61,978g n. 110,000d. 244.0 x x 13.6 metres.
6-cyl. 2 S.C.S.A. (600 x 2,292mm) MAN-B&W 6S60MC type engine (No. AA1587) made by the shipbuilder. 16,680 BHP. 14 kts.
Double hulled crude oil tanker.
7.1.2003: Keel laid by Hyundai Heavy Industries Company Ltd., Ulsan (Yard No. 1403), for The Shipping Corporation Of India, Mumbai. 29.3.2003: Launched. 23.5.2003: Completed.

9278686

TC.68. LYRA PIONEER (2003 - 2004)

28,059g. 11,645n. 173.10 x 32.20 x 18.70 metres
6-cyl 2 SCSA (500 x 2,000mm) made by Mitsui Engineering & Shipbuilding Comoany Ltd, Tamano
14.6.2002: Keel laid by Shin Kurushima Onishi (Yard No. 5186), for Vegapro Shipholding SA (Donnelly Tanker Management, Limassol, managers), under the Panamanian flag. (O.N. 29457-03). 12.6.2003: Launched. 18.10.2003: Completed, (Pacific Carriers (Hartmann Gruppen), operators).

LIGOVSKY PROSPECT

(Courtesy Fotoflite)

9256066

TC.69. LIGOVSKY PROSPECT (2003 -)

63,586g. 34,823n. 115,000d. 239.0 x 44 x metres
5-cyl. 2 S.C.S.A. (700 x 2,800mm) MAN B&W 5S70MC-C type oil engine made by HSD Engine Company Ltd. 18,900 BHP. 15.1 kts.
Double skinned crude oil tanker.
19.5.2003: Keel laid by Daewoo Shipbuilding & Marine Engineering Company Ltd., Ulsan (Yard No. 5231), for Progress Shipping Ltd., Limassol, Cyprus, (Unicom Management Services, Limassol, Cyprus, managers), under the Liberian flag. 23.8.2003: Launched. 28.10.2003: Completed.

STENA CONTENDER (2)

(Internet source / Philippe Holthof)

9256078

TC.70. STENA CONTENDER (2) (2003 -)

63,586g. 34,823n. 115,000d. 239.0 x 44 x metres
5-cyl. 2 S.C.S.A. (700 x 2,800mm) MAN B&W 5S70MC-C type oil engine made by HSD Engine Company Ltd. 18,900 BHP. 15.1 kts.
Double skinned crude oil tanker.
30.6.2003: Keel laid as LITEYNY PROSPECT Daewoo Shipbuilding & Marine Engineering Company Ltd., Ulsan (Yard No. 5232), for Oriental Carriers Ltd., Limassol, Cyprus, (Unicom Management Services, Limassol, Cyprus, managers), under the Liberian flag. 11.10.2003: Launched as STENA CONTENDER. 2.12.2003: Completed.

9256236

TC.71. STENA COMMANDER (2) (2003 -)

41,000g. 16,500n. 72,346d. 228.60(BB) x x 14.00 metres.
5-cyl. 2 S.C.S.A. (600 x 2,400mm) B&W 5S60MC-C type oil engine made by the shipbuilder. 15,350 BHP. 15 kts.
Double skinned tanker.
15.4.2002: Keel laid as BLUE DOLPHIN by Hudong Shipbuilding Group, Shanghai (Yard No. H1302A), for Fratelli D'Amato SpA, Dolphin Tankers (V. Ships Monaco, managers), Italy. 12.8.2002: Launched. 20.3.2003: Completed for Dolphin Tankers (V-Ships Monaco, managers), Italy. 29.3.2003: STENA COMMANDER.

9256248

TC.72. STENA COMANCHE (2) (2003 -)

41,000g. 16,500n. 72,346d. 228.60(BB) x x 14.00 metres.
5-cyl. 2 S.C.S.A. (600 x 2,400mm) B&W 5S60MC-C type oil engine made by the shipbuilder. 15,350 BHP. 15 kts.
Double skinned tanker.
15.5.2002: Keel laid as WHITE DOLPHIN by Hudong Shipbuilding Group, Shanghai (Yard No. H1303A), for Fratelli D'Amato SpA, Dolphin Tankers (V. Ships Monaco, managers), Italy. 9.9.2002: Launched. 14.5.2003: Completed for Dolphin Tankers (V-Ships Monaco, managers), Italy. 17.5.2003: Renamed STENA COMANCHE.

STENA CONQUEROR

(Internet source)

9252448

TC.73. STENA CONQUEROR (2003 -)

27,335g. 14,244n. 47,323d. 182.5(BB) x 32.22 x 12.187 metres.
6-cyl. 2 S.C.S.A. (500 x 1,910mm) B&W 6S50MC type oil engine made by the shipbuilder. 11,665 BHP. 14.5 kts.
Double skinned chemical / oil products tanker.
2002: Ordered as HELLENICA by Uljanik Brodogradiliste dd, Pula (Yard No. 444) for Voyage Ltd., Malta. 8.2.2003: Keel laid. 14.6.2003: Launched. 10.2003: Completed as STENA CONQUEROR, for Gestioni Armatoriali, Naples, (Fulltankers SpA, Naples, managers), Italy.

9259721

TC.74. DA MING HU (2003 -)

85,855g. 52,153n. 159,000d. 274.8(BB) x x metres

6-cyl. 2 S.C.S.A. (700 x 2,674mm) B&W 6S70MC type oil engine made by Dalian Marine Diesel Engine Factory, Dalian. 22,923 BHP. 15 kts.
Double skinned crude oil tanker.
25.7.2002: Keel laid by Bohai Shipyard (Yard No. 159K-1 then 508-1), for Cosco Dalian Shipping Company, China. 29.5.2003: Launched. 28.11.2003: Completed. 12.2003: Chartered by Stena Bulk Ab (proposed to rename STENA COSMOPOLITAN).

DA YUAN HU (Internet source)

9259733
TC.75. DA YUAN HU (2004 -)
85,855g. 52,153n. 159,000d. 274.8(BB) x x metres
6-cyl. 2 S.C.S.A. (700 x 2,674mm) B&W 6S70MC type oil engine made by Dalian Marine Diesel Engine Factory, Dalian. 22,923 BHP. 15 kts.
Double skinned crude oil tanker.
10.6.2003: Keel laid by Bohai Shipyard (Yard No. 159K-2 then 508-2), for Cosco Dalian Shipping Company, China. 29.2.2004: Launched. 22.6.2004: Completed and chartered by Stena Bulk Ab (proposed to rename STENA COSMOGRAPHIC).

STENA ITALICA

(Internet source / L. Van Duivendijk)

9258597
TC.76. STENA ITALICA (2004 -)
27,335g. 14,244n. 47,136d. 182.43(BB) x 32.22 x 12.197 metres.
6-cyl. 2 S.C.S.A. (500 x 1,910mm) MAN B&W 6S50MC type oil engine (No. 347) made by Strojogradnja "Uljanik" d.d., Pula, Croatia. 11,665 BHP. 14.5 kts.
Double skinned chemical / oil products tanker.
8.11.2003: Keel laid by Uljanik Brodogradiliste dd, Pula (Yard No. 447), for for Gestioni Armatoriali, Naples, (Fulltankers SpA, managers), Naples, Italy. 11.7.2004: Completed.

9258612

TC.77. STENA CONSUL (2) (2004 -)

27,335g. 13,852n. 47,171d. 182.5(BB) x 32.22 x 12.200 metres.
6-cyl. 2 S.C.S.A. (500 x 2,000mm) MAN B&W 6S50MC-C type oil engine made by Strojogradnja "Uljanik" d.d., Pula, Croatia. 11,665 BHP. 14.5 kts.
Double skinned chemical / oil products tanker.
14.6.2003: Keel laid by Uljanik Brodogradiliste dd, Pula (Yard No. 449), for Intrigue Shipping, Novorossysk, Russia, (Novoship UK Ltd., London, managers) proposed Liberian flag. 8.11.2003: Launched for Oceansong Shipping Ltd., (Northern Marine Management USA L.L.C., Houston, managers). 26.3.2004: Completed for Compass Ltd., Houston, (same managers), under the Bermudan flag.

STENA CONSUL (2) (Internet source)

STENA CONCERTINA (2) (Internet source)

9004607

TC.78. STENA CONCERTINA (2) (2004 -)

52,048g. 30,143n. 95.833d. 232.04(BB) x 42.03 x 14.2 metres
6-cyl. 2 S.C.S.A. (620 x 2,150mm) Sulzer 6RTA62 type oil engine made by Diesel United Ltd. 12,780 BHP. 13.5 kts.
Double skinned crude oil tanker
9.7.1991: Keel laid as DIANA by Sanoyas Corporation, Mizushima (hull Yard No. 1110), as sub-contract for Sumitomo Heavy Industries Ltd., Oppama Shipyard, Yokosuka. 1.5.1992: Completed as Sumitomo Heavy Industries Ltd., Oppama Shipyard, Yokosuka (Yard No. 1117), for San Martin Shipping Corp, Naples, (Seaarland Shipping Management GmbH, Villach, Austria, managers), under the Liberian flag. 19.5.2002: Sold to Slagen Shipping Company Ltd., Oslo, (C. H. Sorensen Management AS, Oslo, managers), and to Liberian flag. 29.8.2002: Renamed MOSS, under the Liberian flag. 10.9.2004: Transferred to Norway NIS flag. 29.9.2004: Renamed STENA CONCERTINA, (Polyar Tankers AS, Oslo, managers), under Norway NIS flag.

9223253

TC.79. PORT LOUIS (2004 -)

25,065g. 10,064n. 37,791d. 170.36 (BB) x x 11.5 metres

6-cyl. 2S.C.S.A. (460 x 1,932mm) B&W 6S46MC-C type engine made by Hudong Heavy Machinery Company Ltd., Shanghai.
Refined products tanker.
8.6.2001: Keel laid as MERIOM PEARL by Guangzhou Shipyard International, Guangzhou (Yard No. 9130008), for Pearl Maritime Ltd., (Overseas Maritime Carriers S.A. (OMC. S.A., managers), under the Maltese flag. 26.11.2001: Launched. 8.4.2002: Completed. 2004: Sold to International Tanker Management (Germany) GmbH & Company, (International Tanker Management Holding, Dubai, managers), and renamed PORT LOUIS, under the Marshall Islands flag. 2004: To "Port Louis" GmbH & Company KG, (same managers).

9251456
TC.80. PORT STEWART (2004 -)
25,065g. 10,064n. 37,791d. 170.36 (BB) x x 11.5 metres
6-cyl. 2S.C.S.A. (460 x 1,932mm) B&W 6S46MC-C type engine made by Hudong Heavy Machinery Company Ltd., Shanghai
Refined products tanker.
28.6.2002: Keel laid as MERIOM JADE by Guangzhou Shipyard International, Guangzhou (Yard No. 0010015), for Jade Maritime Ltd., (Overseas Maritime Carriers S.A. (OMC. S.A., managers), under the Maltese flag. 19.12.2002: Launched. 12.3.2003: Completed. 2004: Sold to International Tanker Management (Germany) GmbH & Company, (International Tanker Management Holding, Dubai, managers), and renamed PORT STEWART, under the Marshall Islands flag. 2004: To "Port Stewart" GmbH & Company KG, (same managers).

9274525
TC.81. NORDIC RIO (2004 -)
83,120g. 46,633n. 151,294d. 274.5 x 48.00 x 16.4 metres
6-cyl. 2S.C.S.A. (700 x 2,800mm) B&W 6S70ME-C type engine made by HSD Engine Company Ltd., Changwon. 25,320 BHP.
Double skinned, bow loading tanker for offshore installations.
13.11.2003: Keel laid by Samsung Heavy Industries Company Ltd., Koje (Yard No. 1437), for Nordic Rio LLC, (IUM Shipmanagement AS, Grimstad, managers), under the Bahamas flag. 15.2.2004: Launched. 27.4.2004: Completed, (Teekay Marine Services AS, managers).

9205079
TC.82. TITAN GLORY (2004 -)
159,187g. 104,027n. 308,491d. 332.95 x 58.05 x 22.700 metres.
7-cyl. 2 S.C.S.A. (840 x 3,150mm) Sulzer 7RTA84T type engine made by the shipbuilder, 36,931 BHP. 16.4 kts.
Double hulled crude oil tanker.
2.5.200: Keel laid as MILLENNIUM MAERSK by Hyundai Heavy Industries Company Ltd., Ulsan (Yard No 1238), for AS DS Svendborg & DS af 1912 AS, Copenhagen. 9.2000: Completed. 2004: Sold to DS-Rendite-Fonds Nr. 106 VLCC Titan Glory GmbH & Company Tankschiff KG, Hamburg, (Northern Marine Management (Deutschland) GmbH, Hamburg, managers), and renamed TITAN GLORY, under the Panamanian flag.

YOUNARA GLORY

(Internet source)

9289477
TC.83. YOUNARA GLORY (2004 -)
161,235g. 111,798n. 320,050d 333.02(BB) x x 22.587 metres

6-cyl. 2 S.C.S.A. (900 x 3,188mm) 6S90MC-C type engine (No.A1906) made by Hyundai Heavy Industries Company Ltd., Ulsan. 39,989 BHP. 15 kts.
19.7.2004: Keel laid as DELOS by Daewoo Shipbuilding & Marine Engineering Company Ltd., Okpo (Yard No. 5260), for unspecified Greek owners. 31.8.2004: Launched. 29.11.2004: Completed as YOUNARA GLORY for Younara Maritime Ltd., (Northern Marine Management Ltd., Clydebank, UK, managers). 2005: Sold to DS-Rendite-Fonds VLCC Younara Glory GmbH & Company Tankschiff KG, Hamburg, (Northern Marine Management (Deutschland) GmbH Hamburg, managers), under the Panamanian flag.

9102930
TC.84. NORDIC VOYAGER (2005 -)
79,494g. 47,975n. 149,775d. 270.45(BB) x 44.6 x 17.520 metres.
6-cyl. 2 S.C.S.A. (720 x 2,500mm) Sulzer 6RTA72U type engine made by Dalian Marine Diesel Engine Factory. 22,750 BHP. 14 kts.
Double hulled crude oil tanker.
8.9.1995: Keel laid as WILMA YANGTZE by Dalian New Shipyard, Dalian (Yard No. T1500-1), for Parallel Maritime Inc., (Wilhelmsen Marine Services AS, managers Oslo). 31.5.1996: Launched. 28.12.1996: Completed. 2005: Sold to Nordic American Tanker Shipping Ltd., Bermuda, (same managers), and renamed NORDIC VOYAGER, under the Bermudan flag. 2005: Teekay Marine Services AS, appointed as managers.

STENA CONTEST (2)

(Courtesy Stena Ab)

9272199
TC.85. STENA CONTEST (2) (2005 -)
27,357g. 13,857n. 47,171d. 182.5 x 32.23 x 11.0 metres
6-cyl. 2 S.C.S.A. (500 x 2,000mm) B&W 6S50MC-C type oil engine (No. 350) made by Strojogradnja "Uljanik" d.d., Pula, Croatia. 12,870 BHP.
Double skinned tanker.
28.8.2004: Keel laid by Brodogradiliste, Split (Yard No. 450), for Intrigue Shipping, Novorossysk, Russia, (Novoship UK Ltd., London, managers) 1.12.2004: Launched. 21.3.2005: Completed for Oceanswift Ltd., Houston, (Northern Marine Management USA LLC, Houston, managers), under the Bermudan flag.

STENA CONCEPT (2)

(Courtesy Stena Ab)

9272204
TC.86. STENA CONCEPT (2) (2005 -)
27,357g. 13,857n. 47,171d. 182.5 x 32.23 x 11.0 metres

6-cyl. 2 S.C.S.A. (500 x 2,000mm) B&W 6S50MC-C type oil engine (No. 351) made by Strojogradnja "Uljanik" d.d., Pula, Croatia. 12,870 BHP.
Double skinned tanker.
17.10.2004: Keel laid by Brodogradiliste, Split (Yard No. 451), for Intrigue Shipping, Novorossysk, Russia, (Novoship UK Ltd., London, managers). 2005: Completed for Oceansymphony Ltd., (Northern Marine Management USA LLC, Houston, managers), under the Bermudan flag.

SONANGOL LUANDA (Internet source)

9203760

TC.87. SONANGOL LUANDA (2005 -)

81,230g. 50,687n. 149,999d. 274.00 x x 17.020 metres.
6-cyl. 2 S.C.S.A. (700 x 2,674mm) B&W 6S70MC type engine made by Korea Heavy Industries & Construction Company Ltd. (HANJUNG). 22,920 BHP. 15.2 kts.
Double skinned crude oil tanker.
3.4.2000: Keel laid by Daewoo Heavy Industries Ltd., Okpo (Yard No. 5153), for Sociedad Nacional de Combustives de Angola (SONANGOLA), (Frontline Management AS, managers), under the Bahamas flag. 24.6.2000: Launched. 6.9.2000: Completed. 2003: Removed from management. 2004 Wallem Shipmanagement USA LLC., appointed as managers.

SONANGOL KIZOMBA

(Internet source)

9203772

TC.88. SONANGOL KIZOMBA (2005 -)

81,230g. 50,687n. 149,999d. 274.00 x x 17.020 metres.
6-cyl. 2 S.C.S.A. (700 x 2,674mm) B&W 6S70MC type engine made by Korea Heavy Industries & Construction Company Ltd. (HANJUNG). 22,920 BHP. 15.2 kts.
Double skinned crude oil tanker.
21.8.2000: Keel laid by Daewoo Heavy Industries Ltd., Okpo (Yard No. 5154), for Sociedad Nacional de Combustives de Angola (SONANGOLA), (Frontline Management AS, managers), under the Bahamas flag. 11.11.200: Launched. 16.1.2001: Completed. 2003: Removed from management. 2004 Wallem Shipmanagement USA LLC., appointed as managers.

9180114

TC.89. SONANGOL GIRASSOL (2005 -)

81,230g. 50,687n. 149,999d. 274.00 x x 17.020 metres.
6-cyl. 2 S.C.S.A. (700 x 2,674mm) B&W 6S70MC type engine made by Korea Heavy Industries & Construction Company Ltd. (HANJUNG). 22,920 BHP. 15.2 kts.

Double skinned crude oil tanker.
5.7.1999: Keel laid by Daewoo Heavy Industries Ltd., Okpo (Yard No. 5138), for Sociedad Nacional de Combustives de Angola (SONANGOLA), (Frontline Management AS, managers), under the Bahamas flag. 9.10.1999: Launched. 6.1.2000: Completed. 2003: Removed from management. 2004 Wallem Shipmanagement USA LLC., appointed as managers.

9315654
TC.90. SONANGOL KASSANJE (2005 -)
83,469g. n. 159,000d. 269.32 (BB) x 48.0 x metres.
6-cyl. 2 S.C.S.A. (700 x 2,674mm) B&W 6S70MC type engine(No. ML-1629) made by HSD Engine Company Ltd., Changwon. 23,238 BHP. 15.2 kts.
Double skinned crude oil tanker.
7.12.2004: Keel laid by Daewoo Shipbuilding & Marine Engineering Company Ltd., Okpo (Yard No. 5276), for Sociedad Nacional de Combustives de Angola (SONANGOLA). 30.4.2005: Launched. 15.6.2005: Completed for Sonangol Shipping Kassanje Ltd., Hong Kong (Wallem Shipmanagement Ltd., Hong Kong), under the Bahamas flag.

9295074
TC.91. YONG XING ZHOU (2005 –)
43,062g. 21,289n. 74,090d. 228.6 x 32.26 x metres
6-cyl. 2 S.C.S.A. (600 x 2,292mm) B&W 6S60MC type oil engine made by Dalian Marine Diesel Engine Factory, Dalian. 16,642 BHP.
Panamax tanker
8.7.2004: Keel laid by Dalian Shipyard (Yard No. PC700-2), for Nanjing Water Transport Industry Company Ltd., (Nanjing Tanker Corporation, managers), Nanjing, China. 30.12.2004: Launched. 8.6.2005: Completed.

9249087
TC.92. HRVATSKA (2005 -)
84,315g. 55,779n. 166,739d. 281.2 x x 17.00 metres.
6-cyl. 2 S.C.S.A. (700 x 2,000mm) B&W 6S70MC-C engine made by Tvornica Dizel Motora "Split", Split. 25,370 BHP.
Double skinned crude oil tanker.
2001 Ordered from Brodospas Split (Yard No. 434), by Aenona Maritime Ltd., Maltese flag operators. 5.6.2004: Keel laid. 23.12.2004: Launched. 3.6.2005: Completed for Pulzar Maritime Two, (Tankerska Plovidba, managers), Zadar, Croatia.

9299678
TC.93. EURONIKE (2005 -)
85,431g. 53,684n. 164,565d. 274.0 x 50.042 x 17.00 metres
6-cyl. 2 S.C.S.A. (700 x 2,000mm) B&W 6S70MC-C engine made by Tvornica Dizel Motora "Split", Split. 25,370 BHP.
Double skinned crude oil tanker.
2003: Ordered as PROTEAS from Hyundai Heavy Industries Company Ltd., Ulsan (Yard No. 1618), by Apollo Excellence Shipping SA, (Tsakos Shipping & Trading S.A.), Greece. 2004: Proposed name changed to PROMITHEAS (Tsakos Energy Navigation Ltd., managers). 25.4.2005: Keel laid as EURONIKE (Tsakos Shipping & Trading S.A.). 8.7.2005: Launched. 14.9.2005: Completed.

9274094
TC.94. STENA COMPASS (2) (2005 -)
43,000g. n. 72,000d. 228.60 x 32.20 x 12.0.0 metres
6-cyl 2S.C.S.A. (600 x 2,292mm) MAN B&W 6S60MC type oil engine made by Dalian Marine Diesel Engine Factory, Dalian. 16,680 BHP.
Double skinned tanker.
28.9.2004: Keel laid by Dalian Shipyard, Dalian (Yard No. PC720-3), for Concordia Maritime Ab, (Stena Bulk Ab., operating managers). 24.6.2005: Launched. 9.2005: Contract sold to Aries Maritime Transport, G (Magnus Carriers SA., managers), Greece, and vessel bareboat chartered to Stena Bulk Ab. 15.12.2005: Completed.

STENA COMPASS

(Courtesy Stena Ab)

Tankers On Order Or Under Construction.

9295036

TC.95. STENA COMPASSION (2006 -)

43,000g. n. 72,000d. 228.60 x 32.20 x 12.00 metres

6-cyl 2S.C.S.A. (600 x 2,292mm) MAN B&W 6S60MC type oil engine made by Dalian Marine Diesel Engine Factory, Dalian. 16,680 BHP.

Double skinned tanker.

10.10.2004: Keel laid by Dalian Shipyard, Dalian(Yard No. PC720-4), for Concordia Maritime Ab, (Stena Bulk Ab., operating managers). 9.2005: Contract sold to Aries Maritime Transport, G (Magnus Carriers SA., managers), Greece, and vessel bareboat chartered to Stena Bulk Ab. 20.11.2005: Launched.

9322827

TC.96. STENA ANTARCTICA (2) (2006 -)

62,500g. n. 113,600d.

B-max class - ice strengthened double skinned, twin rudder, tanker

2005: Ordered from Samsung Heavy Industries Company Ltd, Koje (Yard No. 1575), for Moon Shipping Services Navegacione (Premuda Tankers, managers), Genoa, Italy.

9322839

TC.97. STENA ATLANTICA (4) (2006 -)

62,500g. n. 113,600d.

B-max class - ice strengthened double skinned, twin rudder, tanker

2005: Ordered from Samsung Heavy Industries Company Ltd, Koje (Yard No. 1576), for Moon Shipping Services Navegacione (Premuda Tankers, managers), Genoa, Italy.

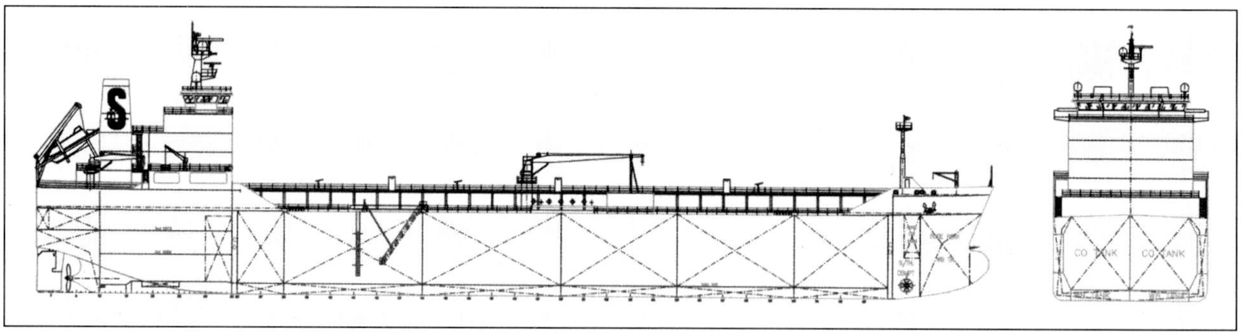

Stena tanker article in The Scandinavian Shipping Gazette of 23rd Dec. 2004 makes reference to a Stena "E-Max" Clean petroleum products/chemical design of 15,000dwt 140 x 25 x 7.6 metres 14.5kts.
Reported also on Maritime Data website and by Galbraith Brokers, **Six VYBORG type** + 2 options, oil / products tankers valued at $17.5 million, for Stena in association with Transpetrol of Moscow - each 8,000g. 15,000d. (3 due **2006)**, (2 due **2007**). (1 due **2008).** At the time of writing however, no confirmation of the order placement has been given.

Part Three - Passenger & Roro-Cargo Operations.

In the autumn of 1962, one Poul Ludvigsen, had attempted to establish a ferry service under the auspices of Skagen - Goteborgs - Linjen AS, utilizing the chartered vessel OSTERSOEN, but after only four days the adventure failed dramatically and the OSTERSOEN hastily returned to her owners.

Having successfully operated hitherto with cargo vessels, Olsson had watched carefully the failed operation and identifying an opportunity decided to turn into reality, his thoughts on the possibility of pleasure trips to Denmark, for people of all walks of life, not just for the wealthy. In a major change of policy by the directorship of the company, Olsson founded ***Skagenlinjen Ab.,*** as a feeler for the passenger market, initially using the chartered OSTERSOEN, taking over where Ludvigsen had left off. OSTERSOEN departed for Skagen on 21 December 1962 thus sowing the seed for what has become Stena Line. She operated the route until Skagen Harbour became icebound on 10 February 1963. When the service reopened the chartered SEUTE DEERN served it. She supplemented with several chartered small modern passenger vessels. Two old second-hand ships were purchased early in 1963. VISBY was purchased in January with agreed delivery in the summer whereupon as SKAGEN II she inaugurated the Lysekil - Skagen route on 17 July. The passenger vessels were to establish a network of routes, some of which however were discontinued after only one season -

1962:
Gothenburg - Skagen (Discontinued in 1965).
Lysekil - Skagen (summer season only)
(Discontinued in 1966).

1963: Gothenburg - Frederikshavn.
Uddevalla - Marstrand - Skagen
(One season only).
Nakskov - Kiel (Discontinued in 1965).

1964: Gothenburg - Läsö (Summer 1964 only).
Halmstad - Helsingör (Summer 1964 only).
Bergkvara - Allinge (Summer 1964 only).
Gothenburg - Larvik (Summer 1964 only).
Trelleborg - Falsterbokanalen - Kastrup
(Discontinued 1967).
Malmo - Kastrup (Discontinued 1966).

AFRODITE on the Kastrup - Malmo route.
(Author's collection)

Satisfied with the earnings, and response from travellers, an order was placed for two small passenger ferries of similar style to the chartered vessels. They subsequently appeared during 1964 as POSEIDON and AFRODITE.

Alongside the passenger only vessels the chartered OSTERSOEN and ISFJORD provided valuable experience in the car ferry principles and with moves toward a much improved passenger service the Company placed orders for two roll-on - roll-off vehicle / passenger ferries. The first of these French built vessels was delivered as STENA DANICA during 1965 for the ferry service between Gothenburg and Frederikshavn. She was the first vessel to carry the "STENA" prefix to the name. At this juncture the Skagen routes were discontinued when Skagen Line was rebranded as Stena Line.

A Change of Direction

The traffic between Gothenburg and Frederikshavn had not developed as fast as anticipated so, with surplus capacity on their hands, the Company looked around for new routes to utilise the second ship. As a result a new service between Tilbury and Calais (UK - France) was inaugurated on 3 July 1965. ***Stena Line / P.D.A., Ltd.,*** was formed to manage this operation, using the STENA NORDICA, which had arrived direct from her builders in France. The new service was known as "THE LONDONER", and the original plans and advertisements showed the ship with this name on the bows only, with her real name on the stern. However, when the ship entered service this logo was carried on the ship's sides, in large red letters, with the ship name fore and aft as normal. The service was operated until 3 October 1965, when it ceased for the winter months, at which juncture the vessel moved to Scandinavia and gained Jatten –Finn on her hull instead of The Londoner. Due to the shortage of employment STENA NORDICA was offered for sale early in 1966, at an asking price of £1.25m. However, she was taken off the market when a charter agreement was reached with the Caledonian Steam Packet, (Irish Services), Ltd. It was their intention to use her on their Larne - Stranraer (N. Ireland - Scotland) service. This was the first ever "charter-out" undertaken by the company, an activity that has since that time, become one of the main features of their operations.

When the French service re-opened in the spring of 1966 it was with the ferry PRINSESSAN CHRISTINA, which had been chartered from the Rederi Ab. Goteborg - Frederikshavn Linjen, (Sessanlinjen), Sweden. This vessel was repainted in STENA colours as "THE LONDONER" for the duration of the season. There proved, however, to be insufficient volumes of traffic for her size, resulting in a decision being taken at the end of the season to reduce the size of vessel for the 1967 season. STENA BALTICA was thus allocated to the route until February 1968 when reluctantly the service was discontinued.

Meanwhile, the new STENA GERMANICA was delivered onto the Kiel - Gothenburg (West Germany - Sweden) route that commenced operation on the 24 April. Passengers were offered the round trip for 68 Swedish Kroner.

During the next three years other trade continued to flourish and more new and second hand vessels entered company service. By the end of the 1960's Stena were operating on three main routes, Gothenburg – Kiel, Gothenburg – Frederikshavn and Stockholm – Mariehamn, but the expansion bubble was about to burst. The Swedish Government introduced new legislation effective from 1 January 1969 that imposed stringent new laws concerning manning levels on all Swedish registered ships. These new laws prompted Stena to offer many of their vessels for sale and place orders for two new larger ferries, to comply with the new regulations. These two new vessels ordered from a Yugoslav shipyard, were designated as night ferries for the Kiel - Gothenburg service. During the interim period the new STENA DANICA was delivered from her builders. To supplement her a second-hand vessel was sought as a stopgap, until the new vessels could be delivered during 1972 - 1973. To this end the SAGA was purchased during 1971 to be renamed STENA ATLANTICA.

Four ships were ordered from Yugoslavia In March 1970. These vessels were to be day ferries, for delivery during 1973 - 1974. Of these four, two were designated for the Goteborg - Frederikshavn route, and the other pair was ordered as options. However, it was subsequently decided that the company would not take up the options. Stena however successfully found a buyer for the options and as a result the contracts for yard No's. 161 and 164, passed to *Rederi Ab. Gotland*, Sweden, in a deal which involved the acquisition of shares in the latter company by Stena Ab. as well as a cash payment. This left Stena with yard No's. 162 and 163, to be completed as STENA JUTLANDICA and STENA DANICA. The specifications of the two contracts that had been sold were altered and the ships were completed as VISBY and GOTLAND with slightly differing superstructure arrangements to those of the Stena sisters.

VISBY (Internet source / Aare Avasulo)

Expansion Into The Ferry Charter-Market

The company was watching the changes in the freight transportation market very carefully and formulating development plans. The old style break-bulk cargo handling methods were giving ground to the innovative unit load system. In the early stages the unit load was being transported on regular passenger RoRo services, but as the system gained momentum, so too did demand for precious deck-space and more frequent sailings. It was those demands that sparked the directorship into action, seeing the potential of new business. In what was becoming a normal for the company, another multiple vessel order was also placed for four RoRo / cargo ferries for delivery during 1970 - 1972. These four newly innovative ships, constructed with a worldwide operating capability, were to be used primarily on charter work, as well as on the company routes operating alongside the passenger RoRo vessels. The first was delivered as STENA CARRIER during 1970 and was arranged with a charter to the Canadian Ministry of Transport. In 1971 STUBBENKAMMER was delivered for charter to the East German Railway Authority, but was purchased outright by her proposed charterers. The third of the quartet was launched as STENA TRAILER. Whilst fitting out a ten-year charter to the British Railways Board was arranged and, at their request, she was completed as DALRIADA for use on their Larne - Stranraer service.

DALRIADA on trials in British Rail colours (Courtesy Stena Ab)

Subsequent to the success of this vessel in their operations the British Railways Board opted to charter the last of the quartet and once again, at their request, Stena ordered the ship to be built as ANDERIDA. On this vessel it was also requested that railway track should be fitted to the deck, thus enabling the vessel to double-up as a train ferry as and when required. During the vessel's fitting out period an agreement was reached that the charterers would purchase her as soon as sea and acceptance trials had been completed.

At this point I would like to point out that when the British Railways Board, through their bankers, in 1974, purchased STENA CARRIER and renamed her ULIDIA they then operated three of the four vessels of this class.

During 1972 the first of the two new night ferries was delivered onto the Gothenburg - Kiel service. She had been named STENA OLYMPICA to commemorate the staging of the Olympic games in Munich in that year. To coincide with her arrival a new route was opened from Kiel – Korsör utilizing the German route vessel during their daytime stopover at Kiel. A Gothenburg – Copenhagen route was also opened but after a few months of poor trading results it was closed.

Following the re-organisation of the company into three divisions, all the administration staff were moved to the newly constructed terminal building, at Masthuggskajen. This new terminal was a welcome time-saver for passengers to Germany, as the mooring site was moved from Skandiahamnen to down town Gothenburg. This also contributed to the return of the former character of the inner harbour, a scene of lively activity, and now a centre for passenger activity.

Pleased with the financial returns on the chartered tonnage the Company ordered three new multi - purpose RoRo cargo ferries from Dutch shipbuilders, for delivery during 1973, a year that witness the arrival of many new vessels and names. STENA SCANDINAVICA, the second vessel for the Gothenburg -Kiel route entered service. Days earlier, STENA SAILER, the first of the Dutch built trio was delivered onto a short charter with British Railways.

The second Dutch built vessel, STENA SEATRADER had been arranged with a charter to the Canadian Ministry of Transport as a replacement for smaller STENA CARRIER. This charter resulted in the STENA prefix being dropped after launching and the vessel being completed as SEATRADER.

The last of the trio was also destined for charter, but this time it was the beginning of a new era for Stena. This vessel was to be "demise chartered", to the Union Steamship Company of New Zealand Ltd. A demise charter was described by the company as "a vessel chartered by another company, registered and operated in their fleet as one of their own vessels with a fee paid to the owner." This differs from a bareboat charter, where the vessel remains registered in the name of the owner but is operated by the charterer for a set time, wearing their colour scheme and name style. The vessel completed her sea trials as STENA SHIPPER. She was however painted in the charterer's colour scheme of bottle green hull and red funnel with black top and two black rings, (similar to funnels of Cunard vessels). Upon completion of her acceptance trials she was renamed UNION WELLINGTON for the duration of her three-year charter.

The new Yugoslav built STENA JUTLANDICA was introduced onto the Danish route, whilst another order was placed for four passenger ferries. This latest order was placed with Rickmers Werft, Bremerhaven, for delivery during 1974 - 1975. Whilst these vessels were under construction a charter to Canadian National Line was arranged resulting in one vessel being renamed whilst fitting out, and another being launched with the charterer's "MARINE" style name prefix.

Further orders were placed for RoRo-cargo ferries for operations within the charter market. During June 1974 three were ordered from Hamburg builders, and in January 1975 a further three near-sister ships from Austrian builders. These new vessels were to be known as the STENA SEAPORTER class and allocated STENA "T" names, were to cost around £8 million each. The three Hamburg vessels were arranged with charters and all given their charterers choice of name before launching. P&O Ferries, who later opted to purchase the vessels whilst they were being fitted out, chartered the BISON and BUFFALO. The UNION MELBOURNE was chartered to the Union Steamship Company of New Zealand Ltd., as a larger replacement for the UNION WELLINGTON, also chartered from the Company. As soon as the UNION MELBOURNE was completed, she was sent for lengthening before delivery onto her charter. In turn, when the UNION WELLINGTON was relieved by the new ship she was sent to Kiel for lengthening, as were her two sister ships, before the trio commenced three separate demise charters.

November 1975 witnessed the placing of the initial phase of what was to become the largest ever order by the company. From South Korea shipbuilders, Rederi Ab. Concordia, ordered five multi-purpose RoRo vessels. These vessels were to be known as the STENA SEARUNNER class and were supplemented during December 1975, with an order for a further batch of six vessels, all of which were scheduled for delivery during 1977 - 1978. This class had been meticulously designed with longevity of service in mind. Company engineers had incorporated many design features that would give versatility. A larger than required engine capacity would meet any need for power in the event of lengthening. The engine-room was designed to accept even larger machinery whilst the hull and superstructure catered for additional decks and accommodation respectively. The careers of this class have proven how prophetic that foresight was.

The earlier decision to build three ships in Austria was soon to be regretted when during 1976 the first of the trio, launched during that long hot summer, was due to begin the journey down the River Danube in sections, under tow. That journey proved to be one full of mishaps and misfortunes. The plan was for all three vessels to have their hulls launched without superstructure. This would be built separately and loaded onto a barge. The hull and barge bearing the superstructure would then be towed down river to Galatz, in Romania, where the superstructure would be lifted into position and the ship completed. That was the plan.

In the case of the first vessel STENA TENDER however, a road bridge collapsed and blocked her intended exit route thus delaying her at Vienna for a few weeks. Because of the exceptionally hot, dry weather of 1976, the river levels were in places lower than desired and the ship had to be bodily dragged along the bottom by her tugs and their long suffering crews. It was now however into October and the rains began with a vengeance and continued well into November by which time the water levels were substantially above normal. When the convoy arrived at Novostad, in Yugoslavia, the hull was only just able to pass under the bridge, but not so the superstructure. The order was given to anchor upstream and wait for the waters to recede. It was nearly six months before it could continue downstream. At this juncture the United Baltic Corporation Ltd., of London, contracted to buy the "vessel", after it had been lengthened and completed. It was arranged that Werft Nobiskrug GmbH, at Rendsburg, West Germany, would undertake this work. This company had also lengthened the UNION MELBOURNE, a near sister ship after her completion at Hamburg, so were familiar with the vessel design and characteristics. The superstructure was lifted aboard and partly welded by the workers who had travelled from Vienna, and who were now living in temporary accommodation built on the vehicle deck. The vessel was not registered, but was towed from the Black Sea to West Germany as a "Steel Structure" and at Rendsburg entered dry dock as STENA TENDER and when lengthened and completed emerged as GOYA. The other two of the trio were completed without mishap as STENA TOPPER and STENA TIMER / JAGUAR. Sold to British owners, STENA TOPPER sailed from Galatz, via Gothenburg, to Belfast, where she was taken in hand by Harland & Wolff Ltd., for alteration to make her more suitable for her charter, to the British Railways Board on their Larne - Stranraer route. Upon the completion of this work the vessel was renamed DARNIA, at Belfast.

The STENA TIMER was also destined to trade from Larne, but on charter to P&O Ferries. Upon her completion of sea trials she was renamed JAGUAR and sailed from Galatz, to join her Hamburg built sisters, BUFFALO and BISON, on the Larne - Fleetwood, and Dublin - Fleetwood routes. When P&O Ferries chartered UNION MELBOURNE, all six of this class of vessel have served the Northern Ireland port of Larne, on various routes and when UNION TRADER (ex UNION MELBOURNE), was purchased by P&O Ferries and renamed PUMA, together with the vessel originally destined as STENA TENDER becoming LEOPARD, five of them have carried their wild-life naming system.

Many events were to affect the group during 1977, the most important of which was achieving the first decade of service to West Germany. To mark the occasion and as a token of appreciation, the City of Kiel presented Sten A. Olsson with the Federal Republic of Germany's "Highest Order of Merit". Minister President Stoltenberg presented this.

Toward the end of the year delivery of the Korean built SEARUNNER class commenced with a variety of names and colour schemes to suit their relevant charterer's requirements. They were also registered under several different flags. The NORSKY was delivered onto the newly opened Ipswich - Rotterdam service, operated by North Sea Ferries Ltd., a company partly owned by P&O, and the Dutch Nedlloyd, groups. The Greek, Arghiris Line, soon chartered STENA RUNNER and was renamed ALPHA PROGRESS, under British registry to supplement ALPHA EXPRESS, under Greek registry, demise chartered from Stena. Agreement was also reached that a sister would be completed as ALPHA ENTERPRISE, also under British registry. Atlantic Container Line contracted to charter two of the vessels building as STENA PROJECT and STENA PROSPER and these were delivered as ATLANTIC PROJECT and ATLANTIC PROSPER. The ELK was chartered to, and later purchased by the P&O group, through their bankers. Tor Line chartered TOR FELICIA for a short period before she was further chartered to the Italian Merzario Line, as MERZARIO GRECIA, to join her sisters, MERZARIO AUSONIA and MERZARIO ESPANIA. These latter vessels replaced a group of smaller,"Tarros" class vessels, on charter to Merzario Line from Sea Containers Inc.

Versatility - Inbuilt To The Ship Design

When STENA SCANDINAVICA was sold a requirement arose for a quick replacement and to this end the Norwegian BOLERO was taken on charter and renamed SCANDINAVICA. She was painted in Stena colours and entered on the Kiel - Gothenburg route, having been transferred to Swedish registry.

By the end of the 1970's Stena Line were operating the routes Gothenburg – Frederikshavn, Gothenburg – Kiel and Oslo – Frederikshavn. Stena following closure by a Norwegian operator had resurrected the latter route.

The versatility of the management was proven during 1979 when, after discussion on the feasibility of a request by a building construction company, the ferry PEER GYNT was purchased and sent for major refurbishment and alteration into a floating hotel. Construction workers at Sullum Voe, in the Shetland Islands, where a new oil refinery was being built, would use her. When this work, which included the fitting of a large helicopter platform, was completed the ship was renamed STENA BALTICA.

This was an example of the willingness of the company to adapt to the needs of the charterers. Further evidence of this type of activity became apparent when the Korean vessels came under further scrutiny from Stena's ship "Tailors", at their design office further developing their design concept. The first stage of their plan was augmented when ALPHA PROGRESS and ALPHA ENTERPRISE were sent to Hapag-Lloyd Werft GmbH, at Bremerhaven, to be deepened by adding a new upper deck which would cover the original upper deck, and to be also widened by adding side sponsons for greater stability. At the same time an extra accommodation block was built aft of the funnel at the top of the existing superstructure block, extending right to the after end of the hull. This provided 160 berths for the lorry drivers. When completed the vessels were renamed HELLAS and SYRIA respectively. Following this MERZARIO HISPANIA was renamed NORDIC FERRY and following a short period, together with STENA TRANSPORTER were similarly converted the latter being renamed BALTIC FERRY. STENA GOTHICA and STENA BRITANNICA were also, later, given the same alterations but without the extra accommodation block. Other vessels of the class have been widened only in a similar manner, but in their case it was to enable a greater quantity of containers to be stacked on the original main deck without loss of stability. SYRIA and HELLAS later returned to the same yard to be lengthened and were transferred to the Cypriot registry upon completion of the work. Of the eleven vessels in the class all have been altered in some way and very few bare any resemblance to their original design profile.

There was an urgent need for increased tonnage and a particular specification required within the fleet late in the 1970's and to meet that demand the three 1973, Dutch built sisters all of which had earlier been lengthened, were brought back into the fold upon the completion of their respective charters.

Consolidation

With the traffic between Oslo and Frederikshavn making good progress further new ships were under serious consideration, and following the enlargement and improvements to the Gothenburg terminal, further new terminals were ordered for Kiel and Frederikshavn. As a direct result of the co-ordination of ferry services, and using vessels of both the Stena and Sessan fleets from Gothenburg, vastly increased volume was achieved. A sister ship to the newly delivered KRONPRINSESSAN

VICTORIA was eventually ordered. It was reported that the name DROTTNING SILVIA was applied for but following objections the vessels was launched without name.

Orders were also placed in France, for two super day ferries for delivery during 1982, and in Poland, for four super night ferries, for delivery during 1983-1984.

By 1982 in anticipation of the new arrivals, together with a slight downturn in the market, some of the older vessels were disposed of. At the end of August however, an opportunistic purchase by the company saw the remnants of Lion Ferry acquired from the Bonnier Group, together with their one vessel EUROPAFARJAN III that was operating their Varberg – Grenaa route. The vessel was quickly sold and replaced with units from the Stena fleet, thus further reducing overcapacity in the fleet.

A shuffle of names took place between the Sessan Line vessels, when the PRINSESSAN BIRGITTA was renamed STENA SCANDINAVICA to release the name for use on the new ship. This came about when the plan to use the name DROTTNING SILVIA was abandoned. STENA JUTLANDICA was renamed JUTLANDICA and transferred to the Bahamas registry, thus releasing the name for use on the second of the French buildings, the first being delivered as STENA DANICA. The Gothenburg – Frederikshavn route underwent a change during May 1983. One of the vessels plying the route was utilized to service a supplementary route from Frederikshavn to Moss to link with the Gothenburg ferry thus developing a triangular service Gothenburg – Frederikshavn – Moss – Frederikshavn.

The first of the much-delayed Polish ships arrived in service during 1987, as STENA GERMANICA and owned by a leasing firm. STENA DANICA and STENA JUTLANDICA were subsequently transferred onto a lease ownership whilst Lion ferry opened a second route from Halmstad to Grenaa.

Within the year Stena was able to expand into North America when it acquired a route and two vessels operating from Victoria in Canada to Seattle in USA. The route was restyled as BC Stena Line in May 1989 but because of a change in USA gambling laws within territorial waters, the service declined in popularity and was wound up in November 1990. Further closure saw Lion Ferry end its Helsingör – Grenaa service leaving only the Halmstad and Varberg to Grenaa routes.

Some old names were revived with the purchase of three RoRo vessels from the Romanian Government they being renamed STENA TIMER, STENA TENDER, and STENA TOPPER. The latter two names had been previously used on vessels, which did not trade for the company, both being sold early in their careers. Further freight ferries were purchased and two of these were sent for lengthening at Cityvarvet Ab. at Gothenburg to make them more readily suited to the charter market, whilst four new freight RoRo ferries, two as options, were ordered from Fosens yard at Oresund, for delivery in 1990-91. The two optional contracts were subsequently sold to Turkish operators who amended the design to suit their particular needs.

European Expansion - Sealink

Having successfully acquired both the Dutch, Crown Line and Sealink British Ferries, the initial phase of reformation was the introduction of a dedicated freight ferry on the Harwich - Hoek van Holland route to absorb the steady increase of traffic being attracted. This vessel was one of a pair of redundant ferries purchased by Stena some time previous but with delivery planned in the spring of 1990. This first unit was refitted and renamed STENA SEATRADER. Subsequently replaced by a new generation of vessels to Harwich she remained based on Hoek van Holland and opened a new freight route to Immingham. STENA SEATRADER and STENA SEARIDER still operate the Immingham – Hoek van Holland route, although both are due for replacement in the coming months. Summer 1991 saw a Southampton – Cherbourg route opened and months later the Folkestone – Boulogne route was closed, that being offset by the implementation of a Dover to Dunkirk freight route.

New construction featured heavily in the early 1990's with HSS 1 and HSS 2 (HSS 1500) the first units of a new design concept in catamaran style fast travel being ordered for Stena Sealink's Holyhead - Dun Laoghaire and Larne - Stranraer routes whilst STENA SEALYNX and later the STENA SEALYNX II were chartered for interim period until arrival of HSS on Holyhead route to get customers used to and build the market for the high speed concept. Subsequently HSS 3 was ordered for Harwich - Hook of Holland service whilst HSS 4 (HSS 1500) was destined for Stena Line's Gothenburg - Frederikshavn route. A new building freight/passenger ferry was ordered from Holland. STENA JUTLANDICA was very similar in appearance to Irish Ferries' ISLE OF INISHFREE, a vessel later to enter Stena service.

Stena Ab announced on 1 November 1995 the placing of orders for ELEVEN RoRo ferries. These were for two differing classes and at different shipyards. One class, a passenger / RoRo, named as Stena Seapacer consisted of two firm orders plus two options of 7,000 dwt was placed in Spain. The other, the freight RoRo Stena 4-runner class consisted of seven firm orders of 12,000 dwt placed in Italy. All were to be capable of 24 knots.

The latter class was subsequently to create problems for the fleet operational planners. Two had been arranged with charters to the British Ministry of Defence and another pair to a Turkish operator who had subsequently opted to purchase upon completion. Subsequently, Stena had entered negotiations with the shipbuilder for the construction of further units of the series to replace the 2 units sold and the 2 chartered to Ministry of Defence. These however failed due in the main to delays being incurred at the shipyard necessitating re-negotiation of schedules with charterers, early in 1998 resulting in a shuffle of names against yard numbers. The delays and associated costs had created financial problems at the yard, that ultimately led to its collapse with all work stopped on the remaining six vessels in 1999, with many of them either launched or in advanced state of build. The existing orders were in doubt as to completion or even commencement.

Exasperated, with the situation Stena subsequently placed an order in China for 3 units assigned as the Stena 4-Runner- Mk2 class

Of the six vessels remaining at the Italian yard, two have since been completed. See ship numbers F. 300 and F. 301.

The remaining four, at the time of writing, are either incomplete or not commenced.

It was also announced that from 12 November 1995 the Stranraer service would operate from Belfast's new Victoria Terminal thus adding approx 45 minutes to crossing but this was addressed with the arrival on the route of the HSS 2 - STENA VOYAGER in July 1996.

Co-operation And Competition

With the 1994 opening of the Channel Tunnel linking the UK with France, all the ferry operators providing services from Dover and Folkestone to Calais, Dunkirk and Boulogne henceforth faced a new challenge. With high-speed rail links to France from London and a rail shuttle service for road vehicles through the tunnel, volumes of ferry traffic began an inevitable decline. From that point ferry operators no longer had the monopoly and were forced to respond by introducing numerous saver packages and other such special offers. Some routes succumbed to dwindling revenues and were closed whilst others held their own, if only just. A fundamental problem facing all operators was potentially over-capacity in face of dwindling trade. P&O had recently had a series of new vessels constructed to address freight trades. Sealink Stena had introduced new vessels also. Both were discovering that whilst vessels were maintaining the schedules, they were often far from full, a false economy. After a couple of years of continued decline, during which Sealink Stena Line had been restyled as Stena Line, both companies held discussions, and the outcome was the creation, in 1998, of P&O Stena, to provide a united front. Fleets were rationalized with P&O the larger participant, holding 60%. Vessels were shuffled to and from various other routes to attain the ideal combination of capacities. The joint venture however, was to last only four-years. P&O Ferries parent organization, in the interim, had commenced a total overhaul of their operations worldwide, one that was to see the disposal of many of their trading divisions over the coming years, together with the creation of joint ventures within others. The re-organisation was to see increased investment in their ferry operations, but only on specific routes. One of the latter was Dover – France, and as a result they arranged the acquisition of Stena's shareholding and other interests on the route, effective from 2002. From that separation Stena was able to acquire P&O's Felixstowe – Rotterdam freight routes, and transferred the Felixstowe base across the river to Harwich. Subsequently P&O offered Stena the opportunity to acquire their Irish Sea freight operations, and offer that was accepted, but was then referred to the U.K. Competition Commission. When the Commission eventually issued their ruling, Stena was able to acquire much less than had been intended by P&O, who were forced to retain their Dublin – U.K. service.

Further expansion had meanwhile, been undertaken in Scandinavian waters, when in 1996, Stena were enabled to acquire Sweferry Ab, the Swedish facet of the multi-national Scandlines operation, whereupon, in 1997 they restyled it as Scandlines Ab. That operation introduced several new vessels and routes to the Stena portfolio. This fleet was a mix of vessel types and sizes, some owned, some managed and others chartered. One vessel was under construction. Following acquisition, minimal changes were undertaken until 2000 when in a surprise move STENA GERMANICA was registered in the ownership of Scandlines Ab.

At the time of publication of this work, Stena Group were operating the following freight and passenger ferry routes / vessels:

SCANDINAVIA

Oslo – Frederikshavn
Stena Saga

Gothenburg – Frederikshavn
Stena Carisma
Stena Danica
Stena Jutlandica
Stena Scanrail

Varberg – Grenaa
Stena Nautica

Gothenburg – Kiel
Stena Germanica
Stena Scandinavica

Goteborg – Travemunde
Stena Carrier
Stena Freighter

Helsingborg – Helsingor
Aurora Af Helsingborg
Hamlet (50%)

Trelleborg – Travemunde
Gotaland

Trelleborg – Rostock
Skane

Trelleborg – Sassnitz
Trelleborg

Karlskrona – Gdynia
Stena Baltica
Stena Nordica

IRISH SEA

Larne – Fleetwood
Stena Leader
Stena Pioneer
Stena Seafarer

Belfast – Stranraer
Stena Voyager
Stena Caledonia

Dublin – Holyhead
Stena Adventurer

Dun Laoghaire – Holyhead
Stena Explorer

Fishguard – Rosslare
Stena Europe
Stena Lynx III

NORTH SEA

Harwich - Hoek Van Holland
Stena Discovery
Stena Hollandica
Stena Britannica

Harwich – Rotterdam
Stena Partner
Stena Transfer
Stena Transporter

Immingham - Hoek Van Holland
Stena Seatrader
Stena Searider
(To be replaced by Stena Trader and
Stena Traveller both under Construction)

Artist's impression of the replacement vessels under construction for the Immingham – Hoek van Holland route.

The Passenger & RoRo-Cargo Fleet

SKAGEN I

(Courtesy Stena Ab)

F.1. SKAGEN I (1963 - 1965)

As built: 937g. 520n. 209.6 x 34.2 x 18.9 feet.
Post 1949: 1,325g. 716n. 233.4 x 34.2 x 18.5 feet.
T.3-cyl. (16½", 27" & 45 " x 27") engine made by shipbuilder.
Passenger ferry.
1914: Completed as HEIMDAL by Akt. Burmeister & Wain, Copenhagen (Yard No. 292), for AS Dampskibsselskabet P. A. A. Bornholm af 1866, Denmark. 1930: Sold to Stockholms Rederi Svea, (Eman Hogborg, manager), Sweden. 1936: Renamed BRYNHILD. 1949: Lengthened. 1959: Sold to Ab Telfa, (Gunnar Andersson, manager), Sweden. 1961: Sold to Rederi Ab Continent Line, Sweden. 1962: Sold to Theodore Sandgren & Others, Sweden. 1963: Sold to Partrederi for SS Brynhild, Sweden. 4.1963: Chartered and renamed SKAGEN I. 8.1963: Released from charter and reverted to BRYNHILD. 2.12.1963: Purchased at auction by Skagenlinien Rederi Ab, (Sten A. Olsson Handels Ab, managers), Sweden, and renamed SKAGEN I. 1963: Transferred to Sten A. Olsson Handels Ab, who restyled, Stena Ab. 1964: Laid up for disposal. 4.1965: Sold to Holmen Bruk, refitted by Lodose Varv, and renamed REGINA, was towed to Halstavik. 12.1967: Sold to ASEA, Vasteras, Sweden, for employment as a floating hostel for visiting German workers. 12.1968: Re-located to Simpvarp near Oskarshamn. Summer 1970 suffered damage and sold to Danish shipbreakers, was demolished at Nakskov.

F.2. VISBY / SKAGEN II (1963 - 1968)

877g. 456n. 300d. 171.0 x 30.5 x 13.7 feet.
T.3-cyl. (17-1/8", 29" & 48" x 30") engine made by the shipbuilder. 12 kts.
Passenger ferry.
1924: Completed by Ab Oskarshamns M V, Oskarshamn (Yard No. 274), for Angf. Ab Gotland, Sweden. 1963: Purchased by Skagenlinien Rederi Ab, (Sten A. Olsson Handels Ab, managers), and later renamed SKAGEN II. 1964: Transferred to Stena Ab. 1965: Transferred to Rederibolaget Sarabande Olsson & Company Kommanditbolag, Sweden. 1966: Transferred to Stena Ab. 1968: Demolished by Persohn & Sonner at Ystad.

5386057

F.3. WAPPEN (1964 - 1965)

3,819g. 1,908n. 2,494d. 341' 3" x 49' 7" x 13' 2".
Two, 16-cyl. 4 S.C.S.A. (400 x 460mm) oil engines made by Ottensener Eisenwerke, (Willy H. Schlieker), K. G., Hamburg, geared to twin screw shafts with controllable pitch propellers. 4,480 BHP. 22 kts. Thwartship thrust propeller forward.
Ice strengthened, 1,800 deck passengers / ferry.
21.9.1961: Keel laid as WAPPEN VON HAMBURG by Blohm & Voss A. G., Hamburg (Yard No. 823), for Hafen Dampfschifffahrts A.G, W. Germany. 18.1.1962: Launched. 21.5.1962: Completed. 11.1963:

Chartered to Skagenlinjen Rederi Ab, (Sten A. Olsson Handels Ab, managers. 4.1964: Released from charter. 9.1964: Purchased by Stena Redeeria GmbH, W. Germany, and renamed WAPPEN. 1965: Sold to Hafen Dampfschiffahrts A. G., W. Germany. 1966: Renamed ALTE LIEBE. 1971: Owners restyled Hadag Seetouristik U Fahrdienst A.G. 1975: Sold to K. G. M. S. Alte Liebe, (Jacobsen, Kroger and Company, managers), W. Germany. 1983: Passenger capacity increased by 180. 1984: Sold to Reederei D. Oltmann GmbH and Company K. G. (Bremer Seebaderdienst D. Oltmann and Company, managers), W. Germany, and renamed HELGOLAND. 1987: Sold to Harle Reederei Warrings, W. Germany. 1990: Sold to Rita Warrings, Germany. 1996: Sold to Bremerhaven Helgoland Linie GmbH & Company A. G., Wittmund, Germany. 2005: Sold to unspecified Netherlands owners, (Supperclub Cruise NV, Amsterdam, managers), and renamed SUPPER CLUBCRUISE 02, under the Panamanian flag.

WAPPEN on the Jatten-Finn route. Note the dummy funnel above the bridge.

(Author's collection)

POSEIDON.

(Author's collection)

6412920

F.4. POSEIDON (1964 - 1973)

As built: 1,358g. 605n. 152d. 214' 11' x 38' 10" x 9' 7".
Post 1993: 1,240g. 421n. 152d.
Two, 8-cyl. 4 S.C.S.A. (320 x 450mm) Deutz RBV8M545 type oil engines made by Kloeckner, Humboldt Deutz, Koeln, geared to twin screw shafts with controllable pitch propellers. 2,640 BHP. 16 kts.
Ice strengthened, 805deck-passenger ferry. 1993: Passenger capacity increased to 827 on deck.
28.4.1964: Launched by Ulstein M.V. AS, Ulsteinvik (Yard No. 26), for Skagenlinjen Rederi, (Sten A. Olsson, manager), Sweden. 21.6.1964: Completed for Stena Ab, Sweden. 1973: Sold to Vedettes Amoricaines, France. 1975: Sold to Zeeland Lloyd B. V., Netherlands. 1976: Sold to A.G. Emms, W. Germany. 1978: Sold to Seetouristik GmbH & Company K. G., W. Germany. 1993: Sold to Forde-Reedeerei GmbH., Germany. 2000: Sold to Seetouristik GmbH & Company K. G., Germany, and renamed POSEIDON IV, under the Panamanian flag. 2003: Sold to Pearl Cruise Line, Colombo, Sri Lanka, and renamed PEARL CRUISE II.

6412413

F.5. AFRODITE (1964 - 1971)

As built: 564g. 246n. 106d. 158' 7" x 26' 4" x 11' 0"
Post 1978: 675g. 412n. 175d. 49.23 x 8.31 x metres.
Post 1998: 672g. 252n. 156d.
Two, 8-cyl. 4 S.C.S.A. (250 x 350mm) MWM TRH435AU type oil engines made by Motorenwerke Mannheim A.G. (MWM), Mannheim, geared to twin screw shafts. 1,650 BHP. 12.5 kts
Ice strengthened, 350 deck passenger ferry.
1978: Passenger capacity increased to 450
13.4.1964: Launched by D.W. Kremer Sohn GmbH & Company, Elmshorm (Yard No. 1108), for Kiel - Nakskov Linjen, (Sten A. Olsson, manager), Sweden. 10.7.1964: Completed for Sten A. Olsson Handels Ab, Sweden. 1967: Transferred to Rederi Ab Concordia, (Stena Ab, managers), Sweden. 1971: Sold to Forde-Reederei GmbH, W. Germany. 1978: Lengthened, widened, and passenger capacity increased to 450. 1998: Sold to Reedeerei Gert Muller GmbH, & Company K. G., Panamanian flag, and renamed NORDLICHT II. 2003: Renamed ATLANTIS II. 2004: Sold to CCC Catamaran, Mallentin, Germany, and renamed GLORIA II.

STENA NORDICA (1)

(Author's collection)

6516544

F.6. STENA NORDICA (1) (1965 - 1973)

2,607g. 1,160n. 615d. 261' 10" x 53' 2" x 12' 8".
Two, 12-cyl. 4 S.C.S.A. (400 x 500mm) oil engines made by Kloeckner, Humboldt - Deutz, Koeln, geared to twin screw shafts with controllable pitch propellers. 6,000 BHP. 17kts. Thwartship thrust propeller forward.
935 deck passengers / roro cargo / ferry, with bow and stern doors.
15.5.1965: Launched by Ateliers et Chantiers de La Seine Maritime, Le Trait (Yard No. 173), for Stena Ab, (Sten A. Olsson, manager), Sweden. 15.6.1965: Completed. 1973: Sold to Consolidata de Ferrys C. A., (CONFERRY), Venezuela, and renamed SANTA ANA. 7.5.1980: When 4 hours out from Puerto La Cruz, vessel caught fire. Subsequently taken in tow, the burning vessel was beached at a position 10.5N., 64.10W., allowed to burn out and settled in shallow water.

STENA DANICA (1)

(Author's collection)

6516532

F.7. STENA DANICA (1) (1965 - 1970)

As built: 2,690g. 1,270n. 640d. 282' 3" x 54' 6" x 12' 8".
Post 1995; 4,245g. 2,482n. 1,000d.
Two, 12-cyl. 4 S.C.S.A. (400 x 500mm) oil engines made by Kloeckner, Humboldt - Deutz, Koeln, geared to twin screw shafts with controllable pitch propellers. 6,000 BHP. 17 kts. Thwartship thrust propeller forward.
1,000 deck passengers / roro cargo / ferry, with bow and stern doors.
3.5.1965: Launched by Ateliers et Chantiers de La Seine Maritime, Le Trait (Yard No. 172), for Stena Ab, (Sten A. Olsson, manager), Sweden. 19.6.1965: Completed. 1970: Sold to the Government of Canada, (Ministry of Transport), (Canadian National Railway Company, managers), Canada, and renamed LUCY MAUD MONTGOMERY. 1977: Owner restyled Government of Canada, (Minister of Transport), (same managers). 1979: Owner restyled Government of Canada, (Ministry of Transport), and removed from management. 1990: Sold to Marine Atlantic Inc., Canada. 1995: Sold to Government of Canada (Transport Canada), (Co-operative de Transport Maritime et Aerien (C. T. M. A.) managers), Canada. 1998: Sold to Robbie Shipping & Port Services Inc., Key West, Florida, and renamed LADY CARIBE I, under Honduras flag.

STENA BALTICA (1)
With charterer's funnel markings.

(Internet source)

6513451

F.8. STENA BALTICA (1) (1966 - 1970)

As built: 1,156g. 430n. 202' 8" x 41' 3" x 10' 4½".
Post 1988: 1,123g. 551n.
Post 1995: 943g. 428n.
Two, 9-cyl. 4 S.C.S.A. (300 x 450mm) MAN G9V30/45ATL type oil engines manufactured in 1964 by Maschinenbau Augsburg-Nuernberg (MAN), Augsburg, geared to twin screw shafts with controllable pitch propellers. Fitted in 1966. 1,335 BHP. 15 kts.
650 deck passengers / roro cargo / ferry with bow door / ramp, and stern door / ramp.
27.3.1965: Launched by AS Langesunds M.V., Langesund (Yard No. 53), for Stena Ab, (Sten A. Olsson, manager), Sweden. 31.3.1966: Completed. 1970: Sold to the Caledonian Steam Packet Company Ltd., Glasgow, and renamed CALEDONIA. 1974: Resulting from an amalgamation, owners restyled as Caledonian, MacBrayne Ltd. 1975: Transferred to Caledonian, MacBrayne (Holdings) Ltd. 1981: Transferred to Caledonian, MacBrayne Ltd. 1988: Sold to John Anthony Doherty, Anstruther, Fife. 1988: Sold to Libera Navigazione Lauro S.a.S., Italy, and renamed HEIDI. 1991: Sold to Traghetti Pozzuoli S.r.L., Naples, Italy. 2004: Sold to Medmar Navi SpA, Naples.

6702155

F.9. STENA GERMANICA (1) (1967 - 1979)

5,195g. 2,735n. 701d. 364' 0"(BB) x 60' 8" x 15' 9¾".
Two, 16-cyl. 4 S.C.S.A. (400 x 540mm) MAN 16V40/54 vee type oil engines made by Maschinenbau Augsburg Nuernberg (MAN), Augsburg, geared to twin screw shafts with controllable pitch propellers. 8,640 BHP. 23.5 kts. Thwartship thrust controllable pitch propeller forward.
Ice strengthened, 384 berthed, 916 deck passengers / roro cargo / ferry, with bow door / ramp, and stern door / ramp.
7.2.1966: Launched by AS Langesunds M.V., Langesund (Yard No. 54), for Stena Ab, (Sten A. Olsson, manager), Sweden. 21.2.1967: Whilst returning from builders sea trials, grounded and sustained severe bottom damage, thus delaying completion. 15.4.1967: Completed. 1978: Chartered out as a ferry for oil

workers between Aberdeen, and the Brent oilfield in the North Sea. This included the fitting of a helicopter platform aft. 1979: Sold to Armatur S. A., Panama, and renamed A. REGINA. 01:10hrs, 15.2.1985: Whilst on a voyage from Mayaguez to San Pedro de Macoris, grounded on a reef, off Mona Island, at a position 40 miles West of Puerto Rico. 143 passengers and 70 crew rescued by 4 American Naval helicopters operating a shuttle to Mona Island. Declared a constructive total loss.

STENA GERMANICA (1)

(Author's collection)

STENA BRITANNICA (1)

(Courtesy Stena Ab)

6717148

F.10. STENA BRITANNICA (1) (1967 - 1968)

As built: 5,073g. 2,660n. 711d. 364' 0"(BB) x 60' 8" x 15' 9¾".
Post 1986: 5,149g. 3,900n. 1,144d.
Post 1990: 5,019g. 2,856n. 1,144d.
Post 1994: 6,942g. 2,710n. 1,144d.
Two, 16-cyl. 4 S.C.S.A. (400 x 540mm) MAN 16V40/55 vee type oil engines made by Maschinenbau Augsburg-Nuernberg (MAN), Augsburg, geared to twin screw shafts with controllable pitch propellers. 8,640 BHP. 23.5 kts. Two, thwartship thrust controllable pitch propellers forward.
Ice strengthened, 432 berthed, 868 deck passengers / roro cargo / ferry with bow door / ramp, and stern door / ramp.
25.11.1966: Launched by AS Langesunds M.V., Langesund (Yard No. 55), for Stena Ab, (Sten A. Olsson, manager), Sweden. Fitted out by Framnaes M.V. AS, Sandefjord. 18.12.1967: Completed. 1968: Sold to the State of Alaska, (Department of Public Works), and renamed WICKERSHAM. 1974: Sold to Rederi Ab Sally, (Algot Johansson, manager), Finland, and renamed VIKING 6. 1980: Chartered to Brittany Ferries Ltd., France, and renamed GOELO. 1982: Reverted to VIKING 6. 1982: Sold to Sol Lines, Cyprus, and renamed SOL OLYMPIA. 1983: Sold to Arena Shipping Company Ltd., (Sol Lines Ltd., managers), Cyprus. 1985: Renamed SUN EXPRESS. 1985: Reverted to VIKING 6. 1986: Sold to Navigazione Arcipelago Maddalenino S.p.A. (NAV.AR.MA), Italy, and renamed MOBY DREAM. 1993: Sold to Sardegna Lines S.p.A., Italy, and renamed SARDEGNA BELLA. 24.9.2001: Arrived at Aliaga for demolition.

6917267

F.11. STENA DANICA (2) (1969 - 1974)

8,807g. 7,071n. 1,205d. 410' 5"(BB) x 67' 9" x 15' 11½".

Two, 16-cyl. 4 S.C.S.A. (400 x 540mm) MAN 16V40/54 vee type oil engines made by Maschinenbau Augsburg-Nuernberg, Augsburg, geared to twin screw shafts with controllable pitch propellers. 7,600 BHP. 22.5 kts. Thwartship thrust propeller forward, and aft.
1,541 passengers / roro cargo / ferry, with bow door / ramp, and stern door / ramp.
16.2.1969: Launched by A.G 'Weser' Werk Seebeck, Bremerhaven (Yard No. 934), for Stena Ab, (Sten A. Olsson, manager), Sweden. 28.6.1969: Completed. 1974: Sold to the Government of Canada, Province of British Colombia, (Ministry of Transport and Communications)(B. C. Ferries), Canada, and renamed QUEEN OF SURREY. 1980: Subsequent to the addition of an extra 200 berths by the Burrard, Yarrow Corporation, at their N. Vancouver shipyard, was renamed QUEEN OF THE NORTH, to release the name for a new building ship. 1983: Owners restyled British Columbia Ferry Corporation, Victoria BC.

STENA DANICA (2)

(The World Ship Society Ltd.)

7033202
F.12. STENA CARRIER (1) (1970 - 1974)
As built: 1,599g. 633n. 2,591d. 347' 5"(BB) x 52' 7" x 16' 2½".
Post 1989: 4,979g. 2,765n. 1,157d.
Two, 9-cyl. 4 S.C.S.A. (250 x 300mm) LDM-9 type (2,431 BHP) and two, 8-cyl. 4 S.C.S.A. (250 x 300mm) LDM-8 type (2,159 BHP) oil engines made by Normo-Gruppen AS, Bergen, one of each type geared to each of two screw shafts, with controllable pitch propellers, 4,590 BHP. 17 kts. Thwartship thrust propeller forward.
Ice strengthened, 16 berthed, 20 deck passengers / roro cargo / ferry, with a stern door / ramp.
30.4.1970: Launched by Kristiansands M.V. AS, Kristiansand (Yard No. 215), for Stena Ab, (Sten A. Olsson, manager), Sweden. 1.10.1970: Completed. 1974: Sold to Barclay's Export and Finance Company Ltd., (British Transport Ship Management (Scotland) Ltd., managers), London, and renamed ULIDIA. 1981: Sold to Corvo Shipping Inc., (Manta Line Inc., managers), Greece, and renamed AUTO TRADER. 1985: Sold to International Agency for Shipping & Trading Co., Egypt. 1986: Renamed RAGA QUEEN. 1988: Sold to AS Team Askoy, (Rutelaget Askoy-Bergen AS, managers), Norway, and renamed FJORDVEIEN. (replaced KYSTVEIEN see ship No.F.16). 1989: Sold to AS Rogaland Kystferer Ab, Norway. 1993: Sold to Rutelaget Askoy-Bergen AS. 1995: Sold to Ab Lillgard, Finland, and renamed FJARDVAGEN. 1995: Sold to Basto Fosen AS, Norway, and renamed HOLGER STJERN. 1999: Sold to Meridiano S.r.l., Lazzaro, Italy, and renamed HOLGER. 2005: Transferred to Turkish flag.

7105081
F.13. STENA TRAILER (1) / DALRIADA (1971 - 1980)
1,600g. 627n. 2,540d. 347' 9"(BB) x 52' 7" x 16' 2½".
Two, 9-cyl. 4 S.C.S.A. (250 x 300mm) LDM-9 type (2,431 BHP) and two, 8-cyl. 4 S.C.S.A. (250 x 300mm) LDM-8 type (2,159 BHP) oil engines made by Normo-Gruppen AS, Bergen, one of each type geared to each of two screw shafts, with controllable pitch propellers, 4,590 BHP. 17 kts. Thwartship thrust propeller forward.
Ice strengthened, 16 berthed, 20 deck passengers / roro cargo / ferry, with a stern door / ramp.
27.2.1971: Launched as STENA TRAILER by Brodrene Lothe AS, Haugesund (Yard No. 31), for Stena Ab, (Sten A. Olsson, manager), Sweden. 12.6.1971: Completed as DALRIADA for charter to the British Railways Board, London.1980: Renamed VIKING TRADER. 1981: Renamed STENA TRADER. 1981: Sold to Finska Foretagsfinans Ab, (Oy Hango Ship Management Ab., managers), Finland. 1983: Sold to Soumen Yritsrahoitus Oy, (Finska Foretags Finans Ab), (Oy Hango Shipowners Ab, managers), Finland. 1984: Transferred to Swedish flag, (Oy Bore Line Ab., managers). 1985: Sold to Kalundborg Autotransport AS., Denmark, and renamed TRADER. 1985: Renamed TRAILER. 1986: Sold to Bente Orla Jorgensen,

Denmark. 1991: Sold to C.I. Vance Investment Ltd., (Polish Scandinavia Shipping Lines Ltd., (Polska Skandynawia Linie Zeglugowe Sp.z.o.o.) managers), Bahamas, and renamed SARMACJA. 1992: Owners and managers both deleted by Lloyds Register and vessel transferred to Polish flag and renamed WOLIN. 1993: Sold to P. T. Perusahaan Angkutan Ferry (Jemla Ferry), Indonesia, and renamed MESUJI. 1993: Sold to Jemla Ferry, Jakarta. 1994: Renamed LAMPUNG.

STENA ATLANTICA (1)

(Author's collection)

6524905

F.14. STENA ATLANTICA (1) (1971 - 1973)

As built: 7,978g. 3,540n. 2,794d. 463' 3" x 68' 9" x 18' 1".
Post 1994: 12,374g. 4,802n. 2,794d.
Four, 6-cyl. 4 S.C.S.A. (400 x 460mm) Pielstick 6PC2L-400 type oil engines made by the shipbuilder, geared in pairs to twin screw shafts with controllable pitch propellers. 10,080 BHP. 18 kts. Thwartship thrust controllable pitch propeller forward.
520 berthed and 680 deck passengers / roro cargo / ferry with stern door.
18.10.1965: Launched as SAGA by Lindholmens Varv Ab, Goteborg (Yard No. 1093), for Ab Svenska Lloyd, Sweden. 2.5.1966: Completed. 1971: Purchased by Stena Ab, Sweden, and renamed STENA ATLANTICA. 1973: Sold to Thomesto Oy., (Finn Lines), Finland, and renamed FINNPARTNER. 1976: Renamed OLAU FINN . 1982: Sold to P.S.P. Finance, Finland and renamed FOLKLINER. 1984: Sold to Minoan Lines Shipping S. A., Greece and renamed FESTOS. 1998: Sold to Diler Feribot Isletmeciliginve Turizm A. S., (Grup Denizcilik ve Ticaret A.S., managers), Turkey, and renamed CAPTAIN ZAMAN I 2001: Sold to Sirene Shipping & Trading Inc., Turkey, (same managers). 2003: Sold to unspecified Turkish owners, (same managers), and renamed SANCAK I. 16.4.2003: Whilst under repair at Tuzla, caught fire. 19.4.2003: Fire extinguished. 26.7.2003: Arrived in tow at Aliaga for demolition by Butoni Denizcilik. 30.7.2003: Beached and work commenced.

STUBBENKAMMER

(Hans Mornhout collection)

7105093

F.15. STUBBENKAMMER (1971)

As built: 1,920g. 810n. 1,746d. 409' 0"(BB) x 55' 0" x 16' 2½".
Post 1990: 6,665g. 3,182n. 3,120d.
Post 1998: 6,207g. 2,981n. 3,200d.
Post 1999: 6,665g. 3,182n. 3,200d.
Two, 9-cyl. 4 S.C.S.A. (250 x 300mm) LDM-9 type (2,431 BHP) and two, 8-cyl. 4 S.C.S.A. (250 x 300mm) LDM-8 type (2,159 BHP) oil engines made by Normo-Gruppen AS, Bergen, one of each type geared to each of two screw shafts, with controllable pitch propellers, 4,590 BHP. 17 kts. Thwartship thrust propeller forward.
Post 1985: Two, 8-cyl. 2 S.C.S.A. (280 x 360mm) Wichmann WX28V8 type oil engines made by AS Wichmann, Rubbestadneset, geared to twin shafts with controllable pitch propellers. 5,652 BHP. 14 kts. Thwartship thrust propeller forward.

Ice strengthened, 12 passengers / roro cargo / rail vehicles / ferry, with bow door / ramp, and stern door / ramp.
5.3.1971: Launched by Trosvik Verksted AS, Brevik (Yard No. 94), for Stena Line Ab, Sweden, for bareboat charter to Deutsche Reichsbahn, East Germany. 10.9.1971: Completed. 10.1971: Sold to charterers. 1983: Owners restyled, Government of the D. R. G., (Deutsche Reichsbahn), (G.D.R. State Railways). 1983: Sold to Fosen Mek. Verksted AS, Norway, and renamed FRENGENFJORD. 1984: Sold to Rutelagat Askoy-Bergen AS, Norway, and renamed KYSTVEIEN. 1985: Re-engined. 1988: Replaced by FJORDVEIEN, (see ship No.F.13), and sold to KS AS Scandi Line, Norway, and renamed BOHUS II. 1991: Sold to Vard AS (KS AS Scandi Line, managers), Norway. 1994: Sold to Elcana Maritime Inc., (Star Cruise Sendirian Berhad, managers), Panama, and renamed SUBIC ADVENTURE. 1995: Sold to Basto Fosen AS, Norway, and renamed EINAR TAMBARSKJELVE. 1997: Sold to Consolidada de Ferrys C. A., (CONFERRYS), Caracas, Venezuela, under St. Vincent & The Grenadines flag. 1998: Transferred to Venezuela flag, and renamed PETRONILA MATA.

ANDERIDA at Dover

(W. J. Harvey)

7222229

F.16. ANDERIDA (1972)

1,600g. 632n. 2,591d. 347' 9"(BB) x 52' 7" x 16' 2½".
Post 1999: 106.5 metres.
Two, 9-cyl. 4 S.C.S.A. (250 x 300mm) Normo LDM9 type (2,431 BHP) and two, 8-cyl. 4 S.C.S.A. (250 x 300mm) Normo LDMC8 type (2,159 BHP) oil engines made by Normo-Gruppen AS, Bergen, one of each type geared to each of two screw shafts, with controllable pitch propellers, 4,590 BHP. 17 kts. Thwartship thrust propeller forward.
Ice strengthened, 16 berthed & 20 deck passengers / roro cargo / rail vehicle / ferry, with bow door / ramp and stern door / ramp.
11.12.1971: Launched by Trosvik Verksted AS, Brevik (Yard No. 95), for Stena Ab, Sweden. 28.4.1972: Completed. 1.5.1972: Sold to Carpass (Shipping) Company Ltd., London. 24.8.1972: Arrived at Dover at the end of delivery voyage. 1976: Transferred to British Railways Board. 1979: Transferred to Sealink (U.K.) Ltd. 1981: Sold to Covenant Shipping Inc., (Manta Line Inc., managers), Greece, and renamed TRUCK TRADER. 1984: Sold to Marlborough Sealink Ltd., Cyprus, and renamed SEALINK. 1985: Transferred to New Zealand flag. 1986: Reverted to the Cypriot flag, and renamed MIRELA. 1988: Sold to O/S. Cooperative de Trans Maritime et Aerien (C.T.M.A.), Canada and renamed C.T.M.A. VOYAGEUR. 1992: Sold to Navigation Madeleine Inc., Cap-aux-Meules QC, Canada (O/S Cooperative de Trans Maritime et Aerien (C.T.M.A.), managers).

STENA OLYMPICA at Kiel

(W. J. Harvey)

7119836

F.17. STENA OLYMPICA (1972 - 1982)

As built: 7,118g. 3,838n. 1,321d. 410' 1" (BB) x 64' 1" x 16' 5"

Post 1987: 11,968g. 5,928n. 1,321d. 143.06(BB) x 19.54 x metres.
Post 2001: 12,087g. 5,928n. 1,321d.
Two, 18-cyl. 4 S.C.S.A. (400 x 460mm) Pielstick 18PC2V-400 type, oil engines made by Lindholmen Motor Ab, Goteborg, geared to twin screw shafts with controllable pitch propellers. 9,000 BHP. 21.5 kts. Thwartship thrust propeller forward.
Ice strengthened, 866 berthed, 634 deck passengers / roro cargo / ferry, with bow door / ramp, and stern door / ramp.
18.9.1971: Launched by "Titovo" Brodogradaliste, Kraljevica (Yard No. 399), for Stena Ab, Sweden. 25.6.1972: Completed for Stena Line Ab. 1982: Sold to Transworld Steamship Company Inc., Panama, and renamed SCOTIA PRINCE. 1987: Lengthened. 1999: Prince of Fungy Cruises Ltd., appointed as managers. 2002: Transferred to under the Bahamas flag. 2004: Sold to Scotia Prince Cruises Ltd., Miami, (International Shipping, Miami, managers), under the Bahamas flag.

STENA TRAILER (2)

(W. J. Harvey)

7227578

F.18. STENA TRAILER (2) (1972 - 1974)

As built: 1,306g. 464n. 1,714d. 343' 5" x 49' 5" x 11' 6¾"
Post 1994: 3,420g. 1,026n. 1,626d.
Two, 9-cyl. 4 S.C.S.A. (250 x 300mm) Normo LSMCB-9 type oil engines made by Normo - Gruppen AS., Bergen, geared to twin screw shafts with controllable pitch propellers. 2,700 BHP. 15 kts. Thwartship thrust controllable pitch propeller forward.
Ice strengthened, 12 berthed passengers / roro cargo /ferry, with bow door / ramp, and stern door / ramp.
22.6.1972: Launched by Trondheims M.V. Aker Trondelag AS, Trondheim (Yard No. 690), for Rederi Ab Concordia, Sweden. 25.9.1972: Completed for Stena Ab, Sweden. 1974: Renamed NOPAL SKY. 1977: Renamed STENA TRAILER. 1978: Transferred to Contrast Shipping Line Ltd., Cayman Islands, and renamed KIRK TRAILER. 1980: Renamed CARIBBEAN TRAILER. 1983: Transferred to Deremar Company Shipping S. A., Panama. 1984: Transferred to Contrast Maritime Ltd., Cayman Islands. 1987: Sold to Palmera Shipping Company Ltd., Las Palmas de Gran Canaria, under Grand Cayman flag. 1995: Transferred to Panamanian flag, Armas Naviera S.A. appointed as managers.

STENA FINLANDICA

(Internet source / J. B. Jensen)

5404964

F.19. STENA FINLANDICA (1972 - 1975)

As built: 2,746g. 1,213n. 464d. 300' 3" x 47' 8" x 14' 0".
Post 1994: 2,890g. 928n. 610d.
Two, 12-cyl. 4.S.C.S.A. (400 x 500mm) Deutz RBV12M350 type oil engines made by Kloeckner Humboldt Deutz, Koeln, geared to twin screw shafts. 6,000 BHP. 18 kts. Thwartship thrust propeller forward.
Ice strengthened, 387 berthed, 175 deck passengers / ferry.
1962: Ordered as HELGOLAND from Hanseatische Werft GmbH, Hamburg (Yard No. 25), by Hafen-Dampschiffahrts A.G., W. Germany. 1962: Shipyard declared bankruptcy, and the order was transferred to Howaldtswerke Hamburg A.G., Hamburg, (Yard No. 943). 9.3.1963: Launched. 24.5.1963: Completed. 10.1963: Chartered to Skagenlinjen Rederi Ab, (Sten A. Olsson Handels Ab, managers. 1964: Renamed LARVIKSPILEN. 6.1966: Released from charter and reverted to HELGOLAND. 10.8.1966: Departed from Hamburg for employment as a hospital ship off Da Nang, South Vietnam, from where she returned in 1972. 1972: Purchased by Stena Reederei GmbH, Kiel and renamed STENA FINLANDICA. 1975: Renamed BALTIC STAR. 1977: Sold to K. G. Seetouristik GmbH & Company, Lubeck. 1993: Sold to Forde-Reedeerei GmbH, Germany. 1995: Sold to Seetouristik GmbH & Company K. G., Lubeck. 2000: Sold to Latin Cruises Ltd., y Holanda Quito, Ecuador, (Galatours S.A., y Holanda Quito, Ecuador, managers), and renamed GALAPAGOS LEGEND, under Grand Cayman flag. 2002: Transferred to Georgia Flag.

STENA TRANSPORTER (2) at Malta with charterer's funnel markings. (The World Ship Society Ltd)

7303308

F.20. STENA TRANSPORTER (1) / JARL TRANSPORTER (1973 - 1975)

1,301g. 464n. 1,714d. 345' 9" x 49' 5" x 11' 6¾"
Two, 9-cyl. 4 S.C.S.A. (250 x 300mm) Normo LSMCB-9 type oil engines made by Normo-Gruppen AS., Bergen, geared to twin screw shafts with controllable pitch propellers. 2,700 BHP. 15 kts. Thwartship thrust controllable pitch propeller forward.
Ice strengthened, 12 berthed passengers / roro cargo / ferry with bow door / ramp, and stern door / ramp.
1972: Laid down as STENA TRANSPORTER by Trondheims M.V. Aker Trondelag AS, Trondheim (Yard No. 691), for Stena Ab, Sweden. 6.11.1972: Launched as JARL TRANSPORTER for Rederi Ab Concordia, Sweden (Stena Ab managers). 21.2.1973: Completed for demise-charter to and registered under Det Nordenfjelske D/S., Norway. 4.1973: Charter terms were altered and vessel appointed as bareboat chartered to Det Nordenfjelske D/S., Norway, reverting to Stena Ab and Swedish flag. 1975: Renamed STENA TRANSPORTER. 1975: Sold to Cie. Phocoenne d'Armement Maritime, France, and renamed LEON R.E. 1984: Sold to Weybourg Shipping Line Ltd., (Weymouth - Cherbourg Ferry Line), London, (to have been renamed WEYBOURG), but was immediately resold to P.T. Putera Master Sarana Penyeberangan, Jakarta, Indonesia, and renamed NUSA DHARMA.

7218668

F.21. STENA JUTLANDICA (1) (1973 - 1982)

As built: 6,333g. 3,246n. 2,100d. 409' 7" (BB) x 70' 6" x 17' 2¾ "
Post 1977: 6,524g. 3,285n. 2,362d. 124.85(BB) x 23.37 x 5.480 metres.
Post 1994: 13,179g. 3,959n. 2,362d.
Two, 18-cyl. 4 S.C.S.A. (400 x 460mm) Pielstick 18PC2V-400 vee type, oil engines made by Lindholmen Motor Ab, Goteborg, geared to twin screw shafts with controllable pitch propellers. 18,000 BHP. 22 kts. Thwartship thrust propeller forward.
Ice strengthened, 114 berthed, 1,838 deck passengers / roro cargo / ferry, with bow door / ramp, and stern door / ramp.

29.5.1972: Launched by Brodogradiliste Jozo Lozovina Mosor, Trogir (Yard No. 162), for Stena Ab, Sweden. 24.5.1973: Completed. 1977: Deepened to increase the upper car deck headroom, and widened by adding side-sponsons for better stability. 1982: Transferred to Bahamas flag, and renamed JUTLANDICA to release the name for a new vessel under construction. 1983: Sold to C. N. Marine Inc., Canada, and renamed BLUENOSE. 1984: Reverted to the Bahamas flag. 1987: Transferred to Marine Atlantic Inc., Nassau. 1997: Sold to Government of Canada (Transport Canada), (Bay Ferries Ltd., managers). 1998: Sold to Bay Ferries Ltd. 1999: Renamed HULL 309. 1999: Sold to Europa Ferrys S.A., Algeciris, Spain, and renamed EUROFERRYS ATLANTICA. 2005: Transferred to Panamanian flag.

STENA JUTLANDICA (1) in later life, following her jumboisation

(W. J. Harvey)

STENA SAILER (1) outward from the New Waterway enroute to Dover.

(Courtesy A Vuyk & Zonen)

7304340

F.22. STENA SAILER (1) (1973 - 1975)

As built: 2,664g. 992n. 3,861d. 378' 1"(BB) x 53' 7" x 14' 9"
Post 1975: 3,206g. 1,352n. 3,861d. 142.22(BB) x 16.34 x 5.90 metres.
Post 1995: 7,955g. 2,386n. 5,376d.
Two, 6-cyl. 4 S.C.S.A. (410 x 470mm) Werkspoor 6TM410 type oil engines made by Werkspoor-Amsterdam N.V., Amsterdam, geared to twin screw shafts with controllable pitch propellers. 7,200 BHP. 16 kts. Thwartship thrust controllable pitch propeller forward.
Ice strengthened, 12 berthed passengers / roro cargo / ferry, with bow door / ramp, and stern door / ramp.
18.1.1973: Launched by A.Vuyk & Zonen's Scheepswerven B.V., Capelle a/d Ijssel (Yard No. 862), for Stena Ab, London. 28.5.1973: Completed for Stena Ab, Sweden. 1975: Lengthened by Howaldtswerke-Deutsche Werft A.G., Kiel, and upon completion, was demise-chartered to Farah Maritime Company Ltd., (Adelphi Vergottis (Hellas) Ltd., S. A., managers), Cyprus, and renamed FARHA. 1981: Transferred to Snowdrop Shipping Ltd., Cyprus, (Triport Ferries, (Management), Ltd., managers), Glasgow, and renamed STENA SEATRADER. 1988: Northern Coasters Inc., appointed as managers. 4.1989: Renamed KIRK TRADER. 1993: Sold to Inter Caribe Ltd., (Jamaica Freight and Shipping Company Ltd., managers), Bahamas, and renamed ISLAND TRADER. 1994: Renamed KIRK TRADER. 1994: Sold to Caricom Investments Ltd., and renamed ISLAND TRADER. 1995: Renamed KIRK MARINA. 1997: Renamed

SEABOARD MARINER (Freight Management Ltd., appointed as managers. 2002: Renamed ISLAND TRADER. 2004: Sold to Marco Shipping, Dubai, U.A.E., and renamed MERDIF 4, under Jordanian flag.

STENA SCANDINAVICA (1)

(Author's collection)

7226603
F.23. STENA SCANDINAVICA (1) (1973 - 1978)
As built: 7,125g. 3,851n. 1,471d. 409' 3" (BB) x 64' 1" x 16' 9½"
Post 1982: 10,256g. 6,341n. 2,676d. 156.85(BB) x 19.59 x 5.217 metres.
Post 1994: 13,638g. 7,578n. 2,676d.
Two, 18-cyl. 4 S.C.S.A. (400 x 460mm) Pielstick 18PC2V-400 vee type, oil engines made by Lindholmen Motorenfabrik Ab, Goteborg, geared to twin screw shafts with controllable pitch propellers. 18,000 BHP. 21.5 kts. Thwartship thrust controllable pitch propeller forward.
Ice strengthened, 873 berthed, 727 deck passengers / roro cargo / ferry, with bow door / ramp, and stern door / ramp.
9.9.1972: Launched by "Titovo" Brodogradaliste, Kraljevica (Yard No. 400), for Stena Line Ab, Sweden. 27.6.1973: Completed. 1978: Sold to Irish Shipping Ltd. and Others, (Irish Continental Line Ltd., managers), Eire, and renamed SAINT KILLIAN. 1979: Transferred to Irish Continental Line Ltd., Dublin. 1981-1982: Lengthened at a cost of £7.5m. by Amsterdamsche Droogdok Maatschaapij, Holland, increasing the passenger capacity to 1,340 berthed, and 626 deck spaces. Renamed SAINT KILLIAN II, vessel was returned to her owners during 2.1982. 1988: Owners restyled Irish Continental Group PLC. (IRISH FERRIES). 1998: Sold to Cape Enterprises Ltd., (Newshipco S.A., managers), Panama, and renamed MEDINA STAR. 2000: Sold to the Commercial Bank Of Greece. 2002: Sold to Egnatia International Shipping S.A., Piraeus, (Hellenic Mediterranean Lines S. A., Piraeus, managers), and renamed EGNATIA III.

SEATRADER outward from the New Waterway.

(Courtesy A Vuyk & Zonen)

7305772
F.24. STENA SEATRADER (1) / SEATRADER (1973 - 1976)
As built: 2,572g. 870n. 3,861d. 378' 1"(BB) x 53' 7" x 19' 1"
Post 1976: 3,209g. 1,340n. 6,726d. 142.22(BB) x 16.34 x 5.944 metres.
Post 1987: 7,504g. 2,251n. 6,726d. 141.90(BB) x 16.34 x 5.944 metres.
Two, 6-cyl. 4 S.C.S.A. (410 x 470mm) Werkspoor 6TM410 type oil engines made by Werkspoor-Amsterdam N.V., Amsterdam, geared to twin screw shafts with controllable pitch propellers. 7,200 BHP. 18 kts. Thwartship thrust controllable pitch propeller forward.

Ice strengthened, 12 berthed passengers / roro cargo / ferry, with bow door / ramp, and stern door / ramp.
1972: Ordered from A. Vuyk & Zonen's Scheepswerven B.V., Capelle a/d Ijssel (Yard No. 863), by Stena Ab, Sweden. 10.2.1973: Sub-contracted hull launched as STENA SEATRADER by Van der Geissen Du Noord, Krimpen and subsequently towed to Capelle a/d Ijssel. 14.8.1973: Completed as SEATRADER by A. Vuyk & Zonen's Scheepswerven B.V. 1976: Lengthened by Howaldtwerke-Deutsche Werft A.G., Kiel, and upon completion was demise chartered to Bahjah Navigation Company, (Adelphi Vergottis (Hellas) Ltd. S. A., managers), Cyprus, and renamed BAHJAH. 1981: Transferred to Stena Ab, Sweden, and renamed STENA SEARIDER. 1982: Transferred to Snowdrop Shipping Ltd., (Triport Ferries (Management) Ltd., managers), Cyprus. 1983: Renamed SEARIDER. 1984: Transferred to Rederi Ab Concordia, (Stena Ab, managers), Sweden, and renamed STENA SEARIDER. 1984: Transferred to Stena Ab, and renamed TRUCKER. 1985: Renamed STENA SEARIDER. 1986: Transferred to Rederi Ab Concordia, (Stena Ab, managers). 8.1987: Delivered to Cityvarvet, Gothenburg, for conversion into a railway vehicle ferry. 1987: Transferred to Stena Rederi, (Liro Shipping Ab, managers), and renamed STENA SCANRAIL. 1988: Transferred to Stena Line Ab, (same managers). 2000: Removed from management. 2000: Transferred to Stena Line Scandinavia Ab.

STENA SHIPPER (1) outward from the New Waterway in the twilight, for overnight sea trials, and already painted in charterer's funnel markings.

(Courtesy A Vuyk & Zonen)

7325241

F.25. STENA SHIPPER (1) (1973)

As built: 2,638g. 798n. 3,861d. 378' 1"(BB) x 53' 7" x 19' 4¼"
Post 1976: 3,514g. 1,296n. 5,555d. 142.27(BB) x 16.34 x 5.925 metres.
Post 1990: 4,078g. 1,799n. 5,555d.
Two, 6-cyl. 4 S.C.S.A. (410 x 470mm) Werkspoor 6TM410 type oil engines made by Werkspoor-Amsterdam N.V., Amsterdam, geared to twin screw shafts with controllable pitch propellers. 7,200 BHP. 18 kts. Thwartship thrust propeller forward.
Ice strengthened, 12 berthed passengers / roro cargo / ferry, with bow door / ramp, and stern door / ramp.
16.6.1973: Launched as STENA SHIPPER by A. Vuyk & Zonen's Scheepswerven B.V., Capelle a/d Ijssel (Yard No. 864), for Stena Ab, Sweden. 24.9.1973: Completed for demise-charter to Union Steamship Company of New Zealand Ltd. 2.11.1973: Renamed UNION WELLINGTON. 1976: Lengthened by Howaldtswerke-Deutsche Werft A.G., Kiel, and upon completion was renamed ALPHA EXPRESS for demise charter to Arghiris Line, Greece. 26.1.1977: Transferred to W. German flag, (O.N. 2198), for acceptance trials. 27.1.1977: Transferred to Greek flag. 1980: Transferred to Stena Line Ltd., (Triport Ferries (Management) Ltd., managers), Glasgow, and renamed STENA SHIPPER. 1981: Converted into a rail vehicle / ferry, and upon completion, renamed SPEEDLINK VANGUARD and transferred to Northern Coasters Ltd., (same managers), London. 1982: Removed from management. During the night of 19/20.12.1982: Collided with and sank the British ferry EUROPEAN GATEWAY (4,263g/75), in the Orwell Estuary, whilst inward bound from Zeebrugge to Harwich. 1987: Renamed CARIBE EXPRESS. 1988: Renamed STENA SHIPPER, then KIRK SHIPPER, Cayman Island flag, (Northern Marine Management (Cyprus) Ltd.), managers. 1988: Transferred to Stena Ferries Ltd. (Northern Marine Inc., managers). 1989: Chartered to Truckline Ferries, and renamed NORMANDIE SHIPPER. 1991: Transferred to Marine Investments Ltd., (Stena Rederi, managers). 1992: Sold to B.A.I.S.A. Brittany Ferries (Bretagne-Angleterre-Irlande), France. 1999: Sold to Bonavista Shipping Corp., Bahamas, and renamed BONAVISTA 2003: Sold to Kittelsen Shipping AS, Stathelle, Norway, (Barber Ship Management India, Mumbai, India managers), and renamed BOA VISTA, under the Panamanian flag.

UNION WELLINGTON showing charterer's modifications. (The World Ship Society Ltd)

F.26. UNION WELLINGTON (1973 - 1976) see ship No.F.25 above.

STENA NORMANDICA in later life with charterer's colour scheme.

(The World Ship Society Ltd)

7360605

F.27. STENA NORMANDICA (1974 - 1985)

As built: 5,443g. 2,675n. 2,845d. 120.78(BB) x 19.51 x 5.9 metres.
Post 1995: 12,108g. 3,623n. 2,541d.
Two, 12-cyl. 4 S.C.S.A. (450 x 550) MaK 12M551AK vee type, oil engines made by Atlas-MaK Maschinenbau GmbH, Kiel, geared to twin screw shafts with controllable pitch propellers. 14,080 BHP. 20.25 kts. Thwartship thrust propeller forward.
Ice strengthened, 116 berthed, 1,084 deck passengers / roro cargo / vehicles / ferry, with bow door / ramp, and stern door / ramp.
11.5.1974: Launched by Rickmers Rhederei GmbH, Rickmers Werft, Bremerhaven, (Yard No. 380), for Stena Ab, Sweden. 11.12.1974: Completed. 1984: Transferred to Stena Shipping Line Ltd., Bahamas. 1985: Sold to Royal Scot Leasing Ltd., (Sealink (UK) Ltd., managers), and renamed ST. BRENDAN, retaining Bahamas flag. 1988: Managers restyled Sealink UK Ltd. (SEALINK BRITISH FERRIES). 1990: Sold to Navigazione Arcipelago Maddalenino S.p.A. (NAV.AR.MA), Italy, and renamed MOBY VINCENT. 1992: Sold to Moby Lines S.r.L., Italy. 1993: Renamed WASA SUN. 1994: Renamed MOBY VINCENT. (LR Supplement 1-10 May 1995 quotes this change from WASA SUN). 1998: Sold to Fion S.p.A., Portugal. 1999: Transferred to Italy register. 2001: Moby SpA., appointed as managers. 2004: Sold to Moby SpA., Portoferraio, Italy.

N.B. Some nautical magazine articles refer to a period in 1976 when vessel was trading as NORMANDICA for North Sea Ferries Ltd., giving her their NOR style of naming system. However this does not appear in any official documents or registers for that period.]

STENA DANICA (3)

(Author's collection)

7321661

F.28. STENA NORDICA (2) / STENA DANICA (3) (1974 - 1981)

As built: 6,333g. 3,246n. 2,134d. 124.85(BB) x 21.87 x 5.265 metres.
Post 1977: 6,538g. 3,178n. 2,362d. 124.85(BB) x 23.37 x 5.480 metres.
Two, 18-cyl. 4 S.C.S.A. (400 x 460mm) Pielstick 18PC2V-400 vee type, oil engines made by Lindholmen Motor AB, Goteborg, geared to twin screw shafts with controllable pitch propellers. 18,000 BHP. 22 kts. Thwartship thrust propeller forward.
Ice strengthened, 114 berthed, 1,838 deck passengers / roro cargo / ferry, with bow door / ramp, and stern door / ramp.
17.6.1973: Launched as STENA NORDICA by Brodogradiliste Jozo Lozovina Mosor, Trogir (Yard No. 163), for Stena Ab, Sweden. 2.6.1974: Completed as STENA DANICA. 1977: Deepened to increase the headroom on the upper car deck, and widened, by adding side sponsons for increased stABility. 1981: Renamed STENA NORDICA. 1983: Transferred to Belgian flag. 1984: Transferred to Nautica (Belgium) N.V., and renamed STENA NAUTICA. 1986: Transferred to Stena Cargo Line Ltd., Bahamas. 1987: Renamed VERSAILLES, (Stena Ab, managers), and transferred to French, Dieppe, flag. 1988: Transferred to Overseas Equipment Company Ltd., (Societe Nationale des Chemins de fer Francaise (S.N.C.F.), managers), France. 1990: Societe Nouvelle d'Armement Trans-Manche (S.N.A.T.) (SEALINK), appointed as managers. 1992: Renamed STENA LONDONER, and transferred to Bahamian Flag. 1993: Sold to G. I. E. Versabail, (same managers). 1996: Sold to SeaFrance S.A., France, and renamed SEAFRANCE MONET. 1998: Sold to Societe Nationale des Chemins de Fer Francais (S.N.C.F.) (SeaFrance S.A., managers). 2000: Sold to Naviera Armas SA, Spain, and renamed VOLCAN DE TACANDE. 2001: Renamed VOLCAN DE TANADE. 2002: Reverted to VOLCAN DE TACANDE. 30.1.2005: Suffered main engine failure resultant from water ingress, in a position 4 miles from Los Christianos, Teneriffe. 29 crew and 60 passengers were evacuated and vessel towed to Las Palmas. Subsequently declared as a constructive total loss. 11.9.2005: Arrived at Aliaga for demolition by Iska Ltd.

F.29. NOPAL SKY (1974 - 1977) see ship No. F.18 above.

7349039

F.30. STENA NAUTICA (1) (1974)

As built: 5,443g. 2,765n. 2,840d. 120.78(BB) x 19.51 x 5.95 metres.
Post 1994: 12,120g. 5,496n. 2,840d.
Two, 12-cyl. 4 S.C.S.A. (450 x 550mm) MaK 12M551AK vee type, oil engines made by Atlas-MaK Maschinenbau GmbH, Kiel, geared to twin screw shafts with controllable pitch propellers. 14,080 BHP. 21.25 kts. Thwartship thrust propeller forward.
Ice strengthened, 116 berthed, 1,084 deck passengers / vehicle /roro cargo / ferry, with bow door / ramp, and stern door / ramp.
4.8.1973: Keel laid by Rickmers Rhederei GmbH, Rickmers Werft, Bremerhaven (Yard No. 379), for Stena Ab, Sweden. 3.2.1974: Launched. 1.10.1974: Completed. 15.11.1974: Renamed MARINE NAUTICA. 1981: Transferred to Roylease Ltd., Canada. 1983: Transferred to Bahamian flag. 1986: Sold to Tourship Company S. A., Panama, and renamed CORSICA MARINA II. 1986: Sold to Dominican Ferrys S. A., Panama. 1994: Sold to Mangrovia Charterers Associates AS, (Tourship Ltd., managers), Panama. 1999: Sold to Dominican Ferrys S.A., (same managers). 2000: Sold to Medcharter SpA., Italy. 2003: Sold to Forship Srl., Savona, Italy, (Tourship Italia SpA., La Spezia, managers), and renamed CORSICA MARINA SECONDA.

F.31. MARINE NAUTICA (1974 - 1986) see ship No. F.30 above.

BISON

(Hans Mornhout collection)

7361570

F.32. STENA TRAILER (3) / BISON (1974 - 1975)

As built: 3,453g. 1,103n. 5,805d. 125.00(BB) x 19.05 x 3.785 metres.
Post 1981: 4,377g. 1,759n. 4,170d. 141.81(BB) x 19.05 x 4.701 metres.
Post 1992: 4,249g. 1,695n. 7,078d.
Post 1994: 11,723g. 3,517n. 7,078d.
Post 1995: 14,387g. 4,316n. 7,078d. 140.1(BB) x 23.40 x 4.701 metres.
Post 1999: 14,387g. 4,316n. 4,670d.
Post 2000: 14,426g. 4,328n. 4,385d. 141.8(BB) x 23.8 x metres.
Two, 12-cyl. 4 S.C.S.A. (370 x 400mm) Deutz RSBV12M540 vee type, oil engines made by Kloeckner Humboldt Deutz, Koeln, geared to twin screw shafts with controllable pitch propellers. 6,000 BHP. 18.5 kts. Two, thwartship thrust propellers forward.
Ice strengthened, 12 berthed passengers / roro cargo / ferry with stern door / ramp.
13.8.1974: Keel laid as STENA TRAILER by J. J. Sietas K. G. Schiffswerke GmbH & Company, Hamburg, (Yard No. 755), for Stena Ab, Sweden, 31.10.1974: Launched as BISON for charter to P&O Group. 24.1.1975: Upon completion was sold to Hain Nourse Ltd., (Belfast Steam Ship Company Ltd., managers), London, (P&O Group). 1976: P&O Ferries Ltd., appointed as managers. 1979: Transferred to P&O Ferries Ltd., (same managers). 1981: Lengthened by Tyne Shiprepairers Ltd., Newcastle, increasing passenger capacity to 76 berths. 1985: Transferred to POETS Fleet Management Ltd. 1991: Transferred to Pandoro Ltd. 1995: Widened. 1997: Renamed EUROPEAN PIONEER, (P&O Ship Management (Irish Sea) Ltd., managers). 2004: Sold to Stena Ropax Ltd., London, (Stena Line Ltd., Ashford, Kent, managers). 2004: Renamed STENA PIONEER, retaining Bermudan flag.

BUFFALO in later life after her first lengthening.

(Hans Mornhout collection)

7361582

F.33. STENA TRAVELLER (1) / BUFFALO (1975)

As built: 3,453g. 1,103n. 5,805d. 125.02(BB) x 19.05 x 3.753 metres.
Post 1988: 10,987g. 5,863n. 4,377d. 141.81(BB) x 19.59 x 5.771 metres.
Post 1991: 10,987g. 3,296n. 4,377d.
Post 1998: 12,879g. 3,864n. 3.933d. 156.50 (BB)x 19.59 x 4.300 metres.
Two, 12-cyl. 4 S.C.S.A. (370 x 400mm) Deutz RSBV12M540 vee type, oil engines made by Kloeckner-Humboldt Deutz, Koeln, geared to twin screw shafts with controllable pitch propellers. 6,000 BHP. 18.5 kts. Two, Thwartship thrust propellers forward.
Ice strengthened, 12 berthed passengers / roro cargo / ferry with stern door / ramp.
31.10.1974: Keel laid as STENA TRAVELLER by J. J. Sietas K. G. Schiffswerke GmbH & Company, Hamburg, (Yard No. 756), for Stena Ab, Sweden 6.1.1975: Launched as BISON for charter to P&O Ferries but was subsequently sold to them. 26.3.1975: Completed for Hain Nourse Ltd., London, (Belfast Steamship Company Ltd., Belfast, managers). 1976: P&O Ferries Ltd., appointed as managers. 1979:

Transferred to P&O Ferries Ltd. 1985: Transferred to POETS Fleet Management Ltd. 1988: Lengthened, by Hall, Russell & Company Ltd., Aberdeen, at Leith, and then taken to Aberdeen for the addition of an extra 33 passenger berths. 1991: Transferred to Pandoro Ltd. 1998: Lengthened and renamed EUROPEAN LEADER, (P&O Ship Management (Irish Sea) Ltd., managers). 2004: Sold to Stena Ropax Ltd., London, (Stena Line Ltd., Ashford, Kent, managers). 2004: Renamed STENA LEADER, retaining Bermudan flag.

UNION MELBOURNE leaving Larne shortly after returning from New Zealand

(W. J. Harvey)

7361594

F.34. STENA TRADER (1) / UNION MELBOURNE (1975 - 1980)

As built: 3,453g. 1,103n. 5,805d. 124.49(BB) x 19.41 x 3.785 metres.
Post 1975: 4,043g. 1,453n. 5,599d. 141.81(BB) x 19.41 x 5.809 metres.
Post 1980: 4,377g. 1,755n. 4,020d.
Post 1992: 4,377g. 1,759n. 4,035d.
Post 1994: 10,957g. 3,287n. 4,035d.
Two, 12-cyl. 4 S.C.S.A. (370 x 400mm) Deutz RSBV12M540 vee type, oil engines made by Kloeckner-Humboldt Deutz, Koeln, geared to twin screw shafts with controllable pitch propellers. 6,000 BHP. 18.5 kts. Thwartship thrust propeller forward.
Ice strengthened, 12 berthed passengers / roro cargo / ferry, with stern door / ramp.
7.1.1975: Keel laid as STENA TRADER by J. J. Sietas K. G. Schiffswerke GmbH & Company, Hamburg, (Yard No. 757), for Stena Line Ltd., London. 3.3.1975: Launched as UNION MELBOURNE. 28.5.1975: Completed for Northern Coasters Ltd., London. 1975: Lengthened by Werft Nobiskrug GmbH, Rendsburg, shortly after completion. 1980: Renamed UNION TRADER. 11.9.1980: Sold to Bovis Proprieties (Southern) Ltd., London, (P&O Group), and sent to Tyne Shiprepairers Ltd., S. Shields, to have additional accommodation built on the upper deck. 20.11.1980: Upon completion renamed PUMA and placed under P&O Ferries Ltd., management. 31.12.1984: POETS Fleet Management Ltd., appointed as managers. 1991: Transferred to Pandoro Ltd. 1994: Transferred to Bermudan flag. 1998: Renamed EUROPEAN SEAFARER, (P&O Ship Management (Irish Sea) Ltd., managers). 2004: Sold to Stena Ropax Ltd., London, (Stena Line Ltd., Ashford, Kent, managers). 2004: Renamed STENA SEAFARER, retaining Bermudan flag.

F.35. STENA TRANSPORTER (1) (1975) see ship No. F.20 above.

7360617

F.36. MARINE ATLANTICA (1975 - 1986)

As built: 5,441g. 2,759n. 2,840d. 120.0(BB) x 19.51 x 5.9 metres.
Post 1992: 5,810g. 2,962n. 2,503d.
Post 1994: 11,637g. 3,606n. 2,840d.
Post 1995: 12,100g. 3,750n. 2,840d.
Two, 12-cyl. 4 S.C.S.A. (450 x 550mm) MaK 12M551AK vee type, oil engines made by Atlas-MaK Maschinenbau GmbH, Kiel, geared to twin screw shafts with controllable pitch propellers. 14,080 BHP. 20.5 kts. Thwartship thrust propeller forward.
Ice strengthened, 116 berthed, 1,084 passengers / roro cargo /vehicles / ferry with bow door / ramp and stern door / ramp.
4.5.1974: Keel laid as STENA ATLANTICA by Rickmers Rhederei GmbH, Rickmers Werft, Bremerhaven (Yard No. 381), for Stena Line Ab, Sweden. 18.12.1974: Launched as MARINE ATLANTICA. 30.5.1975: Completed. 1979: Transferred to Roylease Ltd., Canada. 1983: Transferred to the Bahamian flag. 1986: Sold to Tourship Company S.A., Italy, and renamed CORSICA VERA. 1987: Renamed SARDINIA VERA. 1993: Sold to Nuovo Trans Tirreno Express S.r.L.(Sardinia Ferries), Italy. 1995: Sold to Medinvest S.r.L. 1999: Tourship Italia S.p.A., appointed as managers. 2000: Removed from management. 2004: Sold to

Forship Srl, Savona, Italy, (D'Orbigny Management, Bordeaux, managers). 2005: Tourship Italia Srl, Savona, Italy appointed as managers.

7360629

F.37. STENA NORDICA (3) (1975 - 1978)

As built: 5,443g. 2,765n. 2,793d. 120.78(BB) x 19.51 x 5.9 metres.
Post 1993: 11,717g. 3,564n. 1,521d.
Two, 12-cyl. 4 S.C.S.A. (450 x 550mm) MaK 12M551AK vee type, oil engines made by Atlas-MaK Maschinenbau GmbH, Kiel, geared to twin screw shafts with controllable pitch propellers. 14,080 BHP. 20.25 kts. Thwartship thrust propeller forward.
Ice strengthened, 116 berthed, 1,084 deck passengers / vehicles / roro cargo / ferry, with bow door / ramp, and stern door / ramp.
18.12.1974: Keel laid by Rickmers Rhederei GmbH, Rickmers Werft, Bremerhaven (Yard No. 382), for Stena Ab, Sweden. 15.5.1975: Launched. 28.11.1975: Completed. 1978: Renamed HELLAS. 1979: Renamed STENA NORDICA. 1980: Renamed HELLAS. 1980: Renamed STENA NORDICA. 1981: Renamed STENA NAUTICA. 1982: Transferred to Nautica (Belgium) Ltd. 7.4.1983: Renamed REINE ASTRID and subsequently purchased by (charterers), Regie Voor Maritiem Transport, Belgium, and transferred to Belgian flag. 1997: Sold to Onorato Overseas Transport Maritima Ltda., Funchal, Portugal, and renamed MOBY KISS. 1997: Sold to Compagnie Marocaine de Navigation (COMANAV), Casablanca, Morocco, and renamed AL MANSOUR.

FARHA at Kiel shortly after lengthening.

(W. J. Harvey)

F.38. FARHA **(1975 - 1981)** see ship No. F.22 above.

BALTIC STAR.

(Hans Mornhout collection)

F.39. BALTIC STAR **(1975 - 1977)** see ship No. F.19 above.

ALPHA EXPRESS at Kiel preparing for post-lengthening sea trials.

(W. J. Harvey)

F.40. ALPHA EXPRESS **(1976 - 1980)** see ship No. F.25 above.

BAHJAH

(Courtesy Fotoflite)

F.41. BAHJAH **(1976 - 1981)** see ship No. F.24 above.

7501285

F.42. STENA TENDER (1) (1976)

As launched: 2,905g. 1,021n. 4,150d. 116.95(BB) x 18.14 x 4.779 metres.
As completed: 3,809g. 1,614n. 6,400d. 144.07(BB) x 18.14 x 5.70 metres.
Post 1992: 3,985g. 1,858n. 3,775d.
Post 1994: 9,085g. 2,726n. 3,775d.
Two, 12-cyl. 4 S.C.S.A. (370 x 400mm) Deutz RSBV12M540 vee type, oil engines made by Kloeckner-Humboldt Deutz, Koeln, geared to twin screw shafts with controllable pitch propellers. 11,999 BHP. 18 kts. Two, thwartship thrust propellers forward.
Ice strengthened. 12 berthed passengers / roro cargo / ferry, with bow door / ramp, and stern door / ramp.
1.4.1975: Keel laid by Osterreichische Schiffswerften A.G., Linz - Korneuburg, Korneuburg (Yard No. 709), for Stena Ab, Sweden15.1.1976: Launched. 1976: Whilst awaiting completion the vessel contract was sold to the United Baltic Corporation Ltd., London, who had the "steel structure" towed to Werft Nobiskrug GmbH, Rendsburg, for lengthening and completion. Placed in dry dock as STENA TENDER. 14.10.1977: Completed as GOYA. 1.1980: Sold to Federal Commerce & Navigation (1974) Ltd., Canada. 3.1980: Renamed FEDERAL NOVA. 1981: Sold to Seaforth Fednav Inc., and renamed CARIBBEAN SKY. 1982: Renamed MANAURE VII. 1982: Sold to Philippine Maritime Inc., Panama. 1982: Sold to Timber Shipping Inc., Panama, and renamed OYSTER BAY. 1983: Sold to Cenargo Ltd., (Denholm Ship Management Ltd., managers) Southampton, and renamed VIKING TRADER. 1984: Converted to carry 40 berthed, and 36 deck passengers. 1985: Owners restyled as Cenargo Navigation Ltd., (Townsend Car Ferries Ltd., managers). 1986: Managers restyled as Thoresen Car Ferries Ltd., (TOWNSEND THORESEN). 1987: Managers restyled as P&O European Ferries (Portsmouth) Ltd. 1988: Sold to POETS Fleet Management Ltd., London. 1991: Transferred to Pandoro Ltd. 1996: Renamed LEOPARD. 1998: Renamed EUROPEAN NAVIGATOR, (P&O Ship Management (Irish Sea) Ltd., managers). 2003: Sold to Arab Bridge Maritime Company & Salam International Transport & Trading, Amman, (Arab Ship Management Ltd, (ASM), Amman, managers), and renamed BLACK IRIS, under the Jordanian flag.

7501302

F.43. STENA TIMER (1) / JAGUAR (1977 - 1978)

As built: 2,905g. 1,021n. 3,357d. 116.95(BB) x 18.14 x 4.779 metres.
Post 1995: 6,461g. 2,118n. 3,357d.
Two, 12-cyl. 4 S.C.S.A. (370 x 400mm) Deutz RSBV12M540 vee type, oil engines made by Kloeckner-Humboldt Deutz, Koeln, geared to twin screw shafts with controllable pitch propellers. 10,200 BHP. 18 kts. Two, thwartship thrust propellers forward.
Ice strengthened, 12 berthed passengers / vehicles / roro cargo / ferry, with bow door / ramp, and stern door / ramp.
26.6.1976: Keel laid as STENA TIMER by Osterreichische Schiffswerften A.G., Linz-Korneuburg, Korneuburg (Yard No. 711), for Rederi Ab Concordia, Sweden. 28.1.1977: Launched. 11.4.1977: Upon completion of builders sea trials was transferred to Stena Line Ab, Sweden, and renamed JAGUAR, for a charter to P&O Ferries Ltd. 1978: Renamed STENA TIMER. 1981: Sold to the Government of Mexico,

(Secretaria de Communicaciones y Transportes Servicio de Transbordadores Direccion General), Mexico, and renamed LORETO. 2004: Renamed AJMAN 2. 9.11.2004: Arrived at Chittagong for demolition.

STENA TIMER (1) post acceptance trials

(Author's collection)

JAGUAR leaving Larne

(The late William Darlow)

STENA TOPPER (1) **as DARNIA** leaving Larne.

(W. J. Harvey)

7501297

F.44. STENA TOPPER (1) (1977)

As built: 2,807g. 978n. 3,357d. 114.38(BB) x 18.14 x 5.765 metres.
Post 1982: 3,455g. 1,636n. 1,791d.
Post 1991: 3,549g. 1,530n. 1,791d. 114.01(BB) x 18.14 x 5.764 metres.
Post 1994: 8,547g. 2,537n. 1,791d. 114.02(BB) x 18.14 x 5.764 metres.
Post 1997: 8,547g. 2,537n. 2,150d. 114.02(BB) x 18.14 x 5.760 metres.
Two, 12-cyl. 4 S.C.S.A. (370 x 400mm) Deutz RSBV12M540 vee type, oil engines made by Kloeckner-Humboldt Deutz, Koeln, geared to twin screw shafts with controllable pitch propellers. 10,200 BHP. 18 kts. Two, Thwartship thrust controllable pitch propellers forward.
Ice strengthened, 12 berthed passengers / vehicles / roro cargo / ferry, with bow door / ramp, and stern door / ramp.
23.6.1975: Keel laid by Osterreichische Schiffswerften A.G., Linz - Korneuburg, Korneuburg (Yard No. 710), for Rederi Ab Concordia, Sweden. 22.6.1976: Launched. 27.5.1977: Completed for Stena Line Ab, Sweden.

5.6.1977: Sold to Barclay's Mercantile Industrial Finance Company Ltd., on behalf of J. Fisher & Sons Ltd., Barrow. 8.7.1977: Vessel arrived at Belfast as STENA TOPPER for the fitting of stabilisers, and minor alterations to suit her new role with British Railways. Upon completion of this work, vessel was re-christened DARNIA, without ceremony, at Harland & Wolff Ltd., Belfast shipyard. 1982: Owner restyled J. Fisher & Sons plc, the vessel remaining chartered to and managed by Sealink (UK) Ltd. 1982: Humber Graving Dock Company Ltd. constructed additional accommodation for 412 deck passengers during a refit at Immingham. 1988: Managers restyled Sealink (UK) Ltd. (SEALINK BRITISH FERRIES). 1990: Managers restyled as Sealink UK Ltd. (SEALINK STENA LINE). 1991: Sold to Rederiaktibolag Gotland (Nordstrom & Thulin Ab, managers). 1991: Sold to Orfeus Shipping Ab, (same managers), Sweden, and renamed NORD NEPTUNUS. 1997: Sold to the Estonian Shipping Company (ESCO) (RAS Eesti Merelaevandus), Tallinn and renamed NEPTUNIA. 2000: Sold to Oakbay Ltd., (Sandford Ship Management Ltd., managers), under Gibraltar flag. 2001: Sold to Marseilles Fret S.A., (MARFRET), Marseilles, France, retaining Gibraltar flag.

F.45. STENA TRAILER (2) (1977 - 1978) see ship No. F.18 above.

7528568

F.46. MERZARIO AUSONIA (1977 - 1980)

As built: 4,544g. 1,483n. 8,672d. 151.01(BB) x 21.67 x 7.322 metres.
Post 1981: 5,940g. 2,091n. 8,672d.
Post 1987: 5,497g. 2,606n. 8,911d.
Post 1994: 13,154g. 3,943n. 8,911d.
Two, 12-cyl. 4 S.C.S.A. (400 x 460mm) Pielstick 12PC2-5V-400 vee type oil engines made by Nippon Kokan K.K., Yokohama, geared to twin screw shafts with controllable pitch propellers. 15,600 BHP. 17 kts. Thwartship thrust controllable pitch propeller forward.
12 berthed passengers / 562 x 20'containers / roro cargo / ferry, with stern door / ramp.
21.3.1977: Keel laid by Hyundai S. B. & Heavy Industry, Ulsan (Yard No. 642), for Sten A. Olsson, Sweden. 11.5.1977: Launched. 31.8.1977: Completed for Rederi Ab Concordia, Sweden. 1980: Renamed STENA FREIGHTER. 1981: Transferred to Stena Gulf Line Ltd., Cayman Islands, (O.N.385055). 1982: Renamed JOLLY GIALLO. 1982: Renamed JOLLY TURCHESE. 1983: Renamed STENA FREIGHTER, (Three Crowns Marine Management Ltd., managers). 1984: Transferred to Rederi Ab Concordia (Stena Ab, managers), Sweden. 1986: Swedish Ship Management Ab, appointed as managers. 1987: Transferred to Stena Rederi Ab, (same managers). 1988: Transferred to Stena Line Ab, (same managers). 1995: Ab Stena Marine, appointed as managers. 2000: Removed from management. 2004: Sold to Lillbacka Powerco Oy, Harma, Finland, and renamed GLOBAL FREIGHTER.

STENA RUNNER
May 1978 whilst renaming.

(W. J. Harvey)

7528570

F.47. STENA RUNNER (1977 - 1978)

As built: 5,724g. 2,692n. 8,672d. 151.01(BB) x 21.67 x 7.319 metres.
Post 1979: 6,455g. 3,248n. 8,704d. 151.01(BB) x 25.28 x 7.318 metres.
Post 1981: 8,596g. 4,264n. 8,672d. 184.61(BB) x 25.28 x 6.370 metres.
Post 1994: 21,162g. 6,348n. 8,672d.
Two, 12-cyl. 4 S.C.S.A. (400 x 460mm) Pielstick 12PC2-5V-400 vee type oil engines made by Nippon Kokan K.K., Yokohama, geared to twin screw shafts with controllable pitch propellers. 15,600 BHP. 17 kts. Thwartship thrust controllable pitch propeller forward.
12 berthed passengers / 562 x 20'container / roro cargo / ferry, with stern door / ramp.
1.6.1977: Keel laid by Hyundai S. B. & Heavy Industry, Ulsan (Yard No. 643), for Stena Container Line Ltd., London. 15.7.1977: Launched. 4.11.1977: Completed for Stena Line Ltd., London. 24.5.1978:

Renamed ALPHA PROGRESS. 1979: Deepened by Hapag-Lloyd Werft GmbH, Bremerhaven, converted into a 144 berthed passenger / roro cargo / ferry, and transferred to Samos Pearl Shipping Company, (Hellas Ferries Company Ltd., managers), Greece, renamed HELLAS. 1982: Lengthened by Hapag-Lloyd Werft GmbH, Bremerhaven, including 64 new berths. Transferred to Cypriot flag. 1984: Transferred to Capulet Navigation Ltd., (Stena Line Ab, managers), Cyprus. 1986: Transferred to Lombard Charterhire Ltd., London, (Atlantic Steam Navigation Company Ltd. (TOWNSEND THORESEN), managers), and renamed DORIC FERRY. 1987: Managers restyled as P&O European Ferries (Felixtowe) Ltd. 1992: Renamed EUROPEAN TIDEWAY. 1994: Sold to P&O European Ferries (Felixstowe) Ltd. 1997: Transferred to P&O North Sea Ferries Ltd., London. 2002: Sold to Stena Line Ltd., UK, and renamed IDEWAY. (Tideway was not available for use). 2002: Renamed STENA TRANSFER. 2003: Sold to Stena Ropax Ltd., London.

NORSKY (Hans Mornhout collection)

7528582

F.48. NORSKY (1977 - 1980)

As built: 5,539g. 2,524n. 8,113d. 151.01(BB) x 21.67 x 7.297 metres.
Post 1989: 18,779g. 6,539n. 4,418d. 151.01(BB) x 26.27 x 7.297 metres.
Two, 12-cyl. 4 S.C.S.A. (400 x 460mm) Pielstick 12PC2-5V-400 vee type oil engines made by Nippon Kokan K.K., Yokohama, geared to twin screw shafts with controllable pitch propellers. 15,600 BHP. 17 kts. Thwartship thrust controllable pitch propeller forward.
12 berthed passengers / 562 x 20' container / roro cargo /ferry, with stern door / ramp.
1987: 768 berthed, 832 deck passenger ferry, including 174 cabins, some for handicapped people
14.2.1977: Keel laid by Hyundai S. B. & Heavy Industry, Ulsan (Yard No. 644), for Stena Container Line Ltd., London. 21.6.1977: Launched. 30.11.1977: Completed. 1980: Renamed STENA SHIPPER. 1980: Renamed MERZARIO IONIA, (Triport Ferries (Management) Ltd., managers). 1981: Demise chartered to Entermar Shipping Company S. A., (Constellation Lines S. A., managers), Greece, and renamed CONSTELLATION ENTERPRISE. 1986: Transferred to Stena Challenger Ltd., (Swedish Ship Management Ab, managers), and renamed STENA SHIPPER under Bahamas flag (O.N. 708882). 4.9.1987: Arrived at Blohm & Voss A. G., Hamburg, to be converted on behalf of Nordstrom & Thulin Ab, Stockholm. During this work Nordstrom & Thulin agreed to purchase the vessel which was renamed N&T 700, (Johnson Line, appointed as managers). Upon completion vessel was renamed GRAIP. 1989: Johnson Baltic Traffic Management Ab, appointed as managers. 1998: Sold to The Government of the Peoples Republic of China, Beijing,China, and renamed CHONG MING DAO.

7528594

F.49. ELK (1977 - 1986)

As built: 5,463g. 2,473n. 8,652d. 151.01(BB) x 21.67 x 7.32 metres.
Post 1986: 6,182g. 2,802n. 8,593d. 163.61(BB) x 22.90 x 7.32 metres.
Post 1987: 14,374g. 9,332n. 8,593d.
Post 1990: 14,374g. 4,312n. 9,700d. 163.61(BB) x 21.67 x 7.32 metres.
Two, 12-cyl. 4 S.C.S.A. (400 x 460mm) Pielstick 12PC2-5V-400 vee type oil engines made by Nippon Kokan K.K., Yokohama, geared to twin screw shafts with controllable pitch propellers. 15,600 BHP. 18 kts. Thwartship thrust controllable pitch propeller forward.
12 berthed passengers / 562 x 20'containers / roro cargo / ferry, with stern door / ramp.
14.2.1977: Keel laid by Hyundai S. B. & Heavy Industry, Ulsan (Yard No. 645), for Stena Container Line Ltd., London, for charter to Ferrymasters Ltd. (P&O Group). 21.6.1977: Launched. 28.12.1977: Completed for Stena Line Ltd., London. 28.9.1978: Transferred to the Standard Chartered Merchant Bank & Others, (P&O Ferries Ltd., chartering managers), London. 10.3.1979: Grounded, when arriving at Gothenburg. 13.3.1979: Refloated, but had suffered severe bottom damage, before and during salvage, which was subsequently repaired. 4.4.1982: Requisitioned by the British Government, for use as transport vessel,

during the Falklands conflict. 7.1982: Returned to her owners, who restyled as Elk Leasing Company Ltd., (P&O Ferries Ltd., chartering managers), London. 3.12.1984: Managers restyled POETS Fleet Management Ltd. 1986: Purchased through Elk Leasing Company Ltd. by P&O Ferries Ltd., London. 16.8.1986: Returned to service, upon completion of a lengthening operation, by Ateliers Reunis du Nord et de l'Ouest (A.R.N.O.), Dunkirk. 1995: Sold to the consortium of West Merchant Bank Ltd., BNP Leasing Ltd., C. T. S. B. Leasing and A. E. B. (U.K.) Ltd., London, and removed from management. 1995: Pandoro Ltd., appointed as managers. 1997: P&O Ferrymasters Ltd., appointed as managers. 1998: P&O North Sea Ferries Ltd., appointed as managers. 2000: Sold to DFDS Tor Line. 2001: Renamed TOR BALTICA. 2003: Sold to Baltica Shipping & Trading, (ADG Shipmanagement, Riga, managers), Latvia, and transferred to Belize flag.

ELK as built.

(W. J. Harvey)

ATLANTIC PROSPER

(W. J. Harvey)

7528609

F.50. STENA PROSPER (1) / ATLANTIC PROSPER (1978 - 1981)

As built: 5,466g. 2,485n. 8,672d. 151.01(BB) x 21.67 x 7.322 metres.
Post 1979: Widened 22.97 metres.
Post 1986: 5,738g. 2,677n. 8,672d. 151.01(BB) x 22.97 x 7.319 metres.
Post 1994: 14,059g. 4,217n. 8,672d.
Post 1997: 15,396g. 4,656n. 8,672d.

Two, 12-cyl. 4 S.C.S.A. (400 x 460mm) Pielstick 12PC2-5V-400 vee type oil engines made by Nippon Kokan K.K., Yokahama, geared to twin screw shafts with controllable pitch propellers. 15,600 BHP. 18 kts. Thwartship thrust controllable pitch propeller forward.

12 berthed passengers / 562 x 20'containers / roro cargo / ferry, with stern door / ramp.

18.4.1977: Keel laid as STENA PROSPER by Hyundai S. B. & Heavy Industry, Ulsan (Yard No. 646), for Stena Container Line Ltd., London. 26.8.1977: Launched as ATLANTIC PROSPER for charter to Atlantic Container Line (ACL). 6.2.1978: Completed. 1981: Renamed STENA IONIA. 1981: Transferred to Stena Atlas Line Ltd., Malta, and renamed MERZARIO IONIA. 1982: Renamed STENA IONIA. 1983: Three Crowns Marine Management Ltd., appointed as managers. 1984: Swedish Caledonian Marine Management Ltd., appointed as managers. 1984: Transferred to Stena Caribbean Line Ltd., Cayman Islands. 1985: Transferred to Rederi Ab Concordia, (Liro Shipping Ab, managers), Sweden, and renamed STENA GOTHICA. 1986: Deepened by Hapag Lloyd Werft GmbH, Bremerhaven. 1987: Transferred to Stena

Rederi, (Liro Shipping Ab, managers), Sweden. 1988: Renamed BORE GOTHICA. 1989: Sold to August Lindholms Eftr Ab, (same managers). 1992: Sold to OY Rettig Ab, (OY Bore Line AB, managers), Finland. 1995: Sold to OY Bore Lines Ab, and removed from management.1997: Renamed FINNBIRCH. 1999: Sold to Stromma Turism, & Sjofart Ab. (Lindholm Shipping), Stockholm, Sweden.

ATLANTIC PROJECT (W. J. Harvey)

7528623

F.51. STENA PROJECT (1) / ATLANTIC PROJECT (1978 - 1981)

As built: 5,466g. 2,485n. 8,811d. 151.01(BB) x 21.67 x 7.319 metres.
Post 1979: Widened 22.71 metres.
Post 1986: 5,735g. 2,680n. 8,672d. 151.01(BB) x 22.71 x 7.319 metres.
Post 1995: 15,525g. 4,702n. 8,800d.

Two, 12-cyl. 4 S.C.S.A. (400 x 460mm) Pielstick 12PC2-5V-400 vee type oil engines made by Nippon Kokan K.K., Yokohama, geared to twin screw shafts with controllable pitch propellers. 15,600 BHP. 18 kts. Thwartship thrust controllable pitch propeller forward.

12 berthed passengers / 562 x 20'containers / cargo roro / ferry, with stern door / ramp.

25.6.1977: Laid down as STENA PROJECT by Hyundai Heavy Industries Company Ltd., Ulsan (Yard No. 648) for Stena Line Ltd., London. 13.1.1978: Launched, as ATLANTIC PROJECT, for charter to Atlantic Container Line (ACL). 23.3.1978: Completed for Stena Container Line Ltd., London. 1981: Transferred to Stena RoRo Line Ltd., Malta, and renamed MERZARIO HISPANIA. 1983: Renamed STENA HISPANIA, (Three Crowns Marine Management Ltd., managers). 1984: Swedish Caledonian Marine Management Ltd., appointed as managers. 1984: Renamed KOTKA VIOLET. 1984: Renamed STENA HISPANIA. 1984: Transferred to Stena Caribbean Line Ltd., (Swedish Caledonian Marine Management Ltd., managers), Cayman Islands. 1986: Renamed STENA BRITANNICA, (Stena Ab, managers), and transferred to London flag. 1986: Deepened by Hapag Lloyd Werft, GmbH, Bremerhaven. 1988: Renamed BORE BRITANNICA. 1989: Sold to OY Rettig Ab, Finland. 1992: OY Bore Ab, appointed as managers. 1996: Sold to OY Bore Lines Ab., and renamed FINNFOREST. 1997: Baltic Marine Services Ab., appointed as managers. 1999: Sold to Stromma Turism & Sjofart Ab. (Lindholm Shipping), Stockholm, Sweden, under the Bahamas flag.

TOR FELICIA

(Hans Mornhout collection)

7528611

F.52. TOR FELICIA (1978)

As built: 5,466g. 2,485n. 8,672d. 151.01(BB) x 21.67 x 7.319 metres.
Post 1992: 12,162g. 8,464n. 8,661d.

Post 1994: 13,117g. 3,935n. 8,661d.
Two, 12-cyl. 4 S.C.S.A. (400 x 460mm) Pielstick 12PC2-5V-400 vee type oil engines made by Nippon Kokan K.K., Yokohama, geared to twin screw shafts with controllable pitch propellers. 15,600 BHP. 17 kts. Thwartship thrust controllable pitch propeller forward.
12 berthed passengers / 562 x 20'containers / roro cargo / ferry, with stern door / ramp.
17.10.1977: Keel laid by Hyundai Heavy Industries Company Ltd., Ulsan (Yard No. 647), for Stena Line Ltd., London, for charter to Tor Line Ab. 22.12.1977: Launched. 8.5.1978: Completed. 1978: Renamed MERZARIO GRECIA. 1983: Transferred to Stena Gulf Line Ltd., (Swedish Caledonian Marine Management Ltd., managers), Cayman Islands, and renamed STENA GRECIA. 1986: Stena Ab, appointed as managers. 1987: Sold to Marine Atlantic Inc., North Sydney, Nova Scotia, and renamed ATLANTIC FREIGHTER.

ALPHA ENTERPRISE at Hull

(W. J. Harvey)

7528635
F.53. ALPHA ENTERPRISE (1978 - 1980)
As built: 5,466g. 2,485n. 8,672d. 151.01(BB) x 21.67 x 7.319 metres.
Post 1979: Widened 25.28 metres.
Post 1980: 6,455g. 3,248n. 8,704d. 151.01(BB) x 25.28 x 6.522 metres.
Post 1981: 8,596g. 4,264n. 8,734d. 184.61(BB) x 25.28 x 6.370 metres.
Post 1994: 21,162g. 6,348n. 8,734d.
Two, 12-cyl. 4 S.C.S.A. (400 x 460mm) Pielstick 12PC2-5V-400 vee type oil engines made by Nippon Kokan K.K., Yokohama, geared to twin screw shafts with controllable pitch propellers. 15,600 BHP. 16 kts. Thwartship thrust controllable pitch propeller forward.
12 berthed passengers / 562 x 20'containers / roro cargo / ferry, with stern door / ramp
25.6.1977: Keel laid by Hyundai Heavy Industries Company Ltd., Ulsan (Yard No. 649), for Stena Container Line Ltd., London, for charter to Arghiris Lines, Greece. 1.2.1978: Launched. 31.5.1978: Completed for Stena Line Ltd., London. 1980: Deepened by Hapag-LLoyd Werft GmbH, Bremerhaven, and converted to carry 144 berthed passengers, and upon completion of the work vessel was transferred to Seafarer Maritime Inc., (Hellas Ferries Company Ltd., managers), Greece, and renamed SYRIA. 1981: Lengthened by Hapag-Lloyd Werft GmbH, Bremerhaven, including a further 76 passenger berths. 1982: Transferred to Polyzena Maritime Company Ltd., (same managers), Cyprus. 1983: Renamed STENA TRANSPORTER, (Swedish Caledonian Marine Management Ltd., managers). 1984: Northern Marine Management Ltd., appointed as managers. 1985: Renamed CERDIC FERRY. 1986: Transferred to Lombard Charterhire Ltd., (Atlantic Steam Navigation Company Ltd. (TOWNSEND THORESEN), managers), London. 1987: Managers restyled, P&O European Ferries (Felixtowe) Ltd. 1991: Renamed EUROPEAN FREEWAY. 1994: Sold to P&O European Ferries (Felixstowe) Ltd. 1997: Transferred to P&O North Sea Ferries Ltd., London. 2002: Sold to Stena Line Ltd., UK, and renamed FREEWAY. 2002: Renamed STENA PARTNER. 2004: Sold to Stena Ropax Ltd., London.

7528647
F.54. IMPARCA EXPRESS I (1978 - 1980)
As built: 5,466g. 2,489n. 8,113d. 151.01(BB) x 20.48 x 7.322 metres.
Post 1994: 13,117g. 3,935n. 8,661d.
Two, 12-cyl. 4 S.C.S.A. (400 x 460mm) Pielstick 12PC2-5V-400 vee type oil engines made by Nippon Kokan K.K., Yokohama, geared to twin screw shafts with controllable pitch propellers. 15,600 BHP. 17 kts. Thwartship thrust controllable pitch propeller forward.
12 berthed passengers / 562 x 20'containers / roro cargo / ferry, with stern door / ramp.

11.7.1977: Keel laid by Hyundai Heavy Industries Company Ltd., Ulsan (Yard No. 650), for Stena Atlantic Line Ltd., Bermuda. 17.3.1978: Launched. 30.6.1978: Completed. 1980: Renamed STENA CARRIER. 1980: Renamed IMPARCA MIAMI. 1981: Transferred to Stena Ocean Line Ltd., (Triport Ferries (Management) Ltd., managers), Cayman Islands, and renamed STENA CARRIER. 1982: Renamed JOLLY BRUNO. 1982: Renamed JOLLY SMERALDO. 1983: Renamed STENA CARRIER, (Swedish Caledonian Marine Management Ltd., managers). 1984: Stena Ab, appointed as managers. 1985: Northern Marine Management (Cyprus) Ltd., appointed as managers. 1986: Northern Marine Management Ltd., appointed as managers. 1987: Stcna Ab, appointed as managers. 1988: Transferred to Stena Carrier Ltd., (Wald & Rahm Management Ab, managers). 1995: Ab Stena Marine appointed as managers. 1999: Removed from management. 2000: Sold to Stena Line Shipholding B.V. (Stena Line Ab, managers). 2004: Sold to Lillbacka Powerco, Harma, Finland, and renamed GLOBAL CARRIER.

7528659

F.55. MERZARIO ESPANIA (1978)

As built: 5,466g. 2,485n. 8,672d. 151.01(BB) x 21.67 x 7.319 metres.
Post 1981: 6,455g. 3,284n. 8,704d. widened to 23.58 metres.
Post 1986: 18,732g. 10,578n. 8,704d.
Post 1994: 16,776g. 5,032n. 5,455d. 151.01(BB) x 23.58 x 6.500 metres.
Two, 12 Cyl. 4 S.C.S.A. (400 x 460mm) Pielstick 12PC2-5V-400 vee type oil engines made by Nippon Kokan K.K., Yokohama, geared to twin screw shafts with controllable pitch propellers. 15,600 BHP. 17 kts. Thwartship thrust controllable pitch propeller forward.
12 berthed passengers / 562 x 20'containers / roro cargo / ferry, with stern door / ramp.
11.7.1977: Keel laid by Hyundai Heavy Industries Company Ltd., Ulsan (Yard No. 651), for Stena Container Line Ltd., London. 20.3.1978: Launched. 31.7.1978: Completed for Stena Line Ltd., London. 1978: Renamed MERZARIO HISPANIA. 1981: Deepened by Hapag Lloyd Werft GmbH, Bremerhaven, fitted to carry 114 berthed passengers, and renamed NORDIC FERRY. 5.1982: Requisitioned by the British Government, for use as a transport vessel during the Falklands conflict. 7.1982: Returned to owners. 12.1984: Sold for £10.5m. to Monarch Steamship Company Ltd., (Atlantic Steam Navigation Company Ltd., managers), London. 1986: Converted to carry 350 deck passengers, by Wilton Fijenoord B.V., Rotterdam. 1986: Managers restyled Atlantic Steam Navigation Company Ltd. (TOWNSEND THORESEN). 1987: Managers restyled as P&O European Ferries (Felixtowe) Ltd. 1989: Transferred to P&O European Ferries (Felixtowe) Ltd. 1991: Sold to NatWest Specialist Finance Ltd., (P&O European Ferries (Felixtowe) Ltd., managers), and renamed PRIDE OF FLANDERS. 1997: P&O North Sea Ferries Ltd., appointed as managers. 2000: Sold to Natwest Leasing (GB) Ltd. 2002: Sold to Stena Line Ltd., UK, and renamed FLANDERS. 2002: Renamed STENA TRANSPORTER. 2004: Sold to Stena Ropax Ltd., London.

STENA TRANSPORTER (2) (Author's collection))

7528661

F.56. STENA TRADER (2) / STENA TRANSPORTER (2) (1978 - 1979)

As built: 5,466g. 2,485n. 8,672d. 151.01(BB) x 21.67 x 7.319 metres.
Post 1980: 6,455g. 3,248n. 8,704d. widened to 25.28 metres.
Post 1985: 18,732g. 10,580n. 8,704d.
Post 1995: 16,776g. 5,032n. 5,455d. 151.01(BB) x 25.28 x 6.500 metres.
Two, 12-cyl. 4 S.C.S.A. (400 x 460mm) Pielstick 12PC2-5V-400 vee type, oil engines made by Nippon Kokan K.K., Yokohama, geared to twin screw shafts with controllable pitch propellers. 15,600 BHP. 17 kts. Thwartship thrust controllable pitch propeller forward.
12 berth passengers / 562 x 20'containers / roro cargo / ferry, with stern door / ramp.

3.9.1977: Keel laid as STENA TRADER by Hyundai Heavy Industries Company Ltd., Ulsan (Yard No. 652), for Stena Container Line Ltd., London. 5.7.1978: Launched. 15.9.1978: Completed as STENA TRANSPORTER for Stena Cargo Line Ltd., London. 1979: Renamed FINNROSE. 1980: Renamed STENA TRANSPORTER. 1980: Deepened, widened and fitted with 114 passenger berths by Hapag-Lloyd Werft GmbH, Bremerhaven, and renamed BALTIC FERRY. 1982: Triport Ferries (Management) Ltd., appointed as managers. 5.1982: Requisitioned by the British Government, for use as a transport vessel, during the Falklands conflict. 1983: Returned to owners. 12.1984: Sold for £10.5m. to Monarch Steamship Company Ltd., (Atlantic Steam Navigation Company Ltd., managers), London. 1985: Converted to carry 350 deck passengers, at Rotterdam, by Wilton Fijenoord B.V. 1986: Managers restyled Atlantic Steam Navigation Company Ltd., (TOWNSEND THORESEN). 1987: Managers restyled P&O European Ferries (Felixtowe) Ltd. 1989: Transferred to P&O European Ferries (Felixtowe) Ltd. 1991: Sold to BMBF (No.15) Ltd., (P&O European Ferries (Felixtowe) Ltd., managers), and renamed PRIDE OF SUFFOLK. 1997: P&O North Sea Ferries Ltd., appointed as managers. 2001: Renamed EUROPEAN DIPLOMAT (P&O European Ferries (Irish Sea) Ltd., appointed as managers). 2003: Sold to P&O Ship Management Irish Sea Ltd., Altrincham, (P&O Ferries Ltd., Dover, managers). 2005: Sold to Celtic Link Ferries Ltd., Wexford, Republic of Ireland, (same managers), and renamed DIPLOMAT.

STENA OCEANICA (1) (Author's collection)

6620773

F.57. STENA OCEANICA (1) (1978 - 1979)

As built: 8,897g. 4,071n. 2,591d. 141.2 x 20.96 x 5.49 metres.
Post 1979: 10,034g. 4,933n. 2,591d. widened to 22.61 metres.
Post 1994: 12,764g. 3,924n. 2,591d.

Four, 6-cyl. 4 S.C.S.A. (400 x 460mm) Pielstick 6PC2L-400 type, oil engines made by the shipbuilder, geared in pairs to twin screw shafts with controllable pitch propellers. 10,080 BHP. 20 kts. Thwartship thrust controllable pitch propeller forward.

748 berthed passenger / roro cargo / ferry, with stern door.

1987: Berthed passenger capacity increased to 956.

29.9.1966: Launched as PATRICIA by Lindholmens Varv Ab, Goteborg (Yard No. 1095), for Rederi Ab Svenska Lloyd, Sweden. 15.3.1967: Completed. 1978: Purchased by Stena Ab, Sweden, and renamed STENA OCEANICA. 1979: Widened and deepened, by Smith's Dock Company Ltd., Teesside, to increase car deck head room, and passenger berth capacity to 832. Upon completion vessel was transferred to Stena Line Ab, Sweden, and renamed STENA SAGA. 1987: Stena Line Shipmanagement Hb, appointed as managers. 1988: Transferred to Lion Ferry AB, and renamed LION QUEEN. 1989: Transferred to Stena Line Ab, (Lion Ferry Ab, managers). 1990: Refitted at Rendsburg and transferred to British Columbia Stena Line Ltd., (BC STENA LINE), Canada, and renamed CROWN PRINCESS VICTORIA. 1990: Transferred to Stena Crown Princess Ltd., and renamed CROWN PRINCESS under Bahamian flag. 1991: Renamed PACIFIC STAR. 1993: Renamed SUN FIESTA, (Sun Fiesta Cruises Inc., managers). 1994: Renamed LION QUEEN, transferred to Swedish flag, and Lion Ferry Ab, appointed as managers. 1995: Transferred to Polish flag. 1996: Transferred to Stena (Bermuda) Line Ltd., Bahamas flag, (Northern Marine Management Ltd., appointed as managers). 1997: Sold to Kingsway Shipping Private Ltd., (Sembawang Shipmanagement Pte Ltd., managers), Bahamas, and renamed PUTRI BINTANG. 1998: Sold to Stena (Bermuda) Line Ltd., and renamed AMUSEMENT WORLD. 1999: Sold to Kingsway Management Private Ltd., (New Century Cruise Lines Private Ltd., managers). Singapore, under the Bahamas flag. 2005: Sold to Jackston Maritime Ltd., Singapore, (Universal Shipmanagement Ltd., Singapore, managers), and transferred to Tuvala flag.

F.58. MERZARIO GRECIA **(1978 - 1983)** see ship No. F.52 above.

F.59. MERZARIO HISPANIA (1) **(1978 - 1981)** see ship No. F.55 above.

ALPHA PROGRESS in Bidston Dock, Merseyside (W. J. Harvey)

F.60. ALPHA PROGRESS **(1978 - 1980)** see ship No. F.47 above.

F.61. STENA TIMER (1) **(1978 - 1981)** see ship No. F.43 above.

HELLAS (1) (Hans Mornhout collection)

F.62. HELLAS (1) **(1978 - 1979)** see ship No. F.37 above.

F.63. KIRK TRAILER **(1978 - 1980)** see ship No. F.18 above.

6605450

F.64. STENA BALTICA (2) (1979 - 1982)

As built: 7,481g. 3,798n. 1,626d. 134.52 x 19.92 x 5.722 metres.
Post 1979: 7,586g. 4,419n. 1,900d. 124.85 x 22.53 metres.
Two, 8-cyl. 2 S.C.S.A. (560 x 1,000mm) Sulzer 8TD56 type, oil engines made by Oy Wartsila Ab., Turku / Abo, geared to twin screw shafts with controllable pitch propellers. 14,000 BHP. 21 kts. Thwartship thrust propeller forward.
Ice strengthened 800 berthed, 1,200 deck passengers / roro cargo / ferry with bow and stern doors.
15.12.1965: Launched as FINNPARTNER by Oy Wartsila Ab., Helsingfors (Yard No. 380), for Oy Finn Lines, (Amer Tupakka Oy, managers), Finland. 6.1966: Completed. 1968: Sold to Stockholms Rederi Ab Svea, Sweden and renamed SVEABORG. 1977: Renamed PEER GYNT. 1978: Purchased by Stena Ab, Sweden and renamed STENA BALTICA. 1978 - 1979: Refitted by Werft Nobiskrug GmbH, Rendsburg, as an accommodation ship. 11.3.1979: Conversion completed. 1982: Sold to D.A. Line, Greece, and renamed IALYSSOS, and reverted back into a 1,200 deck, 800 berthed passengers / vehicles roro ferry. 1983:

Owners restyled as Dodekanissiak Anonimos Naftiliaki Eteria (D.A.N.E.). 1995: Owners restyled as D.A.N.E. Sea Line (Dodekanissiak Anonimos Naftiliaki Eteria). 2003: Sold to unspecified Saudi Arabian owners, and renamed SALIM. 2004: Sold to Natalia Shipping SA, and renamed NOURA 1, under Mongolia flag. 2004: Renamed NOURA. 18.5.2004: Officially reported as having been demolished.

STENA BALTICA (2) (Author's collection)

STENA SAGA (1)

Showing clearly the hull modifications incorporated to both increase the turning area on her vehicle deck and for stability.

(Hans Mornhout collection)

F.65. STENA SAGA (1) **(1979 - 1988)** see ship No. F.57 above.

F.66. FINNROSE **(1979 - 1980)** see ship No. F.56 above.

F.67. STENA NORDICA (3) **(1979 - 1980)** see ship No. F.37 above.

F.68. HELLAS (2) **(1979 - 1986)** see ship No. F.47 above.

HELLAS (2) seen at Felixstowe whilst deputizing for requisitioned vessels during the Falklands War

(Author's collection)

STENA SAILER (2)

(Hans Mornhout collection)

7365069

F.69. STENA SAILER (2) (1980 - 1986)

As built: 3,400g. 735n. 2,540d. 119.0 x 16.49 x 4.617 metres.
Post 1999: 6,653g. 735n. 2,495d.
Four, 12-cyl. 4 S.C.S.A. (250 x 300mm) Polar SF112VS-F vee type oil engines made by British Polar Engines Ltd., Glasgow, geared, in pairs, to twin screw shafts with controllable pitch propellers. 8,400 BHP. 17 kts. Thwartship thrust controllable pitch propeller forward.
12 berthed passengers / roro cargo / 70 x 20'containers / ferry, with bow door / ramp, and stern door / ramp.
1993: 37cabins, 122 berthed and 332 deck passengers / RoRo-cargo / ferry.
30.1.1974: Keel laid as DUNDALK by Verolme Cork Dockyards Ltd., Cork (Yard No. 874), for Allied Irish Bank Ltd., (British & Irish Steam Packet Company Ltd., managers), Eire. 12.9.1974: Launched. 4.1.1975: Completed. 12.1980: Purchased by Stena Line Ab, and renamed STENA SAILER, retaining Eire flag. 1982: Transferred to Stena Caribbean Line Ltd., (Triport Ferries (Management) Ltd., managers). 1983: Swedish Caledonian Marine Management Ltd., appointed as managers. 1984: Transferred to Cayman Islands flag. 1985: Northern Marine Management Ltd., appointed as managers. 1987: Renamed LION SAILER. 1987: Reverted to STENA SAILER. 1988: Transferred to Hoginaut International Ltd., (Swecal Ltd., managers), Georgetown, same name. 1988: Sold to Sealink (UK) Ltd., (SEALINK BRITISH FERRIES), and renamed ST. CYBI. 1990: Owners purchased by Stena Ab, and restyled as Sealink Stena Line Ltd. 1991: Sold to Kostas and Christos Miras, Greece, and renamed WIND CYBI. 1992: Sold to Olympia II Shipping Co., (same managers), Greece, and renamed THESEUS. 1.1993: Laid up with surveys overdue. 8.1993: Lloyds Register class withdrawn. 1993: Under conversion. 1995: Sold to Dimitrios Miras & Company, E.N.E., Greece, and removed from management. 1997: Sold to Olympia II Shipping Company, (Dimitrios Miras & Company, E.N.E., managers). Piraeus.

F.70. CARIBBEAN TRAILER (1980 - 1987) see ship No. F.19 above.

F.71. STENA SHIPPER (1) **(1980 - 1981)** see ship No. F.26 above.

F.72. HELLAS (1) **(1980)** see ship No. F.38 above.

F.73. STENA NORDICA (3) **(1980 - 1981)** see ship No. F.37 above.

F.74. STENA SHIPPER (2) **(1980)** see ship No. F.48 above.

F.75. MERZARIO IONIA (1) **(1980 - 1981)** see ship No. F.48 above.

F.76. STENA FREIGHTER (1) **(1980 - 1982)** see ship No. F.46 above.

SYRIA after returning to Bremerhaven for lengthening

(Courtesy Stena Ab)

F.77. SYRIA **(1980 - 1983)** see ship No. F.53 above.

F.78. STENA CARRIER (2) **(1980)** see ship No. F.54 above.

IMPARCA MIAMI

(Hans Mornhout collection)

F.79. IMPARCA MIAMI **(1980 - 1981)** see ship No. F.54 above.

F.80. STENA TRANSPORTER (2) **(1980)** see ship No. F.56 above.

F.81. UNION TRADER **(1980)** see ship No. F.34 above.

F.82. VIKING TRADER **(1980 - 1981)** see ship No. F.13 above.

F.83. BALTIC FERRY **(1980 - 1984)** see ship No. F.56 above.

BALTIC FERRY at Felixstowe, after jumboising.

(Courtesy Stena Ab)

KRONPRINSESSAN VICTORIA arriving at Kiel.

(W. J. Harvey)

7901760

F.84. KRONPRINSESSAN VICTORIA (1981 - 1988)

As built: 14,378g. 7,859n. 3,315d. 149.05(BB) x 26.55 x 6.127 metres.
Post 1987: 17,062g. 10,053n. 3,189d.
Post 1994: 24,828g. 11,969n. 3,189d.
Four, 12-cyl. 4 S.C.S.A. (320 x 350mm) Wartsila 12V32 vee type oil engines made by Oy Wartsila Ab, Vaasa, geared in pairs, to twin screw shafts with controllable pitch propellers. 20,600 BHP. 20.5 kts. Two, Thwartship thrust controllable pitch propellers forward.
Ice strengthened, 1,374 berthed, 702 deck passengers / roro cargo / ferry, with bow door / ramp, and three stern rampdoors.
11.2.1980: Keel laid by Gotaverken, Arendal Ab, Goteborg (Yard No. 908) for Sessan Linjen Ab, (Rederi Ab Goteborg-Frederikshavn Linjen, managers) Sweden. 15.10.1980: Launched. 10.4.1981: Completed for Rederi Ab Goteborg-Frederikshavn Linjen, Sweden. 1981: Owners merged with Stena Ab, and henceforth operated as Stena - Sessan Linjen. 1986: Stena Ab, appointed as managers. 1987: Stena Line Shipmanagement Hb, appointed as managers. 1988: Renamed STENA SAGA. 1989: Managers restyled as Stena Marine Management. 1994: Sold to Rederi Ab Gotland, (Stena Sealink Ltd. (STENA SEALINK LINE), managers), and renamed STENA EUROPE. 1997: Sold to Stena Line Ab, Bahamas flag, and renamed LION EUROPE. 1997: Sold to Lion Ferry Polska (Lion Ferry Ab., managers), Gdynia. 1998: Sold to Stena Lina Ab., (Stena Line Polska Company Ltd., managers) and renamed STENA EUROPE, retaining Polish flag. 2003: Sold to Stena Line Ltd., Ashford, Kent, and transferred to British flag.

7347548

F.85. PRINSESSAN BIRGITTA (1) (1981 - 1982)

As built: 8,753g. 4,401n. 1,600d. 153.02 x 20.05 x 5.62 metres.
Post 1995: 13,336g. 5,806n. 1,600d. 152.41 x 20.05 x 5.62 metres.
Two, 18-cyl. 4 S.C.S.A. (400 x 460mm) Pielstick 18PC2-5V-400 vee type oil engines made by the shipbuilder, geared to twin screw shafts with controllable pitch propellers. 21,600 BHP. 18.5 kts. Two, thwartship thrust controllable pitch propellers forward, and one aft.
Ice strengthened, 889 berthed, 341 deck passengers / roro cargo / ferry, with bow door / ramp, and stern door / ramp.

20.3.1973: Keel laid by Oy Wartsila Ab., Turku (Yard No. 1214), by Sessanlinjen, (Rederi Ab Ragne), Sweden. 28.9.1973: Launched for Rederi Ab Ragne, (Ragnerederierna, managers), Sweden. 9.4.1974: Completed. 1977: Sold to Rederi Ab Goteborg-Frederikshavn Linjen, (same managers), Sweden. 1980: Removed from management. 1981: Acquired by Stena Line Ab (Stena-Sessan Linjen, managers/operators). 1982: Renamed STENA SCANDINAVICA to release name for a new vessel. 1983: Transferred to Sessanlinjen Ab, Sweden. 1986: Transferred to Rederi Ab Goteborg-Frederikshavn Linjen, (Stena Ab, managers). 1987: Transferred to Stena Ab, renamed SCANDINAVICA. 1988: Proposed to rename LION QUEEN but vessel was subsituted by STENA SAGA that was thus renamed. 1988: Transferred to Stena Line Ab, (Stena Line Shipmanagement Hb, managers), Bahamas flag, O.N. 715399. 1988: Transferred to Stena Line Ltd., (Stena Marine Management, managers). 5.1989: Renamed TARAK L. 1989: Transferred to Scandinavica Ltd., (Northern Marine Management Ltd., managers), and reverted to SCANDINAVICA. 1990: Sold to Norway Line Invest KS, (Kosmos Ship Management AS, managers), Norway, and renamed VENUS. 1990: Owners restyled as Colour Line, (S&C Marine AS appointed as managers). 1994: Sold to DFDS AS, Denmark, and renamed KING OF SCANDINAVIA. 2000: Sold to DFDS Seaways (DFDS AS, managers), Denmark.). 2002: Sold to Reca Marmara, Monaco, (V. Ships Leisure, Monaco, managers), and renamed CESME, under the Turkish flag.

PRINSESSAN BIRGITTA (1).

(W. J. Harvey)

7037806

F.86. PRINSESSAN DESIREE (1981 - 1983)

As built: 5,799g. 2,875n. 1,848d. 123.37 x 19.61 x 5.169 metres.
Post 1994: 8,772g. 2,631n. 1,968d.
Post 1999: 9,149g. 2,744n. 1,968d.
Eight, 12-cyl. 4 S.C.S.A. (250 x 300mm) Polar SF112VS-E vee type oil engines made by Nydqvist & Holm Ab, Trollhattan, four geared to each of twin screw shafts with controllable pitch propellers. 15,600 BHP. 20.5 kts. Thwartship thrust controllable pitch propeller forward.
145 berthed, 1,255 deck passengers / roro cargo / ferry, with bow and stern doors.
20.11.1970: Launched by Aalborg Vaerft AS, Aalborg (Yard No. 190), for Rederi Ab Goteborg-Frederikshavn Linjen (Sessan Linjen), Sweden. 3.6.1971: Completed. 1981: Stena-Sessan Line Ab, Sweden, appointed as managers / operators. 1983: Renamed EUROPAFARJAN. 1984: Transferred to Stena Line Ab (Varberg - Grena Linjen Ab, managers), Sweden. 1984: Transferred to Varberg - Grena Linjen Ab. 1985: Transferred to Lion Ferry Ab, and renamed EUROPAFARJAN II. 1987: Renamed LION PRINCESS. 1988: Transferred to Stena Ab. 1989: Transferred to Stena Line Ab, (Lion Ferry Ab, managers). 1994: Sold to Vard AS, (KS AS Scandi Line, managers), Norway, and renamed BOHUS. 1997: Sold to Color Line ASA., (Color Line Marine AS, managers), Oslo. 2005: Transferred to MV Color Bohus AS, (same managers).

F.87. STENA SEARIDER (1) **(1981 - 1983)** see ship No. F.24 above.

F.88. STENA SEATRADER (2) **(1981 - 1989)** see ship No. F.22 above.

F.89. SPEEDLINK VANGUARD **(1981 - 1987)** see ship No. F.25 above.

F.90. STENA NORDICA (2) **(1981 - 1984)** see ship No. F.28 above.

F.91. STENA NAUTICA (2) **(1981 - 1983)** see ship No. F.37 above.

F.92. CONSTELLATION ENTERPRISE **(1981 - 1986)** see ship No. F.48 above.

F.93. STENA IONIA (1) **(1981)** see ship No. F.50 above.

F.94. MERZARIO HISPANIA (2) **(1981 - 1983)** see ship No. F.51 above.

F.95. STENA CARRIER (3) (1981 - 1982) see ship No. F.54 above.

F.96. MERZARIO IONIA (2) (1981 - 1982) see ship No. F.50 above.

NORDIC FERRY at Felixstowe, after jumboising. (Courtesy Stena Ab)

F.97. NORDIC FERRY (1981 - 1984) see ship No. F.55 above.

F.98. STENA TRADER (1) (1981) see ship No. F.13 above.

PRINSESSAN BIRGITTA (2)

(W. J. Harvey)

7901772

F.99. PRINSESSAN BIRGITTA (2) (1982 - 1983)

As built: 14,378g. 7,859n. 3,315d. 149.05(BB) x 26.55 x 6.127 metres.
Post 1983: 17,043g. 10,104n. 3,315d.
Post 1994: 24,872g. 9,314n. 3,315d.
Four, 12-cyl. 4 S.C.S.A. (320 x 350mm) Wartsila 12V32 vee type oil engines made by Oy Wartsila Ab., Vaasa, geared in pairs, to twin screw shafts with controllable pitch propellers. 20,600 BHP. 20.5 kts. Two, thwartship thrust controllable pitch propellers forward.
Ice strengthened, 1,100 berthed, 1,000 deck passengers / roro cargo / ferry, with bow door / ramp, and three stern rampdoors.
1979: Ordered as DROTTNING SILVIA from Gotaverken Arendal Ab, Goteborg (Yard No. 909), by Sessanlinjen Ab, Sweden. 10.11.1980: Keel laid. 22.5.1981: Launched without name for Rederi Ab Goteborg-Frederikshavn Linjen, Sweden. Whilst fitting out the owners merged with Stena Ab. 19.5.1982: Completed as PRINSESSAN BIRGITTA for Stena-Sessan Line Ab, Sweden. 6.1983: Transferred to Hill Samuel Trading (No. 26) Ltd., (Stena Ferry Ab, managers), London, and renamed ST. NICHOLAS. 1986: Transferred to Ibos Finance Ltd; Squarehorn Ltd; Ellstree Platforms Ltd., and A. Moir & Company Ltd., (same managers), London. 1987: Transferred to McAlpine Aviation; Elstree Platforms Ltd. & Others, (same managers), London. 1987: Transferred to M.C.C., Leasing (No.6) Ltd., and N.W.S. 6 Ltd., London, (same managers). 1988: Sold to Paxro 1 Ltd., (Sealink UK Ltd. (SEALINK BRITISH FERRIES) managers), and transferred to Bahamas flag, (O.N.703472). 1990: Owners purchased by Stena Ab, and restyled as Sealink UK Ltd., (SEALINK STENA LINE). 1990: Transferred to Rederi Ab Gotland, (Stena Sealink Ltd. (STENA SEALINK LINE), managers), Bahamas flag. 1991: Renamed STENA NORMANDY. 1997: Renamed

NORMANDY under Estonian flag, (Hansatee Ltd, (A. S. Hansatee manager), Managers). 1998: Sold to Irish Continental Group plc (IRISH FERRIES), Dublin, Ireland, under the Bahamas flag. 2005: Transferred to Irish Ferries Ltd., (Dobson Fleet Management Ltd., Dublin, managers).

7350090

F.100. EUROPAFARJAN III (1982 - 1983)

As built: 4,775g. 2,153n. 1,321d. 118.67(BB) x 18.55 x 5.011 metres.
Post 1994: 8,798g. 5,371n. 1,321d.
Post 2000: 8,871g. 2,874n. 1,321d.
Four, 9-cyl. 4 S.C.S.A. (320 x 450mm) MaK 9M453AK type oil engines made by Atlas-Mak Maschinenbau, Kiel, geared in pairs to twin screw shafts with controllable pitch propellers. 12,624 BHP. 20.75 kts. Thwartship thrust propeller forward.
Ice strengthened, 124 berthed, 1,076 deck passengers / roro cargo / ferry, with bow door / ramp, and stern door / ramp.
24.10.1973: Keel laid by Werft Nobiskrug GmbH, Rendsburg (Yard No. 683), for Lion Ferry Ab, Sweden. 25.5.1974: Launched. 6.9.1974: Completed. 7.1982: Owners and vessel purchased by Stena Ab, Sweden, but retained their own identity. 3.1983: Sold to Tourship Company S.A., Panama, and renamed CORSICA SERENA II. 1995: Tourship Ltd., appointed as managers. 1997: Sold to Mangrovia Charterers Associates AS., (same managers). 1999: Sold to Medinvest SpA., Italy. 2004: Sold to Forshipo Srl., Savona, Italy, (Medinvest SpA, Savona, managers), and renamed CORSICA SERENA SECONDA.

7427752

F.101. MARINER * (1982 - 1983)

As built; 3,642g. 1,536n. 5,675d. 126.35(BB) x 19.44 x 6.579 metres.
Post 1993: 9,737g. 2,921n. 5,675d.
16-cyl. 4 S.C.S.A. (400 x 480mm) Sulzer 16ZV40/48 vee type oil engine made by Hitachi Zosen, Hiroshima Works, Innishima, geared to shaft with controllable pitch propeller. 10,400 BHP. 18.5 kts. Two, thwartship thrust controllable pitch propellers forward, and one aft.
Ice strengthened, 12 berthed passengers / roro cargo / ferry, with stern door / ramp.
10.10.1975: Keel laid as SEASPEED DANA by Trosvik Verksted AS, Brevik (Yard No. 114), for Seaspeed Ferry Company Ltd., (Morland Navigation, London), Greece. 24.1.1976: Launched. 11.5.1976: Completed. 1981: Sold to Kara Shipping Company Ltd., Malta, and renamed DANA. 1982: Purchased, in a damaged condition, by Stena Line Ab, Sweden, and renamed MARINER*. 29.12.1982: Departed from Wallham, in tow of the tugs THETIS (200g/61) and ERLAND (309g/74), arriving at Drammen next day, for repairs. 1983: Renamed STENA MARINER, (Swedish Caledonian Marine Management Ltd., managers), Sweden. 1984: OT Shipping Ab, appointed as managers. 1985: Transferred to Stena Caribbean Line Ltd. (Northern Marine Management Ltd., managers), Cayman Islands. 1988: Northern Marine Inc., appointed as managers. 1990: Transferred to Stena Mediterranean Line Ltd., (Matina Lines, managers), Malta, and chartered to Compagnie Tunisienne de Navition, and renamed SALAH L, (as a replacement for for MONAWAR L, q.v.). 1992: Transferred to Stena Rederei Ab, (Issomarine Maritime Enterprises Ltd., managers), Malta. 1993: Transferred to Stena Mediterranean Line Ltd., (Marship Services Inc., managers), Malta, and renamed SENATOR, (O.N.7081). 1994: Renamed STENA MARINER. 1995: Sold to Exxtor Ferries Ltd., (European Maritime Services A.G., and renamed EXCALIBUR, under Bahamian flag. 1996: Barber Ship Management AS., appointed as managers. 1997: Sold to Kalingrad Key Line Ltd., (same managers) Malta, and renamed CALIBUR. 1998: Transferred to Estonia flag, (Estonian Shipping Company (ESCO) (RAS Eesti Merelaevandus) appointed as managers). 2000: Sold to Kalingrad Key Line Plc, Oslo, Norway, (V Ships Norway AS, Oslo, managers), under the Maltese flag.

*N.B. Although the vessel carried the name MARINER for the short voyage from Wallham to Drammen and was recorded as such in Lloyds Shipping Index at the time, it does not appear in Lloyd's Register as a name that was registered although the owners have confirmed the allocation for the voyage.

6918560

F.102. PRINSESSAN CHRISTINA (2) (1982 - 1983).

As built: 5,697g. 2,823n. 1,848d. 123.45 x 19.61 x 5.250 metres.
Post 1994: 8,909g. 2,733n. 1,845d.
Post 2000: 8,893g. 3,340n. 1,845d.
Eight, 12-cyl. 4 S.C.S.A. (250 x 300mm) Polar SF112VS-E vee type oil engines made by Nydqvist & Holm AB, Trollhattan, four geared to each of twin screw shafts with controllable pitch propellers. 15,600 BHP. 20.5 kts. Thwartship thrust controllable pitch propeller forward.
145 berthed, 1,255 deck passengers / roro cargo / ferry, with bow and stern doors.
9.5.1969: Launched by Aalborg Vaerft AS, Aalborg (Yard No. 180), for Rederi Ab Goteborg-Frederikshavn Linjen, (Sessan Linjen), Sweden. 9.12.1969: Completed. 1981: Sold to Safe Ship Rederi Ab, Sweden, and

renamed SAFE CHRISTINA. 1982: Purchased by Stena Line Ab, Sweden, and renamed PRINSESSAN CHRISTINA. 1983: Renamed STENA NORDICA. 1985: Transferred to Lion Ferry Ab, Sweden, and renamed EUROPAFARJAN I. 1987: Renamed LION PRINCE. 1988: Transferred to Stena Ab, Sweden. 1989: Transferred to Stena Line Ab, (Lion Ferry Ab, managers). 1998: Renamed STENA PRINCE. 1999: Sold to Freedom Ferries, (TR.I.S. Traghetti Isole Sarde S.r.l, managers), Italy, and renamed COMMODORE. 2003: Sold to Enermar SpA, Genoa, and renamed PALAU under the Italian flag. 2005: Sold to D & P Cruises, Augusta, (Naviservice Srl, Augusta, managers).

F.103. JOLLY GIALLO **(1982)** see ship No. F.46 above.

F.104. JOLLY TURCHESE **(1982 - 1983)** see ship No. F.46above.

F.105. STENA IONIA (1) **(1982 - 1985)** see ship No. F.50 above.

F.106. JOLLY BRUNO **(1982)** see ship No. F.54 above.

F.107. JOLLY SMERALDO **(1982 - 1983)** see ship No. F.54 above.

STENA SCANDINAVICA (2)

(Author's collection)

F.108. STENA SCANDINAVICA (2) **(1982 - 1987)** see ship No. F.85 above.

F.109. JUTLANDICA **(1982 - 1983)** see ship No. F.21 above.

STENA DANICA (4)

(Author's collection)

7907245

F.110. STENA DANICA (4) (1983 -)

As built: 15,899g. 8,061n. 2,950d. 152.23(BB) x 28.48 x 6.317 metres.
Post 1994: 28,727g. 8,700n. 2,950d.

Four, 12-cyl. 4 S.C.S.A. (400 x 480mm) Sulzer 12ZV40/48 vee type oil engines made by Cie. de Const.Mec.Sulzer (CCM Sulzer), Mantes, geared in pairs to twin screw shafts with controllable pitch propellers. 34,800 BHP. 21 kts. Two, thwartship thrust controllable pitch propellers forward.
Ice strengthened, 96 berthed, 2,204 deck passengers / roro cargo / ferry, with bow door / ramp, and two stern rampdoors.
2.4.1980: Keel laid by Chantiers Du Nord et de la Mediterrane, Dunkerque (Yard No. 309), for Stena Line Ab, Sweden. 30.8.1980: Launched. 10.2.1983: Completed. 1987: Transferred to Stena Danicas Interessenter Kb, (Stena Ab, managers, under a lease agreement), Sweden. 1987: Management transferred to Stena Line Shipmanagement Hb. 1989: Managers restyled as Stena Marine Management. 1992: Transferred to Stena Line Danica Ab, (Stena Line Service Ab, managers). 1994: Transferred to Stena Line Ab and removed from management. 1995: Stena Line Service Ab re-appointed as managers. 1996: Transferred to Stena Danicas Interessenter Kb, (Stena Line Scandinavia Ab., managers). 2000: Sold to Stena Line Ab., (removed from management). 2004: Sold to Stena Danicas Interessenter Kb, (Stena Line Scandinavia Ab., managers).

7907257

F.111. STENA JUTLANDICA (2) (1983 - 1996)

As built: 15,811g. 8,020n. 2,950d. 154.90(BB) x 28.48 x 6.317 metres.
Post 1994: 28,727g. 8,618n. 2,950d.
Post 1996: 28,559g. 8,568n. 2,950d.
Post 2000: 28,558g. 8,568n. 3,810d. 156.2(BB) metres.
Four, 12-cyl. 4 S.C.S.A. (400 x 480mm) Sulzer 12ZV40/48 vee type oil engines made by Cie. de Const. Mec. Sulzer (CCM Sulzer), Mantes, geared in pairs to twin screw shafts with controllable pitch propellers. 34,800 BHP. 21 kts. Two, thwartship thrust controllable pitch propellers forward.
Ice strengthened, 86 berthed, 2,204 deck passengers / roro cargo / ferry, with bow door / ramp, and two stern rampdoors.
4.8.1980: Keel laid by Chantiers Du Nord et de la Mediterrane, Dunkerque (Yard No. 310), for Stena Line Ab, Sweden. 22.12.1980: Launched. 29.3.1983: Completed. 1987: Transferred to B & B Finans Projekt Ab, (Stena Line Shipmanagement Hb, managers, under a lease agreement), Sweden. 1988: Transferred to Wallenius, Safe Jasminia Ab, (same managers). 1989: Managers restyled as Stena Marine Management. 1990: Transferred by Stena Line Ab. 1990: Transferred to Wallenius, Safe Jasminia Ab, (Ab Stena Marine, managers). 1995: Transferred to Stena Rederi Ab. 1996: Stena Line Ltd., appointed as managers, transferred to London flag, and renamed STENA EMPEREUR. 1998: Transferred to P&O Stena Line Ltd., (P&O Stena Line Ship Management Ltd., managers), and renamed P&OSL PROVENCE. 2000: Sold to P&O Stena Line Short Sea Ltd., (same managers). 2001: Sold to P&O Stena Invicta Ltd., (same managers). 2002: Sold to P&O Ferries Invicta Ltd., (P&O Ferries Ship Management Ltd., managers), Dover, and renamed P O PROVENCE. 2003: Renamed PRIDE OF PROVENCE. 2004: Sold to Mili Shipping Company SA, Greece, and renamed ALKMINI A. 2005: Sold to Kystlink AS Langesund, Norway and renamed PRIDE OF TELEMARK.

STENA MARINER

(Hans Mornhout collection)

F.112. STENA MARINER (1983 - 1990) see ship No. F.101 above.

STENA BALTICA (3) spent only a short time in the fleet.

(Internet source / Bertil Soderberg)

7224459

F.113. STENA BALTICA (3) (1983)

As built: 8,528g. 3,949n. 2,100d. 128.02(BB) x 22.05 x 5.919 metres.
Post 1994: 12,281g. 4,098n. 1,775d.
Four, 9-cyl. 2 S.C.S.A. (400 x 480mm) Sulzer ZH40/48 type, oil engines made by the shipbuilder, geared in pairs to twin screw shafts with controllable pitch propellers. 18,000 BHP. 22 kts. Thwartship thrust controllable pitch propeller forward.
377 berthed, 823 deck passengers / roro cargo / ferry with bow door / ramp, and stern door / ramp.
1972: Ordered as BORE I from Oy Wartsila Ab, Turku / Abo (Yard No. 1199), by Silja Rederiet Ab, Finland. 11.7.1972: Launched for Angf. Ab Bore, Finland. 15.3.1973: Completed. 1980: Sold to Finska Angfartygs Ab (EFFOA), (Finland Steamship Company Ltd.), Finland, and renamed SKANDIA. 1983: Purchased by Stena Line Ab, Sweden, and renamed STENA BALTICA, under Bahamian flag. 1983: Sold to USSR-Baltic Shipping Company, Leningrad, and renamed ILYICH. 9.1996: Sold by auction to unspecified owners, and renamed ANASTASIA V. 1.1997: Sold to Windward Venture Ltd., (Windward Lines Ltd., managers), and renamed WINDWARD PRIDE. 4.1997: Sold to the Estonian Shipping Company (ESCO) (RAS Eesti Merelaevandus) (Tschudi & Eitzen ESCO Ship Management Ltd., managers), Estonia, and renamed BALTIC KRISTINA. 2003: Sold to Rigas Juras Linija, Riga.

F.114. STENA GRECIA **(1983 - 1986)** see ship No. F.52 above.

F.115. STENA CARRIER (4) **(1983 - 2004)** see ship No. F.54 above.

F.116. STENA NORDICA (4) **(1983 - 1985)** see ship No. F.102 above.

EUROPAFARJAN

(Hans Mornhout collection)

F.117. EUROPAFARJAN **(1983 - 1985)** see ship No. F.86 above.

F.118. ST. NICHOLAS **(1983 - 1989)** see ship No. F.99 above.

F.119. SEARIDER **(1983 - 1984)** see ship No. F.24 above.

REINE ASTRID

(Author's collection)

F.120. REINE ASTRID **(1983)** see ship No. F.37 above.

F.121. STENA FREIGHTER (2) **(1983 - 2004)** see ship No. F.46 above.

F.122. STENA HISPANIA (1) **(1983 - 1984)** see ship No. F.51 above.

F.123. STENA TRANSPORTER (3) **(1983 - 1985)** see ship No. F.53 above.

STENA DRIVER

(Hans Mornhout collection)

7826867

F.124. STENA DRIVER (1984 - 1985)

As built: 5,088g. 2,345n. 6,235d. 148.44(BB) x 20.22 x 9.341 metres.
Post 2000: 13,294g. 3,988n. 4,798d. 171.06(BB) x 20.25 x 5.270 metres.
As built: Two, 12-cyl. 4 S.C.S.A. (330 x 360mm) vee type oil engines made by Motorenwerke Mannheim A.G., (MWM), Mannheim, geared to twin screw shafts with controllable pitch propellers. 12,000 BHP. 17 kts. Thwartship thrust controllable pitch propeller forward.
Post 1993: Two, 12-cyl. 4 S.C.S.A. (320 x 350mm) Wartsila 12V32E vee type oil engines made by Wartsila Diesel Oy, Vaasa/Vasa. 13,418 BHP. 18.5 kts.
Post 1999: Two, 12-cyl. 4 S.C.S.A. (320 x 350mm) Wartsila 12V32E vee type oil engines made by Wartsila Diesel Oy, Vaasa/Vasa. 13,378 BHP. 18.5 kts.
32 berthed passengers / roro cargo / ferry, with a stern door.
2000: 20 cabins. 46 berthed and 135 deck passenger.
20.5.1980: Keel laid as LUCKY RIDER by Nuovi Cantieri Apvania S.p.A., Marina di Carrara (Yard No. 2120), for Castello Shipping Corp & Navyglad Shipping Corp, Greece16.1.1981: Launched. 30.12.1981:

Completed but delivery suspended. 3.1982: Delivered to Castello Hellas Shipping Company, (Delpa Maritime Company Ltd., managers), Greece. 1982: Transferred to Navyglad Hellas Shipping Company, Greece, (same managers). 1984: Purchased by Stena Ab, Sweden, and transferred to Stena Challenger Ltd., (Stena Ab, managers), Bahamas, and renamed STENA DRIVER. 1985: Sold to Sealink (UK) Ltd., London, and renamed SEAFREIGHT FREEWAY, under the Bermudan flag. 23.5.1988: During a voyage from Dover to Zeebrugge, suffered an engine room fire, caused by a break in a fuel pipe. The fire was put out, but vessel was disabled and subsequently towed to Dunkirk for repair. One of her engineers was killed, and another badly burned, by the fire. 1988: Sold to Navigation Maritime Bulgare, Bulgaria, and renamed SERDICA. 1988: Transferred to So Mejdunaroden Automobilen Transport (S.M.A.T.), Bulgaria. 1990: Sold to Hornet Shipping Company, Denmark, and renamed NORDIC HUNTER. 1991: Sold to Arka Marine AS, Denmark, and renamed ARKA MARINE. 1991: Sold to Akra Marine II KS., (Blaesbjerg Marine AS, managers), Denmark, and renamed ASK. 11.1993: Re-engined. 1997: Sold to Scandlines AG., Copenhagen, Denmark. 5.1999: Re-engined. 2000 Lengthened.

7048219

F.125. STENA BALTICA (4) (1984)

As built: 10,513g. 5,269n. 2,100d. 142.14(BB) x 22.20 x 5.515 metres.
Post 1996: 12,574g. 4,422n. 2,100d.
Two, 16-cyl. 4 S.C.S.A. (400 x 460mm) Pielstick 16PC2V-400 vee type oil engines made by Chantiers de l'Atlantique, St. Nazaire, geared to twin screw shafts with controllable pitch propellers. 15,780 BHP. 20 kts. Two, thwartship thrust controllable pitch propellers forward.
874 berthed passengers / roro cargo / ferry, with stern door.
1970: Ordered as MASSALIA from Dubigeon-Normandie S.A., Prairie au Duc, Nantes (Yard No. 124), by Charguer Ruenis. 29.1.1971: Launched for Cie. de Paquebots, France. 5.7.1971: Completed. 1984: Purchased by Stena Cargo Line Ltd., Sweden, and renamed STENA BALTICA. 1984: Renamed ISLAND FIESTA, and transferred to Bahamas flag. 1984: Renamed SCANDINAVIAN STAR. 1987: Stena Ab appointed as managers, and passenger berths reduced to 810. 16.3.1988: Whilst on a voyage from Cozumel to St. Petersburg, suffered a serious engine room fire, at a position 60 miles N.N.E., from Cancun, Mexico. Subsequently taken in tow. 23.3.1988: Arrived at Miami, Florida, for repairs, expected to take two months. 1990: Sold to unspecified Norwegian interests. 4.1990: Suffered a severe fire resulting in the vessel being gutted and the death of 158 people. At the time ownership was in dispute. 1990: Arrived under tow at Hull, for reconstruction by Humber Shiprepairers Ltd. 1990: Towed to Southampton for completion of work, following the financial collapse of the Humber repair contractors. 1990: Sold to VR Shipping ApS, and renamed CANDI. 1990: Sold to KS Scandinavian Star. 1994: Renamed REGAL VOYAGER. 1995: Sold to St. Thomas Cruises Ltd., (International Shipping Partners Inc., managers). 19.5.2004: Unspecified shipbreakers commenced work.

F.126. ISLAND FIESTA **(1984)** see ship No. F.125 above.

SCANDINAVIAN STAR

(Hans Mornhout collection)

F.127. SCANDINAVIAN STAR **(1984 - 1990)** see ship No. F.125 above.

F.128. STENA SEARIDER (1) **(1984)** see ship No. F.24 above.

F.129. TRUCKER **(1984 - 1985)** see ship No. F.24 above.

F.130. KOTKA VIOLET **(1984)** see ship No. F.51 above.

F.131. STENA HISPANIA (1) **(1984 - 1986)** see ship No. F.51 above.

F.132. STENA NAUTICA (3) **(1984 - 1987)** see ship No. F.28 above.

F.133. STENA SEARIDER (1) **(1985 - 1987)** see ship No. F.24 above.

CERDIC FERRY (Hans Mornhout collection)

F.134. CERDIC FERRY **(1985 - 1991)** see ship No. F.53 above.

F.135. EUROPAFARJAN I **(1985 - 1987)** see ship No. F.102 above.

F.136. EUROPAFARJAN II **(1985 - 1987)** see ship No. F.86 above.

F.137. STENA GOTHICA (2) **(1985 - 1988)** see ship No. F.50 above

STENA NORDICA (5) (Hans Mornhout collection)

7230599

F.138. STENA NORDICA (5) **(1986 - 1988)**

As built: 6,801g. 3,370n. 1,200d. 128.12(BB) x 19.99 x 5.50 metres.
Post 1994: 10,154g. 4,730n. 1,200d.
Post 1997: 10,514g. 4,730n. 1,132d.
Four, 8-cyl. 4 S.C.S.A. (410 x 470mm) Werkspoor 8TM410 type oil engines made by Soc., Dresser - Dujardin, Lille, geared, in pairs, to twin screw shafts with controllable pitch propellers. 20,400 BHP. 23 kts. Thwartship thrust controllable pitch propeller forward.
Ice strengthened, 634 berthed, 866 deck passengers / roro cargo / ferry, with bow door / ramp, and stern door / ramp.
23.10.1972: Launched as PETER WESSEL by Societe Nouvelle des Ateliers et Chantiers du Havre, Le Havre (Yard No. 212), for AS Larvik-Frederikshavnferjen, Norway. 20.7.1973: Completed. 1984: Sold to Admiral Shipping (Nassau) Ltd., (AS Larvik-Frederikshavnferjen, managers), Bahamas, and renamed ZEELAND.

1986: Purchased by Stena Ab, Sweden, and renamed STENA NORDICA. 1988: Transferred to Stena Line Ab, (Stena Line Ship Management Hb, managers). 1988: Sold to Jadranska Linijska Plovidba (Jadrolinija), Jugoslavia, and renamed MARKO POLO. 1992: Transferred to Croatia flag. 1992: Owners restyled as Javno Poduzece "Jadrolinja" P.O. 1994: Sold to Adriatic General Shipping Company Ltd., Rijeka, (Jadrolinja Cruises Ltd., Rijeka, managers), Croatia.

F.139. STENA SHIPPER (2) (1986 - 1987) see ship No. F.48 above.

DORIC FERRY

(Hans Mornhout collection)

F.140. DORIC FERRY (1986 - 1991) see ship No. F.47 above.

STENA BRITANNICA (2) (Courtesy Stena Ab)

F.141. STENA BRITANNICA (2) (1986 - 1988) see ship No. F.51 above.

7705130

F.142. BORNHOLM EXPRESS (1986 - 1989)

195g. 102n. 30d. 26.65 x 9.02 x metres.

Two, 12-cyl. 4 S.C.S.A. (175 x 205mm) 12V493TY70 vee type oil engines made by M.T.U. Friedrichshafen GmbH, Friedrichshafen. 2,200 BHP. 26 kts.

Twin hulled aluminium alloy, 166 deck passenger ferry.

9.12.1976: Keel laid as STEIGTIND by Westermoen Hydrofoil AS., Alta (Yard No. 65), for Saltens D/S AS, Norway. 15.6.1977: Launched. 23.6.1977: Completed. 1986: Purchased by Stena Danicas Interessenter

Kb, (Stena Ab, managers), Sweden, and renamed BORNHOLM EXPRESS. 1989: Sold to Jens Carlsson, Sweden. 1990: Sold to Rotainer Chartering Ab., Sweden. 1991: Sold to P/R for m.v. Skagen Exress, (Rotainer Chartering Ab, managers), Sweden, and renamed SKAGEN EXPRESS. 1992: Sold to P/R for M/S Sundskatten, (same managers), and renamed SUNDSKATTEN. 1993: Sold to Michael Kopp, (Peene Werft GmbH, managers), Wolgast, Germany, and renamed HAFFSKATTEN.

7907659

F.143. STENA SCANDINAVICA (3) / STENA GERMANICA (3) (1987 - 2001)

As built: 24,967g. 14,092n. 4,500d. 175.37(BB) x 29.04 x 6.701 metres.
Post 1988: 26,071g. 14,815n. 4,500d.
Post 1994: 38,772g. 24,324n. 4,500d.
Post 1999: 39,178g. 22,089n. 4,500d.
Four, 16-cyl. 4 S.C.S.A. (400 x 480mm) Sulzer 16ZV40/48 vee type oil engines made by "Zgoda" Zaklady Urzadzen Technicznych, Swietochlowice, geared in pairs, to twin screw shafts with controllable pitch propellers. 40,000 BHP. 23 kts. Two thwartship thrust controllable pitch propellers forward.
Ice strengthened, 2,204 berthed, 196 deck passengers / roro cargo / ferry, with bow door / ramp, and two stern rampdoors.
1979: One of four sisters ordered in Poland by Stena Line Ab, Sweden. 30.10.1980: Keel laid. 22.8.1981: Launched as STENA SCANDINAVICA by Stocznia im "Komuny Paryskiej" Gdynia, Poland (Yard No. B.494/01), for Stena Line Ab, Sweden. 11.1986: Renamed STENA GERMANICA, whilst fitting out. 20.2.1987: Sea trials for PR Finans Ab, (Stena Ab, managers), Sweden. 21.2.1987: Departed incomplete from the Lenin Shipyard, for berthing trials at Kiel thence to Gothenburg for completion of her interior decor. 11.4.1987: Completed for restyled, PK Finans Ab, (Stena Line Shipmanagement Hb, managers), Sweden. 6.4.1987: Maiden service voyage (6-years late). 1987: Transferred to Stena Ab, (same managers). 1988: Transferred to Stena Line Ab, (same managers). 1988: Managers restyled as Stena Marine Management Hb. 1990: Transferred to Carcorp Forvalting Ab., (Volvo Group) (same managers). 1991: Transferred to Stena Line Ab. 1992: Transferred to Stena Rederei Ab, (Ab Stena Marine, managers). 1999: Sold to Stena Line Scandinavia Ab. (removed from management). 1.2001: Sold to Scandlines Ab, Helsingborg, Sweden. 4.2001: Stena Line Scandinavia Ab, appointed as managers.

F.144. LION SAILER (1987) see ship No. F.69 above.

F.145. STENA SAILER (2) (1987 - 1988) see ship No. F.69 above.

7705714

F.146. STENA TRAILER (4) (1987 - 1991)

As built: 6,301g. 3,012n. 10,145d. 148.01(BB) x x 8.019 metres.
Post 1994: 15,406g. 9,209n. 10,145d.
Two, 6-cyl. 4 S.C.S.A. (520 x 550mm) MAN 6L52/55A type oil engines made by the shipbuilder, geared to a single shaft with a controllable pitch propeller. 12,165 BHP. 18 kts Thwartship thrust controllable pitch propeller forward.
Roro cargo / ferry / 556 TEU container carrier, with stern door / ramp.
28.7.1977: Keel laid as VENTUARI by Kawasaki Heavy Industries Ltd., Kobe (Yard No. 1269), for Langton Maritime Shipping Inc., (Century Greyhound Leasing & Finance, managers), Liberia. 18.10.1977: Launched. 30.6.1978: Completed for Naviera Neptuno Cia., (Maritime Transport Overseas GmbH, managers), Venezuela. 1981: Sold to Lancaster Transport Company Ltd., Liberia, and renamed BALDER CARRIER. 1985: Sold to Chester Transport Company Ltd., (Kawasaki Heavy Industries Ltd., managers), Liberia, and renamed CHESTER. 1987: Purchased by Seaburg Inc., (Northern Marine Management (Cyprus) Ltd., managers), Liberia, and renamed STENA TRAILER. 1988: Northern Marine Inc., appointed as managers. 1990: Transferred to Stena (Bermuda) Line Ltd., (Northern Marine Management Ltd., managers), Bermuda. 1991: Renamed TRAILER. 1991: Renamed STENA TRAILER. 1993: Renamed MEDFERRY EXPRESS. 1999: Sold to Sea Malta Ltd., Marsa, Malta and renamed MALTESE FALCON.

7705726

F.147. STENA TRADER (3) (1987 - 1991)

As built: 6,280g. 2,992n. 10,065d. 148.01(BB) x x 8.002 metres.
Post 1994: 6,974g. 2,992n. 10,065d.
Post 1996: 15,347g. 4,604n. 10,065d.
Two, 6-cyl. 4 S.C.S.A. (520 x 550mm) MAN 6L52/55A type oil engines made by the shipbuilder, geared to a single screw shaft with a controllable pitch propeller. 12,000 BHP. 18 kts. Thwartship thrust controllable pitch propeller forward.
RoRo cargo / 544 x 20'container carrier / ferry, with stern door / ramp.

28.9.1977: Keel laid as AFRICAN SOUL by Kawasaki Heavy Industries Ltd., Kobe, (Yard No. 1273), for Jacoby Shipping Corp., (Century Greyhound Leasing & Finance, managers), Liberia. 10.2.1978: Launched. 27.7.1979: Completed for Lancaster Transport Company Ltd., Liberia. 1981: Renamed BALDER FREIGHTER. 1985: Sold to Fortlee Transport Company Ltd., (Kawasaki Heavy Industries Ltd., managers), Liberia, and renamed FORTLEE. 1987: Purchased by Vikon Enterprises Ltd., (Northern Marine Management (Cyprus) Ltd., managers), Liberia, and renamed STENA TRADER. 1988: Northern Marine Inc., appointed as managers. 1990: Transferred to Stena America Line Ltd., (Northern Marine Management Ltd., managers), Bermuda, (O.N. 715340). 1991: Sold to Societe Nationale Maritime Corse Mediterrannee (S.N.C.M.), France, and renamed SAINTE BAUME. 1993: Sold to Overseas Freighters Ltd., Bahamas, and renamed SOUTHERN TRADER. 1994: Stim D'Orbigny, appointed as manager. 1997: Managers restyled as Compagnie de Management d'Orbigny (CMO). 2001: Sold to Societe Mediteranneene D'Investissement et de Participations, under the Bahamas flag. 2004: Sold to Fast Line, Alexandria, (Levant Shipping & Technical, Marseilles, managers), and renamed FAST ARROW, under the Maltese flag.

LION PRINCE

(Hans Mornhout collection)

F.148. LION PRINCE (1987 - 1998) see ship No. F.102 above.

LION PRINCESS (Hans Mornhout collection)

F.149. LION PRINCESS (1987 - 1994) see ship No. F.86 above.

F.150. SCANDINAVICA (2) (1987 - 1989) see ship No. F.85 above.

SCANDINAVICA (2) with Sealink funnel colours.

(Hans Mornhout collection)

F.151. CARIBE EXPRESS (1987 - 1988) see ship No. F.25 above.

F.152. STENA SCANRAIL (1987 -) see ship No. F.24 above.

F.153. VERSAILLES (1987) see ship No. F.28 above.

7907661
F.154. STENA GERMANICA (2) /STENA SCANDINAVICA (4) (1988 -)

As built: 26,088g. 14,786n. 4,500d. 175.39(BB) x 29.01 x 6.701 metres
Post 1994: 38,756g. 24,315n. 4,500d.
Post 1997: 39,169g. 22,084n. 4,500d.
Four, 16-cyl. 4 S.C.S.A. (400 x 480mm) Sulzer 16ZV40/48 vee type oil engines made by Zgoda Zaklady Urzadzen Technicznych, Swietochlowice, geared in pairs to twin screw shafts, with controllable pitch propellers. 40,000 BHP. 23 kts. Two, thwartship thrust controllable pitch propellers forward.
Ice strengthened, 2,312 berthed & 196 deck passenger / RoRo cargo / ferry, with a bow door / ramp, and two stern rampdoors.
1979: One of four sisters ordered in Poland by Stena Line Ab, Sweden. 31.8.1981: Launched. 16.4.1983: Launched as STENA GERMANICA by Stockznia Gdanska im Lenina, Gdansk, Poland (Yard No. B.494/02), for Stena Line Ab, Sweden. 11.1986: Renamed STENA SCANDINAVICA whilst fitting out. 29.11.1987: Departed, incomplete, from Gdansk. 1.12.1987: Arrived at Goteborg for completion. 10.2.1988: Christened at Kiel by Queen Silvia of Sweden. 29.2.1988: Completed. 1988: Stena Marine Management, appointed as managers. 1992: Managers restyled as Stena Marine Ab. 2000: Transferred to Stena Line Scandinavia Ab., and removed from management.

7722621
F.155. STENA PROGRESS (1988 - 1989)

As built: 5,778g. 2,943n. 9,332d. 140.85(BB) x 23.19 x 7.652 metres.
Post 1994: 14,444g. 4,391n. 9,332d.
Two, 8-cyl. 4 S.C.S.A. (400 x 480mm) Sulzer 8ZL40/80 type, oil engines made by Sumitomo Heavy Industries Ltd., Tamashima Works, Kurashiki, geared to twin screw shafts with controllable pitch propellers. 12,000 BHP. 17.5 kts. Thwartship thrust controllable pitch propeller forward.
RoRo cargo / vehicle / 510 x 20' container / ferry, with a slewing stern ramp.
10.4.1978: Keel laid as TFL PROGRESS by Minami-Nippon Zosen K.K., Usuki (Yard No. 520), for Gursan Shipping Corp, Greece. 7.7.1978: Launched. 26.10.1978: Completed. 1981: Renamed MERZARIO EMILIA. 1982: Renamed TFL PROGRESS. 1983: Transferred to Progress Shipping Company Ltd., (International Cruises S.A., managers), Bermuda, and renamed UNION DUNEDIN. 1987: Renamed PROGRESS ATLANTIC, under the Greek flag. 1988: Purchased by Stena Ab, transferred to Fernwood Inc., (Northern Marine Management (Cyprus) Ltd., managers), Liberia, and renamed STENA PROGRESS. 1989: Northern Marine Inc., appointed as managers. 1989: Sold to Societe Navale et Commerciale Delmas-Vieijeux (SNCDV), (Euronavis Gestion et Affretement Navires, managers), Bahamas, and renamed C. R. TANGER. 1991: Transferred to SCAC-Delmas-Vieljeux (S.D.V.), (Maritime Delmas Vieljeux, managers, subsequently restyled as Delmas Armement). 2001: Sold to E. P. E. Simantonis, (Aegean Carriers Naftiki Eteria, managers), Greece, and renamed AEGEAN PEARL. 2002: Sold to Pasifai Shipping S.A., Piraeus, (Aegean Cargo Naftiki Eteria, Piraeus, managers).

STENA PROGRESS

(Hans Mornhout collection)

7911545

F.156. SILVIA REGINA (1988 - 1991)

As built: 25,677g. 14,070n. 3,898d. 166.10(BB) x 29.04 x 6.719 metres.
Post 1989: 26,671g. 14,738n. 3,898d.
Post 1994: 33,750g. 17,528n. 3,898d.
Four, 12-cyl. 4 S.C.S.A. (400 x 460mm) Pielstick 12PC2-5V-400 vee type, oil engines made by the shipbuilder, geared in pairs to twin screw shafts with controllable pitch propellers. 31,198 BHP. 20 kts. Two, Thwartship thrust controllable pitch propellers forward.
Ice strengthened, 1,544 berthed, 416 deck passenger / roro cargo/ ferry, with bow door / ramp, and 2 stern door / ramps.
1980: Ordered as SILJA STAR from Oy Wartsila Ab, Turku / Abo (Yard No. 1252), by OY Svea Line, (Silja Line, managers). 22.4.1980: Keel laid. 21.10.1980: Launched as SILVIA REGINA for Oy Svea Line (Finland) Ab, (Stockholms Rederi Ab Svea, managers), Finland. 10.6.1981: Completed. 1982: Sold to Finnish Corporate Finance Ltd., (Finska Angfartygs Ab (EFFOA) (Finland Steamship Company Ltd.), managers), Finland. 1983: Sold to Suomen Yritysrahoitus Oy, (Finska Foretags Finans Ab), (same managers), Finland. 1986: Sold to Johnson Line Ab, (Johnson Shipmanagement Ab, managers), Sweden. 1988: Purchased by Stena Line Ab, (same managers), Sweden. 1989: Transferred to Stena Ab, (same managers). 1990: Oy Silja Line Ab., appointed as managers. 7.1991: Transferred to Sealink Stena Line Ltd., and renamed STENA BRITANNICA. 1994: Transferred to Stena Line Ab, and renamed STENA SAGA. 1995: Transferred to Stena Rederi Ab (Ab Stena Marine, managers), Sweden. 2000: Sold to Stena Sphere Ab., (Stena Line Scandinavia Ab., managers).

LION QUEEN

(Hans Mornhout collection)

F.159. LION QUEEN (1988 - 1990) see ship No. F.57 above.

F.158. BORE GOTHICA (1988 - 1989) see ship No. F.51 above.

F.159. STENA SHIPPER (1) (1988) see ship No. F.26 above.

F.160. STENA SAGA (2) (1988 - 1994) see ship No. F.84 above.

7350442

F.161. SCANDINAVIAN SAGA (1988 - 1991)

As built: 5,259g. 2,752n. 1,361d. 131.98 x 19.84 x 5.284 metres.
Post 1991: 7,764g. 2,752n. 1,361d.
Post 1992: 5,259g. 2,752n. 1,361d.
Post 2001: 9,511g. 3,479n. 1,361d.
Two, 8-cyl. 4 S.C.S.A. (450 x 550mm) MaK 8M551AK type oil engines made by Atlas Mak Maschinenbau, Kiel, geared to twin screw shafts. 8,000 bhp. 17 kts.
550 berthed passenger / roro cargo / 66 x 20' container / ferry, with stern doors.
10.2.1972: Keel laid as CASTALIA by Kynossoura Dock Yard Company Ltd., Salamis (Yard No. 82), for Hellenic Mediterranean Lines Company Ltd., Greece. 10.1.1974: Launched. 14.11.1974: Completed. 1988: Purchased by Stena Gulf Line Ltd., (Stena Ab, managers), Bahamas, and renamed SCANDINAVIAN SAGA. 1991: Transferred to SeaEscape Ltd. Miami, and renamed PRIDE OF SAN DIEGO. 1992: Transferred to Stena America Line Ltd., Bahamas, and renamed TROPIC STAR II. 1995: Renamed STENA ARCADIA. 1997: Sold to Yacatan Shipping Inc., and renamed EMERALD EMPRESS. 1998: Sold to unspecified owners, and renamed SOFIA. 2000: Sold to Albuferra Investments Inc, and renamed ENCHANTED SUN. 2001: Sold to Cardinham International Inc., (Rederi Ab Hoginaut, Sweden, managers), and renamed TALISMAN, under the Bahamas flag. 2001: Sold to Competent Shipping Ltd., Miami, (International Shipping Partners Inc., Miami, managers), and renamed MANISTAL, under the Bahamas flag. 2003: Renamed ST. TROPEZ. 2005: Sold to S Navigation II Ltd., Hialeah, Florida, (Seahawk North America, managers).

7383138

F.162. STENA PROJECT (2) (1988)

As built: 4,452g. 1,935n. 7,207d. 137.70(BB) x 21.04 x 7.16 metres.
Post 1988: 4,112g. 2,035n. 7,207d.
Post 1991: 14,406g. 4,231n. 11,927d. 188.67(BB) x 21.04 x 6.98 metres.
Two, 12-cyl. 4 S.C.S.A. (400 x 460mm) Pielstick 12PC2-2V-400 vee type oil engines made by Lindholmen Motor Ab, Gothenburg, geared to twin screw shafts. 12,000 BHP. 16 kts. Thwartship thrust propeller forward.
Roro cargo, with stern door / ramp, and 324 TEU container ship, with deck guides.
15.2.1973: Ordered as TOR FLANDRIA from Framnaes M.V., Sandefjord (Yard No. 183), by Salenredierna Ab, Sweden, for use in the Tor Line fleet. 14.12.1973: Contract sold and keel laid for Blandford Shipping Company Ltd., (F. Olsen, manager), London. 2.1974: Contract sold to the Australian Shipping Commission, Melbourne. 27.6.1974: Launched as MELBOURNE TRADER. 22.1.1975: Completed and The Australian National Line, appointed managers. 1988: Sold to Bulk Enterprises Ltd., Malta, and renamed RAILRO 2. 1988: Purchased by Stena Ab, and renamed STENA PROJECT. 1988: Transferred to Stena RoRo Line Ltd., (Stena Ab, managers), Malta, chartered to Compagnie Tunisienne de Navition, and renamed MONAWAR L. 1991: Lengthened, transferred to Stena Line Ab, Sweden, and renamed STENA GOTHICA. 1992: Transferred to Scandinavica Ltd., (Ab Stena Marine, managers). 1995: Transferred to Stena Line Ab. 1996: Transferred to Stena Marine Ab. (Stena Line Scandinavia Ab., managers). 2000: Sold to Stena Line Ab., (removed from management). 2004: Sold to Stena Marine Ab., Gothenburg. 2004: Transferred to RoRo Partners Ltd., Cyprus, (Interorient Navigation Ltd., Cyprus, managers), and renamed RORO GOTHICA. under Marshall Islands flag.

F.163. MONAWAR L (1988 - 1991) see ship No. F.162 above.

7320332

F.164. PRINZ HAMLET / STENA BALTICA (6) (1988)

As built: 5,829g. 3,036n. 1,127d. 118.83(BB) x 18.55 x 5.201 metres.
Post 1994: 8,697g. 3,629n. 1,127d.
Four, 6-cyl. 4 S.C.S.A. (410 x 470mm) Werkspoor 6TM410 type oil engines made by Stork-Werkspoor Diesel N.V., Amsterdam, geared in pairs to twin screw shafts with controllable pitch propellers. 16,000 BHP. 20 kts. Thwartship thrust propeller forward.
Ice strengthened, 626 berthed, 294 deck passenger / roro cargo / ferry, with stern door / ramp.
26.5.1973: Launched as PRINZ HAMLET by Werft Nobiskrug GmbH, Rendsburg (Yard No. 679), for Fahrschiffsges Prinz Malcolm, Prinzenlinie, W. Germany. 11.1973: Completed for Prinzenlinien Schiffahrts

GmbH & Co., W. Germany. 1987: Sold to D.F.D.S. AS, Denmark, and renamed PRINS HAMLET. 29.9.1988: Purchased by Sail Pride Inc, Liberia, (Stena Ab). 3.10.1988: Renamed STENA BALTICA. 12.1988: Renamed NIEBOROW for charter to (with an option to purchase) and transferred to Polish Baltic Shipping Company, (Polska Zegluga Baltycka), Poland. 1989: Sold to Polish Baltic Shipping Company, (Polska Zegluga Baltycka), Poland. 1990: Sold to Sail Pride Inc., (Stena Ab, managers), Bahamas, same name. 1993: Polish Baltic Shipping Company, (Polska Zegluga Baltycka), appointed as managers. 2002: Sold to Adriatic Lines, Serbia & Montenegro, (Monship Navigation, managers), and renamed SVETI STEFAN II under the Bahamas flag. 2005: Removed from management.

PRINZ HAMLET arriving at Hamburg in the summer of 1975.

(W.J. Harvey)

VANCOUVER ISLAND PRINCESS

(Internet source / Ted Blank)

5284998

F.165. VANCOUVER ISLAND PRINCESS (1988 - 1993)

5,554g. 2,430n. 416' 0" x 65' 5" x 14' 10¼".

Four, 7-cyl. 4 S.C.S.A. (430 x 545mm) oil engines made by the National Gas & Oil Engine Company, Ashton-under-Lyne, single reduction geared in pairs to twin screw shafts. 700 BHP each.

Post 1974: Four, 12-cyl. 2 S.C.S.A. (230 x 240mm) 12-645-87 vee type oil engines made by General Motors Corp., Electro - Motive Division, La Grange, U.S.A. 4,200 BHP. Thwartship thrust propeller forward.

348 deck passenger / roro cargo / ferry, with bow and stern doors.

7.3.1955: Launched as PRINCESS OF VANCOUVER by A. Stephen and Sons Ltd., Glasgow (Yard No. 646), for Canadian Pacific Railway Company, Canada. 5.5.1955: Completed. 1973: Owners restyled, Canadian Pacific Ltd. 5.1974: Re-engined. 1979: Coastal Marine Operations, appointed as managers. 1981: Owners restyled, Government of Canada, (Ministry of Transportation and Highways for the Province of British Columbia. 1982: Converted from a train / passenger ferry. 1987: Transferred to British Columbia Steamship Company (1975) Ltd., and renamed VANCOUVER ISLAND PRINCESS. 1988: Purchased by Stena Ab. 5.1989: Company restyled as British Colombia Stena Line Ltd. (BC Stena Line). 11.1990: BC Stena Line Ltd. ceased operation. 1993: Sold to Kangda Shipping Company Ltd., China, and renamed NAN HAI MING ZHU. 2001: Sold to Haveton Shipping Ltd., Hong Kong, and renamed PEARL OF SOUTH CHINA SEA, under Panama register.

5284900

F.166. PRINCESS MARGUERITE (1988 - 1991)

5,911g. 2,379n. 373.8 x 56.1 x 25.8 feet.

Two, steam turbines, made by British, Thompson - Houston Company Ltd., Rugby, each driving a generator, powering an electric motor, connected to twin screw shafts. 7,500 BHP. 19 kts.

1,814 deck passenger / roro cargo / ferry, with 2 doors on both port, and starboard sides.

26.5.1948: Launched by Fairfield Company Ltd., Govan, Glasgow (Yard No. 729), for Canadian Pacific Railway Company, Canada. 3.1949: Completed. 1973: Owners restyled Canadian Pacific Ltd. 1975:

Transferred to Province of British Columbia, Department of Lands and Forests, B.C. Steamships., (British Columbia Steamship Company (1975) Ltd., managers), Canada. 1978: Owners restyled Province of British Columbia, (Minister of Transport & Communications - B.C. Ferries), (same managers). 1979: Owners restyled Government of Canada, (Ministry of Transport & Communications for the Province of British Columbia), (same managers). 1983: Owners restyled Government of Canada, (Ministry of Transportation & Highways, for the Province of British Columbia), and removed from management. 1985: Transferred to British Columbia Steamship (1975) Ltd., Canada. 1988: Purchased by Stena Ab. 5.1989: Company restyled as British Colombia Stena Line Ltd. (BC Stena Line). 11.1990: BC Stena Line Ltd. ceased operations. 9.1991: Sold to Seaco Holdings Inc. 1992: Transferred to Vessel Holdings Ltd., Bahamas. 1995: Placed in lay-up at Singapore. 28.6.1996: Lloyds Register class deleted as vessel to be demolished.

PRINCESS MARGURITE (Courtesy Stena Ab)

F.167. KIRK SHIPPER (1988 - 1989) see ship No. F.25 above.

F.168. NIEBOROW (1988 - 1989) see ship No. F.164 above.

F.169. BORE BRITANNICA (1988 - 1989) see ship No. F.51 above.

7807744

F.170. TURELLA (1988 - 1989) / STENA NORDICA (6) (1989 - 1996)

As built: 10,604g. 5,539n. 3,700d. 119.41 x 24.21 x 13.64 metres.
Post 1994: 16,630g. 6,850n. 3,100d.
Post 1994: 16,405g. 7,404n. 3,100d.
Four, 12-cyl. 2 S.C.S.A. (400 x 460mm) Pielstick 12PC2-2V-400 vee type oil engines made by the shipbuilder, geared in pairs to twin screw shafts with controllable pitch propellers. 24,000 BHP. 21.25 kts. Two thwartship thrust propellers forward.
Ice strengthened, 750 berthed & 950 deck passenger / roro cargo / ferry with bow door / ramp and two stern doors / ramps.
10.8.1978: Keel laid by Oy Wartsila Ab, Turku/Abo (Yard No. 1242), for SF Line Ab, Finland. 24.11.1978: Launched. 15.4.1979: Completed. 10.1988: Purchased by Stena Ab. 1.1989: Renamed STENA NORDICA. 1996: Renamed LION KING. 1997: To Estonian flag, (Hansatee Ltd, (A. S. Hansatee manager), appointed as managers). 1998: Sold to Tallink Line Ltd., (HT Shipmanagement Ltd., managers), Estonia, and renamed FANTAASIA. 1999: Sold to Hansatee Ltd, (A. S. Hansatee), Estonia. 2001: Sold to Tallink Group Ltd.

F.171. TARAK L (1988 – 1989) see ship No. F.85 above.

8009014

F.172. STENA TENDER (2) (1989)

As built: 2,831g. 1,437n. 5,000d. 121.49 x 21.03 x 5.301 metres.
Post 1994: 7,817g. 2,346n. 5,000d.
Two, 9-cyl. 4 S.C.S.A. (320 x 420mm) MaK 9M453AK type oil engines made by Krupp MaK. Maschinenbau GmbH, Kiel, geared to twin screw shafts with controllable pitch propellers. 7,200 BHP. 15.5 kts. Thwartship thrust controllable pitch propeller forward.
784 x 20' container / roro cargo carrier, with two stern doors / ramps.
1983: Completed as BALDER SUND by Santierul Naval Galatz, Galatz (Yard No. 764), for KS AS Balder RoRo 2 (Parley Augustsson) (Balder Management AS, managers), Norway. 1985: Sold to Intreprenderee Mecanica Navala, Romania, and renamed BAZIAS 6. 1986: Transferred to Navimpex. 1988: Reverted to Intreprenee Mecanica Navale. 1989: Purchased by Snowdrop Shipping Ltd., (Northern Marine Inc.,

managers), Cyprus, and renamed STENA TENDER. 1989: Transferred to Aubrey Shipping Corp., (Stena Marine Management Hb, managers), Sweden, and renamed TENDER. 1991: Transferred to Stena Tender Line Ltd., (Eaglehurst Ship Management Ltd., managers), Isle of Man, and renamed CITY OF PORT MELBOURNE. 1994: Transferred to Stena Rederi, (Brambles Shipping Division, managers). 1999: Sold to Stena Tender Line Ltd., (Northern Marine Management Ltd., managers), and renamed STENA TENDER, under Isle of Man flag. 2004: Sold to ADNATCO, Abu Dhabi, United Arab Emirates, (same managers), and renamed AL RUWAIS.

8009038

F.173. STENA TIMER (2) (1989)

As built: 2,831g. 1,437n. 5,000d. 121.49 x 21.03 x 5.301 metres.
Post 1994: 7,817g. 2,346n. 5,000d.
Two, 9-cyl. 4 S.C.S.A. (320 x 420mm) MaK 9M453AK type oil engines made by Krupp MaK. Maschinenbau GmbH, Kiel, geared to twin screw shafts with controllable pitch propellers. 7,200 BHP. 15.5 kts. Thwartship thrust controllable pitch propeller forward.
784 x 20' container / roro cargo carrier, with two stern doors / ramps.
1984: Completed as BALDER STRAND by Santierul Naval Galatz, Galatz (Yard No. 766), for KS AS Balder RoRo 2 (Parley Augustsson) (Balder Management AS, managers), Norway. 1985: Sold to Intreprenee Mecanica Navale, Romania, and renamed BAZIAS 8. 1986: Transferred to Navimpex. 1988: Reverted to Intreprenee Mecanica Navale. 1989: Purchased by Stena Challenger Ltd., (Brambles Holdings Ltd., managers), Cyprus, and renamed STENA TIMER. 4.1989: Renamed TASMANIA B. 1991: Renamed CITY OF BURNIE. 1994: Transferred to Stena Rederi, (Brambles Shipping Division, managers). 1999: Sold to Stena RoRo & Ferry Division (Northern Marine Management Ltd., managers), and renamed STENA TIMER, under Isle of Man flag. 2004: Sold to ADNATCO, Abu Dhabi, United Arab Emirates, (same managers), and renamed AL DHAFRAH.

8009026

F.174. STENA TOPPER (2) (1989)

As built: 2,462g. 963n. 5,000d. 121.49 x 21.03 x 5.331 metres.
Post 1994: 7,817g. 2,346n. 5,000d.
Two, 9-cyl. 4 S.C.S.A. (320 x 420mm) MaK 9M453AK type oil engines made by Krupp MaK. Maschinenbau GmbH, Kiel, geared to twin screw shafts with controllable pitch propellers. 7,200 BHP. 15.5 kts. Thwartship thrust controllable pitch propeller forward.
784 x 20' container / roro cargo carrier, with two stern doors / ramps.
1982: Ordered as BALDER VIK, from Santierul Naval Galatz, Galatz (Yard No. 765), by KS AS Balder RoRo 2 (Parley Augustsson), Norway. 1983: Completed for Almira Shipping Corporation, (Balder Management AS, managers), Liberia. 1986: Sold to Intreprenee Mecanica Navale, (Ocean wide Ship Management B.V., managers), Romania, and renamed BAZIAS 7. 1986: Transferred to Navimpex. 1988: Reverted to Intreprenee Mecanica Navale, (Oceanwide Ship Management B.V., managers). 1989: Purchased by Snowdrop Shipping Ltd., (Northern Marine Inc., managers), Cyprus, and renamed STENA TOPPER. 4.1989: Renamed SALAR. 1993: Demise chartered to Belfast Freight Ferries Ltd., (Marine Management Services Ltd., managers), Bahamas, and renamed RIVER LUNE. 1996: Sold to Belfast Freight Ferries Ltd., (Celtic Marine Ltd., appointed as managers). 1999: Sold to Cenargo Navigation (Hong Kong) Ltd., (V-Ships Management Ltd., appointed as managers). 2001: Bluewater Marine management Ltd., appointed as managers. 2004: Sold to Norsemerchant Ferries Ltd., Heysham, (Meridian Marine Management Ltd., Liverpool, managers). 2005: Sold to Swedish Orient Line (Bahamas) Ltd., (OSM Ship Management Ab, Gothenburg, and renamed HANSALAND, under the Bahamas flag.

7525322

F.175. STENA TRANSFER (1) (1989 - 1994)

As built: 4,543g. 1,573n. 6,580d. 140.90(BB) x 21.37 x 7.087 metres.
Post 1989: 15,115g. 9,817n. 9,709d. 179.50(BB) x 21.37 x 6.930 metres.
Two, 12-cyl. 4 S.C.S.A. (400 x 480mm) Sulzer 12ZV40/48 vee type oil engines made by Compagnie de Mecanique Sulzer (CCM), Mantes, geared to twin screw shafts with controllable pitch propellers. 17,400 BHP. 17 kts. Two thwartship thrust controllable pitch propellers forward.
RoRo cargo / 170 x 20' container carrier with stern door / ramp.
1.1.1977: Keel laid as LOTUS by Ankerlokken Verft Floro AS., Floro (Yard No. 108), for Zim Israel Navigation Company Ltd., Israel. 5.1978: Completed. 5.1979: Commissioned. 1989: Purchased by Barbi Shipping Corp., (Stena Ab, managers), Liberia, and renamed STENA TRANSFER. 1989: Lengthened by Cityvarvet Ab, Gothenburg. 1990: Transferred to Stena Ferry Line Ltd., (Northern Marine Management Ltd., managers), Bermuda (O.N.715325). 1994: Demise chartered to Und RoRo Isletmereli A.S., (Northern

Marine Management Ltd., managers), Turkey, and renamed UND TRANSFER. 2002: Sold to Armatori Sardi Srl., Livorno, Italy, and renamed DELFINO GRIGIO.

8416308

F.176. KONINGIN BEATRIX (1989 - 2002)

31,189g. 15,170n. 3,060d. 161.80(BB) x x 6.201 metres

Four, 8-cyl. 4 S.C.S.A. (400 x 450mm) MAN type oil engines made by MAN-B.& W. Diesel GmbH, Augsburg, geared in pairs to twin screw shafts, with controllable pitch propellers. 24,348 BHP. 21 Kts. Two thwartship thrust controllable pitch propellers forward.

557 berthed & 1,543 deck passenger / RoRo cargo / ferry, with two bow doors with one ramp, and three stern door-ramps.

28.1.1985: Keel laid by Van der Giessen-de Noord B.V., Krimpen a/d Ijssel (Yard No. 935), for Stoomvaart Maatschappij Zeeland (Koniklijke Nederlandsche Postvaart N. V.), Holland. 9.11.1985: Launched. 1986: Completed. 1989: Owners restyled as Crown Line B.V. 4.1989: Purchased with Company by Stena Ab, Sweden. 1990: Owners restyled as Stena Line Holland B.V. 1997: Transferred to London flag (Stena Line Ltd., managers). 2000: Sold to Stena Line Ltd. 2002: Transferred to Stena Line B. V., (Stena Line Services Ab., Gothenburg, managers, and renamed STENA BALTICA, under the Bahamas flag. 2004: Sold to Stena Line Ltd., Ashford, Kent, (same managers).

F.177. KIRK TRADER (1989 - 1993) see ship No. F.22 above.

F.178. TASMANIA B (1989 - 1991) see ship No. F.173 above.

F.179. TENDER (1989 - 1991) see ship No. F.172 above.

STENA TRANSPORTER (4)

(Hans Mornhout collection)

7525310

F.180. STENA TRANSPORTER (4) (1989 - 1994)

As built: 4,543g. 1,573n. 6,580d. 140.9(BB) x 21.37 x 7.087 metres.

Post 1989: 15,225g. 9,817n. 9,709d. 179.5(BB) x 21.37 x 6.930 metres.

Post 1992: 15,225g. 4,567n. 9,709d.

Two, 12-cyl. 4 S.C.S.A. (400 x 480mm) Sulzer 12ZV40/48 vee type oil engines made by Compagnie de Mecanique Sulzer (CCM), Mantes, geared to twin screw shafts with controllable pitch propellers. 17,400 BHP. 19 kts. Thwartship thrust controllable pitch propeller forward.

RoRo cargo / 170 x 20' container carrier with stern door / ramp.

11.1977: Completed as JASMINE by Ankerlokken Verft Floro AS., Floro (Yard No. 107), for Zim Israel Navigation Company Ltd., Israel. 1989: Purchased by Surf Pride Inc., (Northern Marine Management Ltd., managers), Liberia, and renamed STENA TRANSPORTER. 9.8.1989: Arrived to be lengthened by Cityvarvet AB, Gothenburg. 10.1989: Work completed and transferred to Stena Pacific Line Ltd., Bermudan flag. 1992: Stena Rederi Abappointed as managers. 1994: Demise chartered to Und RoRo Isletmereli A.S., (Northern Marine Management Ltd., managers), Turkey, and renamed UND TRANSPORTER. 2002: Sold to Armatori Sardi Srl., Italy, and renamed DELFINO BIANCO.

7724241

F.181. STENA PROSPER (2) (1989)

As Built: 2,211g. 611n. 5,200d. 133.05 x 21.05 x 5.031 metres.

Post 1994: 9,377g. 2,813n. 5,200d.

Two, 12-cyl. 4 S.C.S.A. (320 x 420mm) MaK 12M453AK vee type oil engines made by MaK Maschinenbau GmbH, Kiel, geared to twin screw shafts with controllable pitch propellers. 9,000 BHP. 15.5 kts. Thwartship thrust propeller forward.

Ice strengthened 6 berthed passenger / roro cargo / 524 x 20' container carrier, with two stern door / ramps.
1.1.1978: Keel laid as NORWEGIAN CONQUERER by AS. Bergens M.V., Bergen (Yard No.796), for KS AS Stewi II, Steineger & Wiik AS, Norway. 30.3.1979: Launched. 5.2.1980: Completed. 1980: Renamed JOLLY BRUNO. 1982: Sold to Medorient Shipping Line Inc., Panama, and renamed SUSAN A. 4.1989: Purchased by Stena Ab, Sweden, and renamed STENA PROSPER. 5.1989: Chartered to Swedish operators and renamed NORDIC PRIDE with option to purchase for Norwegian NIS flag. 1990: Sold to Partrederi for M.S. Nordic Pride (Rederi Ab Hornet (Hornet Shipping Company), managers). 1994: Sold to Bul Pride Maritime Ltd., (Navigation Maritime Bulgare (NAVIBULGAR), managers), and renamed BUL PRIDE under St. Vincent & The Grenadines flag. 2004: Sold to Fencore Aviation Services Ltd., Waterford, Ireland, (Gotech Fibre Ltd., Waterford, managers), and renamed KILCOE.

STENA PROSPER (2) as **JOLLY BRUNO**
(Hans Mornhout collection)

F.182. NORDIC PRIDE **(1989 - 1990)** see ship No. F.181 above.

F.183. NORMANDIE SHIPPER **(1989 - 1992)** see ship No. F.25 above.

F.184. SCANDINAVICA (2) **(1989 - 1990)** see ship No. F.85 above.

G AND C ADMIRAL
(Hans Mornhout collection)

7616377
F.185. G AND C ADMIRAL (1989 - 1993)
13,379g. 7,487n. 22,858d. 197.52(BB) x 32.26 x 10.027 metres.
Two, 14-cyl. 4 S.C.S.A. (520 x 550mm) MAN 14V52/55A vee type oil engines made by the shipbuilder's Kobe works, geared to a single screw shaft with a controllable pitch propeller. 28,000 BHP. 20 kts. Two, thwartship thrust controllable pitch propellers forward, and a thwartship thrust propeller aft.
Heavy load RoRo cargo / 1315 x 20' container carrier, with side doors / ramps and stern door / ramp.
20.12.1976: Keel laid as SEASPEED AMERICA by Kawasaki Heavy Industries Ltd., Sakaide (Yard No. 1259), for RoRo Charterers Corp., Greece. 15.3.1977: Launched. 26.7.1977: Completed. 11.1977: Sold to Transocean RoRo Corp., (Marship Corp, managers), Greece. 1983: Removed from management. 1986: Transferred to Panamanian flag, (Shipping Management S. A. M. (V.SHIPS), appointed as managers). 1987: Sold to West Side Shipping S. A., Bahamas, and renamed G AND C ADMIRAL. 1989: Purchased by Stena

Ab, (to have been renamed STENA AMERICA), but having had her charter renewed by Grimaldi and Cobelfret, (G AND C) was transferred to Sun Pride Inc. (Marship (Services) Inc., managers), Liberia. 1991: Transferred to Stena Admiral Line Ltd., (same managers), Bahamas. 1993: Renamed STENA AMERICA. 1993: Sold to the Government of The United States of America (Department of Transportation). 5.4.1993: Departed from Le Havre on delivery voyage. 15.4.1993: Arrived at Hampton Roads, and was subsequently renamed CAPE RACE. 22.4.1993: Reported as listed under United States Reserve Fleet. Entry removed from Lloyd's Register – Military service only.

5216147

F.186. STEFAN (3) (1989 - 1991)

11,693g. 5,637n. 7,170d. 153.42 x 21.09 x 8.764 metres.
Two steam turbines manufactured in 1945 by General Elactric Co., Erie, double reduction geared to screw shaft. 8,500 BHP. 16.5 kts.
Passenger ship being used as an accommodation vessel.
7.1952: Completed as MAASDAM by Dok en Werf Mij. Wilton-Fijenoord N.V., Schiedam (Yard No. 733), for Holland America Line N. V. Holland. 1968: Sold to Polish Ocean Lines, Poland, and renamed STEFAN BATORY. 1988: Sold to Erne Compania Maritima S. A., (Hellenic - Polish Shipping & Trading Enterprises Ltd., managers), Panama. 1989: Purchased by City Shipping International Inc., (Stena Rederi, managers), Bahamas, converted into an accommodation ship for refugees, renamed STEFAN, permanantly moored and connected to all municiple services at Gothenburg. 1991: Sold to Courage Maritime S.A., (Marship (Services) Inc., managers), Greece. 17.9.1991: Arrived at Piraeus and laid up. 1992: Tony Travel & Agency Ltd., appointed as managers. 12.1994: Laid up - Surveys Overdue. 12.1996: Damaged by stranding. 1999: Lloyds Register delete managers – to be demolished.

SALAR

(Hans Mornhout collection)

F.187. SALAR (1989 - 1993) see ship No. F.174 above.

F.188. CROWN PRINCESS VICTORIA (1990) see ship No. F.57 above.

F.189. CROWN PRINCESS (1990 - 1991) see ship No. F.57 above.

CAMBRIDGE FERRY

(Internet source)

6400044

F.190. CAMBRIDGE FERRY (1990 - 1992)

3,061g. 1,007n. 1,854d. 122.84 x 18.70 x 3.431 metres.
Two, 7-cyl. 4 S.C.S.A. (381 x 508mm) National Gas KLSSDM-6 type oil engines made by Mirrlees National Ltd., Stockport, geared to twin shafts with controllable pitch propellers. 3,720 BHP. 13.5 kts.
6 cabins, 12 berthed passengers / RoRo cargo / 35 rail vehicles ferry.
6.5.1963: Keel laid by Hawthorn, Leslie (Shipbuilders) Ltd., Hebburn (Yard No. 754), for the British Railways Board. 1.11.1963: Launched. 19.12.1963: Completed. 1979: Owners restyled as Sealink U.K. Ltd. 1990: Purchased by Stena Ab. 1990: Restyled as Sealink UK Ltd., (SEALINK STENA LINE). 3.1992: Sold to Barion S.r.L., Italy, and renamed ITA UNO, under the Maltese flag. 1992: Sold to Sincomar Malta Ltd., (Barion S.r.L., managers), Malta, and renamed SIRIO. 1998: Transferred to Panamanian flag. 26.5.2003: Unspecified shipbreakers commenced work.

7814462

F.191. FANTASIA (1990)

As built: 8,919g. 3,801n. 10,500d. 163.51(BB) x 23.04 x 7.922 metres.
Post 1990: 25,122g. 11,331n. 10,500d. x 27.63 x 8.60 metres.
Post 1999: 25,122g. 11,331n. 3,451d.
Two, 7-cyl. 2 S.C.S.A. (560 x 1,150mm) Sulzer 7RLB56 type oil engines made by Kockums M.V. AB, Malmo, geared to twin screw shafts with controllable pitch propellers. 17,701 BHP. 21 kts. Two tunnel thwartship thrust propellers forward.
Post 1998: Two, 7-cyl. 2 S.C.S.A. (560 x 1,150mm) Sulzer 7RLA56 type oil engines made by Sumitomo Heavy Industries Ltd., Tamashima. 17,701 BHP. 18 kts.
Ice strengthened, 70 cabin, 175 berthed passenger / RoRo cargo/ ferry, with two stern door/ramps.
3.5.1979: Keel laid as SCANDINAVIA by Kockums Varv (Shipyard) Ab. Malmo (Yard No. 569), for Rederi Ab Nordo, Sweden. 1.12.1979: Launched. 17.3.1980: Completed. 1982: Sold to the Government of Bulgaria, and renamed TZAREVETZ. 1988: Sold to Sea Containers Group, Bahamas, and renamed FIESTA. 1989: Transferred to Ro-Ro 1 Ltd., (Sealink U.K. Ltd. (SEALINK BRITISH FERRIES), managers). 1990: Renamed FANTASIA. 1990: Purchased by Stena Ab. 1990: Restyled as Sealink UK Ltd., (SEALINK STENA LINE). 1990: Transferred to Stena Fantasia (FL) Ltd., (same managers), and renamed STENA FANTASIA. 1993: Managers restyled as Stena Sealink Ltd., (STENA SEALINK LINE). 1.1996: Managers restyled as Stena Line Ltd. 1999: Transferred to Stena Equipment & Aircraft Leasing Ltd., (P&O Stena Line Ship Management Ltd., managers), and renamed P&OSL CANTERBURY and re-registered at Dover. 2000: Transferred to Ixora Ltd, (same managers). 2002: Renamed P O CANTERBURY. 2004: Sold to Duana Shipping, (G. A. Shipping, managers), Greece, and renamed ALKMINI A. 2004: Sold to ADABAR, Kolobrzeg, Poland, (Polish Baltic Shipping, managers), Poland, and renamed WAWEL, retaining Bahamas flag.

FIESTA

(Internet source)

7806099

F.192. FIESTA (1990 - 1996)

As built: 8,919g. 3,801n. 10,500d. 163.51(BB) x 23.04 x 7.922 metres.
Post 1990: 25,122g. 11,331n. 10,500d. x 27.63 x 8.60 metres.

Two, 7-cyl. 2 S.C.S.A. (560 x 1,150mm) Sulzer 7RLB56 type oil engines made by Kockums M.V. AB, Malmo, geared to twin screw shafts with controllable pitch propellers. 17,700 BHP. 21 kts. Thwartship thrust propeller forward.
Ice strengthened, 70 cabin, 175 berthed passenger / RoRo Cargo/ Ferry, with two stern door/ramps.
16.3.1979: Keel laid as ARIADNE by Kockums Varv (Shipyard) Ab, Malmo (Yard No. 568), for Rederi Ab Nordo, Sweden. 13.10.1979: Launched. 25.1.1980: Completed. 1980: Renamed SOCA. 1982: Sold to the Government of Bulgaria, and renamed TRAPEZITZA. 1989: Sold to Sea Containers Group, Bahamas, and renamed FANTASIA. 1989: Transferred to Ro-Ro 2 Ltd., (Sealink U.K. Ltd. (SEALINK BRITISH FERRIES), managers), renamed CHANNEL SEAWAY. 1990: Renamed FIESTA. 1990: Sold 51% to Societe Proprietaire des Navires SPN (Societe Nouvelle d'Armement Transmanche (S.N.A.T.)(SEALINK), managers), Paris, France. 1990: 49% share purchased by Stena Ab. 1992: Stena Ab increased their shareholding to 51%. 1996: Renamed SEAFRANCE CEZANNE, (SeaFrance S.A., managers). 2000: Stena sold their holding to SeaFrance S.A., France.

COTE D'AZUR

(Internet source / Andreas Worteler)

7920534

F.193. COTE D'AZUR (1990 - 1995)

8,862g. 2,950n. 1,865d. 130.03(BB) x 23.02 x 5.001 metres.
Two, 18-cyl. 4 S.C.S.A. (400 x 460mm) Pielstick 18PC2-5V-400 vee type oil engines made by Alsthom-Atlantique, Montoir St.Nazaire, geared to twin controllable pitch propellers forward. 22,500 BHP. 18 kts. Twin thwartship thrust controllable pitch propellers forward.
Two cabin, 4 berthed and 1,596 deck passenger ferry with bow & stern doors.
18.4.1980: Keel laid by Societe Nouvelle des Ateliers & Chantiers de Havre, Le Havre (Yard No. 256), for Societe Nationale des Chemins de Fer Francaise (S.N.C.F.), France. 22.12.1980: Launched. 30.9.1981: Completed. 1990: Sold 51% to Societe Proprietaire des Navires (SPN), France & 49% to Sealink UK Ltd., (Societe Nouvelle d'Armement Transmanche (S.N.A.T.)(SEALINK), managers), France. 1990: 49% share purchased by Stena Ab. 1992: Stena Ab increased their shareholding to 51%. 1.1996: Renamed SEAFRANCE RENOIR, (SeaFrance S. A., managers). 2000: Stena sold their holding to SeaFrance S.A., France.

7719430

F.194. GALLOWAY PRINCESS (1990 - 1991)

As built: 6,630g. 3,181n. 1,895d. 129.42(BB) x 21.62 x 4.739 metres.
Post 1994: 12,175g. 3,625n. 1,895d.
Two, 16-cyl. 4 S.C.S.A. (400 x 460mm) Pielstick 16PC2-5V-400 vee type oil engines made by Crossley Premier Engines Ltd., Manchester, geared to twin screw shafts with controllable pitch propellers. 16,000 BHP. 18.5 kts. Twin thwartship thrust propellers forward.
13 cabin, 26 berthed & 974 deck passengers / RoRo cargo / ferry, with stern door & bow door/ramp.
29.9.1978: Keel laid by Harland & Wolff Ltd., Belfast (Yard No. 1713), for the British Railways Board. 24.5.1979: Launched. 31.3.1980: Completed. 18.4.1980: Delivered to Midland Montague Leasing Ltd., (Sealink (Scotland) Ltd., managers), London. 1990: Purchased by Stena Ab. 1990: Restyled as Sealink UK Ltd., (SEALINK STENA LINE). 1991: Sold to NWS 11 Ltd., and renamed STENA GALLOWAY. 1993: Managers restyled as Stena Sealink Ltd., (STENA SEALINK LINE). 1.1996: Managers restyled as Stena Line

Ltd. 1998: Transferred to P&O Stena Line Ltd., (same managers). 1999: Transferred to Stena Line Ltd. 2000: Sold to NWS 11 Ltd. 2002: Sold to Internationa Maritime Transport Group (I.M.T.G.), Casablanca, Morocco, and renamed LE RIF.

HENGIST

(Internet source / Andreas Worteler)

7205063

F.195. HENGIST (1990 - 1991)

As built: 5,590g. 2,008n. 1,030d. 118.09 x 19.84 x 4.117 metres.
Post 1994: 8,129g. - n. 1,050d.
Post 1998: 5,122g. 2,610n. 1,050d.
Two, 16-cyl. 4 S.C.S.A. (400 x 460mm) Pielstick 16PC2-2V-400 vee type oil engines manufactured, Port side by Atelier & Chantier de Nantes (Bretagne-Loire), Nantes, & starboard side by Chantiers de l'Atlantique, Nantes, geared to twin screw shafts with controllable pitch propellers. 15,000 BHP. 19.5 kts. Thwartship thrust propeller forward.
7 cabin, 24 berthed & 1,376 deck passenger /RoRo cargo / ferry, with bow & stern doors.
15.4.1971: Keel laid by Arsenal de la National Francaise, Brest (Yard No. CF.1), for the British Railways Board. 10.2.1972: Launched. 19.5.1972: Completed. 1979: Owners restyled as Sealink U.K. Ltd. 1990: Purchased by Stena Ab. 1990: Restyled as Sealink UK Ltd., (SEALINK STENA LINE). 1991: Renamed STENA HENGIST. 3.1992: Sold to Tilos Shipping Company S.A., Greece, and renamed ROMILDA. 1993: Sold to Apollon Express 2 Shipping Company, (Ventouris Sea Lines, managers), Greece, and renamed APOLLON EXPRESS. 2.1996: Sold to Mios Naftiki Eteria, (Agapitos Lines, managers), Greece, and renamed PANAGIA EKATONTAPYLIANI. 2000: Sold to Minoan Flying Dolphins Maritime S.A., Greece, and renamed EXPRESS ARTEMIS. 2001: Sold to Hellas Flying Dolphins Maritime S.A., Piraeus, Greece, and renamed PANAGIA HRISOVALANTOU. 2004: Renamed AGIOS GEORGIOS. 2005: Sold to Panagia Odigitria Shipping SA, Piraeus.

HORSA

(Internet source / Gordon Hislip)

7205075

F.196. HORSA (1990 - 1991)

As built: 5,590g. 2,008n. 1,030d. 118.09 x 19.84 x 3.960 metres.
Post 1994: 7,685g. –n. 1,014d.
Post 1998: 5,109g. 2,581n. 1,014d.
Two, 16-cyl. 4 S.C.S.A. (400 x 460mm) Pielstick 16PC2-2V-400 vee type oil engines manufactured, Port side by Attelier & Chantiers de Nantes (Bretagne-Loire), Nantes, & starboard side by Chantiers de l'Atlantique, Nantes, geared to twin screw shafts with controllable pitch propellers. 15,000 BHP. 19.5 kts. Thwartship thrust propeller forward.
7 cabin, 24 berthed & 1,376 deck passenger / RoRo cargo / ferry, with bow & stern doors.
15.4.1971: Keel laid by Arsenal de la National Francaise, Brest (Yard No. CF.2), for the British Railways Board. 10.2.1972: Launched. 27.7.1972: Completed. 30.7.1972: Arrived at Dover. 1979: Owners restyled as Sealink U.K. Ltd. 1990: Purchased by Stena Ab. 1990: Restyled as Sealink UK Ltd., (SEALINK STENA LINE). 1991: Renamed STENA HORSA. 1992: Sold to Agoudimos Lines Shipping Company, Greece, and renamed PENELOPE A. 1995: Flanmare Shipping Inc., appointed as managers. 2000: Sold to Minoan Flying Dolphins Maritime S.A., Greece, and renamed EXPRESS PENELOPE. 2001: Owners restyled as Hellas Flying Dolphins Maritime S.A., Piraeus. 2004: Sold to Aegean Islands Shipping S.A., Piraeus, (Hellas Flying Dolphins Shipping S.A., managers), and reverted to PENELOPE A.

7813937

F.197. ST. ANSELM (1990)

As built: 7,405g. 3,659n. 1,829d. 129.65(BB) x 21.62 x 5.011 metres.
Post 1994: 12,705g. 3,811n. 1,895d.
Two, 16-cyl. 4 S.C.S.A. (400 x 460mm) Pielstick 16PC2-5V-400 vee type oil engines made by A. P. E. Crossley Ltd., Manchester, geared to twin screw shafts with controllable pitch propellers. 20,800 BHP. 19.5 kts. Two thwartship thrust propellers forward.
15 cabin, 30 berthed & 1370 deck passengers / RoRo cargo / ferry, with stern door & bow door/ramp.
22.2.1979: Keel laid by Harland & Wolff Ltd., Belfast (Yard No. 1715), for the British Railways Board. 5.12.1979: Launched. 16.10.1980: Completed for Lloyds Leasing Ltd., (Sealink U.K. Ltd., managers), London. 1990: Managers purchased by Stena Ab, and restyled as Sealink Stena Line Ltd. 1990: Restyled as Sealink UK Ltd., (SEALINK STENA LINE). 10.1990: Purchased by R. B. Equipment and Aircraft Leasing Ltd., and renamed STENA CAMBRIA, during refit on Tyneside. 1992: Owners restyled as R. B. Equipment Leasing Ltd., (same managers). 1993: Managers restyled as Stena Sealink Ltd., (STENA SEALINK LINE). 1.1996: Managers restyled as Stena Line Ltd. 1999: Sold to Umafisa Cataluna S. A., (Umafisa Lines, managers) Ibiza, Spain, and renamed ISLA DE BOTAFOC.

ST CHRISTOPHER

(Internet source / Andreas Worteler)

7813949

F.198. ST. CHRISTOPHER (1990 - 1991)

As built: 7,399g. 3,655n. 2,092d. 129.62(BB) x 21.62 x 5.011 metres.
Post 1994: 12,711g. 3,813n. 2,092d.
Two, 16-cyl. 4 S.C.S.A. (400 x 460mm) Pielstick 16PC2-5V-400 vee type oil engines made by A. P. E. Crossley Ltd., Manchester, geared to twin screw shafts with controllable pitch propellers. 20,800 BHP. 19.5 kts. Two thwartship thrust propellers forward.
15 cabin, 30 berthed & 1,370 deck passengers / RoRo cargo / ferry, with stern door & bow door/ramp.
18.6.1979: Keel laid by Harland & Wolff Ltd., Belfast (Yard No. 1716), for the British Railways Board. 20.3.1980: Launched. 9.3.1981: Completed for Barclays Mercantile & Industrial Finance Ltd., (Sealink

U.K. Ltd. managers), London. 1990: Managers purchased by Stena Ab, and restyled as Sealink Stena Line Ltd. 1990: Restyled as Sealink UK Ltd., (SEALINK STENA LINE). 1991: Renamed STENA ANTRIM. 1993: Transferred to Stena Equipment and Aircraft Leasing Ltd., (STEAL), (same managers). 1993: Managers restyled as Stena Sealink Ltd., (STENA SEALINK LINE). 1.1996: Managers restyled as Stena Line Ltd. 1998: Sold to Lignes Maritimes du Detroit SA., (LIMADET), Tangier, Morocco, and renamed IBN BATOUTA.

ST COLUMBA

(Internet source)

7507019

F.199. ST. COLUMBA (1990 - 1991)

As built: 7,836g. 3,790n. 1,945d. 129.22 x 21.24 x 4.676 metres.
Post 1994: 11,690g. 3,539n. 1,945d.
Two, 16-cyl. 4 S.C.S.A. (410 x 470mm) Werkspoor 167M410 vee type oil engines made by Stork-Werkspoor Diesel B.V., Amsterdam, geared to twin screw shafts with controllable pitch propellers. 18,000 BHP. 19.5 kts. Thwartship thrust propeller forward.
26 cabins, 52 berthed & 2,209 deck passengers / RoRo Cargo / Ferry, with bow door/ramp & stern door.
28.11.1975: Keel laid by Aalborg Vaerft AS., Aalborg (Yard No. 214), for the British Railways Board. 17.7.1976: Launched. 1.4.1977: Completed. 1979: Owners restyled as Sealink U.K.Ltd. 1990: Purchased by Stena Ab. 1990: Restyled as Sealink UK Ltd., (SEALINK STENA LINE). 1991: Renamed STENA HIBERNIA. 1993: Owners restyled as Stena Sealink Ltd., (STENA SEALINK LINE). 1.1996: Owners restyled as Stena Line Ltd. 2.1996: Renamed STENA ADVENTURER. 1997: Sold to Express Tinos Shipping Company (Agapitos Express Ferries, managers) Greece, and renamed EXPRESS APHRODITE. 2000: Sold to Minoan Flying Dolphins Maritime S.A., Greece. 2001: Owners restyled as Hellas Flying Dolphins Maritime S.A. 2005: Renamed EXPRESS APHRODITI.

ST CYBI

(Hans Mornhout collection)

F.200. ST. CYBI (1990 - 1991) see ship No. F.69 above.

ST DAVID

(Internet source / Aubrey Dale)

7910917

F.201. ST. DAVID (1990 - 1991)

As built: 7,196g. 3,543n. 2,206d. 129.65(BB) x 21.62 x 4.841 metres.
Post 1994: 12,619g. 3,652n. 2,206d.
Post 2000: 132.00(BB) metres.
Two, 16-cyl. 4 S.C.S.A. (400 x 460mm) Pielstick 16PC2-5V-400 vee type oil engines made by A. P. E. Crossley Ltd., Manchester, geared to twin screw shafts with controllable pitch propellers. 20,800 BHP. 18.5 kts. Two thwartship thrust propellers forward.
23 cabin, 46 berthed & 1,154 deck passengers / RoRo cargo / ferry, with stern door & bow door/ramp.
12.12.1979: Keel laid by Harland & Wolff Ltd., Belfast (Yard No. 1717), for the British Railways Board. 25.9.1980: Launched. 23.7.1981: Completed for Barclays Mercantile & Industrial Finance Ltd., (Sealink U.K. Ltd. managers), London. 1990: Managers purchased by Stena Ab, and restyled as Sealink Stena Line Ltd. 1990: Restyled as Sealink UK Ltd., (SEALINK STENA LINE). 1991: Purchased by Stena Equipment and Aircraft Leasing Ltd. (STEAL), and renamed STENA CALEDONIA. 1993: Managers restyled as Stena Sealink Ltd., (STENA SEALINK LINE). 1.1996: Managers restyled as Stena Line Ltd. 1998: Sold to P&O Stena Line Ltd., (same managers). 1998: Sold to City Leasing Ltd., London, (same managers). 1999: Sold to Stena Line Ltd., Ashford. 2001: Sold to Stena Florida Line Ltd., Clydebank, (same managers).

ST NICHOLAS shortly after entering the Sealink Harwich – Hook of Holland charter – still with a Stena -Sessan colour scheme less the S on the funnel

(Internet source / Cees De Bijl)

F.202. ST. NICHOLAS (2) (1990 - 1991) see ship No. F.99 above.

6417047

F.203. EARL WILLIAM (1990 - 1992)

As built: 3,984g. 1,943n. 928d. 99.50 x 17.73 x 4.420 metres.
Post 1994: 5,739g. 2,546n. 928d.
Post 1997: 3,984g. 2,546n. 928d.

Two, 12-cyl. 4 S.C.S.A. (400 x 460mm) Pielstick 12PC2-2V-400 vee type oil engines made by Lindholmens Varv Ab, Goteborg, geared to twin controllable pitch propellers. 12,000 BHP. 18 kts. Thwartship thrust propeller forward.
42 cabin, 126 berthed and 1,118 deck passenger/ RoRo cargo/ ferry with bow door/ramp & stern door/ramp.
1964: Completed as VIKING II by Kaldnes M.V. AS, Tonsberg (Yard No.160), for Thoresen Car Ferries, Norway. 1964: Renamed CARFERRY VIKING II. 1977: Sold to Lloyds Leasing Ltd., London, on behalf of Sealink UK Ltd., who were appointed as lease managers, and renamed EARL WILLIAM. 1987: Used as an accommodation ship, at Harwich, for illegal immigrants. 1990: Charterers / managers purchased by Stena Ab, and restyled as Sealink UK Ltd., (SEALINK STENA LINE). 3.1992: Sold to Barion S.r.L., Italy, and renamed WILLIAM, under the Maltese flag. 1992: Sold to Adonis Shipping Company Ltd., Malta, and renamed PEARL WILLIAM. 1994: Ionian Ferries Ltd., appointed as managers. 1996: Sold to P. & L. Ferries Shipping Company S.A., and renamed MAR JULIA under the Maltese flag. 1997: Sold to Lucky Shipping S. A., St. Vincent & The Grenadines, and renamed CESME STERN 2001: Sold to Windward Lines Ltd., (Windward Agencies Ltd., managers), St Michael, Barbados, and renamed WINDWARD II., retaining St Vincent & The Grenadines flag.

EARL WILLIAM

(Internet source / Terence Mitchell)

7301491

F.204. STENA SEATRADER (3) (1990 -)

As built: 5,160g. 1,598n. 2,985d. 148.01 x 22.13 x 5.538 metres.
Post 1982: 6,926g. 2,874n. 6,850d. 182.73 x 22.13 x 6.220 metres.
Post 1994: 17,991g. 5,379n. 6,850d.
Two, 8-cyl. 4 S.C.S.A. (400 x 460mm) Pielstick 8PC2L-400 type oil engines (centre)
Two, 6-cyl. 4 S.C.S.A. (400 x 460mm) Pielstick 6PC2L-400 type oil engines (wings)
All made by Lindholmen Motor Ab, Gothenburg, single reduction geared to twin screw shafts with controllable pitch propellers. 14,000 BHP. 17.5 kts. Two thwartship thrust controllable pitch propellers forward.
Ice strengthened, 32 berthed & 4 deck passenger / Roro cargo ferry, with a port and starboard quarter stern door / ramp.
Post 1996: 100 berth.
19.5.1972: Keel laid as SVEALAND by AS Nakskov Skibsvaerft, Nakskov (Yard No. 199), for Lion Ferry Ab, Sweden. 11.1.1973: Launched. 12.9.1973: Completed. 1982: Lengthened and renamed SVEALAND AV MALMO. 1987: Sold to Rederi Ab Nordo-Link, Sweden, and renamed SVEA LINK. 1990: Purchased by Stena Line B.V., Holland, and renamed STENA SEATRADER. 1990: Transferred to Fernwood Inc., (Northern Marine Management Ltd., managers), Bahamas. 1990: Transferred to Lily Shipping B.V., Amsterdam. 1997: Transferred to Stena Line Holland B. V. 1998: Transferred to P&O Stena Line Ltd., (Stena Line Ltd., managers). 1999: Transferred to Stena Line Ltd. 2000: Sold to Stena Line B.V. 2001: Sold to Stena Line Holland B.V., Hoek van Holland, (Northern Marine Management Ltd., Clydebank, managers).

6915881

F.205. STENA SEARIDER (2) (1990 - 1991)

As built: 6,209g. 2,275n. 4,650d. 137.34 x 24.54 x 5.716 metres.
Post 1984: 5,863g. 2,519n. 4,725d. 178.70 x 24.54 x 5.716 metres.
Post 1987: 20,914g. 6,274n. 14,800d. 178.70 x 24.54 x 5.716 metres.

Two, 12-cyl. 4 S.C.S.A. (400 x 460mm) Pielstick 12PC2-2V-400 vee type oil engines made by the shipbuilder at Turko/Abo, reduction geared to twin controllable pitch propellers. 11,160 BHP. 18 kts. Thwartship thrust propeller forward.
Ice strengthened, passenger / RoRo cargo / rail vehicle ferry with two stern door/ramps.
6.6.1968: Keel laid as FINNCARRIER by Oy Wartsila Ab, Helsinki / Helsingfors (Yard No. 390), for Merivienti Oy, (Oy Finnlines Ltd., managers), Finland. 26.3.1969: Launched. 15.11.1969: Completed. 1972: Sold to Enso-Gutzeit Oy, (same managers), Finland. 1975: Renamed POLARIS. 1980: Sold to Finska Angfartygs Ab (EFFOA) (Finland Steamship Company Ltd), Finland. 1984: Sold to Rederi Ab Nordo, Sweden, and renamed SCANDINAVIA. 1987: Sold to Rederi Ab Nordo-Link, Sweden, lengthened and renamed SCANDINAVIA LINK. 1990: Purchased by Stena Ab, and renamed STENA SEARIDER. 1991: Transferred to Fernwood Inc., (Northern Marine management Ltd., managers), Bahamas. 1991: Renamed SEARIDER. 1992: Transferred to Stena Searider Ltd., (same managers), and renamed STENA SEARIDER. 1992: Renamed NORSE MERSEY for charter to Norse Irish Ferries Ltd. 1995: Transferred to Stena Line Treasury Ab, Sweden, and renamed STENA SEARIDER. 1995: Transferred to Stena Marine Ab, Sweden. 1996: Transferred to Stena Line Treasury Ab, (Stena Line Scandinavia Ab, managers). 1997: Sold to Stena Line Ltd., and transferred to London flag. 1998: Sold to P&O Stena Line Ltd., (Stena Line Ltd., managers). 1999: Sold to Stena Line Ltd. 2000: Sold to Stena Line Scandinavia Ab., (Stena Line Ltd., managers), retaining British flag. 2004: Northern Marine Management Ltd., Clydebank, appointed managers.

STENA SEARIDER (2) (Internet source)

6405434

F.206. EMPRESS (1990 - 1991)

As built: 12,037g. 6,657n. 2,880d. 135.64 x 21.52 x 6.116 metres.
Post 1985: 8,187g. 3,853n. 2,353d.
Post 1991: 13,176g. 5,032n. 2,725d.
Two, 10-cyl. 2 S.C.S.A. (570 x 800mm) MAN type oil engines made by Maschinenfabrik - Augsburg - Nuernburg (MAN), Hamburg, geared to twin screw shafts. 13,500 BHP. 17 kts.
124 cabins, 260 berthed, 190 deck passenger/ vehicle roro ferry with a stern door/ramp.
Post 1991: 301 cabins, 623 berthed passenger vessel.
11.9.1962: Keel laid as EMPRESS OF AUSTRALIA by Cockatoo Docks Sydney (Yard No. 220), for the Australian Coastal Shipping Commission, (Australian Navigation Line, managers). 18.1.1964: Launched. 8.1.1965: Completed for the Australian National Line. 1972: Modified by New South Wales Government Engineering & Shipbuilding Undertaking (State Dockyard), Newcastle N.S.W. which involved internal reconstruction and alteration to passenger capacities. 1985: Sold to Falcon Maritime Company, (Tony Travel & Agency Ltd., managers), Greece, and renamed EMPRESS. 1990: Purchased by Stena Ab, (same managers), for conversion into a passenger vessel to be renamed STENA EMPRESS. 1991: Sold to Anchor of the Seas Ltd., (same managers), Nassau, and renamed ROYAL PACIFIC. 8.1992: Sunk following a collision with an unspecified Taiwanese trawler.

8317954

F.207. NIELS KLIM (1990 - 1991)

As built: 19,763g. 6,180n. 2,568d. 134.02(BB) x 24.62 x 5.541 metres.
Post 1992: 11,602g. 6,154n. 2,568d.
Post 1996: 19,763g. 5,928n. 2,500d.

Two, 8-cyl. 2 S.C.S.A. (450 x 1,200mm) B&W 8L45GB type oil engines made by B&W Maskfabrik Division of B&W Diesel AS, Copenhagen, geared to twin screw shafts with controllable pitch propellers. 14,420 BHP. 17 kts. Two thwartship controllable pitch propellers forward & one aft.
Ice strengthened, 74 cabins, 148 berthed & 1,852 deck passengers / RoRo cargo / ferry, with bow door/ramp & two stern door/ramps 1 x port & starboard.
21.11.1984: Keel laid by AS Nakskov Skibsvaerft, Nakskov (Yard No. 234), for the Government of the Kingdom of Denmark (Danske Statsbaner). 29.5.1985: Launched. 21.4.1986: Completed. 1990: Purchased by Stena Ab. 1991: Renamed STENA NAUTICA. 1992: Transferred to Stena Nautica Line Ltd., (Sealink U.K. Ltd., (SEALINK STENA LINE), managers), Bermuda, and renamed ISLE OF INNISFREE, (O.N. 716308) for charter to Irish Continental Group plc (IRISH FERRIES). 1992: Irish Continental Group plc (IRISH FERRIES), appointed as managers. 1995: Released from charter reverted to but not registered as STENA NAUTICA and laid up at Dunkirk. 1995: Lion Ferry Ab appointed as managers, and renamed LION KING. 30.4.1996: Renamed LION KING II 6.5.1996: Renamed STENA NAUTICA, (same managers). 1998: Transferred to Bermudan flag. 2000: Sold to Stena Sphere Ab., (Stena Line Scandinavia Ab., managers). 2003: Sold to Stena Nautica Ab, Gothenburg, (same managers). 2.2004: Whilst on passage from Grenaa to Varberg in thick fog, suffered collision damage from the St Vincent registered JOANNA. It was intended to beach vessel to prevent sinking but tugs succeeded in stabilising and towing her into Varberg, temporary repairs undertaken and vessel towed to Gothenburg's Cityvarvet for permanent repairs.

8317942

F.208. PEDER PAARS (1990 - 1991)

19,763g. 6,180n. 2,813d. 134.02(BB) x 24.62 x 5.650 metres.
Two, 8-cyl. 2 S.C.S.A. (450 x 1,200mm) B&W 8L45GB type oil engines made by B&W Maskfabrik Division of B&W Diesel AS, Copenhagen, geared to twin screw shafts with controllable pitch propellers. 14,420 BHP. 17 kts. Two thwartship controllable pitch propellers forward & one aft.
Ice strengthened, 74 cabins, 148 berthed & 1,852 deck passengers / RoRo cargo / ferry, with bow door/ramp & two stern door/ramps 1 x port & starboard.
4.5.1984: Keel laid by AS Nakskov Skibsvaerft, Nakskov (Yard No. 233), for the Government of the Kingdom of Denmark (Danske Statsbaner). 21.11.1984: Launched. 18.10.1985: Completed. 2.1.1986: Delivered. 1990: Purchased by Stena Ab. 7.1991: Transferred to Stena Empress Ltd., (Sealink U.K. Ltd., (SEALINK STENA LINE), managers), and renamed STENA INVICTA, (O.N.704405). 1993: Managers restyled as Stena Sealink Ltd., (STENA SEALINK LINE). 1998: Sold to P&O Stena Line Ltd., (Stena Line Ltd., managers). 1999: Sold to Stena Line Ltd. 2000: Sold to P&O Stena Line (Ships) Ltd., (P&O Stena Line Ship Management Ltd., managers), and renamed COLOR VIKING. 2001: Sold to Color Line ASA, Oslo, (Color Line Marine AS, Sandefjord, managers).

NIEBOROW

(Hans Mornhout collection)

F.209. NIEBOROW **(1990 - 2002)** see ship No. F.164 above.

F.210. STENA FANTASIA **(1990 - 1999)** see ship No. F.191 above.

F.211. STENA CAMBRIA **(1990 - 1999)** see ship No. F.197 above.

STENA CAMBRIA

(Hans Mornhout collection)

F.212. SALAH L. (1990 - 1993) see ship No. F.101 above.

F.213. STENA GOTHICA (3) (1991 - 2004) see ship No. F.162 above.

F.214. STENA HENGIST (1991 - 1992) see ship No. F.195 above.

F.215. STENA HORSA (1991 - 1992) see ship No. F.196 above.

F.216. STENA HIBERNIA (1991 - 1996) see ship No. F.199 above.

STENA CALEDONIA

(Hans Mornhout collection)

F.217. STENA CALEDONIA (1991 -) see ship No. F.201 above.

STENA GALLOWAY although constructed with the same hull form as her three sisterships, she had a different superstructure.

(Internet source / Marko Stampehl)

F.218. STENA GALLOWAY (1991 - 2002) see ship No. F.194 above.

F.219. STENA ANTRIM (1991 - 1999) see ship No. F.198 above.

STENA ANTRIM

(Hans Mornhout collection)

F.220. STENA NORMANDY **(1991 - 1997)** see ship No. F.99 above.

F.221. PACIFIC STAR **(1991 - 1993)** see ship No. F.57 above.

F.222. STENA NAUTICA (4) **(1991 - 1992)** see ship No. F.207 above.

F.223. STENA INVICTA **(1991 - 2000)** see ship No. F.208 above.

STENA CHALLENGER (2)

(Internet source / Marko Stampehl)

8917388

F.224. STENA CHALLENGER (2) (1991 - 2000)

18,523g. 5,556n. 4,650d. 154.00(BB) x 24.30 x 5.515 metres.

Two, 8-cyl. 4 S.C.S.A. (400 x 560mm) Sulzer 8ZA40S type oil engines made by Oy Wartsila Ab, Turku/Abo, geared to twin screw shafts with controllable pitch propellers. 14,346 BHP. 17.5 kts.

RoRo cargo / 92 berthed 500 deck passenger ferry, with bow and stern door/ramps and a container capacity for 240 TEU.

13.3.1990: Keel laid by Bruces Verkstads Ab, Landskrona (Yard No.20) as a sub-contract to Fosens Mekaniska Verkstaeder, Fevaag. 26.9.1990: Launched. 24.5.1991: Completed by Fosens Mekaniska Verkstaeder, Fevaag (Yard No. 50), for Stena RoRo Ab. 7.1991: Additional refinements completed for Stena Equipment & Aircraft Leasing Ltd., (Sealink U.K. Ltd., (SEALINK STENA LINE), managers). 1993: Managers restyled as Stena Sealink Ltd., (STENA SEALINK LINE). 1998: Sold to P&O Stena Line Ltd., (Stena Line Ltd., managers). 1999: Sold to Stena Line Ltd. 2000: Sold to Marine Atlantic Inc., North Sydney N.S., Canada, and back-chartered until delivery of STENA FORWARDER in 2001. 2001: Renamed LEIF ERICSON. under the Canada flag.

F.225. STENA TRAILER (4) **(1991 - 1993)** see ship No. F.146 above.

F.226. CITY OF BURNIE **(1991 - 1999)** see ship No. F.173 above.

F.227. CITY OF PORT MELBOURNE **(1991 - 1999)** see ship No. F.172 above.

F.228. TRAILER **(1991)** see ship No. F.146 above.

STENA BRITANNICA (3)

(Hans Mornhout collection)

F.229. STENA BRITANNICA (3) **(1991 - 1994)** see ship No. F.156 above.

F.230. SEARIDER (2) **(1991 - 1992)** see ship No. F.205 above.

F.231. EUROPEAN FREEWAY **(1991 - 1994)** see ship No. F.52 above.

F.232. PRIDE OF SAN DIEGO **(1991 - 1992)** see ship No. F.161 above.

STENA TRAVELLER (2)

(Hans Mornhout collection)

8917390

F.233. STENA TRAVELLER (2) (1991 - 1992)

18,332g. 5,499n. 6,003d. 154.00(BB) x 24.33 x 5.515 metres.

Two, 8-cyl. 4 S.C.S.A. (400 x 560mm) Sulzer 8ZA40S type oil engines made by Oy Wartsila Ab, Turku/Abo, geared to twin screw shafts with controllable pitch propellers. 12,203 BHP. 18 kts. Thwartship thrust controllable pitch propellers forward and aft.

RoRo cargo / 92 berthed 500 deck passenger ferry, with bow and stern door/ramps and a container capacity for 240 TEU.

9.10.1990: Keel laid by Bruces Verkstads Ab, Landskrona (Yard No.21) as a sub-contract to Fosens Mekaniska Verkstaeder, Fevaag. 26.3.1991: Launched. 5.1991: Externally completed. 4.9.1991: Completed by Fosens Mekaniska Verkstaeder, Fevaag (Yard No. 51), for Stena RoRo Ab, Sweden. 1992: Transferred to Stena Rederi Ab, and renamed TT TRAVELLER. 1995: Reverted to STENA TRAVELLER. 1996: Transferred to Stena RoRo & Ferry Division, (Stena Line Ltd., managers), and reverted to TT TRAVELLER. 2002: Renamed STENA TRAVELLER. 2004: Sold to Aukse Multipurpose Shipping Ltd, (Lisco Baltic Service Ab, Klaipeda, managers), Lithuania, and renamed LISCO PATRIA.

F.234. EUROPEAN TIDEWAY **(1992 - 1994)** see ship No. F. 47 above.

F.235. STENA SEARIDER (2) **(1992)** see ship No. F.205 above.

F.236. ISLE OF INNISFREE **(1992 - 1995)** see ship No. F.207 above.

F.237. TROPIC STAR II **(1992 - 1995)** see ship No. F.161 above.

F.238. NORSE MERSEY (1) **(1992 - 1995)** see ship No. F.205 above.

STENA LONDONER

(Hans Mornhout collection)

F.239. STENA LONDONER (1992 - 1996) see ship No. F. 28 above.

STENA PARISIEN

(Hans Mornhout collection)

8208763

F.240. STENA PARISIEN (1992 - 1996)

15,093g. 8,965n. 2,430d. 130.21(BB) x 23.02 x 5.022 metres.
Two, 16-cyl. 4 S.C.S.A. (400 x 460mm) Pielstick 16PC2-6V-400 vee type oil engines made by Alsthom-Atlantique, St. Nazaire, geared to twin screw shafts with controllable pitch propellers. 21,537 BHP. 21 kts. Two thwartship thrust controllable pitch propellers forward.
2 cabin / 4 berthed and 1,800 deck passenger / roro cargo ferry with bow door and ramp and stern door ramp.
30.11.1982: Keel laid as CHAMPS ELYSEES by Chantiers Dubigeon S.A. Prairie-au-Duc, Nantes (Yard No.167), for Societe Nationale des Chemins de Fer Francais (S.N.C.F.), France. 20.12.1983: Launched. 2.10.1984: Completed. 1992: Purchased and renamed STENA PARISIEN, registered owners remaining Societe Nationale des Chemins de Fer Francais (S.N.C.F.), France. 1996: Transferred to SeaFrance S.A., and renamed SEAFRANCE MANET.

F.241. TT TRAVELLER (1992 - 1995) see ship No. F.233 above.

F.242. SENATOR (1993 - 1994) see ship No. F.101 above.

F.243. SUN FIESTA (1993 - 1994) see ship No. F. 57 above.

F.244. MEDFERRY EXPRESS (1993 – 1999) see ship No. F.146 above.

F.245. RIVER LUNE **(1993 – 1996)** see ship No. F.174 above.

F.246. LION QUEEN **(1994 - 1997)** see ship No. F. 57 above.

F.247. STENA MARINER **(1994 - 1995)** see ship No. F.101 above.

F.248. UND TRANSFER **(1994 - 2002)** see ship No. F.175 above.

F.249. UND TRANSPORTER **(1994 - 2002)** see ship No. F.182 above.

STENA CLIPPER

(Hans Mornhout collection)

7724710

F.250. STENA CLIPPER **(1994 - 2003)**

As built: 6,341g. 3,281n. 11,020d. 147.89(BB) x 24.03 x 8.114 metres.
Post 1994: 15,365g. 4,609n. 11,020d.
12-cyl. 4 S.C.S.A. (520 x 550mm) MAN 12V52/55A type oil engine made by the shipbuilder, geared to a controllable pitch propeller. 12,660 BHP. 18 kts. Thwartship thrust propeller forward.
RoRo cargo / 568 TEU container carrier with an angled side door/ramp and two stern door/ramps.
10.2.1978: Keel laid as BUTTERFLY by Kawasaki Heavy Industries Ltd., Kobe (Yard No. 1276), for Boxley Shipping Ltd., Singapore. 21.7.1978: Launched. 27.10.1978: Completed. 1982: Sold to Lancaster Transport Company Ltd., Liberia, and renamed BALDER TRADER. 1982: Renamed NOPAL TRADER. 1982: Reverted to BALDER TRADER. 1985: Sold to Riverdale Transport Company Ltd., Liberia, and renamed RIVERDALE. 1987: Sold to Foramco Shipping Ltd., Liberia, and renamed KUMASI. 1989: Sold to Al Baraka Investment & Development Company, (Compagnie Marocaine de Navigation (COMONAV), Morocco, managers), Panama, and renamed ASNI. 1994: Sold to Stena Admiral Line Ltd., (Northern Marine Management Ltd., managers), Bahamas flag, and renamed STENA CLIPPER. 2003: Sold to unspecified Belize flag operators, and renamed CLIPPER. 1.11.2003: Beached at Alang for demolition.

F.251. STENA EUROPE **(1994 - 1997)** see ship No. F. 84 above.

F.252. STENA SAGA (3) **(1994 -)** see ship No. F.156 above.

LION KING (1)

(Hans Mornhout collection)

F.253. LION KING (1) **(1995 - 1996)** see ship No. F.207 above.

F.255. STENA NAUTICA (4) **(1995)** see ship No. F.207 above.

F.255. STENA SEARIDER (2) **(1995 -)** see ship No. F.205 above.

STENA SHIPPER (3)

(Hans Mornhout collection)

7909621

F.256. STENA SHIPPER (3) (1995 - 2005)

As built: 5,200g. 2,600n. 9,325d. 168.81(BB) x 20.22 x 6.452 metres.
Post 1981: 5,120g. 2,569n. 9,235d. x 6.460 metres.
Post 1996: 12,337g. 3,701n. 8,765d.
As built: 8-cyl. 4 S.C.S.A. (620 x 660mm) oil engine made by Stork-Werkspoor Diesel B.V., Amsterdam. 13,000 BHP. 18.5 kts. Thwartship propeller forward and aft.
Post 1983: 6-cyl. 4 S.C.S.A. (580 x 600mm) 6M601AK type oil engine made by Krupp MaK Maschinenbau GmbH, Kiel, geared to a controllable pitch propeller. 7,995 BHP. 17 kts. Thwartship propeller forward and aft.
Post 1995: 8-cyl. 4 S.C.S.A. (580 x 640mm) MAN/B&W 8L58/64 type oil engine made by MAN B&W Diesel AG, Germany, geared to a controllable pitch propeller. 11,120 BHP. 17 kts. Thwartship propeller forward and aft.
Post 1986: Ice strengthened, RoRo Cargo / vehicles ferry / 600 TEU container carrier, with angled stern door/ramps.
Ice strengthened, RoRo Cargo / vehicles ferry / 600 TEU container carrier, with slewing stern door/ramp.
28.3.1979: Keel laid as NESTOR by Jos L. Meyer, Papenburg (Yard No. 588), for Reederei Gerhard Schepers, W. Germany. 12.1979: Completed. 1981: Sold to m.s. "Nestor" Schiffahrts GmbH & Co. K.G., W.Germany. 1984: Renamed NESTOR I. 1985: Renamaed NESTOR. 1986: Sold to Sorinco-Marinw S.a.r.L., Togo. 1987: Renamed AFRICAN GATEWAY. 1989: Scorpion Schiffahrts-gesellschaft m.b.H., appointed as managers, and renamed NESTOR. 1990: Renamed CARIBBEAN STREAM. 1991: Mammoet-Hansa Linie A.G, appointed as managers and renamed NESTOR. 1995: Purchased by Stena Florida Line Ltd., (Northern Marine Management Ltd., Clydebank, managers), Bahamas, and renamed STENA SHIPPER. 24.3.1995: Arrived at Hamburg to be re-engined by Blohm and Voss. 1999: Transferred to U.K. flag. 2004: Transferred to Global Navigation Ltd., Bemuda, (Stena RoRo Ab, Gothenburg, managers), retaining British flag. 3.2005: Renamed VOLGA HIGHWAY for charter, (Northern Marine Management Ltd., Clydebank, managers).

F.257. STENA TRAVELLER (2) **(1995 - 1996)** see ship No. F.233 above.

F.258. STENA ARCADIA **(1995 - 1997)** see ship No. F.161 above.

9080194

F.259. STENA EXPLORER (2) (1996 -)

19,638g. 5,892n. 1,500d. 126.6 x 40.0 x 27.5 height & 4.5 draught metres.

Two General Electric LM2500 and two LM1600 type gas turbines made by Kvaerner Brug AS, Norway, double reduction geared and driving four KaMeWa steerable water jet propulsion units. 67,975 BHP. 40 Kts. Two Contra-rotating KaMeWa type bow thrusters.
1,520 passenger Catamaran type ferry and RoRo ferry for 375 cars or 50 artic-trucks and 120 cars. 4 stern doors.
28.9.1984: Keels laid by Finnyards, Rauma (Yard No. 404), for Stena Ab, Sweden. 19.5.1995: Launched. 16.2.1996: Completed ready for trials. 11.4.1996: Delivered to Stena Ferries Ltd., (Stena Line Ltd., Ashford, managers) London. 2004: Sold to Stena International Ltd., Ashford, Kent, (same managers).

STENA EXPLORER (2) (Courtesy Alan Geddes)

F.260. LION KING II / STENA NAUTICA (4) **(1996 -)** see ship No. F.207 above.

F.261. LION KING (2) **(1996 - 1998)** see ship No. F.170 above.

STENA ADVENTURER (1)

(Courtesy Alan Geddes)

F.262. STENA ADVENTURER (1) **(1996 - 1997)** see ship No. F.199 above.

F.263. STENA EMPEREUR **(1996 - 1998)** see ship No. F.111 above.

9125944

F.264. STENA JUTLANDICA III (1996)

26,691g. 9,046n. 6,750d. 182.50 (BB) x 28.30 x 6.00 metres.
Two, 9-cyl. 4 S.C.S.A. (400 x 540mm) MAN 9L40/54 type oil engines made by MAN B&W Diesel A.G., Germany, geared to twin screw shafts with controllable pitch propellers. 35,238 BHP. 22 kts. Twin thwartship thrust controllable pitch propellers forward.
200 berthed & 1,500 deck passenger / RoRo / Rail vehicle/ ferry with bow and stern doors& ramps and two side doors and ramps on port side.

17.7.1995: Keel laid: by Van Der Giessen du Noord, B.V., Krimpen aan den Ijssel (Yard No. 967), for Stena Rederi, Sweden. 2.3.1996: Launched. 6.1996: Completed. 1996: Renamed STENA JUTLANDICA. 2000: Sold to Stena Sphere Ab., (Stena Line Scandinavia Ab., managers).

STENA VOYAGER moving stern first to her berth at Belfast

(Courtesy Alan Geddes)

9080209

F.265. STENA ENTERPRISE (2) / STENA VOYAGER (1996 -)

19,638g. 5,892n. 1,320d. 126.6 x 40.0 x 27.5 height & 4.5 draught metres.
Two General Electric LM2500 and two LM1600 type gas turbines made by Kvaerner Brug AS, Norway, double reduction geared and driving four KaMeWa steerable water jet propulsion units. 67,975 BHP. 40 kts. Two Contra-rotating KaMeWa type bow thrusters.
1,520 passenger Catamaran type ferry and RoRo ferry for 375 cars or 50 artic-trucks and 120 cars. 4 stern doors.
15.5.1995: Keel laid as STENA ENTERPRISE by Finnyards, Rauma, (Yard No. 405), for Stena Ab, Sweden. 23.2.1996: Launched as STENA VOYAGER. 5.6.1996: Completed for Stena Line Ltd., London. 2004: Sold to Stena International Ltd., Ashford Kent, (Stena Line Ltd., Ashford, managers).

STENA JUTLANDICA (3)

(Hans Mornhout collection)

F.266. STENA JUTLANDICA (3) (1996 -) see ship No. F.264 above.

F.267. TT TRAVELLER (1996 - 2002) see ship No. F.233 above.

9107590

F.268. STENA ENDEAVOUR (2) /STENA DISCOVERY (1997 -)

19,638g. 5,891n. 1,500d. 126.6 x 40.0 x 27.5 height & 4.5 draught metres.
Two General Electric LM2500 and two LM1600 type gas turbines made by Kvaerner Brug AS, Norway, double reduction geared and driving four KaMeWa steerable water jet propulsion units. 67,975 BHP. 42 Kts. Two Contra-rotating KaMeWa type bow thrusters.
1,520 passenger Catamaran type ferry and RoRo ferry for 375 cars or 50 artic-trucks and 120 cars. 4 stern doors.

11.3.1996: Keel laid as STENA ENDEAVOUR by Finnyards, Rauma, (Yard No. 407), for Stena Ab, Sweden. 14.12.1996: Launched as STENA DISCOVERY. 17.4.1997: Completed for Stena Line B. V. Hoek van Holland. 2000: Sold to Stena Line Ab., (Stena Line Holland B. V., managers). 2001: Sold to Stena Line Ships B.V., Hoek van Holland.

STENA DISCOVERY moving stern first to her berth at Belfast

(Courtesy Alan Geddes)

STENA CARISMA

(Hans Mornhout collection)

9127760

F.269. STENA CARISMA (1997 -)

8,361g. 2,589n. 480d. 88.0 x 30.00 x 3.900 metres.

Two gas turbines made by ABB Stal Ab, Finspang, geared to steerable water jet propulsion units. 44,861 BHP. 38 kts.

850 passenger Catamaran type ferry and RoRo ferry for cars or artic-trucks / stern doors.

11.9.1995: Keel laid by Westamarin AS, Norway, (Yard No. 238) for Stena Line Ab, (Stena Line Scandinavia Ab, managers), Sweden. 28.6.1996: Launched. 6.1997: Completed. 2000: Transferred to Stena Line Scandinavia Ab, and removed from management.

LION EUROPE

(Hans Mornhout collection)

F.270. LION EUROPE (1997 - 1999) see ship No. F.84 above.

STENA ROYAL

(Internet source / Marko Stampehl)

8908466

F.271. STENA ROYAL (1998 - 1999)

28,833g. 11,853n. 4,694d. 163.40(BB) x 27.70 x 6.500 metres

Four, 8-cyl. 4 S.C.S.A. (400 x 560mm) Sulzer 8ZAL40S type engines made by Jugoturbina Diesel d.d., Karlovac, geared in pairs to twin controllable pitch propellers. 28,713 BHP. 21 kts. Twin thwartship tunnel thrusters forward.

121 cabin / 434 berthed 918 deck passengers/ Roro cargo / ferry with bow and stern doors.

2.5.1990: Keel laid as PRINS FILIP by N. V. Boelwerf S. A., Tamise (Yard No. 1534) for Ship Finance N.V., (Regie Voor Maritiem Transport, managers), Belgium. 1.3.1991: Launched. 27.4.1992: Completed. 22.5.1997: Laid up. 23.11.1998: Sold to Stena Ferries Ltd., (Stena RoRo & Ferry Division, managers), London, and renamed STENA ROYAL. Under the Bermudan flag. 1999: Renamed P&OSL AQUITAINE, (P&O Stena Line Ship Management Ltd., managers), registered at Dover. 2002: Renamed P O AQUITAINE. 2003: Renamed PRIDE OF AQUITAINE. 2004: Sold to Stena International Ltd., Ashford, (P&O Ferries Ship Management Ltd., Dover, managers). 1.9.2005: Placed in lay-up upon closure of route. 9.2005: Renamed NORMAN SPIRIT. 12.2005: Sold to Louis Dreyfus Lines SAS, (V.Ships Leisure, Monaco, managers), under the Italian flag.

STENA PARTNER (1)

(Hans Mornhout collection)

7909982

F.272. STENA PARTNER (1) (1998)

As Built: 15,952g. 6,751n. 20,450d. 199.39(BB) x 28.02 x 9.002 metres

Post 1994: 33,652g. 10,183n. 20,972d.

Two, 6-cyl. 2 S.C.S.A. (680 x 1250mm) Sulzer 6RND68M type engines made by H. Ceglielski Zaklady Przemyslu Metalowego, Poznan, geared to screw shafts. 21,230 BHP. 19 kts. Twin thwartship thrust controllable pitch propellers forward.

1,050 TEU container carrier / RoRo cargo ferry with a slewing stern ramp port & starboard aft.

15.6.1981: Keel laid as FINNCLIPPER by Kockums Ab, Malmo (Yard No. 579) for Ab Skarhamn Oljetransport, (O. T. Rederierna, managers), Sweden. 24.10.1981: Launched. 17.12.1981 Completed. 1983: Sold to Zenit Dry Cargo Ab., (Zenit Shipping Ab, managers), Sweden, and renamed ZENIT CLIPPER. 1986: Sold to to American Transport Lines (AMTRANS), (Pacific-Gulf Marine Inc., managers), San

Francisco, and renamed AMERICAN FALCON. 1987: Crowley Maritime Corp., appointed as managers. 1994: Sold to Crowley American Transport Inc., Miami. 1998: Stena Rederi, and renamed STENA PARTNER. 1998: Renamed TOR FLANDRIA. 2000: Sold to DFDS Tor Line Ab. 2003: Sold to Scandinavian RoRo Ab, (DFDS Tor Line Ab, managers), Gothenburg.

7909970

F.273. STENA PORTER (1998)

As Built: 15,952g. 6,751n. 20,731d. 193.61(BB) x 28.02 x 9.219 metres
Post 1994: 33,652g. 10,183n. 20,972d.
Two, 6-cyl. 2 S.C.S.A. (680 x 1250mm) Sulzer 6RND68M type engines made by H. Ceglielski Zaklady Przemyslu Metalowego, Poznan, geared to screw shafts. 21,230 BHP. 19 kts. Twin thwartship thrust controllable pitch propellers forward.
1,050 TEU container carrier / RoRo cargo ferry with a slewing stern ramp port & starboard aft.
26.6.1980: Keel laid as KUWAIT EXPRESS by Kockums Ab, Malmo (Yard No. 578) for Lars Georg Johansson, Sweden. 24.1.1981: Launched. 13.4.1981 Completed. 1983: Sold to Zenit Dry Cargo Ab., (Zenit Shipping Ab, managers), Sweden, and renamed ZENIT EXPRESS. 1984: Sold to Automar II Corp., (Pacific-Gulf Marine Inc., managers), San Francisco, and renamed AMERICAN CONDOR. 1987: Sold to to American Transport Lines (AMTRANS), (Crowley Maritime Corporation, managers). 1994: Sold to Crowley American Transport Inc., Miami. 1998: Stena Rederi, and renamed STENA PORTER. 1998: Renamed TOR SCANDIA. 2000: Sold to DFDS Tor Line Ab. 2001: Sold to Orondo Ltd., (DFDS Tor Line Ab, managers. 2003: Sold to Scandinavian RoRo Ab, (DFDS Tor Line Ab, managers), Gothenburg.

SEA CENTURION

(Internet source / Tom Grootenboer)

9138783

F.274. STENA AUSONIA / SEA CENTURION (1998 - 2003)

21,104g. 6,331n. 12,350d. 179.30 x x 7.400 metres.
Four, 8-cyl. 4 S.C.S.A. (400 x 560mm) Sulzer 8ZA40S type engines made by New Sulzer Diesel France, Mantes, geared in pairs to twin controllable pitch propellers. 31,323 BHP. 22 kts.
Ice strengthened, 12 berthed passenger - RoRo cargo ferry with stern door ramp and container capacity of 800 TEU.
15.6.1996: Keel laid by Societa Esercizio Cantieri S.p.A., Viareggio, Italy (Yard No. 1546) by Stena Rederi. 7.1997: Launched as STENA AUSONIA for Stena RoRo Line Ltd. 1997: Chartered / sold to Und RoRo Isletereli A.S., Turkey, and was to have been completed as UND EGE. 1998: Deliveries of Yard No. 1546 and 1548 were exchanged. 7.1998 Completed for Stena International Ltd (Northern Marine Management Ltd., Glasgow, managers), as SEA CENTURION for charter to the Royal Fleet Auxiliary / Ministry of Defence, London. 2003: Stena International Ltd., Ashford, Kent, (Northern Marine Management Ltd., Clydebank, managers), and renamed MONT VENTOUX. 2005: Renamed STENA FORWARDER.

F.275. TOR FLANDRIA (1998 - 2000) see ship No. F.272 above.

F.276. TOR SCANDIA (1998 - 2000) see ship No. F.273 above.

F.277. STENA PRINCE (1998 - 1999) see ship No. F.102 above.

F.278. STENA EUROPE (1998 -) see ship No. F. 84 above.

STENA EUROPE

(Internet source)

F.279. STENA TENDER (2) (1999 - 2004) see ship No. F.172 above.

F.280. STENA TIMER (2) (1999 - 2004) see ship No. F.173 above.

FINNCLIPPER

(Hans Mornhout collection)

9137997
F.281. STENA SEAPACER 1 / FINNCLIPPER (1999 - 2001)
30,500g. 7,000d. 188.30 (BB) x 29.30 x 6.50 metres.
Four 8-cyl. 4 S.C.S.A. (400 x 560mm) Sulzer 8ZAL40S type engines made by New Sulzer Diesel France, Mantes, geared in pairs to twin controllable pitch propellers. 31,323 BHP. 22 kts. 2 thwartship thrust propellers forward.
191 cabins / 440 berthed passengers RoRo cargo ferry.
14.2.1997: Keel laid as STENA SEAPACER 1 by Astilleros Espanoles S. A. (AESA) Factoria de Puerto Real, Cadiz (Yard No. 78). 1.2.1998: Launched for Stena Line Ab. 1998: Charter agreed with Finnlines. 18.5.1999: Completed as FINNCLIPPER for Stena Ferries Ltd., (Stena Line Ltd., managers), and registered at Luebeck, Germany. 2001: Sold to Poseidon Schiffahrt AG., Germany. 2002: Sold to Finnlines Deutschland GmbH & Company. 2002: Sold to Finnlines Oy, Finland. 2005: Sold to Ropax 1 Clipper Ab, Malmo, (Finnlines Ship Management Ab, Malmo, managers).

9138006
F.282. STENA SEAPACER 2 / FINNEAGLE (1999 - 2001)
30,500g. 7,000d. 188.30 (BB) x 29.30 x 6.50 metres.
Four 8-cyl. 4 S.C.S.A. (400 x 560mm) Sulzer 8ZAL40S type engines made by New Sulzer Diesel France, Mantes, geared in pairs to twin controllable pitch propellers. 31,323 BHP. 22 kts. 2 thwartship thrust propellers forward.
191 cabins / 440 berthed passengers RoRo cargo ferry.
26.6.1997: Keel laid as STENA SEAPACER 2 by Astilleros Espanoles S. A. (AESA) Factoria de Puerto Real, Cadiz (Yard No. 79). 18.4.1998: Launched for Stena Line Ab. 1998: Charter agreed with Finnlines. 10.1999: Completed as FINNEAGLE for Stena Ferries Ltd., (Stena Line Ltd., managers), and registered at Luebeck, Germany. 2001: Sold to Poseidon Schiffahrt AG., Germany (FG Shipping Oy Ab, Sweden,

managers), and transferred to Swedish flag. 2004: Sold to Nordo-Link Ab., Malmo (Nordo-Link Management Ab, managers), Malmo. 2005: Finnlines Ship Management Ab, Malmo, appointed as managers.

FINNEAGLE

(Hans Mornhout collection)

STENA BRITANNICA (4)

(Internet source / Cees De Bijl)

9145164

F.283. STENA SEAPACER 3 / STENA BRITANNICA (4) (2000 - 2003)

33,769g. 10,630n. 7,456d. 188.30 (BB) x 29.30 x 6.310 metres.
Four 8-cyl. 4 S.C.S.A. (400 x 560mm) Sulzer 8ZAL40S type engines made by New Sulzer Diesel France, Mantes, geared in pairs to twin controllable pitch propellers. 31,323 BHP. 22 kts. 2 thwartship thrust propellers forward.
192 cabins / 452 berthed passengers RoRo cargo ferry.
3.3.1999: Keel laid as STENA SEAPACER 3 from Astilleros Espanoles S. A. (AESA) Factoria de Puerto Real, Cadiz (Yard No. 80), for Stena Marine Ab 21.12.1999: Launched as STENA HOLLANDICA for Baobab Ltd., (Stena Line Ltd., managers). 25.8.2000: Completed for Stena Line Ltd., (Stena Line Holland B. V. managers), London. 2003: Sold to Finnlines Plc., and renamed FINNFELLOW under Swedish flag. 2004: Sold to Nordo-Link Ab., (Nordo-Link Management Ab, managers), Malmo. 2005: Finnlines Ship Management Ab, Malmo, appointed as managers.

9145176

F.284. STENA SEAPACER 4 / STENA HOLLANDICA (2001 -)

33,769g. 10,630n. 7,456d. 188.30 (BB) x 29.30 x 6.310 metres.
Four 8-cyl. 4 S.C.S.A. (400 x 560mm) Sulzer 8ZAL40S type engines made by New Sulzer Diesel France, Mantes, geared in pairs to twin controllable pitch propellers. 31,323 BHP. 22 kts. 2 thwartship thrust propellers forward.
192 cabins / 452 berthed passengers RoRo cargo ferry.
4.6.1999: Keel laid as STENA SEAPACER 3 from Astilleros Espanoles S. A. (AESA) Factoria de Puerto Real, Cadiz (Yard No. 81), for Stena Marine Ab 6.5.2000: Launched as STENA HOLLANDICA. 11.2000: Scheduled delivery to Baobab Ltd., (Stena Line Ltd., managers). 5.2.2001: Completed for Stena Ferries Ltd., Ashford, Kent, (Stena Line Holland B. V., Hoek van Holland, managers), London.

STENA HOLLANDICA

(Internet source)

STENA FORETELLER

(Internet source / Dirk Jankowsky)

9214666

F.285. STENA FORETELLER (2001 - 2002) Stena 4-runner Mk2 class.

24,688g. 7,407n. 12,300d. 195.30 (BB) x 26.80 x7.300 metres

Four 8-cyl. 4 S.C.S.A. (400 x 500mm) Sulzer 8ZA40S type engines made by New Sulzer Bros. Ltd., Winterthur, geared in pairs to twin controllable pitch propellers. 32,628 BHP. 22.5 kts. Twin thwartship thrust propellers forward.

Ice strengthened Ro-Ro cargo vessel with stern door ramp and container capacity of 849 TEU.

12.4.2000: Keel laid by Dalian Shipyard, Dalian, China (Yard No. RO123-1), for Stena RoRo Line Ab, Gothenburg, (Northern Marine Management Ltd., Clydebank, managers), under the Swedish flag. 14.10.2000: Launched. 25.12.2001: Completed. 2002: Renamed CETAM MASSILIA. 1.12.2003: Renamed STENA FORETELLER.

CETAM MASSILIA

(Internet source / Lars Helge Isdahl)

F.286. CETAM MASSILIA (2002 - 2003) see ship No. F. 285 above.

FLANDERS

(Hans Mornhout collection)

F.287. FLANDERS / STENA TRANSPORTER (5) (2002 -) see ship No. F. 55 above.

STENA TRANSPORTER (5)

(Hans Mornhout collection)

FREEWAY

(Hans Mornhout collection)

F.288. FREEWAY / STENA PARTNER (2) (2002 -) see ship No. F. 53 above.

STENA PARTNER (2)

(Hans Mornhout collection)

IDEWAY

(Internet source / Rob De Visser)

F.289. IDEWAY / STENA TRANSFER (2) (2002 -) see ship No. F. 47 above.

STENA TRANSFER (2)

(Internet source)

F.290. STENA TRAVELLER (2) (2002 - 2004) see ship No. F. 233 above.

F.291. STENA BALTICA (7) (2002 -) see ship No. F. 176 above.

F.292. P O AQUITAINE (2002 - 2003) see ship No. F. 271 above.

F.293. PRIDE OF AQUITAINE (2003 - 2005) see ship No. F. 271 above.

STENA BRITANNICA (5)

(Internet source / Cees De Bijl)

9235517

F.294. STENA BRITANNICA II / STENA BRITANNICA (5) (2003 -)

43,487g. 18,963n. 9,763d. 210.80(BB) x 29.88 x 6.3 metres

Four 9-cyl. 4 S.C.S.A. (400 x 540mm) MAN 9L40/54 type 8,810bhp oil engines made by MAN B&W Diesel AG, Germany, geared in pairs to twin controllable pitch propellers. 35,240 BHP. 22 kts. Twin thwartship thrust propellers forward.

Roro / 900 passenger (298 deck; 602 berthed in 246 cabins) ferry with bow ramp and visor and stern ramp door.

4.2.2002: Keel laid by Hyundai Heavy Industries Company Ltd., Ulsan (Yard No. 1392), for Seaspray Leasing Ltd., London, (Stena Line Holland B.V., Hoek van Holland, operating managers). 31.5.2002: Launched. 7.1.2003: Completed. 2003: Renamed STENA BRITANNICA.

STENA ADVENTURER (2)

(Courtesy Trevor Kidd)

9235529

F.295. STENA ADVENTURER (2) (2003 -)

43,532g. 17,935n. 9,487d. 210.80(BB) x 29.88 x 6.3 metres

Four 9-cyl. 4 S.C.S.A. (400 x 540mm) MAN 9L40/54 type 8,810bhp oil engines made by MAN B&W Diesel AG, Germany, geared in pairs to twin controllable pitch propellers. 35,240 BHP. 22 kts. Twin thwartship thrust propellers forward.

Roro / 900 passenger (298 deck; 602 berthed in 246 cabins) ferry with bow ramp and visor and stern ramp door.

3.6.2002: Keel laid by Hyundai Heavy Industries Company Ltd., Ulsan (Yard No. 1393), for Swan National Ltd., London, (Stena Line Ltd, Ashford, operating managers). 6.10.2002: Launched. 16.5.2003: Completed.

STENA FORECASTER

(Internet source / Jan Moller)

9214678

F.296. STENA FORECASTER (2003 -) Stena 4-runner Mk2 class.

24,688g. 7,407n. 12,300d. 195.30 (BB) x 26.80 x 7.300 metres

Four 8-cyl. 4 S.C.S.A. (400 x 500mm) Sulzer 8ZA40S type engines made by New Sulzer Bros. Ltd., Winterthur, geared in pairs to twin controllable pitch propellers. 32,628 BHP. 22.5 kts. Twin thwartship thrust propellers forward.

Ice strengthened Ro-Ro cargo vessel with stern door ramp and container capacity of 849 TEU.

12.7.2000: Keel laid by Dalian Shipyard, Dalian, China (Yard No. RO123-2), for Stena RoRo Ab, Gothenburg, (Northern Marine Management Ltd., Clydebank, managers), under the Swedish flag. 26.12.2000: Launched. 28.4.2003: Completed.

9227259

F.297. STENA FORERUNNER (2003 -) Stena 4-runner Mk2 class.

24,688g. 7,407n. 12,300d. 195.30 (BB) x 26.80 x 7.300 metres

Four 8-cyl. 4 S.C.S.A. (400 x 500mm) Sulzer 8ZA40S type engines made by New Sulzer Bros. Ltd., Winterthur, geared in pairs to twin controllable pitch propellers. 32,628 BHP. 22.5 kts. Twin thwartship thrust propellers forward.
Ice strengthened Ro-Ro cargo vessel with stern door ramp and container capacity of 849 TEU.
27.12.2000: Keel laid by Dalian Shipyard, Dalian, China (Yard No. RO123-3), for Stena RoRo Ab, Gothenburg, (Northern Marine Management Ltd., Clydebank, managers), under the Swedish flag. 26.4.2001: Launched. 29.8.2003: Completed.

STENA FORERUNNER

(Internet source / Jan Moller)

MONT VENTOUX (1)

(Internet source / Lars Helge Isdahl)

F.298. MONT VENTOUX (1) (2003 - 2005) see ship No. F.274 above.

OIHONNA

(Internet source / Dirk Jankowsky)

8222111

F.299. OIHONNA (2003)

20,203g. 6,061n. 12,870d. 155.00(BB) x 25.15 x 8.465 metres

Two 12-cyl. 4 S.C.S.A. (400 x 460mm) Pielstick 12PC2-6V-400 vee type oil engines made by Oy Wartsila Ab, Turku, geared to twin controllable pitch propellers. 17,944 BHP. 17.25 kts. Thwartship thrust controllable pitch propeller forward and aft.

Paper carrying RoRo-cargo vessel with 6 cabins for 12 berthed passangers and a container capacity for 608 TEU.

22.4.1983: Keel laid as OIHONNA by Rauma Repola Oy, Rauma (Yard No. 284), for Effoa – Finska Angfartygs Ab, Helsingfors, Finland. 21.10.1983: Launched. 27.4.1984: Completed. 1986: Sold to Oy Finncarriers Ab, Helsingfors. 2001: Transferred to Finnlines Oy, Helsingfors. 11.2.2003: Sold to Stena RoRo Ab, Gothenburg. 1.4.2003: Delivered. 11.4.2003: Sold to Imperial RoRo Ab, Gothenburg, (OSM Ship Management Ab, Gothenburg, managers), and renamed VASALAND.

STENA CARRIER II

(Internet source / Dirk Jankowsky)

STENA CARRIER (5)

(Courtesy Stena Ab)

9138800

F.300. STENA GRECIA / GRECIA / SEA CENTURION / UND EGE (Proposed) /STENA CARRIER II / STENA CARRIER (5) (2004 -)

21,089g. 6,327n. 12,350d. 182.77(BB) x 25.52 x 6.600 metres.

Four, 8-cyl. 4 S.C.S.A. (400 x 560mm) Sulzer 8ZA40S type engines made by New Sulzer Diesel France, Mantes, geared in pairs to twin controllable pitch propellers. 31,323 BHP. 22 kts.

Ice strengthened, 12 berthed passenger, Ro-Ro cargo vessel with stern door ramp and container capacity of 800 TEU.

18.10.1997: Keel laid by Societa Esercizio Cantieri S.p.A., Viareggio, (Yard No. 1548), for 1998 delivery to Stena RoRo Line Ltd. 23.10.1999: Launched as STENA GRECIA for Stena RoRo Line Ltd., and fixed with a long-term charter to the Ministry of defence (Navy), London, whilst fitting out and was to have been completed as SEA CENTURION for operation by the Royal Fleet Auxiliary, London. 1998: Yard No. 1546 and 1548 were swopped and this one was to have been completed as UND EGE for sale / charter to Und RoRo Isletereli A.S. Turkey, but shipyard encountered financial difficulties and closed. 11.2000: Vessel incomplete and offered for sale as charter cancelled. 15.3.2004: Completed by Nuovi Cantieri Apuania SpA., di Carrara (Yard No.1231), as ARONTE for Finanzaria Navigazione, Italy, under Ireland flag. 2004: Purchased by Stena RoRo Line Ab., Gothenburg, and renamed STENA CARRIER II then STENA CARRIER. 2005: Transferred to Stena Line Scandinavia Ab, Gothenburg.

STENA FREIGHTER (3)

(Internet source / Dirk Jankowsky)

9138795

F.301. STENA HISPANICA (2) / SEA CHIEFTAIN / STENA SEAFREIGHTER / STENA FREIGHTER (3) (2004 -)

14,500g. 7,800n. 10,048d. 182.76 x 25.52 x 6.500 metres.

Four, 8-cyl. 4 S.C.S.A. (400 x 560mm) Sulzer 8ZA40S type engines made by New Sulzer Diesel France, Mantes, geared in pairs to twin controllable pitch propellers. 31,323 BHP. 22 kts.

Ice strengthened, 12 berthed passenger, Ro-Ro cargo vessel with stern door ramp and container capacity of 800 TEU.

19.2.1997: Keel laid as STENA HISPANICA by Societa Esercizio Cantieri S.p.A., Viareggio, Italy (Yard No. 1547), for Stena RoRo Line Ltd. 9.5.1998: Launched for Stena RoRo Line Ltd., but fixed with a long-term charter to the Ministry of Defence (Navy), London, whilst fitting out. 1999: To be completed as SEA CHIEFTAIN for charter to the Royal Fleet Auxiliary / Ministry of Defence, London, but shipyard encountered financial difficulties and closed. 12.3.2004: Completed by Elektromehanika d.o.o., Rijeka, as STENA SEAFREIGHTER, for Wheelhouse (Bermuda) Ltd., Bermuda.. 2004: Sold to Stena Freighter Ab., (Stena Line Scandinavia Ab, managers), Gothenburg, and renamed STENA FREIGHTER.

ENVOY

(Internet source / Rolf Formo)

7716074

F.302. EUROPEAN ENVOY / ENVOY (2004)

As built; 6,310g. 2,091n. 5,024d. 150.02(BB) x 21.77 x 13.01 metres.
Post 1996: 18,653g. 5,595n. 4,267d. 150.02(BB) x 24.43 x 5.115 metres.
Two 12-cyl. 4 S.C.S.A. (420 x 450mm) Mitsui 12V42M vee type oil engines made by the shipbuilder, geared to twin controllable pitch propellers. 18,000 BHP. 18.75 kts. Three thwartship thrust controllable pitch propellers forward and one aft.
Post 1996: 70 deck passenger / roro cargo vessel
11.9.1978: Keel laid as IBEX by Mitsui Engineering & Shipbuilding Company Ltd., Tamano, (Yard No. 1163), for P&O Ferries Ltd. 27.12.1978: Launched. 15.5.1979: Completed. 30.12.1980: Renamed NORSEA. 31.12.1984: Transferred to POETS Fleet Management Ltd. 23.8.1986: Renamed NORSKY. 1995: Transferred to Pandoro Ltd., (P&O European Ferries (Irish Sea) Ltd., managers), and renamed IBEX, under the Bermudan flag. 1996: Widened and converted. 1997: Renamed EUROPEAN ENVOY. 2004: Sold to Stena Line Ltd. 2004: Renamed ENVOY. 2004: Sold to KystLink AS, Langesund, same name.

EUROPEAN LEADER at Larne whilst in transition, with the funnel painted red. (Courtesy Trevor Kidd)

F.303. EUROPEAN LEADER / STENA LEADER (2004 -) see ship No. F.33 above.

EUROPEAN SEAFARER leaving Larne whilst in transition, with the bottom of the funnel painted red. (Courtesy Trevor Kidd)

F.304. EUROPEAN SEAFARER / STENA SEAFARER (2004 -) see ship No. F. 34 above.

EUROPEAN PIONEER leaving Larne whilst in transition, with the Stena funnel almost painted . (Courtesy Trevor Kidd)

F.305. EUROPEAN PIONEER / STENA PIONEER (2004 -) see ship No. F. 32 above.

STENA PIONEER

(Internet source / Rob De Visser)

STENA NORDICA (7)

(Internet source / Preben Morgensen)

9215505

F.306. EUROPEAN AMBASSADOR / STENA NORDICA (7) (2004 -)

24,206g. 12,201n. 4,884d. 170.51(BB) x 25.82 x 6.00 metres.
Two, (centre) 18-cyl. 4 S.C.S.A. (380 475mm) Wartsila 18V38 vee type oil engines made by Wartsila Nederland B.V., Zwolle. (32,302 BHP).
Two, (wings) 12-cyl. 4 S.C.S.A. (380 475mm) Wartsila 12V38 vee type oil engines made by Wartsila Nederland B.V., Zwolle. (21,535 BHP).
Engines geared in pairs to twin controllable pitch propellers. 25.5 kts. Twin thwartsip thrust controllable pitch propellers forward.
80 cabins 222 berthed and 183 deck passenger / roro-cargo ferry bow and stern door/ramp.
28.1.2000: Keel laid by Mitsubishi Heavy Industries Ltd., Shimoneseki (Yard No. 1068), for Lombard Facilities Ltd., (P&O European Ferries (Irish Sea) Ltd., managers), London. 18.8.2000: Launched. 12.12.2000: Completed. 4.2004: Sold to Stena Line Scandinavia Ab. 5.2004: Renamed STENA NORDICA.

9129328

F.307. STENA LYNX III (2004 -)

4,113g. 1,721n. 310d. 80.61 x x 3.145 metres.
Four, 16-cyl. 4 S.C.S.A. (270 x 305mm) Ruston 16RK270 vee type oil engines made by Ruston Paxman Diesels Ltd., Newton le Willows, reduction geared to four water jet propulsion units. 29,909 BHP. 45 kts.
Twin hulled 677 deck passenger / RoRo cargo ferry.
2.7.1995: Keel laid by Incat Australia Pty.Ltd., Tasmania (Yard No. 040) for American Fast Ferries, (Stena Line Ltd., chartering managers), Nassau. 8.5.1996: Launched. 18.5.1996: Completed 1998: Renamed

ELITE. 1998: Renamed P&O STENA ELITE. 1998: Reverted to STENA LYNX III. 2004: Sold to Stena Ropax Ltd., London, (Northern Marine Management Ltd., Clydebank, managers).

STENA LYNX III

(Internet source)

LINDAROSA

(Hans Mornhout collection)

9129586

F.308. LINDAROSA (2005)

18,469g. 13,364n. 8,000d. 183.10(BB) x 25.22 x 7.80 metres
8-cyl. 4 S.C.S.A. (580 x 640mm) MAN 8L58/64 type oil engine made by MAN B&W AS., Copenhagen, geared to a controllable pitch propeller. 15,118 BHP. 19.7kts. Two thwartship thrust fixed pitch propellers forward and one aft.
10 cabins, 20 berths for drivers, roro cargo vessel with stern ramp.
7.11.1994: Keel laid by C. N. "Visentini" di Visentini Francesco & Ci, Donada (Yard No. 170), for Levantina Trasporti S.r.l., Italy. 5.8.1995: Launched. 4.3.1996: Completed. 2.2005: Sold to Stena North Sea Ltd., Clydebank, (Northern Marine Management Ltd., Clydebank, managers). 10.2005: Renamed MONT VENTOUX.

F.309. STENA FORWARDER (2) (2005 - 2006) see ship No. F. 274 above.

F.310. MONT VENTOUX (2) (2005 -) see ship No. F. 308 above.

F.311. VOLGA HIGHWAY (2005 -) see ship No. F. 256 above.

VOLGA HIGHWAY

(Internet source / Marko Stampehl)

NORMAN SPIRIT at Dunkirk

(Internet source / Jose Verove)

F.310. NORMAN SPIRIT (2005) see ship No. F. 271 above.

9188427

F.313. SVEALAND (2005 -)

As built: 25,000g. 7,500n. 7,500d. 186.0(BB) x x 6.5 metres.
Post 1999: 25,206g. 7,741n. 7,500d. 186.0(BB) x x 6.5 metres.
Two, 9-cyl. 4 S.C.S.A. (480 x 600mm) MAN 9L48/60 type oil engine made by MAN B&W Diesel AG, Augsburg, geared to a twin controllable pitch propellers. 25,695 BHP. 21.5 kts. Twin thwartship thrust controllable pitch propellers forward.
As built 240 deck passenger / roro cargo ferry.
Post 1999: 78 cabins, 72 berthed and 168 deck passenger / RoRo cargo ferry .
25.6.1997: Keel laid as ALYSSA by C. N. "Visentini" di Visentini Francesco & C, Donada (Yard No. 185), for Royal Maritime Ltd., Malta. 19.12.1998: Launched. 8.6.1999: Completed. 1999: Converted. 2000: Sold to

Levantina Trasporti Srl, Italy. 6.2001: Chartered by Stena Line Ab, for the Gothenburg – Travemunde route. 7.2001: Renamed SVEALAND. 7.2001: Chartered by Scandlines Ab, for the Trelleborg – Travemunde route. 2003: Transferred to Scandline Hansa charter. 2004: Transferred to the Bahamas flag. 2005: Sold to Stena Bermuda Ltd., (Northern Marine Management Ltd., Clydebank, managers),

Vessels On Order.

9331177

STENA SEABRIDGER 1 / STENA TRADER (4) (2006 -)

25,000g. n. 7,500d. 212.0 x 26.7 x metres.
22 kts.
Stena Seabridger class - 100 passenger RoRo freight ferry .
9.2004: Ordered from Fosens Mekaniske Verksted, Norway, and hull sub-contracted to Baltijsky Zavod Shipyard, Skrovet / Ryssland (Yard No. 74), for Stena Line Hook of Holland – Killingholme service. 10.12.2004: Keel laid. 5.2006: Scheduled completion.

9331189

STENA SEABRIDGER 2 / STENA TRAVELLER (3) (2006 -)

25,000g. n. 7,500d. 212.0 x 26.7 x metres.
22 kts.
Stena Seabridger class - 100 passenger RoRo freight ferry .
9.2004: Ordered from Fosens Mekaniske Verksted, Norway, and hull sub-contracted to Baltijsky Zavod Shipyard, Skrovet / Ryssland (Yard No. 75), for Stena Line Hook of Holland – Killingholme service. 14.6.2005: Keel laid. 11.2006: Scheduled completion.

9367140

STENA MODIFIED SEABRIDGER 1 (2008 -)

37,500g. n. 8,500d. 212.0 x 26.7 x 15.5 metres.
300 passenger – 100 cabins / RoRo freight ferry 22 kts.
8.2005: Ordered from Baltijsky Zavod Shipyard, St Petersburg (Yard No. 05443), by Stena
2008: Scheduled completion

9367152

STENA MODIFIED SEABRIDGER 2 (2008 -)

37,500g. n. 8,500d. 212.0 x 26.7 x 15.5 metres.
300 passenger – 100 cabins / RoRo freight ferry 22 kts.
8.2005: Ordered from Baltijsky Zavod Shipyard, St Petersburg (Yard No. 05444), by Stena
2008: Scheduled completion

STENA MODIFIED SEABRIDGER 3 (OPTION -)

37,500g. n. 8,500d. 212.0 x 26.7 x 15.5 metres.
300 passenger – 100 cabins / RoRo freight ferry 22 kts.
8.2005: Ordered from Baltijsky Zavod Shipyard, St Petersburg (Yard No. 05445), by Stena

STENA MODIFIED SEABRIDGER 4 (OPTION -)

37,500g. n. 8,500d. 212.0 x 26.7 x 15.5 metres.
300 passenger – 100 cabins / RoRo freight ferry 22 kts.
8.2005: Ordered from Baltijsky Zavod Shipyard, St Petersburg (Yard No. 05446), by Stena

The Troubled Stena 4-Runner Class.

Of the six vessels remaining at the Italian yard at the time of its financial collapse, two have since been completed. See ship numbers F. 300 and F. 301.

9138812

A. STENA ESPANIA (1) / UND KARADENIZ (PROPOSED)

14,500g. 12,350 dwt
Ice strengthened, 12 berthed passenger, Ro-Ro cargo vessel with stern door ramp and container capacity of 800 TEU.

28.4.1998: Keel laid as STENA ESPANIA by Societa Esercizio Cantieri S.p.A., Viareggio, Italy (Yard No. 1549). 1998: Charter to Und RoRo Isletereli A.S. Turkey, agreed and to be completed as UND KARADENIZ for 1999 delivery. Lloyds Shipowning Groups - March 2000 edition quotes "for completion 2000". 11.2000: Vessel incomplete with future undecided as charter cancelled. 2000: Buquebus International Ltd., entered into negotiations to take over the contract but these failed. 12/2005: Equasis database / website reported as Italian flag, "in build" and for sale.

9138824

B. STENA IONIA (2) (PROPOSED)

14,500g. 12,350 dwt

Ice strengthened, 12 berthed passenger, Ro-Ro cargo vessel with stern door ramp and container capacity of 800 TEU.

5.11.1998: Keel laid by Societa Esercizio Cantieri S.p.A., Viareggio, (Yard No. 1550). Lloyds Shipowning Groups - March 2000 edition quotes "for completion 2000" 12.2005: Lloyd's Register records stated that construction had been discontinued. 12/2005: Equasis database / website reported as Yard No. 1550 Swedish flag, "in build" for Stena RoRo Line Ab.

9138836

C. STENA ESPANIA (2) (PROPOSED)

14,500g. 12,350 dwt

Ice strengthened, 12 berthed passenger, Ro-Ro cargo vessel with stern door ramp and container capacity of 800 TEU.

On order from Societa Esercizio Cantieri S.p.A., Viareggio (Yard No. 1551) . 12.2005: Lloyd's Register records stated that construction had not been commenced. 12/2005: Equasis database / website reported as Yard No. 1551 Italian flag, "in build" and for sale.

9138848

D. STENA BELGIA (PROPOSED)

14,500g. 12,350 dwt

Ice strengthened, 12 berthed passenger, Ro-Ro cargo vessel with stern door ramp and container capacity of 800 TEU.

On order from Societa Esercizio Cantieri S.p.A., Viareggio (Yard No. 1552). 12.2005: Lloyd's Register records stated that construction had not been commenced. 12/2005: Equasis database / website reported as Yard No. 1552 Swedish flag, "in build" for Stena RoRo Line Ab.

Cancelled Ferries.

Constructed For Others.

7907673

Can. 1. STENA BALTICA (5) (1984 launched then 1986 CANCELLED)

As built: 26,088g. 14,786n. 4,500d. 175.39(BB) x 29.01 x 6.701 metres

Post 1992: 38,261g. 20,073n. 4,500d. 173.00(BB) x 29.00 x 6,700 metres.

Four, 16-cyl. 4 S.C.S.A. (400 x 480mm) Sulzer 16ZV40/48 vee type oil engines made by Zgoda Zaklady Urzadzen Technicznych, Swietochlowice, geared in pairs to twin screw shafts, with controllable pitch propellers. 40,000 BHP. Two, thwartship thrust controllable pitch propellers forward.

Proposed = Ice strengthened, 2,312 berthed & 196 deck passenger / RoRo cargo / ferry, with a bow door / ramp, and two stern rampdoors.

1979: One of four sisters ordered in Poland by Stena Line Ab, Sweden. 2.7.1983: Keel laid by Stocknia im "Komuny Paryskiej" Gdynia, Poland (Yard No. B.494/03). 27.10.1984: Launched. 1986: Cancelled, due to continued excessive delays at shipyard. 1988: Sold incomplete to Fred Olsen Group, Norway, for completion as BONANZA - reportedly at Bremer Vulcan, Vegesak. 6.1992: Completed as BONANZA – 650 cabins; 1600 berthed & 1,400 deck passenger / RoRo cargo ferry with two stern door ramps. 1992: Sold to Anonymos Neftiliaki Eteria Kritis A.A. (A.N.E.K.), Chania, Greece and renamed ELEFTHERIOS VENIZELOS. (EL. VENIZELOS = Abbreviated on ship)

7907685

Can. 2. STENA POLONICA (1985 launched then 1986 CANCELLED)

Proposed: 26,088g. 14,786n. 4,500d. 175.39(BB) x 29.01 x 6.701 metres

Post 1991: 24,000g. 14,000n. 4,500d.

Four, 16-cyl. 4 S.C.S.A. (400 x 480mm) Sulzer 16ZV40/48 vee type oil engines made by Zgoda Zaklady Urzadzen Technicznych, Swietochlowice, geared in pairs to twin screw shafts, with controllable pitch propellers. 40,000 BHP. Two, thwartship thrust controllable pitch propellers forward.
Proposed = Ice strengthened, 2,312 berthed & 196 deck passenger / RoRo cargo / ferry, with a bow door / ramp, and two stern rampdoors.
1979: One of four sisters ordered in Poland by Stena Line Ab, Sweden. 15.8.1985: Keel laid by Stocznia im "Komuny Paryskiej" Gdynia, Poland (Yard No. B.494/04), for Stena Line Ab, Sweden. 1986: Cancelled, due to continued excessive delays at shipyard. 1989: Sold as a steel structure to unspecified Greek buyer (Tony Travel & Agency Ltd., agent / managers). 6.1990: Launched. 18.6.1991: Arrived in tow at Piraeus from Chalkis as REGENT SKY. 16.6.1992: Departed from Pireaus bound to Chalkis for completion. 17.6.1992: Arrived. 1998: Owners suffered financial collapse. 4.2000: Offered for sale by auction whilst still lying incomplete at the Greek shipyard. 7.6.2004: Jay Management S.A., Athens appointed as managers.

8818300

Can. 3. STENA ENDEAVOUR (1) (proposed)

As Proposed: 18,332g. 5,499n. 6,003d. 154.00(BB) x 24.33 x 5.515 metres.
As built: 18,653g. 5,595n. 6,934d. 158.00(BB) x 24.33 x 5.901 metres.
As proposed: Two, 8-cyl. 4 S.C.S.A. (400 x 560mm) Sulzer 8ZA40S type oil engines manufactured by Oy Wartsila Ab, Turku/Abo, geared to twin screw shafts with controllable pitch propellers. 12,203 BHP. 18 kts. Thwartship thrust controllable pitch propellers forward and aft.
As built: Two, 6-cyl. 4 S.C.S.A. (400 x 560mm) Sulzer 6ZA40S type oil engines made by Oy Wartsila Ab, Turku/Abo, geared to twin screw shafts with controllable pitch propellers. 10,767 BHP. 17 kts. Thwartship thrust controllable pitch propellers forward and aft.
As proposed: RoRo cargo / 92 berthed 500 deck passenger ferry, with bow and stern door/ramps and a container capacity for 240 TEU.
As built: RoRo cargo / 60 cabins 120 berthed passenger ferry, with bow and stern door/ramps and a container capacity for 313 TEU.
1990: One of four STENA CHALLENGER type sisterships ordered, this as an option, by Stena RoRo Ab, Sweden, but the contract was sold and design amended. 5.6.1989: Keel laid by Bruces Verkstads Ab, Landskrona (Yard No.19), as a sub-contract to Fosens Mekaniska Verkstaeder, Fevaag, 10.3.1990: Launched as KAPTAN BURHANETTAN ISIM. 21.12.1990: Completed by Fosens Mekaniska Verkstaeder, Fevaag (Yard No. 43), for D.B. Deniz Nakliyati T.A.S. Genel Mudurlugu (Turkish Cargo Lines), Turkey. 2004: Sold to Baltic Ferries / MB & H Corporation, (Unity Line Sp.z.o.o., managers), Poland and renamed GRYF, under the Bahamas flag. 2004: Sold to Gryf Line Ltd., (same managers).

8818312

Can. 4. STENA ENTERPRISE (1) (proposed)

As Proposed: 18,332g. 5,499n. 6,003d. 154.00(BB) x 24.33 x 5.515 metres.
As built: 18,653g. 5,595n. 6,934d. 158.00(BB) x 24.33 x 5.901 metres.
As proposed: Two, 8-cyl. 4 S.C.S.A. (400 x 560mm) Sulzer 8ZA40S type oil engines manufactured by Oy Wartsila Ab, Turku/Abo, geared to twin screw shafts with controllable pitch propellers. 12,203 BHP. 18 kts. Thwartship thrust controllable pitch propellers forward and aft.
As built: Two, 6-cyl. 4 S.C.S.A. (400 x 560mm) Sulzer 6ZA40S type oil engines made by Oy Wartsila Ab, Turku/Abo, geared to twin screw shafts with controllable pitch propellers. 10,767 BHP. 17 kts. Thwartship thrust controllable pitch propellers forward and aft.
As proposed: RoRo cargo / 92 berthed 500 deck passenger ferry, with bow and stern door/ramps and a container capacity for 240 TEU.
As built: RoRo cargo / 60 cabins 120 berthed passenger ferry, with bow and stern door/ramps and a container capacity for 313 TEU.
1990: One of four STENA CHALLENGER type sisterships ordered, this as an option, by Stena RoRo Ab, Sweden, but the contract was sold and design amended. 4.4.1991: Keel laid by Bruces Verkstads Ab, Landskrona (Yard No.22), as a sub-contract to Fosens Mekaniska Verkstaeder, Fevaag. 24.10.1991: Launched as KAPTAN ABIDIN DORAN. 8.5.1992: Completed by Fosens Mekaniska Verkstaeder, Fevaag (Yard No. 44), for D.B. Deniz Nakliyati T.A.S. Genel Mudurlugu (Turkish Cargo Lines), Turkey. 3.2002: Reported as sold to undisclosed operators. 2005: Sold to Shandong Bohai Ferry Company, Peoples Republic of China, and renamed BO HAI MING ZHU.

Not Constructed

Can. 5. HSS 1500 Finnyards Yard No.406 - cancelled 1996.

Can. 6. HSS 900 Westamarin, Yard No. 239 - 1996 delivery Stena Line Ab. cancelled

Can. 7. HSS 700 8.1996: Issue of a letter of intent to order four from Finnyard for 1997/98 delivery. 2.1997: Cancelled.

OSTERSOEN

(Internet source)

5266441

FC.1. OSTERSOEN (1962 - 1963)

As built: 1,102g. 696n. 204d. 175' 0" x 34' 6" x 11' 3"
Post 1960: 1,389g. 633n. 310d. 197' 0" x 34' 5" x 11' 8"
Post 1993: 777g. 278n. 315d.
8-cyl. 2 S.C.S.A. (350 x 620mm) B&W 8-35VF-62 type oil engine made by Burmeister & Wain, Copenhagen. 1,998 BHP.
600 passengers / car ferry with side doors.
Post 1982: 250 berthed & 250 deck passengers / RoRo cargo - ferry.
16.10.1953: Launched. by Svendborg Skibsvaerft AS., Svendborg (Yard No.67), for AS Dampsklsk. paa Bornholm af 1866, Denmark. 1954: Completed. 1960: Lengthened. **20.12.1962: Chartered by Skagenlinjen Rederi Ab, (Sten A.Olsson, manager). 15.3.1963: Released from charter.** 1973: Sold to Roselco Shipping Company Ltd., Cyprus, and renamed ROANA. 1976: Sold to Redalis Shipping Company Ltd., Cyprus. 1990: Sold to Prem Lines Ltd., Cyprus. 1993: Transferred to St. Vincent & The Grenadines flag. 12.1995: Demolition commenced.

ISEFJORD

(Internet source)

5164277

FC.2. ISEFJORD (1963 - 1965)

As built: 625g. 316n. 200d. 196' 10" x 35' 4" x 10' 6"
Post 1965: 498g. 193n. 200d.
Two, 6-cyl. 2 S.C.S.A. (390 x 430mm) B&W type oil engines made by AS Volund, Copenhagen. 3,400 BHP
Post 1963: Two, 7-cyl. 2 S.C.S.A. (280 x 500mm) oil engines manufactured in 1954 by Burmeister & Wain Maskin og Skipsbyggeri, Copenhagen. 2,260 BHP. 1978: Total engine output regraded at 3,400 BHP.

500 passengers / car ferry with stern ramp.
1935: Completed by Aalborg Maskfabrikin och Skeppsbyggeri, Aalborg (Yard No. 51), for AS Grenaa-Hundested Faergefart, (Henning Arup, manager), Denmark. **7.1963: Purchased by the Kiel-Nakskov Linien, (Sten A. Olssen, was a principal shareholder).** 1963: Re-engined. 1965: Sold to Agostino Lauro, Italy, and sent for reconstruction. 1966: Renamed AGOSTINO LAURO. 1975: Owners restyled as Libera Navigazione Lauro S.a.S. 1991: Sold to Agostino Lauro S.r.l., Italy. 1994: Sold to Achille Lauro Lines S.r.l., Italy. 2000: Owner restyled as Linee Lauro S.r.l. 2000: Sold to Medmar SpA, Naples.

SEUTE DEERN

(Internet source / Cees De Bijl)

5321124

FC.3. SEUTE DEERN (1963)

As built: 640g. 303n. 0d. 188' 7" x 31' 3" x 7' 3"
Post 1979: 769g. 446n. 0d. 64.17 x 10.05 x 2.350 metres
Two, 8-cyl. 4 S.C.S.A. (250 x 350mm) oil engines made by Motorenwerke Mannheim A.G., Mannheim. 1,440 BHP.
645 passenger ferry. Post 1979: 770 deck passengers.
12.4.1961: Launched by Rheinstahl Nordseewerke, Emden (Yard No.335), for Partenreederei "Seute Deern", (Cassens Eils, manager), W. Germany. 16.5.1961: Completed. **1963: Chartered for the summer season by Skagenlinjen Rederi Ab.** 1969: Owners restyled as Reederei Cassens Eils. 1979: Lengthened. 1981: Owners restyled as Reedeerei Cassens Eils GmbH & Co.K.G.

HEIN GODENWIND

(Internet source)

5145673

FC.4. HEIN GODENWIND (1963)

As built: 1,024g. 433n. 152d. 195' 9" x 36' 6" x 10' 6"
Post 1969: 981g. 414n. 154d.
Two, 8-cyl. 4 S.C.S.A. (230 x 300mm) MaK 8M281AK type oil engines made by Maschinenwerke Kiel A.G., Kiel. 1,600 BHP.

Ice strengthened 860 deck passenger ferry.
9.7.1960: Launched by J.J. Sietas K.G. Schiffswerft GmbH & Company, Hamburg (Yard No.467), for Hafen-Dampfschiffahrt A.G., Hamburg. 10.9.1960: Completed. **1963: Chartered by Skagenlinjen Rederi Ab.** 1969: Sold to HADAG Seetouristik u Fahrdienst A.G., W. Germany, and renamed KOBENHAVN. 1975: Sold to Forde-Reedeerei GmbH, W. Germany, and renamed NORDSEE 1. 1998: Sold to unspecified Spanish flag buyers, and renamed ESTRELLA DEL MARE. 2004: Sold to unspecified Gibraltar flag operators, and renamed IRRATIONAL EXUBRANCE.

FC.5. WAPPEN VON HAMBURG (1963 - 1964) see No. F.4 above.

HELGOLAND

(Internet source)

FC.6. HELGOLAND/LARVIKSPILEN (1963 - 1966) see No. F.20 above.

SEEBAD WARNEMUNDE (Internet source)

5317238

FC.7. SEEBAD WARNEMUNDE (1964) (1965) (1966)

399g. 186n. 62d. 141' 10" x 25' 0" x 7' 3"
Two, 6-cyl. 4 S.C.S.A. (240 x 360mm) S.K.L. 6NVD36IU type oil engines made by Maschinenbau Halberstadt, Halberstadt. 520 BHP.
305 deck passenger ferry.
1961: Completed by V. E. B. Schiffswerft "Edgar Andre", Magdeburg, (Yard No. 3), for Fahrgastschiffahrt Stralsund, E. Germany. **1964 -1966: Chartered in season by Skagenlinjen Rederi Ab.** 1993: Sold to Weisse Flotte GmbH., Germany. 1996: Sold to Societe Arcachon Bateaux Croisieres S.A., France, and renamed ATLANTIC PRINCESS 2002: Sold to Diva S.a.r.l., Martinique, (Day Charter S.A., managers), Martinique.

5317226

FC.8. SEEBAD HERINGSDORF (1964) (1965) (1966)

399g. 186n. 62d. 141' 10" x 25' 0" x 7' 3"
Two, 6-cyl. 4 S.C.S.A. (240 x 360mm) S.K.L. 6NVD36IU type oil engines made by Maschinenbau Halberstadt, Halberstadt. 520 BHP.
243 deck passenger ferry.
1961: Completed by V. E. B. Schiffswerke "Edgar Andre", Magdeburg (Yard No. 4), for Fahrgastschiffahrt Stralsund, E. Germany. **1964-1966: Chartered in season by Skagenlinjen Rederi Ab.** 1993: Sold to Weisse Flotte GmbH., Germany. 1995: Sold to Weisse Flotte GmbH, Stralsund, Germany, and renamed WISMARIA.

GORCH FOCK

(Internet source)

5404586

FC.9. GORCH FOCK (1964)

980g. 478n. 106d. 180' 6" x 34' 3" x 10' 4"
Two, 6-cyl. 4 S.C.S.A. (300 x 450mm) MAN G6V30/45 type oil engines made by Maschinenwerke Augsburg-Nurnberg A.G., Augsburg. 1,490 BHP. 14 kts.
Ice strengthened 650 deck passenger ferry.
23.2.1963: Launched by J. J. Sietas Schiffswerft GmbH. & Company K.G., Hamburg (Yard No.520), for Hafen-Dampfschiffahrt A.G., Hamburg. 10.4.1963: Completed. **1964: Chartered by Skagenlinjen Rederi Ab.** 1974: Sold to Reedeerei Peter Dielman, W.Germany, and renamed NORDWELLE. 1976: Sold to m.s."Dolfijn I" Schiffahrts GmbH, W.Germany, and renamed DOLFIJN I. 1980: Renamed DOLFIJN II. 1981: Sold to Ocean Wagons Inc., (m.s."Dolfijn I" Schiffahrts GmbH, managers), Panama. 1986: Sold to Kamstra Beheer B.V., (Rederij Kamstra B.V., managers), Panamanian flag. 2003: Sold to At Sea, (Pomorska Zegluga, managers), Szcezcin, Poland, retaining Panamanian flag.

5383304

FC.10. VOLKERFREUNDSCHAFT (1966 - 1985*)

As built: 12,442g. 6,555n. 2,772d. 524' 8" x 69' 1" x 24' 9"
Post 1978: 12,068g. 6,287n. 4,775d.
Post 1983: 11,970g. 6,101n. 2,020d. x x 7.541 metres.
Post 1994: 16,144g. 5,931n. 2,020d.
Two, 8-cyl. 2 S.C.S.A. (760 x 1300mm) oil engines made by the shipbuilder. 12,000 BHP.
Post 1994: Two, 16-cyl. 4 S.C.S.A. (320 x 350mm) Wartsila 16V32 vee type oil engines made by Oy Wartsila Ab, Finland. 7,477 BHP.
Ice strengthened 568 passenger cargo liner.
Post 1994: 250cabins, 566 berthed passengers.
9.9.1946: Launched as STOCKHOLM by Ab Gotaverken, Goteborg (Yard No. 611), for Svenska Amerika Linjen, Sweden. 2.1948: Completed. 1960: Sold to Freir Deutsche Gerwerkschafts-Bund, (Deutsche Seerreederei, managers), E. Germany, and renamed VOLKERFREUNDSCHAFT. **1966: Chartered for the first time by Stena Line Ab, for a series of Christmas-New Year and Easter cruises. 28.12.1966: Departed from Goteborg on a 32 day cruise to the Caribbean and Abores. 21.12.1984 until 24. 1.1985: Undertook final 35 day cruise charter for Company, to the W.Indies.** 1978: Sold to V.E.B.DeutscheFracht / Seereedeerei. 1985: Sold to unspecified Panama buyers, and renamed VOLKER. 1986: Sold to Neptunus Rex Enterprises Inc., Panama, and renamed FIDTJOF NANSEN. 1993: Sold to Nina SpA., Italy, and renamed ITALIA 1 then ITALIA PRIMA. 1994: Re-engined and converted into a full passenger ship. 2000: Renamed VALTURE PRIMA. 2003: Sold to Festival Grociere, Piraeus, (Festival Shipping, managers), Greece., and renamed CARIBE, retaining Italian flag. 2005: Sold to CIC Classic International Cruises SA, Athens, (Arcalia Shipping SA, Lisbon, managers), and renamed ATHENA, under the Portugese flag.

N.B. During this period vessel was not on permanent charter, only for the various cruises arranged by the Company.

5285411

FC.11. PRINSESSAN CHRISTINA (1) (1966)

2,240g. 1,096n. 594d. 286' 6" x 48' 5" x 13' 9".
Two, 5-cyl. 2 S.C.S.A. (500 x 700mm) Polar type, oil engines made by Nydqvist and Holm Ab., Trollhattan, geared to twin screw shafts with controllable pitch propellers. 4,000 BHP. 17 kts. Thwartship thrust controllable pitch propeller forward.
809 passenger / vehicle RoRo / ferry.

28.9.1959: Launched by Aalborg Vaerft AS., Aalborg (Yard No.130), for Goteborg - Frederikshavn Linjen, Sweden. 24.3.1960: Completed. **1966: Taken on charter by Stena Ab., for use on their summer "LONDONER" service.** 1967: Sold to O.Y. Vaasa Umea AB., Finland, and renamed BOTNIA EXPRESS. 1975: Sold to Navegacion Atlantida S.A., Uruguay, and renamed GENERAL JOSE ARTIGAS. 1977: Sold to Consolodata de Ferrys C.A., (CONFERRY), Venezuela, and renamed SANTA MARGARITA DOS. 3.11.1987: Sank at her berth at Cumana with the loss of five lives.

PRINSESSAN CHRISTINA (1)

(Internet source)

5121835

FC.12. FRITZ HECKERT (1968 - 1970*)

As built: 8,120g. 3,654n. 1,800d. 463' 1" x 57' 8" x 18' 3"
Post 1981: 7,363g. 3,401n. 1,800d.
Six, free piston gas generators 2 S.C.S.A. (340 x 904mm) and two Pescara type gas turbines, made by Turbinfabrik, Dresden, double reduction geared to shafts, each 2,900 SHP.
Also, Two, 8-cyl. 2 S.C.S.A. (480 x 720mm) oil engines made by Diesel Motorenwerk, Rostock.
377 passenger cruise liner.
1961: Completed by Mathias-Thesen-Werft, Wismar (Yard No.199), for Freir Deutsche Gerwerkschafts-Bund, (Deutsche Seereederei, managers), E. Germany. **1968: Commenced occasional cruise charters by Stena Line Ab.** 1978: Sold to Volkswerft Stralsund, E. Germany, and converted into an accommdation ship for 349 people. 1982: Entry removed from Lloyd's register due to being "no longer seagoing". No further details known.

* N.B. During this period vessel was not on permanent charter, only for the various cruises arranged by the Company.

FC.13. VIKING II (1971) see ship No. F. 203 above,

Chartered for the Gothenburg – Frederikshavn route January to March.

DROTTNINGEN (Internet source)

6800402

FC.14. DROTTNINGEN (1976)

6,550g. 2,573n. 955d. 377' 4" x 59' 2" x 15' 6"

Four, 6-cyl. 4S.C.S.A. (400 x 460mm) Pielstick 6PC2L-400 vee type oil engines made by Ab Lindholmens Varv, Goteborg, geared in pairs to twin screw shafts. 7,160 BHP. 17 kts. Thwartship thrust controllable pitch propeller forward.

308 berthed and 88 deck passenger / RoRo cargo ferry / rail vehicles.

8.11.1967: Launched by Uddevallavarvet Ab, Uddevalla (Yard No. 280), for Svenska Statens Jarnvagar, Sweden. 4.1968: Completed. **1976: Chartered by Stena Line Ab, to cover an emergency repair period following the summer grounding STENA JUTLANDICA.** 1977: Sold to Federal Arab Maritime Company, Egypt, and renamed ALZAHRAA. 1979: Owners restyled as Federal Arab Maritime Company, (FAMCO). 1984: Sold to Strintzis Lines S.A., Cyprus, and renamed IONIAN VICTORY. 1985: Sold to Freeway Navigation Ltd., Cyprus, and renamed PALOMA. 1993: Sold to Guangdong Shantou Navigation Company, China, and renamed JIN HU. 2001: Sold to Wealthy Bright Holding Ltd., Hong Kong, Eurasia International China Ltd., Hong Kong, managers). 2005: Reported as demolished.

CONDOR

(Internet source / Bertil Soderberg)

7221512

FC.15. CONDOR (1976)

1,547g. 733n. 1,778d. 98.74(BB) x 15.88 x 3.849 metres.

Two, 8-cyl. 4 S.C.S.A. (360 x 450mm) MWM TBD501-8 type oil engines made by Motoren Werke Mannheim A.G., Mannheim, geared to twin screw shafts. 5,400 BHP. 15.5 kts. Thwartship thrust propeller forward.

Ice strengthened roro-cargo vessel.

10.9.1971: Keel laid as CONDOR by A Vuijk en Zonen's Scheepswerven N.V., Capelle aan den Ijssel (Yard No. 861), for Condor Reederei & Schiffahrtges mnH., Germany. 26.4.1972: Launched. 29.7.1972: Completed as SAINT GEORGE. 1974: Renamed CONDOR. 1976: Chartered by Stena Line Ab., for the Gotherburg – Kiel route. 1980: Sold to Naviera Interoceangas S. A., (NISA), Chile, and renamed EVANGELISTAS. 1995: Sold to Nisa Navegacion S.A., (Naviera Magalennes S.A. (NAVIMAG) managers). 2.6.2003: Demolition commenced.

DANA SIRENA seen 5.1975 during a 3-month charter to Prinzenlinien on their Harwich – Hamburg route

(Internet source)

6930207

FC.16. DANA SIRENA (1978)

As built: 7,697g. 3,890n. 1,021d. 124.85 x 19.31 x 5.21 metres.
Post 1971: 7,672g. 3,669n. 1,083d.
Post 1979: 7,988g. 3,883n. 1,100d.

Two, 12-cyl. 2 S.C.S.A. (420 x 900mm) B&W 1242-VT2BF-90 vee type oil engines made by the shipbuilder's Ancona works Geared to twin controllable pitch propellers. 12,000 BHP. 21 kts. Thwartship thrust propeller forward.
1,100 passenger / car ferry with bow, stern and side doors.
20.3.1967: Keel laid as AALBORGHUS by Cantieri Navali del Tirreno e Riuniti, Riva Trigoso, Genoa (Yard No.208), for D.F.D.S. AS, Denmark. 2.7.1969: Launched. 23.7.1969: Completed. 1970/71: Rebuilt by Societe des Anciens Etablissement Groignard S.A., Marseilles, and renamed DANA SIRENA. 3.11.1975: Renamed OLAU DANA. 3.5.1976: Renamed DANA SIRENA. 21.4.1977: Renamed ROBIN HOOD. 23.12.1977: Renamed DANA SIRENA. **15.1.1978 until 23.2.1978: Time chartered by Stena Line Ab, for their Goteborg-Kiel route.** 9.5.1978: Renamed ROBIN HOOD. 4.10.1978: Renamed DANA SIRENA. 18.5.1979: Renamed ROBIN HOOD. 1.10.1979 until 28.11.1979: Rebuilt by Aalborg Vaerft AS, Aalborg, and renamed DANA CORONA. 6.2.1985: Sold to China Ocean Shipping Co. COSCO), Peoples Republic of China. 6.3.1985: Delivered and renamed TIAN E, and subsequently transferred to Dalian Steam Ship Co., (DALIAN COSCO). 2000: Sold to China Shipping Passenger Liner, Dalian.

SCANDINAVICA

(Hans Mornhout collection)

7221433

FC.17. SCANDINAVICA (1) (1978 - 1981).

11,344g. 6,350n. 1,829d. 141.46 x 21.98 x 5.5 metres.
Two, 12-cyl. 4 S.C.S.A. (480 x 520mm), vee type, oil engines made by Ch.de L'Atlantique, St.Nazaire, geared to twin screw shafts. 24,400 BHP. 22 kts.
1,051 passengers / Vehicles roro / ferry, with bow and stern doors.
1972: Ordered as PRINCE OF FUNDY II from Dubigeon-Normandie S.A., Nantes (Yard No.133a), by Fred Olsen; Fearnley & Eger; AS Mowinckels; Roald P. Aukner and Swedish interests. 13.6.1972: Launched as BOLERO for Fred Olsen & Consortium Scandinavia, Norway. 15.2.1973: Completed. **1978: Chartered by Stena Ab, for the Gothenburg - Kiel service, transferred to Swedish flag, renamed SCANDINAVICA, (Stena Ab, managers). 1982: Released from charter**, and transferred to Sameiet Bolero, (Fred Olsen & Co., managers), Norway, and reverted to BOLERO, under Norwegian flag. 3.5.1983: Whilst on a voyage from Stavanger to Hirtshals suffered severe fire damage off Jossingfjord. Subsequently repaired and returned to service. 1991: Sold to Color Line AS., (Color Line Marine AS, managers), Norway, and renamed JUPITER. 1994: Renamed CRUCERO EXPRESS. 1998: Renamed SEMINOLE EXPRESS. 1999: Sold to Alberta Trading, Haifa, (Caspi Shipping, Haifa, managers), and renamed MAGIC I under the Bahamas flag. 2003: Renamed MIRAGE I. 2005: Sold to Magic 1 Cruise Line Corp., (Lance Shipping Company Ltd., managers), and placed in lay-up. (per DNV)

7613404

FC.18. THOMAS WEHR (1978 - 1979)

As built: 1,599g. 627n. 2,900d. 116.31 x 18.22 x 5.281 metres.
Post 1982: 7,628g. 2,288n. 4,322d. 141.31 x 17.43 x 5.230 metres.
Two 8-cyl. 4S.C.S.A. (320 x 420mm) MaK 8M453AK type oil engines made by MaK Maschinenbau GmbH, Kiel, geared to twin controllable pitch propellers. 6,000 BHP. 17 kts. Thwartship thrust propeller forward.
As built: 12 berthed passengers /Roro-cargo ferry with a container capacity for 140 TEU.
Post 1982: 12 berthed passengers /Roro-cargo ferry with a container capacity for 341 TEU.

4.8.1976: Keel laid as THOMAS WEHR by Rickmers Rhederei GmbH Rickmers Werft, Bremerhaven (Yard No. 388), for Partenreederei m.s. Thomas Wehr, (Reederei Oskar Wehr KG (GmbH & Company), managers), Hamburg. 18.11977: Launched. 22.41977: Completed as WACRO EXPRESS. 1978: Renamed THOMAS WEHR **and chartered by Stena Ab for the Kiel - Gothenburg route**. 1979: Released from charter. 1982: Lengthened and renamed TOR NEERLANDIA. 1985: Renamed DANA GERMANIA. . 1986: Renamed THOMAS WEHR. 1993: Renamed MANA. 1993: Renamed SANTA MARIA. 1993: Renamed FULDATAL. 1994: Renamed HORNLINK. 1994: Renamed THOMAS WEHR. 2001: Sold to Milieu Corp., Ostend, Belgium, (Ferryways N.V, Ostend, managers), and renamed ANGLIAN WAY, under the Panamanian flag.

THOMAS WEHR The "S" on funnel not quite complete

(Internet source / Jurgen Stein)

FULDATAL in ice conditions

(Internet source / Hans Joachim Reinecke)

7041015

FC.19. FULDATAL (1980 - 1981)

As built: 1,597g. 694n. 2,920d. 114.86 (BB) x 17.43 x 5.322 metres.
Post 1992: 1,873g. 613n. 2,920d.
Two 8-cyl. 4 S.C.S.A. (450 x 550mm) MaK 8M551AK type oil engines made by Atlas-MaK Maschinenbau, Kiel., geared to twin controllable pitch propellers. 6,800 BHP. 17.5 kts. Thwartship thrust propeller forward.
Ice strengthened 6-cabins, 12 berthed passengers, RoRo cargo vessel with bow door/ramp and two stern door/ramps and a container capacity of 128TEU.
12.12.1970: Launched as FULDATAL by Rickmers Rhederei GmbH Rickmers Werft, Bremerhaven (Yard No. 363), for Partenreederei m.s. "Fuldatal", (J. A. Reinecke (GmbH & Company), managers), W. Germany. 1971: Completed as FALCON 1972: Renamed NORCOVE. 1975: Renamed FULDATAL. **1980 until 1981: Chartered by Stena Line Ab, for the Gothenburg-Frederikshavn route.** 1989: Sold to Marinzulich Capitano Claudia Armatore & C. Srl, Palermo, Italy, and renamed FULL. 1992: Sold to Sea Containers Italia SpA, (Marinzulich Capitano Claudia Armatore & C. Srl, managers). 1993: Sold to Putera Master Sarana Penyeberangan, Indonesia, and renamed NUSA MULIA.

ARGO

(Hans Mornhout collection)

7501613

FC.20. ARGO (1981 - 1986)

As built: 3,932g. 1,698n. 5,485d. 127.03(BB) x 19.89 x 6.554 metres.
Post 9,079g. 2,776n. 5,485d.
Two, 18-cyl. 4 S.C.S.A. (280 x 290mm) Pielstick 18PA6V280 vee type oil engines made by Kloeckner Humboldt Deutz, Koeln, geared to twin screw shafts with controllable pitch propellers. 12,000 BHP. 19.5 kts. Thwartship thrust propeller forward.
54 berthed passenger / RoRo cargo ferry.
11.12.1975: Keel laid by Kroegerwerft GmbH & Company KG, Rendsburg (Yard No. 1391), for Argo Reederei Richard Adler and Sohne, Bremen. 19.6.1976: Launched. 29.9.1976: Completed. 1977: Renamed BRABANT. 1978: Renamed ARGO-HELLAS. 1980: Renamed ARGO. **1981 until 3.1.1986: Chartered by Stena Line Ab, for the Gothenburg-Frederikshavn route.** 1992: Renamed NORCOVE. 1994: Sold to Argo Reedeerei Richard Adler & Sohne, (Interorient Navigation Company Ltd., managers), Cyprus, and renamed SAGA ARIES. 1995: Renamed SALLY EUROWAY. 1997: Renamed EUROWAY. 1998: Sold to Landi Shipping Company Ltd., (same managers), and renamed LANDI. 2000: Renamed EUROLANDIA. 2002: Sold to Lerma Sorel, Palma de Mallorca, Spain, (Tramp Shipping, Madrid, managers), Spain, and renamed PATRICIA DEL MAR. 2005: Iscomar SA, appointed managers.

RORO ANGLIA

(Internet source / Reinhard Nerlich)

7211969

FC.21. RORO ANGLIA (1981 - 1983)

499g. 192n. 1,165d. 105.34(BB) x 15.22 x 3.271metres.
Two, 12-cyl. 4 S.C.S.A. (250 x 300mm) engines made by Nydqvist & Holm Ab., Trollhattan, geared to twin controllable pitch propellers. 3,900 BHP. 17 kts. Thwartship thrust propeller forward.
RoRo cargo / vehicle ferry with stern ramp/door.
1972: Completed as SAILORMARK by Ankerlokken Verft Glommen AS, Frederikstad (Yard No. 179), for ms "Sailormark" Edwin Heyer Schiffahrts K.G., (Christian F. Ahrienkel, managers), Bremen. 1974: Renamed RORO ANGLIA. 1977: Sold to RoRo Anglia "Palm" Schiffahrtges. m.b.h. & Company K.G., (same managers). 1979: Transferred to Panamanian flag. **1.9.1983: Chartered to Stena Line Ab, for the Gothenburg – Travemunde Route. 1983: Released from charter.** 1985: Sold to Trennel Shipping Company Ltd, remaining under the Panamanian flag. 14.1.1987: Sustained severe grounding damage off Baia, declared a compromised total loss and subsequently laid up at Piraeus. 1989: Sold to Apollonia Shipping Company

Ltd., Greece, and renamed RORO APOLLONIA WINNER. 1989: Sold to Mykonos Anonymos Naftiki Eteria, Piraeus, and renamed MYKONOS II. 2004: Sold to N. Korea owners, and renamed SARMAT. 10.2004: Reported as having been demolished in India.

SAINT PATRICK II

(Hans Mornhout collection)

7310260

FC.22. SAINT PATRICK II (1985 - 1986)

7,210g. 3,234n. 1,923d. 125.63(BB) x 21.65 x 5.265 metres.
Two, 16-cyl. 4 S.C.S.A. (410 x 470mm) Werkspoor vee type oil engines made by Stork-Werkspoor Diesel, Amsterdam, geared to twin screw shafts with controllable pitch propellers. 18,900 BHP. 23 kts. Thwartship thrust controllable pitch propeller forward.
328 berthed & 1,172 deck passengers / RoRo cargo ferry with bow and stern doors.
6.1973: Completed as AURELLA by J. J. Sietas K.G. Schiffswerke GmbH. & Company K.G., Hamburg (Yard No. 702), for SF Line Ab, Finland. 1982: Sold to Irish Continental Line Ltd., Dublin, and renamed SAINT PATRICK II. **9.1985: Chartered by Stena Line Ab. 5.1986: Released from charter.** 1989: Owners restyled as Irish Continental Group plc., (IRISH FERRIES). 1993: Transferred to Estonia flag. 1994: Reverted to Irish flag. 1998: Sold to Ironside Ltd., (The Hellenic Mediterranean Lines Company Ltd., managers), and renamed EGNATIA II, under the Maltese flag. 2000: Renamed VILLE DE SETE. 2000: Renamed EGNATIA II. 2000: Renamed CITY OF CORK. 2002: Sold to Madeleine Navigation Corp., Cap aux Meules, Canada, (Cooperative de Transport Maritime et Aerien (C.T.M.A.), managers), and renamed C.T.M.A. VACANCIER.

SAUDI EXPRESS

(Internet source / Fotohaus Pamperin)

7430735

FC.23. SAUDI EXPRESS (1986)

8,708g. 4,640n. 14,522d. 183.14 x x 8.468 metres.
6-cyl. 2 S.C.S.A. (760 x 1550mm) Sulzer 6RND76M type oil engine made by H. Cegielski, Poznan. 12,000 BHP.
RoRo cargo ferry.
5.8.1977: Keel laid as BANDAR ABBAS EXPRESS by Oskarshamns Varv, Oskarshamn (Yard No.425) for OT Rederierna, Sweden. 21.2.1978: Launched. 13.7.1978: Completed. 1980: Renamed SAUDI EXPRESS. 1983: Renamed JOLLY AVORIO. 1986: Sold to Ab Shipinvest, Sweden, and renamed SAUDI EXPRESS. **1986: Chartered by Stena Ab.** 1986: Sold to Bow Marine Ltd., Cayman Islands, charter cancelled, and renamed KARAWA. 1987: Sold to Vinta Maritime Company Inc., (Fred Olsen & Company, managers,),

Philippines, and renamed BORACAY. 1990: Transferred to Pebble Beach Shipping Inc., (same managers), Norway (NIS). 1998: Sold to DFDS AS, Denmark, and renamed DANA MINERVA. 2001: Sold to DFDS Tor Line AS, and renamed TOR MINERVA, under the Norway NIS flag. 2003: Sold to Como Maritime AS, Oslo, (Goliat Shipping, Oslo, managers).

STENA DAN (Hans Mornhout collection)

8501476

FC.24. STENA DAN (1988 - 1991)

19,689g. 9,257n. 14,103d. 163.81(BB) x x 8.802 metres
6-cyl. 4 S.C.S.A. (580 X 600mm) MaK 6M601AK type oil engine made by Krupp MaK. Maschinenbau GmbH, Kiel, geared to a controllable pitch propeller. 9,000 BHP. 16 kts. Thwartship thrust controllable pitch propeller forward.
RoRo cargo ferry / container carrier.
4.9.1987: Keel laid by Danværft AS., Frederikshavn (Yard No.424), for Mercandia Rederierne, (Per Henriksen), Denmark, but order cancelled at early stage of construction. 3.5.1988: Launched as ROSA DAN for Danværft AS., (J.Lauritzen AS, manager and the shipyard owners), Denmark. 4.9.1988: Completed. **11.1988: Renamed STENA DAN, for employment on the Stena - Tor Line service from Harwich. 8.1991: Released from charter**, transferred to Lauritzen Shipping (Bahamas) Ltd., (same managers), and renamed ROSA DAN. 1992: Renamed CARACAS. 1993: Renamed ROSA DAN. 1994: Sold to Pan Aurora Maritime Pte.Ltd., Singapore, and renamed TJOET NYA DHIEN. 1997: Sold to Und RoRo Isletmereli A.S., (Crescent Ship Management Ltd., managers), Turkey, and renamed UND MARMARA 2003: Sold to CR Americas Shipping Company Ltd., (Interorient Navigation Company Ltd., Limassol, managers), and renamed CROWLEY AMERICAS. under the Cypriot flag.

BELINDA (Internet source / Cees De Bijl)

7389194

FC.25. BELINDA (1987 - 1988)

As built: 5,551g. 2,899n. 9,018d. 161.37 x 18.04 x 6.71 metres
Post 19 : 11,125g. 3,338n. 8,538d.
Two, 8-cyl. 4 S.C.S.A. (400 x 480mm) Sulzer 8ZL40/48 type engine made by "Zgoda" Zaklady Urzadzen Technicznych, Swietochlowice, Poland. geared to twin screw shafts. 10,400 BHP. 17.25 kts.
RoRo cargo / vehicle carrier.

23.12.1977: After section keel laid as LINNEA. 25.4.1978: Launched. 27.4.1978: Forward section keel laid as LINNEA. 7.9.1978: Launched. 1.2.1979: Completed as LINNE by Lodose Varv Ab, Lodose (Yard No. 180), for Skarhamns Oljetransport Ab, Sweden. 20.1.1982: Owners in receivership with control passing to Handelsbanken, SE-Banken, PK Banken and Riksgaldsfullmaktige. 4.9.1985: Following numerous periods on lay-up was sold at auction in Gothenburg to Belinda Shipping S.A., (Knud I. Larsen, manager), and renamed BELINDA,under the Panamanian flag. 1987: Sold to Kaprifol Shipping S.A., (Ole Frellsen, manager), Panama. **10.9.1987: Chartered to Stena Line Ab, for the Gothenburg - Travemunde route.** 1.10.1987: Weco-Shipping IS, denmark appointed as managers. **4.1988: Released from charter.** 3.10.1988: Sold to PR Vendila (Holdingaktieselskabet Dannebrog), and transferred to Denmark International Register. 6.10.1988: Renamed NORDBORG. 31.12.1989: Sold to Vendila Rederi AS. 17.7.1991: Sold to Dannebrog Rederi AS, resultant from a merger.10.1994: Sold to DFDS AS, Denmark, and renamed DANA HAFNIA. . 28.9.1999: Renamed KATTEGAT SYD. . 11.1999: Reverted to DANA HAFNIA. 9.1.2001: Transferred to DFDS Tor Line AS, and renamed TOR HAFNIA. 5.2001: Sold to Strade Blu Srl, Italy, (Portunato E. C. Srl, Servizi Armatoriali, managers), and renamed STRADA CORSARA, under the Italian flag.

STENA FELICITY

(Internet source)

7826788

FC.26. FELICITY / STENA FELICITY (1990 - 1997)

As built: 15,001g. 8,420n. 2,700d. 145.62(BB) x 24.52 x 5.514 metres.
Post 1994: 23,775g. 11,056n. 2,700d.
Four, 8-cyl. 2 S.C.S.A.(450 x 900mm) B&W 8K45GFC type oil engines made by Ab Gotaverken, Gothenburg, geared in pairs to twin screw shafts with controllable pitch propellers. 29,600 BHP. 19 kts. Two thwartship thrust propellers forward.
Ice strengthened, 1142 berthed and 872 deck passengers / RoRo cargo ferry with bow door/ramp and three stern ramp doors.
15.10.1979: Keel laid as VISBY by Oresundsvarvet Ab, Landskrona (Yard No.278), for Rederi Ab Gotland, Sweden. 15.1.1980: Launched. 10.10.1980: Completed. 1990: Chartered by Sealink U.K. Ltd., and renamed FELICITY. **1990: Charterers purchased by Stena Ab, and charter retained. 1990: Renamed STENA FELICITY, (Sealink U.K.Ltd., (SEALINK STENA LINE), charterers / managers). 1993: Charterers / managers restyled as Stena Sealink Ltd., (STENA SEALINK LINE). 1.1.1996: Charterers / managers restyled as Stena Line Ltd. 1997: Released from charter** and renamed VISBY. 2003: Renamed VISBORG 7.2003: Sold to Adabar Company Ltd., (Polish Baltic Shipping Company (Polska Zegluga Baltycka SA), Kolobrzeg, managers), Kolobrzeg, and renamed SCANDINAVIA.

7214727

FC.27. VINZIA E (1993 - 1994)

As built: 1,597g. 694n. 2,850d. 114.86 (BB) x 17.43 x 5.322 metres.
Post 1993: 1,935g. 764n. 2,850d.
Post 199 : 5,617g. 1,686n. 2,850d.
Two 8-cyl. 4 S.C.S.A. (450 x 550mm) MaK 8M551AK type oil engines made by Atlas-MaK Maschinenbau, Kiel., geared to twin controllable pitch propellers. 6,800 BHP. 17.5 kts. Thwartship thrust propeller forward.

Ice strengthened 6-cabins, 12 berthed passengers, RoRo cargo vessel
6.5.1972: Launched as WESERTAL by Rickmers Rhederei GmbH Rickmers Werft, Bremerhaven (Yard No. 367), for Partenreederei m.s. "Wesertal", (J. A. Reinecke (GmbH & Company), managers), W. Germany. 1972: Completed. 1972: Renamed MEYER EXPRESS. . 1973: reverted to WESERTAL. 1992: Renamed NORCREST. 1993: Sold to Co. Na. Tir S.p.A., Italy, and renamed VINZIA E. **1993: Chartered by Sealink Stena Line for the Newhaven - Dieppe route.** 1994: Sold to Clare Business Ltd., (Goliat Shipping AS, managers) and renamed DANA BALTICA under Norway (NIS) flag. 1996: Renamed CLARE. 1997: Sold to NL-Group IS, (same managers). 1999: Sold to unspecified buyers (Rederiet Otto Danielsen AS, Copenhagen, managers). 2001: Sold to Clare Maritime, Frederikshavn, (Dania Marine, managers), under the Bahamas flag. 2004: H&L Intercontinental AS, Frederikshavn, managers, and transferred to Norway NIS flag.

VINZIA E with Sealink funnel colours

(Hans Mornhout collection)

STENA SEALYNX

(Internet source)

9001538

FC.28. STENA SEALYNX (1993 - 1996)

3,232g. 969n. 700d. 74.15 x 26.00 x 3.98 metres.
Four, 16-cyl.4 S.C.S.A.(270 x 305mm) 16RK270 vee type oil made by Ruston Diesels Ltd., Newton-Le-Willows, each powering a water-jet propulsion unit. 22,008 BHP. 31 Kts.
Twin aluminium alloy hulled- RoRo cargo/ferry for 430 deck passengers and 90 cars.
11.2.1992: Keel laid by International Catamarans Tasmania Pty. Ltd., Hobart (Yard No.31), **for Buquebus International Ltd., (Stena Sealink Ltd., (STENA SEALINK LINE), managers), Bahamas.** 4.2.1993: Launched. 12.6.1993: Completed. **1.1.1996: Charterers restyled as Stena Line Ltd. 1996: Renamed STENA LYNX.** 1999: Sold to Buquebus International Ltd., (Virtu Ferries Ltd., managers), Bahamas and renamed AVANT. 2002: Sold to Dae A Express, Pohang, S. Korea, and renamed OCEAN FLOWER. 2004: Renamed MANDARIN.

9081693

FC.29. STENA SEALYNX II (1994 - 1996)

3,989g. 1,327n. 250d. 77.46 x x 2.728 metres.
Four, 16-cyl. 4 S.C.S.A. (280 x 300mm) Caterpillar 3616TA vee type oil, made by Caterpillar Inc., U.S.A., each powering a water-jet propulsion unit. 23,492 BHP. 35 Kts.

Twin aluminium alloy hulled- RoRo cargo/ferry for 600 deck passengers and 151 cars.
14.6.1993: Keel laid by Intcat Australia Pty.Ltd., Hobart (Yard No.33), **for Buquebus International Ltd., (Stena Sealink Ltd., (STENA SEALINK LINE), managers), Bahamas.** 12.3.1994: Launched. 5.1994: Completed. **1.1.1996: Charterers restyled as Stena Line Ltd. 1996: Renamed STENA LYNX II.** 1998: Renamed RONDA MARINA. 2003: Sold to Adriatic Fast Ferries, Hobart, (Wavelord Navigation SA, Piraeus, managers), and renamed THUNDERCAT 2, retaining the Bahamas flag. 2005: Renamed JAUME I, and transferred to the Spanish flag, Balearia SA, Denia, Spain, appointed as managers.

STENA SEALYNX II

(Internet source)

NORRONA

(Internet source)

7302914
FC.30. NORRONA (1994) & (1995)
As built: 7,457g. 4,011n. 1,799d. 129.01(BB) x 21.04 x 4.900 metres.
Post 1986: 7,838g. 4,211n. 4,211d.
Post 1996: 11,999g. 4,922n. 4,211d.
Four, 6-cyl. 4 S.C.S.A. (410 x 470mm) Werkspoor 6TM410 type engines made by Stork Werkspoor Diesel, Amsterdam, geared in pairs to twin controllable pitch propellers. 16,000 BHP. 22kts. Thwartship thrust propeller forward.
As built; 600 berthed & 440 deck passenger, roro cargo, vehicle ferry, with bow and stern doors
Post 1992; 800 berthed & 250 deck passenger, roro cargo, vehicle ferry, with bow and stern doors
Post 1993; 752 berthed & 288 deck passenger, roro cargo, vehicle ferry, with bow and stern doors
12.5.1973: Completed as GUSTAV VASA, by Werft Nobiskrug, Rendsburg, (Yard No. 678), for Lion Ferry Ab, Halmstad. (O.N. 11327). 1983: Sold to Smyril Line, Faroes, and renamed NORRONA (O.N. 396). 1991: Owners restyled as Smyril Line p/f. **1994 and 1995: Chartered by Stena Sealink Line for relief duties on the Irish sea routes.** 2004: Sold to Operation Mobilisation Logos Ltd, Malta, (Gute Bucher Fur Alle, managers, Germany), and renamed LOGOS HOPE, retaining Faroes registry.

7429229
FC.31. ROSEBAY (1994 - 1996) & (1998 - 2001)
5,631g. 2,754n. 5,233d. 135.49(BB) x 21.75 x 6.050 metres.
Two, 6-cyl. 4 S.C.S.A. (520 x 55mm) MAN 6L52/55A type oil engines made by Maschinenbau Augsburg-Nuernburg (MAN), Augsburg, geared to twin controllable pitch propellers. 12,660 BHP. Thwartship thrust propeller forward.
Ice strengthened 21 cabin, 63 berthed passenger / RoRo cargo ferry.
4.7.1976: Keel laid as TRANSGERMANIA by J.J. Sietas GmbH & Co.K.G. Schiffswerke, Hamburg, (Yard No.792), for Partreederei m.s. "Transgermania", (Veba Poseidon Schiffahrtges.m.b.H., managers), W.Germany. 27.8.1976: Launched. 30.10.1976: Completed. 1993: Sold to Poseidon Schiffahrt OHG., (same managers), Cyprus, and renamed ROSEBAY. **1994: Chartered for employment by Stena Sealink Line Ltd., as a winter dry-dock relief vessel. 1995: Retained on charter by Stena Line. 1996:**

Realeased from charter. 1997: Sold to Maritime Company Ltd., Cyprus, and renamed EUROSTAR. 1997: renamed EUROCRUISER. 1998: Reverted to ROSEBAY and **chartered to Stena Line Ltd.** 2000: Sold to Oddysy Maritime Company Ltd., (Denval Marine Consultants Ltd., managers), Cyprus. 2001: Sold to Engship, Finland renamed TRANSPARADEN. 2004: Sold to Rederi Ab Eckero, Mariehamn, Finland, and renamed TRANSLANDIA.

ROSEBAY (left) during her first charter period in the original freight livery, and (above) in her second charter period in the revised livery (both Internet source / Cees De Bijl)

MARINE EVANGELINE

(Internet source / Andreas Wortelen)

7369118

FC.32. MARINE EVANGELINE (1995 - 1996)

As built: 2,794g. 981n. 3,548d. 110.14 (BB) x 17.51 x 5.776 metres.
Post 1988: 2,793g. 1,601n. 1,856d.
Post 1995: 7,564g. 2,270n. 1,856d.
Post 1998: 7,564g. 2,270n. 1,642d.
Four 16-cyl. 4 S.C.S.A. (250 x 300mm) Normo KVM-16 vee type engines made by Normo Gruppen AS, Bergen, geared in pairs to controllable pitch propellers. 10,202 BHP. 18.5 kts. Thwartship thrust propeller forward.
50 berthed passenger / Roro cargo vessel
1973: Laid down as CORD ADELER by Kristiansands Mekaniska Verksteder AS, Kristiansand (Yard No. 221), for AS Larvik – Frederikshavnferjen, Norway, and was renamed DUKE OF YORKSHIRE before launch. 6.6.1974: Completed for charter to Norfolk Line BV, Scheveningen, Holland. 15.11.1975: Sold to Norfolk Lijn B. V., Holland. 3.1978: Sold to Rideau Shipping Company Ltd., Canada, and renamed MARINE EVANGELINE. 1978: Transferred to Roylease Ltd., Canada. 1986: Transferred to Marine Atlantic, under French flag. 1987: Sold to Societe Nationale des Chemins de Fer Francais (SNCF), France. 1988: Sold to Marine Atlantic Inc., and reverted to Canada flag. 1992: Transferred to Bahamas flag. 4.7.1993: Renamed SPIRIT OF BOULOGNE for charter purposes, (Sandford Ship Management Ltd., managers). 3.1995: Renamed MARINE EVANGELINE 21.6.1995: **Chartered to Sealink Stena Line for the Newhaven – Dieppe, Stranraer – Larne and Newhaven - Dieppe routes respectively. 10.1996: Released from charter.** 1998: Hansatee Oy, Estonia, appointed as managers, and renamed KAPELLA, under Estonia flag. 2000: Sold to Tallink Group Ltd., Estonia

FC.33. STENA LYNX (1996 - 1999) see No. FC.28 above.

FC.34. STENA LYNX II (1996 - 1998) see No. FC.29 above.

FC.35. STENA LYNX III (1996 - 1998) see No. F. 307 above.

STENA PEGASUS

(Internet source / Andreas Wortelen)

9125891

FC.36. STENA PEGASUS (1996 - 1997)

3,971g. 1,191n. 405d. 95.00 x x 4,600 metres.
Four, 20-cyl. 4 S.C.S.A. (230 x 280mm) M.T.U. 20V1163TB73 vee type oil engines made by MTRU Friedrichshafen GmbH, Friedrichshafen, geared to four water jet propulsion units. 32,628 BHP. 36 kts. Thwartship thrust propeller forward.
7.8.1995: Keel laid as PEGASUS ONE by Fincantieri-Cant. Navale Italiani S.p.A., Riva, Italy, (Yard No.5965) for Ocean Bridge Investments S.A. Italy. 23.2.1996: Launched. 11.5.1996: Completed. **1996: Renamed STENA PEGASUS for a "high speed service" evaluation charter on the Newhaven - Dieppe service.** 1997: Renamed PEGASUS ONE. 1997: Renamed MARGARITA EXPRESS. 2000: Reverted to PEGASUS ONE, Consolidada de Ferrys C.A., appointed as managers. 6.2000: Sold to Africa & Affairs SAL ,(International Bakhsh, managers), Madrid. 8.2000: Sold to Bridge Shipmanagement,Jeddah, (Consolidada de Ferrys C.A., managers). 10.2000: Sold to Ocean Bridge Investments SA, Genova. 8.2002: Sold to DMF Investment, Georgetown, Grand Cayman, (Lothian Shipping Services Ltd., managers), and renamed ST. MATTHEW. 6.2003: Meridian Marine Management Ltd., appointed as managers. 2004: Sold to Tallink Autoexpress Ltd., Nicosia, Cyprus, (Tallink Group Ltd, Tallinn, Estonia, managers), and renamed TALLINK AUTOEXPRESS 4, under Estonia flag.

CONDOR 10 with stena funnel markings

(Internet source)

9001526

FC.37. CONDOR 10 (1996)

3,241g. 1,004n. 660d. 74.15 x 26.00 x 3.142 metres.
Four, 16-cyl. 4 S.C.S.A. (270 x 305mm) Ruston 16RK270 vee type oil engined made by Ruston Diesels Ltd., Newto-le-Willows, powering four waterjet propulsion units. 22,024 BHP. 38 kts.
Aluminium alloy, twin-hulled RoRo cargo /574 deck passenger / ferry with a capacity for 90 cars.
10.11.1991: Keel laid by International Catamarans Tasmania Pty. Ltd., Hobart (Yard No. 030), for Enterprise Trading Private Ltd., Singapore, (Condor Marine Services Ltd., managers). (O.N. 385519). 5.9.1992: Launched 2.2.1993: Completed. **17.5.1996: Chartered for a "high speed service" on the Fishguard - Rosslare route. 14.10.1996: Released from charter.** 2000: Timur Management Private Ltd., appointed as managers. 2005: Sold to Condor Ltd, (Condor Marine Services Ltd., Poole, managers), under the Bahamas flag.

FC.38. ELITE (1998)

see No. F. 307 above.

ELITE

Internet source)

FC.39. P&O STENA ELITE (1998) see No. F. 307 above.

FC.40. STENA LYNX III (1998 -) see No. F.307 above.

SOUTHERN CARRIER (Hans Mornhout collection)

7800758

FC.41. SOUTHERN CARRIER (1999)

As built: 4,546g. 2,126n. 6,950d. 143.29 (BB) x 21.04 x 5.381 metres.
Post 1988: 16,947g. 5,085n. 8,400d. 170.26 (BB) x 21.04 x 5.381 metres.
Post 1988: Two, 12-cyl. 4 S.C.S.A. (320 x 350 Wartsila type oil engines made by Oy Wartsila Ab, Vaasa, Geared to twin screw shafts. 12,227 BHP. 15 kts.
13.11.1978: Keel laid as ANNA ODEN by Gotaverken Oresundsvarvet Ab, Landskrona (Yard No. 269), for Nordsjofrakt Ab., Sweden. 3.1.1979: Launched. 27.4.1979: Completed. 1988: Lengthened by Flensburger Schiffbau-Ges.mbH & Company KG, Flensburg (new hull section reference N), re-engined and renamed TOR FLANDRIA. 1994: Sold to B&N Bylock & Nordsjofrakt Ab., (B&N Shipmanagement Ab., managers), Sweden. 1997: Sea Partner Sweden Ab, appointed as managers. 1997: Sold to Partrederi Tor Flandria, (same managers). 1998: Sold to Partrederi Southern Carrier, (same managers), Sweden, and renamed SOUTHERN CARRIER. **1999: Chartered by Stena Line Ab, for the Gothenburg - Travemunde route.** 2000: Ab Nordsjofrakt RoRo, appointed as managers. 2002: Sold to Rederi Ab Anna Oden, (B&N Nordsjofrakt, managers), Skarhamn, and renamed ANNA ODEN. 2003: Sold to Cobelfret Ab, (Transatlantic Rederi Ab, Skarhamn, managers), Sweden.

FC.42. STENA CHALLENGER (2) (2000 - 2001) see ship No. F.226 in above.

9243435

FC.43. STENA FORWARDER (1) (2001 - 2003)

25,000g. 7,500n. 7,500d. 186.49 x x 6.500 metres
Two 9-cyl. 2 S.C.S.A. (480 x 600mm) MAN 9L48/60 type oil engines made by MAN B&W Diesel AG, Augsburg, geared to twin controllable pitch propellers. 25,695 BHP. 24 kts. Two thwartship thrust propellers forward.
78 cabins, 1,000 deck passenger roro cargo vessel.
21.7.2000: Keel laid by Cantieri Navale "Visentini" di Visintini Francesco & Ci, Donada (Yard No. 195), for Levantina Trasporti Srl, Italy. 28.10.2000: Launched. 21.7.2001: Completed. 2003: Renamed CALIFORNIA STAR. 2005: Sold to California Srl, Contarina, Italy, (Levantina Trasporti Srl, managers).

STENA FORWARDER (1) (Internet source)

NORSE MERSEY (2)

(Hans Mornhout collection)

9108568

FC.44. NORSE MERSEY (2) (2001)

16,009g. 4,802n. 11,000d. 174.5(BB) x x 6.5 metres.
9-cyl. 4 S.C.S.A. (460 x 580mm) Wartsila 9R46 type oil engine made by Wartsila Diesel Oy, Turku, geared to a controllable pitch propeller. 11,073 BHP. 19.5 kts. Thwartship thrust controllable pitch propeller forward and aft.
100 passenger RoRo cargo ferry with a container capacity of 750 TEU.
10.10.1993: Keel laid by C. N. "Visentini" di Visentini Francesco & C, Donada (Yard No. 167), for Levantina Trasporti Srl, Italy. 21.7.1994: Launched. 8.5.1995: Completed. **7.2001: Chartered for the Gothenburg – Travemunde route.** 2002: Renamed CETAM MASSILIA. 2002: Reverted to NORSE MERSEY. 2005: Sold to Inarme Srl, Naples, (Grimaldi Group, Naples, managers), and renamed EUROCARGO NAPOLI.

FC.45. ALYSSA (2001) see ship No. F.313 above.

6.2001: Chartered by Stena Line Ab, for the Gothenburg – Travemunde route.

BORE MARI

(Internet source / Dirk Jankowsky)

8912376

FC.46. BORE-MARI (2004)

5,972g. 1,791n. 4,750d. 114.4(BB) x x 6.169.
16-cyl. 4 S.C.S.A. (320 x 350mm) Wartsila 16V32D vee type oil engine made by Wartsila Diesel Oy, Vaasa, geared to a controllable pitch propeller, 8,048 BHP. 16.5 kts. Thwartship thrust propelle forward.
Ice strengthened, 2 cabins -4 berthed passengers, paper carrying RoRo cargo vessel with stern door, and a container capacity of 143 TEU.
4.10.1989: Keel laid by Nordfjord Skipsindustri AS Nordfjordied (Yard No.49). 7.11.1990: Hull launched. 26.9.1991: Completed as ANN-MARI by Hjorungavaag Verksted AS, Hjorungavaag, (Yard No. 49), for Rederi Ab Lillgard, Finland. 1997: Sold to Oy Rettig Ab Bore, Turku, Finland, and renamed FINNBEAVER. 2002: Renamed BORE-MARI. **January until April 2004: Chartered by Stena Line Ab, for the Gothenburg – Travemunde route.** 2004: Sold to Marin Maritime Company SA, Athens, (Superfast Ferries SA, Athens, managers), and renamed MARIN.

GLOBAL FREIGHTER

(Internet source / Jan Moller)

FC.47. GLOBAL FREIGHTER (2004) see ship No. F.46 above.

9-12.4.2004: Chartered by Stena Line Ab, for the Gothenburg – Travemunde route.

9107942

FC.48. STENA CHALLENGER (3) (2005)

22,365g. 6,732n. 5,794d. 181.60 (BB) x 23.90 x 5.600 metres
Four 8-cyl. 4 S.C.S.A. (400 x 560mm) Sulzer 8ZA40S type oil engines made by Adriadiesel d.d., Karlovac, geared in pairs to twin controllable pitch propellers. 31,323 BHP. 19 kts. Two thwartship thrust controllable pitch propellers forward.
36 cabins, 132 berthed and 1,518 deck passenger, roro cargo, ferry.
3.8.1994: Keel laid as ISLE OF INISHFREE by van der Geissen-de Noord B.V., Krimpen aan den Ijssel (Yard No. 963), for Irish Continental Group plc (IRISH FERRIES), Dublin. 27.1.1995: Launched. 13.5.1995: Completed. 3.2002: Renamed PRIDE OF CHERBOURG. **7.2.2005: Chartered by Stena Line Ab, and renamed STENA CHALLENGER for the Karlskrona - Gdansk route, proposed until May. 7.6.2005: Released from charter**, and renamed CHALLENGER. 28.6.2005: Departed from Karlskrona enroute to New Zealand. 2005: Sold to Toll New Zealand Consolidated Ltd., Auckland, (Interislander Ltd, Wellington, managers).

STENA CHALLENGER (3)

(Internet source / Frank Lose)

SEA RUNNER

(Internet source / Ulrich Streich)

7606645

FC.49. SEA RUNNER (2006)

As built: 4,156g. 846n. 3,884d 120.33 x 20.5 x 5.901 metres.
Two, 12-cyl. 4 S. C.S.A. (320 x 420mm), MaK 12M453AK type oil engines made by MaK Maschinenbau GmbH, Kiel, geared to twin controllable pitch propellers. 8,000 BHP. 16kts. Thwartship thrust propeller forward.
Roro cargo vessel with stern door / ramp and container capacity of 140 TEU.
3.5.1977: Keel laid as LE MANS by Dubegion-Normandie S.A. Prairie-au-Duc, Nantes, France (Yard No. 159), for Societe Francaise de Transports Maritimes (SFTM) & Walon S.A., (Compagnie Morbihannaise de Navigation, managers), Nantes. 13.3.1978: Launched. 24.5.1978: Completed. 1985: Sold to Compagnie Maritimes des Chargeurs Reunis (CMCR), Le Havre, and renamed C R CASABLANCA. 1990: Sold to Sword Sea Shipping Inc., Nassau, and renamed RAVEL. 1992: Sold to Dalian Steam Shipping Company, Dalian, China, and renamed LAN QIAO. 1996: Sold to Cambridge Shipping Company Ltd., Malta, and renamed SEA RUNNER. **1.2006: Chartered by Stena Line Ltd., for the Larne – Fleetwood service**.

FC. . STENA LYNX IV (1996/7 -)

Twin hulled 677 deck passenger / RoRo cargo ferry.
A report implied that this was a vessel under construction by Incat in Tasmania, (Yard No. 043) and which had been refused because it failed to attain the minimum specifications. No further reference was located.

The Subsidiary And Associated Ferry Fleets

Scandlines Ab

Acquired as a subsidiary by Stena Ab - 1997
Formerly
Sweferry Ab – 1997
Scandinavian Ferry Lines Ab – 1991

7229514

Sc.1. GOTALAND (1997 -)

18,060g. 9,708n. 5,209d. 183.09 x 22.5 x 5.8 metres.
Two, (centre) 8-cyl. 4 S.C.S.A. (400 x 460mm) Pielstick 8PC2L-400 vee type oil engines made by Lindholmen Motor Ab, Gothenburg. (7,200 BHP).
Two, (wings) 6-cyl. 4 S.C.S.A. (400 x 460mm) Pielstick 6PC2L-400 vee type oil engines made by Lindholmen Motor Ab, Gothenburg. (5,400 BHP).
Engines geared in pairs to twin controllable pitch propellers. 18 kts. Twin thwartship thrust controllable pitch propellers forward.
74 cabins, 148 berthed and 400 deck passenger / roro-cargo / rail vehicle ferry.

5.10.1972: Launched by AS Nakskov Skibsvaerft, Nakskov (Yard No. 198), for Government of the Kingdom of Sweden (Statens Jarnvagar Farjedriften)(Swedish State Railways). 4.1973: Completed. 1989: Owners restyled as Government of the Kingdom of Sweden (Statens Jarnvagar Farjedriften)(Swedish State Railways & Ferries). 1991: Sold to Ab Sydspedition (SweFerry Ab, managers). 1997: Sold to Scandlines Ab, Helsingborg.

GOTALAND

(Hans Mornhout collection)

TRELLEBORG

(Hans Mornhout collection)

7925297

Sc.2. TRELLEBORG (1997 -)

As built: 10,882g. 3,626n. 3,800d. 170.19 x 23.8 x 5.817 metres.
Post 1994: 20,028g. 6,471n. 3,800d.
Four 8-cyl. 4 S.C.S.A. (400 x 450mm) MAN 8L40/45 type oil engines made by Maschinenbau Augsbug-Neurnberg (MAN), Augsburg, geared in pairs to twin controllable pitch propellers. 23,927 BHP. 17 kts. Two thwartship thrust propellers forward.
23 cabins, 50 berthed and 900 deck passengers / roro-cargo / rail vehicles ferry.
8.12.1980: Keel laid by Oresundsvarvet Ab., Landskrona (Yard No. 271), for Government of the Kingdom of Sweden (Statens Jarnvagar Farjedriften)(Swedish State Railways). 19.5.1981: Launched. 28.5.1982: Completed. 1989: Owners restyled as Government of the Kingdom of Sweden (Statens Jarnvagar Farjedriften)(Swedish State Railways & Ferries). 1991: Sold to Ab Sydspedition (SweFerry Ab, managers). 1993: Sold to Sweferry Ab. 1997: Sold to Scandlines Ab, Helsingborg.

9133915

Sc.3. SKANE (1998 - 2005)

42,705g. 21,731n. 7,290d. 200.20(BB) x 29.6 x 6.500 metres.
Four 8-cyl. 4 S.C.S.A. (480 x 600mm) MAN 8L48/60 type oil engines made by MAN B&W Diesel AG., Augsburg, geared in pairs to twin controllable pitch propellers. 39,399 BHP. 21 kts. Three thwartship thrust propellers forward.

Ice strengthened, 80 berthed drivers, 150 cabins, 600 berthed passengers, / roro-cargo / rail vehicles ferry with stern door.
21.11.1996: Keel laid by Astillieros Espanoles S.A. (AESA), Puerto Real (Yard No. 77) for Sweferry Ab, Sweden. 9.7.1997: Launched for Scandlines Ab, Helsingor, Sweden. 22.6.1998: Completed. 2005: Sold to Skane 97 Statutory Trust , (Scandlines Ab, Helsingor, operating managers).

SKANE

(Hans Mornhout collection)

7907659
Sc.4. STENA GERMANICA (3) (2000 -) see ship No. F.143 above.

Managed.

ORESUND

(Internet source / Marko Stampehl)

8420842
ScM.1. ORESUND (1997 – 2004)
16,925g. 5,882n. 6,772d. 186.902(BB) x 23.7 x 5.638 metres.
Four 6-cyl. 4 S.C.S.A. (400 x 450mm) MAN 6L40/45 type oil engines made by Maschinenbau Augsbug-Neurnberg (MAN), Augsburg, geared in pairs to twin controllable pitch propellers. 17,946 BHP. 18 kts. Two thwartship thrust propellers forward and 1 aft.
Ice strengthened Roro-cargo / rail vehicles ferry withbow door.
19.3.1985: Keel laid by Moss Frederikstad Verft AS, Moss (Yard No. 204), for Government of the Kingdom of Sweden (Statens Jarnvagar Farjedriften)(Swedish State Railways).28.2.1986: Launched. 13.10.1986: Completed 1991: Sold to Swedcarrier Shipping Ab. 1993: Sold to SweFerry Ab. 1994: Partenrederiet Oresund Ab (SweFerry Ab, managers). 1997: Partenrederiet Oresund ANS (Sweferry Ab, managers) and transferred to Norwegian flag. 1998: Transferred to Bahamas flag. 1999: Scandlines Ab appointed as managers. 2004: Sold to SC Ropax 1 Ab, Stockholm, (SeaWind Line Ab, Turku, managers), and renamed SEA WIND, under the Swedish flag.

9007128
ScM.2. AURORA AF HELSINGBORG (1997 -)
10,918g. 3,275n. 2,300d. 111.20 x 28.22 x 5.00 metres.

Four, 6-cyl. 4 S.C.S.A. (320 x 350mm) Wartisla 6R32E oil engines made by Wartsila Diesel Oy, Vaasa, (13,405 BHP) Each engine drives a generator, powering four 2,039 SHP., electric motors, connected to a controllable pitch propeller. Two propellers aft and directional propellers forward. 13.5kts.
Double ended diesel electric, quadruple drive, roro-cargo / rail vehicle / 1,250 deck passanger ferry.
29.11.1990: Keel laid by Tangen Verft AS, Kragero (Yard No. 157), as sub-contract. 4.7.1991: Hull launched. 2.1992: Completed by Langsten Slip & Baatbyggeri AS, Tomrefjord (Yard No. 157), for Aurora 93 Trust, Helsingborg, (SweFerry Ab., managers), Helsingborg. 1997: Scandlines Ab, Helsingborg, appointed as operating managers.

AURORA AF HELSINGBORG

(Hans Mornhout collection)

ScM.3. SKANE (2005 -) see ship No. Sc.3. above.

Chartered.

FELIX E (Hans Mornhout collection)

9140918

ScC. 1. FELIX E (2000 - 2001)

5,307g. 1,593n. 373d. 82.30(BB) x 23.30 x 2.680 metres.
Four 20-cyl. 4 S.C.S.A. (230 x 280mm) MTU 20V1163TB73 vee type oil engines made by MTU Friedrichshafen GmbH, Friedrichshafen driving four water-jet propulsion units. 35 kts. Two thwartship thrust propellers forward.
Twin-hulled aluminium roro cargo / 680 deck passenger ferry.
4.7.1995: Keel laid as FELIX by Austal Ships Pty. Ltd., Fremantle W.A. (Yard No.52), for Speedinvest Ltd., (Sea Containers Ltd., managers), London. 24.6.1996: Launched. 1.10.1996: Completed. 1996: Renamed FELIX I. 1997: Renamed FELIX. 2000: Renamed FELIX E. 2001: Renamed FELIX. 2002: Renamed CROAZIA JET. 2004: Aliscafi SpA, Naples, appointed as managers.

9188427

ScC.2. SVEALAND (2001 - 2003) see ship No. F.313. above.

7.2001 - 2003: Chartered by Scandlines Ab, for the Trelleborg – Travemunde route.

ScC.3. ASK (2003) see ship No.F.124 above.

2003: Chartered by Scandlines Ab for the Trelleborg – Travemunde route.

ASK

(Internet source / Andreas Wortelen)

Scandlines Ab & Scandlines AS

Associated Company

HAMLET

(Internet source / Tim Vogel)

9150030
ScD.1. HAMLET (2) (1997 -)

10,067g. 3,020n. 2,864d. 111.20 x 28.22 x 5.5 metres.
Four, 9-cyl. 4 S.C.S.A. (200 x 280mm) Wartsila 9L20 type oil engines (each 2,080 bhp) made by Wartsila Diesel Oy, reduction geared to twin directional propellers forward and aft. 8,320 BHP. 13 kts.
Vehicle / 1000 deck passenger ferry with bow and stern door and ramp.
4.12.1996: Keel laid by Finnyards Oy, Rauma (Yard No. 412), for joint owners, Scandlines AS, Denmark, and Sweferry Ab, Sweden. 14.3.1997: Launched for Scandlines AS, Denmark and Scandlines Ab, Sweden. 12.6.1997: Completed. 1998: Scandlines AS restyled as Scandlines Danmark AS, and vessel henceforth registered under that title although Scandlines Ab retain their 50%.

P & O Stena Line Ltd.

Associated Company 1998 - 2002
60% P & O – 40% Stena

PO.1. STENA CALEDONIA (1998 - 1999) see ship No. F.201 above.

PO.2. STENA CHALLENGER (2) **(1998 - 1999)** see ship No. F.224 above.

PO.3. STENA GALLOWAY **(1998 - 1999)** see ship No. F.194 above.

PO.4. STENA INVICTA **(1998 - 1999)** see ship No. F.208 above.

PO.5. STENA SEARIDER (2) **(1998 - 1999)** see ship No. F.205 above.

PO.6. STENA VOYAGER **(1998 - 1999)** see ship No. F.265 above.

P&OSL PROVENCE

(Internet source / Soren Lund Hviid)

PO.7. P&OSL PROVENCE **(1998 - 2002)** see ship No. F.111 above.

P&OSL CANTERBURY

(Internet source / Soren Lund Hviid)

PO.8. P&OSL CANTERBURY **(1998 - 2002)** see ship No. F.191 above.

8517736

PO.9. PRIDE OF DOVER / P&OSL DOVER (1998 -)

26,433g. 11,399n. 4,213d. 179.4(BB) x 28.3 x 6.27 metres.

Four, 14-cyl. 4S.C.S.A. (400 x 560mm) Sulzer 14ZA40S vee type oil engines made by Compagnie de Construcion Mec. Sulzer CCM., Mantes, geared to twin controllable pitch propellers. 31,405 BHP. 22 kts. Twin thwartship thrust propellers forward. Thwartship thrust Asymetric thruster unit.
45 cabins, 90 berthed and 2,220 deck passenger / roro-cargo / ferry.
9.4.1986: Keel laid as PRIDE OF DOVER by Schichau -Unterweser AG, Bremen (Yard No. 93), for Stanhope Steamship Company Ltd., (Townsend Car Ferries Ltd., managers). 20.9.1986: Launched. 27.5.1987: Delivered. 31.12.1987: Transferred to P&O European Ferries (Dover) Ltd. 1998: Sold to P&O Stena Line Ltd., (P&O Stena Line Ship Management Ltd., managers). 1999: Renamed P&OSL DOVER. 2002: Sold to P&O Ferries Ltd., Dover, and renamed P O DOVER. 2003: Renamed PRIDE OF DOVER.

P&OSL DOVER

(Internet source / Soren Lund Hviid)

P&OSL KENT

(Internet source / Cees De Bijl)

7820473

PO.10. PRIDE OF KENT / P&OSL KENT (1998 - 2002)

As built: 7,951g. 3,439n. 2,492d. 131.96 x 23.17 x 5.719 metres
Post 1992: 20,446g. 6,133n. 3,379d. 163.40 x 26.18 x 5.536 metres.
Three, 12-cyl. 4S.C.S.A. (400 x 480mm) Sulzer 12ZV40/48 vee type oil engines made by Compagnie de Construcion Mec. Sulzer CCM., Mantes, geared to twin controllable pitch propellers. 28,713 BHP. 20 kts. Thwartship thrust controllable pitch propeller forward.
48 berthed and 1,777 deck passenger / roro-cargo / ferry.
19.12.1978: Keel laid as SPIRIT OF FREE ENTERPRISE by Schichau-Unterweser AG, Bremerhaven (Yard No. 2279), for Townsend Car Ferries Ltd. 21.7.1979: Launched 1.1980: Completed. 31.12.1987: Transferred to P&O European Ferries (Dover) Ltd. and renamed 1992: Lengthened. 1998: Sold to P&O Stena Line Ltd., (P&O Stena Line Ship Management Ltd., managers), and renamed P&OSL KENT. 2002: Renamed P O KENT. 2003: Sold to Lakythra Shipping, (G. A. Shipping, managers), Greece, and renamed ANTHI MARINA.

7820497

PO.11. PRIDE OF BRUGES / P&OSL PICARDY (1998 - 2001)

7,951g. 3,439n. 2,492d. 131.96 x 23.17 x 5.719 metres
Three, 12-cyl. 4S.C.S.A. (400 x 480mm) Sulzer 12ZV40/48 vee type oil engines made by Compagnie de Construcion Mec. Sulzer CCM., Mantes, geared to twin controllable pitch propellers. 23,998 BHP. 22 kts. Thwartship thrust controllable pitch propeller forward.
25 cabins, 48 berthed and 1,278 deck passenger / roro-cargo / ferry.

26.6.1979: Keel laid as PRIDE OF FREE ENTERPRISE by Schichau–Unterweser AG, Bremerhaven (Yard No. 2281), for Townsend Car Ferries Ltd. 31.5.1980: Launched. 11.1980: Completed. 11.12.1987: Renamed PRIDE OF BRUGES. 31.12.1987: Transferred to P&O European Ferries (Dover) Ltd. and renamed 1998: Sold to P&O Stena Line Ltd., (P&O Stena Line Ship Management Ltd., managers). 1999: Renamed P&OSL PICARDY. 2001: Sold to Seaborne Navigation, Koper, Slovenia, (Transeuropa Shipping Lines, Koper, Slovenia, managers), Slovenia, and renamed OLEANDER, under the Cypriot flag.

P&OSL PICARDY

(Internet source / Andreas Worteler)

P&OSL AQUITAINE

(Internet source / Andreas Worteler)

PO.14. P&OSL AQUITAINE (1999 - 2002) see ship No. F.273 above

P & O Stena Line Ship Management Ltd.

Associated Company.

9015254

POM.1. PRIDE OF BURGUNDY / P&OSL BURGUNDY (1998 - 2002)

28,138g. 8,648n. 5,875d. 179.4(BB) x 28.3 x 6.27 metres.

Four, 8-cyl 4 S.C.S.A. (400 x 560mm) Sulzer 8ZA40S type oil engines made by Jugoturbina Diesel d.d., Karlovac, geared to twin controllable pitch propellers. 28,713 BHP. 21 kts. Twin thwartship thrust propellers forward.

79cabins, 196 berthed and 1,224 deck passenger / roro-cargo / ferry.
12.6.1991: Keel laid as EUROPEAN CAUSEWAY by Schichau Seebeckwerft AG, Bremerhaven (Yard No. 1074), for P&O European Ferries (Dover) Ltd. 16.5.1992: Launched as PRIDE OF BURGUNDY. 30.3.1993: Completed. 1998: Sold to Sutten Ltd., (P&O Stena Line Ship Management Ltd., managers), and renamed P&OSL BURGUNDY. 2002: Renamed P O BURGUNDY. 2003: Sold to P&O Ferries Ltd., Dover, and renamed PRIDE OF BURGUNDY.

P&OSL BURGUNDY

(Internet source / Andreas Worteler)

EUROPEAN HIGHWAY as built

(Internet source / Peter Inpijn)

EUROPEAN HIGHWAY reconstructed **as PRIDE OF KENT**

(Internet source / Christian Eckardt)

9015266

POM.2. EUROPEAN HIGHWAY (1998 - 2002)

22,986g. 6,895n. 7,550d. 179.70(BB) x 28.28 x 6.27 metres.
Four, 8-cyl 4 S.C.S.A. (400 x 560mm) Sulzer 8ZAL40S type oil engines made by Jugoturbina Diesel d.d., Karlovac, geared to twin controllable pitch propellers. 28,713 BHP. 21 kts. Twin thwartship thrust propellers forward.
81cabins, 200 berthed passenger / roro-cargo / ferry.

10.8.1991: Keel laid by Schichau Seebeckwerft AG, Bremerhaven (Yard No. 1073), for Hampton Ltd., (P&O European Ferries (Dover) Ltd., managers). 14.12.1991: Launched. 12.6.1992: Completed. 1998: Sold to Sutten Ltd., (P&O Stena Line Ship Management Ltd., managers). 2002: Jumboised. 2003: Sold to P&O Ferries Ltd., (P&O Ferries Ship Management Ltd., managers), Dover, and renamed PRIDE OF KENT.

EUROPEAN PATHWAY as built

(Internet source / Rob De Visser)

EUROPEAN PATHWAY reconstructed **as PRIDE OF CANTERBURY**

(Internet source / Frank Lose)

9007295

POM.3. EUROPEAN PATHWAY (1998 - 2002)

22,986g. 6,895n. 7,509d. 179.40(BB) x 28.3 x 6.27 metres.
Four, 8-cyl 4 S.C.S.A. (400 x 560mm) Sulzer 8ZAL40S type oil engines made by Jugoturbina Diesel d.d., Karlovac, geared to twin controllable pitch propellers. 28,713 BHP. 21 kts. Twin thwartship thrust propellers forward.
81cabins, 200 berthed passenger / roro-cargo / ferry.
2.4.1991: Keel laid by Schichau Seebeckwerft AG, Bremerhaven (Yard No. 1076), for Sutten Ltd., (P&O European Ferries (Dover) Ltd., managers) 10.8.1991: Launched. 23.12.1991: Completed. 1998: P&O Stena Line Ship Management Ltd., managers. 2003: Sold to P&O Ferries Ltd., Dover, jumboised and renamed PRIDE OF CANTERBURY.

9007283

POM.4. EUROPEAN SEAWAY (1998 - 2002)

22,986g. 6,895n. 7,432d. 179.70(BB) x 28.28 x 6.25 metres.
Four, 8-cyl 4 S.C.S.A. (400 x 560mm) Sulzer 8ZAL40S type oil engines made by Jugoturbina Diesel d.d., Karlovac, geared to twin controllable pitch propellers. 28,713 BHP. 21 kts. Twin thwartship thrust propellers forward.
81cabins, 200 berthed passenger / roro-cargo / ferry.

15.10.1990: Keel laid by Schichau Seebeckwerft AG, Bremerhaven (Yard No. 1075), for Sutten Ltd., (P&O European Ferries (Dover) Ltd., managers). 20.4.1991: Launched. 2.10.1991: Completed. 1998: P&O Stena Line Ship Management Ltd., managers. 2003: P&O Ferries Ship Management Ltd., Dover, managers. 2005: Sold to P&O, London, (same managers).

EUROPEAN SEAWAY

(Internet source / Andreas Worteler)

P&OSL CALAIS

(Internet source / Andreas Worteler)

8517748

POM.5. PRIDE OF CALAIS / P&OSL CALAIS (1998 - 2002)

26,433g. 11,399n. 4,213d. 179.4(BB) x 28.3 x 6.27 metres.
Four, 14-cyl. 4S.C.S.A. (400 x 560mm) Sulzer 14ZA40S vee type oil engines made by Compagnie de Construcion Mec. Sulzer CCM., Mantes, geared to twin controllable pitch propellers. 31,405 BHP. 22 kts. Twin thwartship thrust propellers forward. Thwartship thrust Asymetric thruster unit.
45cabins, 90 berthed and 2,220 deck passenger / roro-cargo / ferry.
30.6.1986: Keel laid as PRIDE OF CALAIS by Schichau –Unterweser AG, Bremen (Yard No. 94), for Stanhope Steamship Company Ltd., (Townsend Car Ferries Ltd., managers). 11.4.1987: Launched. 26.11.1987: Completed. 31.12.1987: Transferred to P&O European Ferries (Dover) Ltd. 1998: Sold to P&O Stena Line (Ships) Ltd., (P&O Stena Line Ship Management Ltd., managers). 1999: Renamed P&OSL CALAIS. 2002: Renamed P O CALAIS. 2003: Sold to P&O Ferries Ships Ltd., Dover, (P&O Ferries Ship Management Ltd., managers)and renamed PRIDE OF CALAIS.

POM.6. COLOR VIKING (2000) see ship No. F.208 above.

SeaFrance S. A.

Associated Company 1996 - 2000.

SF.1. SEAFRANCE MANET (1996 -) see ship No. F.240 above

SEAFRANCE NORD PAS DE CALAIS

(Internet source / Cees De Bijl)

8512152
SF.2. SEAFRANCE NORD PAS DE CALAIS (2000 -)
7,264g. 2,492n. 4,284 160.08 (BB) x 23.02 x 5.941 metres.
Two, 16-cyl. 4 S.C.S.A. (400 x 480mm) Sulzer 16ZAV40 type oil engines made by Compagnie de Construcion Mec. Sulzer CCM., Mantes, geared to twin controllable pitch propellers. 24,501 BHP. 21.5 kts.
80 passenger / roro-cargo / rail vehicle ferry.
18.8.1986: Keel laid as NORD PAS DE CALAIS by NORMED-Constructions Navales du Littoral, Loc. Ger., Dunkirk (Yard No. 325), for Societe Nationale des Chemins de Fer Francais (S.N.C.F.), France. 15.4.1987: Launched. 14.12.1987: Completed. 1996: Sold to G.I.E. Nordlink (SeaFrance S.A., managers), and renamed SEAFRANCE NORD PAS DE CALAIS. 2000: Sold to SeaFrance S.A., Paris

SEAFRANCE RODIN

(Internet source / Rob De Visser)

9232527
SF.3. SEAFRANCE RODIN (2001 -)
33,796g. 0n. 5,700d. 186.00 x x 6,500 metres.
Two (centre) 12-cyl. 4 S.C.S.A. (460 x 580mm) Wartsila 12V46 vee type oil engines made by Wartsila Finland Oy, Finland. (31,812 BHP)
Two (wings) 8-cyl. 4 S.C.S.A. (460 x 580mm) Wartsila 8R46 type oil engines made by Wartsila Finland Oy, Finland. (21,208 BHP)
Engines geared in pairs to twin controllable pitch propellers. 25kts.
1,900 deck passenger RoRo cargo / ferry with bow and stern doors.

21.11.2000: Keel laid by Aker Finnyards Oy, Rauma (Yard No. 437), for SeaFrance S.A., Paris. 19.5.2001: Launched. 13.11.2001: Completed.

9305843
SF.4. SEAFRANCE BERLIOZ (2005 -)
33,796g. 0n. 5,700d. 186.00 x x 6,500 metres.
Two (centre) 12-cyl. 4 S.C.S.A. (460 x 580mm) Wartsila 12V46 vee type oil engines made by Wartsila Finland Oy, Finland. (31,812 BHP)
Two (wings) 8-cyl. 4 S.C.S.A. (460 x 580mm) Wartsila 8R46 type oil engines made by Wartsila Finland Oy, Finland. (21,208 BHP)
Engines geared in pairs to twin controllable pitch propellers. 25kts.
1,900 deck passenger RoRo cargo / ferry with bow and stern doors.
16.12.2003: Keel laid by Chantiers d'Atlantique Dunkirk (Yard No. 032), for SeaFrance S.A., Paris. 16.10.2004: Launched. 4.4.2005: Completed.

Managed vessels

SEAFRANCE CEZANNE

(Internet source)

SFM.1. SEAFRANCE CEZANNE. (1996 -) see ship No. F.192 above.

SFM.1. SEAFRANCE MONET (1996 - 2000) see ship No. F.28 above.

SEAFRANCE RENOIR

(Internet source)

SFM.1. SEAFRANCE RENOIR (1996 -) see ship No. F.193 above.

SFM.1. SEAFRANCE NORD PAS DE CALAIS (1996 – 2000) see ship No.SF. 2 above.

Part Four - Offshore Support Operations.

Stena Offshore Ltd
Coflexip Stena Offshore Ltd.
Stena Drilling Ltd

During 1976 another page was turned in the Company history when they agreed to take over the contracts for two Oil Rig Supply Vessels, (ORSV's)/ pipe carriers, which had been under construction for Norwegian owners. These were scheduled for delivery during 1977 but had been placed on the market when the contracts had been cancelled at an early stage. The shipbuilders approached STENA knowing the Company was always looking for avenues to further develop its services to the customer. The offer to STENA was that because the drawings had been done and materials purchased the price would be much less than a fresh order. Following market research STENA agreed the deal but, with the proviso that the vessels should be built 12 metres longer. This figure was conceived as the maximum length of vessel able to manoeuvre under anchor chains to deliver pipes to the pipe - laying barges then entering service in the North Sea. However, things became a little unstuck when by the time STENA PIPER the first of the two vessels was delivered the super - efficient pipe - layers had all but completed their work, leaving STENA with two vessels and no work. This was only short lived as the STENA PIPER, with three times the capacity of the average supply ship was soon fixed with a charter to British Petroleum, for employment in the Forties Field. This large capacity which had been insisted upon was soon to turn from worry to glee as this vessel, being much bigger and more heavily built was able to stand her ground off the rigs in most storms whilst her smaller counterparts had to run for shelter using expensive fuel and time on non - earning voyages both to and from sheltered havens.

Investment in the oil and gas industry continued to increase and in March 1979, Rederi Ab. Concordia placed a massive $100m., order for four ships of a totally new concept in offshore support craft. These vessels to be known as the STENA SEASPREAD class were to be capable of fire fighting, repairing structures both above and below sea level, and supporting diving operations. They were also a direct result of the success of the STENA PIPER in proving that big ships were needed and were successful in the North Sea. Whilst these vessels were building the two older vessels, STENA PIPER and STENA WELDER, were sent for lengthening and conversion into repair ships.

The company continued to further invest in offshore activity an exploration-drilling rig was ordered from Japan. It was proposed to name her STENA CHALLENGER. The rig, to have been capable of anchoring in 600 metres of water and drilling to depths of 9000 metres, proved to be a bit of a problem. Shortly after construction commenced there came a dramatic slump in the market for this operation leaving it grossly over tonnaged. To deal with this hitch delivery was delayed by two years and subsequently a partner was sought in the deal. This resulted in the DYVI organisation coming on the scene. When completed during 1984 the rig would be named DYVI STENA, having had the necessary modifications carried out to keep up with the ever-changing requirements of the market place.

An interesting, three ways, deal was struck between STENA, Brown & Root Ltd., and the British Government after the Falklands conflict. The British Government agreed to purchase STENA INSPECTOR, following the successful operation of both her and STENA SEASPREAD as heavy repair ships. However one stipulation was that they required two vessels in the South Atlantic, one being STENA SEASPREAD. If STENA INSPECTOR were to return to the U.K. for refit it would leave a shortfall. At this time STENA PROTECTOR was in the process of being sold to Brown & Root Ltd. STENA agreed the sale and that the vessel could be renamed BAR PROTECTOR for her new owners but with the proviso that she would be delivered to them after a period of service with the Royal Navy when replaced by H.M.S. DILIGENCE, (ex STENA INSPECTOR). It was therefore agreed that BAR PROTECTOR would remain operated by Stena until 1984.

Early in 1984, STENA placed an order, worth SEK 1.2 billion, for two sophisticated offshore support ships with British Shipbuilders Ltd., Sunderland. These two vessels to be called the STENA SEAWELL class were scheduled for delivery during 1986 - 1987.

Stena Offshore Ltd., on 5 March 1986 ordered two sophisticated support ships from Danish shipbuilders for delivery during 1987. Whilst these vessels were building lease agreements were drawn up and both vessels were delivered into the ownership of a Danish Finance Organisation, as STENA MAYO and STENA MARIANOS.

An opportunity arose late in the 1980's wherein the C.Y. Tung group of Hong Kong had previously acquired the Furness, Withy group, and having little interest in the offshore activities offered those for re-sale. The package included drilling rigs, both leased, chartered or owned, a large work barge and other associated plant. Stena successfully acquired the business and in so doing rapidly expanded their offshore division.

Also through the acquisition came an association with the French controlled Comex Group, specialist in undersea pipelines and associated activities. Subsequently that association developed into a partnership in 1995, and continued to flourish until 2001 when the French partner acquired Stena's shareholding in all but the drilling rigs.

Stena had also entered into a partnership in 1989, with Essar Shipping Ltd., to co-own and operate support craft under the Indian flag. In 1995 that operation was further expanded when both partners entered a co-operation with Peerless Shipping & Oilfield Ltd. Stena's participation in this arrangement was also concluded in 2001. Henceforth, Stena's only presence offshore is maintained through the activities of Stena Drilling.

The Offshore Fleet

STENA PIPER

(Author's collection)

7432264

OFF.1. STENA PIPER (1976 - 1981)

As built: 2,416g. 1,147n. 4,034d. 84.77 x 18.50 x 5.250 metres.
Post 1980: 3,722g. 1,096n. 4,034d. 95.33 x 18.50 x 5.374 metres.
Post 1995: 4,531g. 1,359n. 4,034d.
Two, 16-cyl. 4 S.C.S.A. (250 x 300mm) vee type, oil engines made by AS Bergens N/Y, Bergen, geared to twin screw shafts with controllable pitch propellers. 5,600 BHP. 13.5 kts.
Post 1980: Three thwartship thrust propellers forward, and two aft.
Oil rig support / deck cargo / pipe carrier.
2.12.1975: Keel laid as SEA PIPER by Trondheims M.V. Aker Trondelag AS, Trondheim (Yard No. 732), for unspecified Norwegian interests. 3.5.1976: Launched as STENA PIPER for Stena Ab, (Rederi Ab Concordia, managers), Sweden. 20.9.1976: Completed. 1980: Converted into a fire fighting / diving support ship, by Rickmers Rhederei GmbH, Rickmers Werft, Bremerhaven, which included the addition of a moonpool, a 100 ton crane, and a new hull section. Upon completion transferred, to Stena Line Ab, Sweden, and renamed STENA SEAHORSE. 1985: Demise-chartered to Mexicana de Servicios Maritimos S. A. de C.V., Mexico, and renamed TZIMIN. 1986: Transferred to La Metarie Corp, (Stena Ab, managers), Panama, and renamed SEAHORSE II. 1989: Transferred to Solent Water Shipping Corp. (Northern Coasters Ltd., managers), Panama. 1990: Sold to Oceanic Services Inc., (Servicios Maritimos de Campeche S. A. de C. V., managers), Panama, and renamed OCEANIC I. 1993: Transferred to the Mexico flag.

7432276

OFF.2. STENA SUPPLIER / STENA WELDER (1977 - 1981)

As built: 2,416g. 1,135n. 4,024d. 84.77 x 18.50 x 5.227 metres.

Post 1988: 3,401g. 1,573n. 4,034d. 96.63 x 18.50 x 5.340 metres.
Post 1995: 3,375g. 1,013n. 3,120d.
Two, 16-cyl. 4 S.C.S.A. (250 x 300) vee type, oil engines made by AS Bergens M.V., Bergen, geared to twin screw shafts with controllable pitch propellers. 5,600 BHP. 13.5 kts
Post 1988: Three thwartship thrust propellers forward and two aft.
Oil rig support / deck cargo / pipe carrier.
4.8.1976: Keel laid as SEA SUPPLIER by Trondheims M.V. Aker Trondelag AS, Trondheim, (Yard No. 733), for Norwegian interests. 19.1.1977: Launched as STENA SUPPLIER for Rederi Ab Concordia, (Stena Ab, managers), Sweden. 23.6.1977: Completed as STENA WELDER for Stena Line Ltd., Aberdeen. 1980: Lengthened by Schichau Unterweser, Bremerhaven, and converted into a fire fighting / diving support vessel, which included the addition of a moonpool hull section and a 100 ton crane. Upon completion, transferred to Rederi Ab Concordia, (Stena Line Ab, managers), Sweden, and renamed STENA WORKHORSE. 1984: Transferred to Stena Line Ltd., Cayman Islands. 1987: Transferred to Stena Ab, (Northern Coasters Ltd., managers). 1989: Transferred to Stena Offshore Ships Two Ltd., (same managers). 1989: Sold to unspecified owners, for reversion into a fire fighting pipe carrier, by G. Eides Sonner, Norway. 1990: Sold to Crusader Shipping Company Ltd. (Denholm Ship Management (UK) Ltd., managers), Isle of Man, and renamed ALPHA CRUSADER. 1993: Sold to Blackmoor Ltd., (Seaforth Marine Services Ltd., managers), Bahamas, and renamed CRUSADER. 1994: Renamed CRUSA. 1995: Sold to Adams Offshore Ltd., (same managers), and renamed ADAMS CHALLENGE. 1997: Sold to Algosaibi Diving & Marine Services, Dammam, Saudi Arabia, retaining Bahamas flag.

STENA CONSTRUCTOR

(Author's collection)

7814424

OFF.3. STENA CONSTRUCTOR (1980 - 1995)

As built: 5,823g. 2,810n. 4,670d. 111.49 x 20.99 x 6.701 metres.
Post 1994: 6,989g. 2,097n. 4,670d.
Post 2001: 9,640g. 2,893n. 6,799d. 126.30 x 28.40 x 7.250 metres.
Five, 16-cyl. 4 S.C.S.A. (250 x 300mm) Polar F216V-B vee type, oil engines made by Ab Bofors Nohab, Trollhattan, driving five generators, each powering four electric motors, geared to screw shaft with controllable pitch propeller. 14,400 BHP. 15.5 kts. Two, directional thrust propellers aft, and two thwartship thrust propellers forward.
Ice strengthened, fire fighting /diving, maintenance support ship for offshore installations. Fitted with a two, diving moonpools.
28.5.1979: Keel laid by Oresundsvarvet Ab, Landskrona (Yard No. 274), for Rederi Ab Concordia, (Stena Line Ab, managers), Sweden. 3.8.1979: Launched. 4.1.1980: Completed. 1987: Transferred to Stena Cargo Line Ltd., (Northern Coasters Ltd., managers), Bahamas. 1988: Transferred to Stena Offshore Ships One Ltd., (same managers). 1992: Stena Offshore Ltd., appointed as managers. 1995: Coflexip Stena Offshore Ships One Ltd., and renamed CSO CONSTRUCTOR. 2001: Sold to Technip Ships One Ltd., Aberdeen, (Technip Offshore UK Ltd., Aberdeen, managers), lengthened, widened and converted into a pipe-laying vessel.

7814436

OFF.4. STENA SEASPREAD (1980 - 1992)

As built: 6,061g. 2,672n. 4,835d. 112.02 x 20.99 x 6.839 metres.
Post 1994: 7,114g. 2,134n. 4,835d.

Five, 16-cyl. 4 S.C.S.A. (250 x 300mm) Polar F216V-B vee type, oil engines made by Ab Bofors Nohab, Trollhattan, driving five generators, each powering four electric motors, geared to screw shaft with controllable pitch propeller. 14,400 BHP. 15.5 kts. Two, directional thrust propellers aft, and two thwartship thrust propellers forward.
Ice strengthened, fire fighting / diving, maintenance support ship for offshore installations. Fitted with two diving moonpools.
6.8.1979: Keel laid by Oresundsvarvet Ab, Landskrona (Yard No. 275), for Stena Atlantic Line Ltd., (Stena Line Ab, managers), London. 12.10.1979: Launched. 25.3.1980: Completed. 1982: Chartered by British Government as a repair ship both during and after the Falklands conflict. 4.1983: Returned to owners. 1989: Transferred to Midland Montague Equipment Finance (UK) Ltd., (Northern Coasters Ltd., managers). 1992: Renamed SEASPREAD, Stena Offshore Ltd., appointed as managers. 1994: Sold to Cable & Wireless (Marine) Ltd., London, and converted into a cable-layer & repair ship. 2002: Sold to Cal Dive International Inc., Morgan City, USA, converted into a cable layer / repair, and renamed ECLIPSE under the Bahamas flag.

STENA SEASPREAD

(Author's collection)

7814448

OFF.5. STENA INSPECTOR (1981 - 1984)

As Built: 5,814g. 2,806n. 4,885d. 111.49 x 20.99 x 6.839 metres.
Post 1982: 6,060g. 2,672n. 4,670d.
Post 1984: 8,048g. 2,414n. 4,041d. 111.49 x 20.99 x 6,700 metres
Five, 16-cyl. 4 S.C.S.A. (250 x 300mm) Polar F216V-B vee type oil engines made by Ab Bofors Nohab, Trollhattan, driving five generators, each powering four electric motors, geared to screw shaft with controllable pitch propeller. 14,400 BHP. 15.5 kts. Two, directional thrust propellers aft, and two thwartship thrust propellers forward.
Ice strengthened, fire fighting / diving, maintenance support ship for offshore installations. Fitted with a two, diving moonpools.
28.1.1980: Keel laid by Oresundsvarvet Ab, Landskrona (Yard No. 276), Rederi Ab Concordia, (Stena Line Ab, managers), Sweden. 3.4.1980: Launched. 12.1.1981: Completed. 1982: Transferred to Stena Caribbean Line Ltd., London. (O.N. 399182) for charter to the British Government, for use as a repair ship, during and after the Falklands conflict. 1984: Sold to the Government of the United Kingdom (The Secretary of State for Defence) (Commodore Royal Fleet Auxiliary) London, and renamed DILIGENCE.

STENA PROTECTOR

(Author's collection)

7814450

OFF.6. STENA PROTECTOR (1981 - 1983)

As built: 5,814g. 2,805n. 4,885d. 111.49 x 20.99 x 6.839 metres.
Post 1984: 6,987g. 2,096n. 4,670d.
Five, 16-cyl. 4 S.C.S.A. (250 x 300mm) Polar F216V-B vee type oil engines made by Ab Bofors Nohab, Trollhattan, driving five generators, each powering four electric motors, geared to screw shaft with controllable pitch propeller. 14,400 BHP. 15.5 kts. Two directional thrust propellers aft, and two thwartship thrust propellers forward.
Ice strengthened, fire fighting / diving, maintenance support ship for offshore installations. Fitted with two diving moonpools.
8.4.1980: Keel laid by Oresundsvarvet Ab, Landskrona (Yard No. 277), for Rederi Ab Concordia, (Stena Line Ab, managers), Sweden. 19.6.1980: Launched. 13.3.1981: Completed. 1983: Sold to Brown & Root Construction Ltd., (Stena (UK) Ltd., managers), renamed BAR PROTECTOR, for delivery upon the completion of a charter to the British Government as a repair vessel. (Relieved by H.M.S.DILIGENCE, ex STENA INSPECTOR qv). 1984: Delivered and transferred to Bahamas flag, (Denholm Ship Management Ltd., managers). 1988: Sold to European Marine Contractors Ltd., New Maldon, UK, and removed from management.

STENA WORKHORSE

(Author's collection)

OFF.7. STENA WORKHORSE (1981 - 1989) see ship No. OFF.2 above.

STENA SEAHORSE

(Author's collection)

OFF.8. STENA SEAHORSE (1981 - 1985) see ship No. OFF.1 above.

6508315

OFF.9. CARIBBEAN WIND (1982 - 1985)

As built: 473g. 32n. 303d. 62.01 x 10.32 x 4.141 metres.
Post 1998: 371g.
12-cyl. 4 S.C.S.A. (400 x 500mm) Deutz RBV12M350 vee type oil engine made by Kloeckner - Humboldt Deutz, Koeln. 3,000 BHP. 14 kts.
Salvage tug.
2.7.1964: Launched as HEROS by F. Schichau GmbH, Bremerhaven (Yard No. 1729), for Bugsier Reederei-u-Bergungs A. G., Hamburg. 31.10.1964: Completed. 1979: Sold to Arne Avelin Bogserbats Ab, Sweden, and renamed WIROS. 1982: Purchased by Contrast Maritime Ltd., Cayman Islands, and renamed CARIBBEAN WIND. 1985: Sold to Polaris Towing Company Ltd., Malta, and renamed POLARIS. 1985: Sold to Spector Shipping Company S.A., Panama, and renamed SCAN SALVOR. 1987: Sembawang Johnson

Management Pte. Ltd., appointed as managers. 1988: Sold to Carena Naviera S.A., Cayman Islands, and renamed KERVEROS. 1992: Sold to Omega II Shipping Company SA, Thessaloniki, Greece. 2000: Zouros Shipping S.A., appointed as managers. 2004: Thessaloniki Maritime S.A., appointed as managers.

CARIBBEAN WIND as **SCAN SALVOR** (Author's collection)

BAR PROTECTOR

(Author's collection)

OFF .10. BAR PROTECTOR (1983 - 1984) see ship No. OFF.6 above.

8751095

OFF.11. STENA CHALLENGER (1) / DYVI STENA (1984 - 2001)

12,881g. 7,351n. 367'5" x 223'1" x 111'7"
Service draft 65'7". Transit draft 22'3½".
Four columns 39'4" diameter. Four columns 23' diameter.
Drill depth 30,000' maximum.
Non powered exploration drilling rig.
1982: Launched as STENA CHALLENGER by Mitsubishi Heavy Industries Ltd., Hiroshima (Yard No. 326), for Stena Ab, Sweden. 1984: Completed as DYVI STENA for Stena Shipping Ab, London, (operated by Dyvi Offshore AS). 1991: Transferred to Barclays Mercantile Industrial Finance Ltd., (Stena Offshore Ltd.,

managers). 2001: Sold to Stena Houlder Ltd., and renamed STENA DEE. 2004: Transferred to Stena Drilling Ltd., Aberdeen.

DYVI STENA

(Author's collection)

8112524

OFF.12. STENA SEAPEARL (1984)

As built: 1,599g. 746n. 2,972d. 67.21 x 17.51 x 6.082 metres.
Post 1994: 1,924g. 675n. 2,972d.
Four, 8-cyl. 4 S.C.S.A. (220 x 240mm) Wartsila 8R22 type oil engines (6,960 BHP) made by Oy., Wartsila Ab., Vaasa / Vasa, powering four generators, each driving two 2,000 SHP., electric motors, geared to twin screw shafts with controllable pitch propellers. 12.5 kts. Two thwartship thrust controllable pitch propellers forward.
Oil rig supply / deck cargo vessel.
18.9.1981: Keel laid as SEA PEARL by Drammen Slip & Verks., Drammen (Yard No. 95), for K.S Bugge Supply Ships VI AS, (AS N. R. Bugge, managers), Norway. 31.8.1982: Launched. 3.7.1983: Completed. 4.1984: Purchased by Stena Ocean Line Ltd., Cayman Islands, and renamed STENA SEAPEARL. 10.1984: Demise chartered to B.U.E. Offshore Vessels, and renamed BRITISH AMETHYST. 1988: Transferred to Northern Coasters Ltd., renamed MAERSK ATTENDER and transferred to the Danish flag, for charter to but was sold to Maersk Supply Service, (A. P. Moller, managers), Denmark. 1994: Transferred to A. P. Moller Singapore (Pte) Ltd. 1995: A.P. Moller appointed as managers. 1998: Sold to PR International Offshore Services ANS, Aalsund, Norway, (Australian Offshore Services, managers), and renamed LADY KARI-ANN, under Norway NIS flag. 2003: Farstad Shipping Indian Pacific Ltd., Melbourne, Australia, appointed as managers.

OFF.13. BRITISH AMETHYST (1984 - 1988) see ship No. OFF.12 above.

OFF.14. TZIMIN (1985 - 1986) see ship No. OFF.1 above.

OFF.15. SEAHORSE II (1986 - 1990) see ship No. OFF.1 above.

8324567

OFF.16. STENA SEAWELL (1987 - 1995)

9,158g. 2,747n. 4,615d. 111.41 x 22.96 x 7.260 metres.
Six, 18-cyl. 4 S.C.S.A. (210 x 210mm) Hedamora V18B/12 vee type oil engines made by Hedemora Verkstader Ab, Hedemora, geared to 3 directional thrust controllable pitch propellers aft, and 3 thwartship thrust controllable pitch propellers forward. 17,220 BHP. 15 kts.
Diving, maintenance support / fire fighting vessel, for offshore installations.
1983: Ordered from Sunderland Shipbuilders Ltd., Sunderland, (Yard No. 24), by Stena Ab. 25.6.1984: Keel laid. 12.3.1986: Launched for Northern Coasters Ltd., London. 31.3.1987: Completed for Lombard

Leasing Services Ltd., (Northern Coasters Ltd., managers), London. 1990: Stena Offshore Ltd., appointed as managers. 1995: Transferred to Coflexip Stena Offshore Ltd., and renamed CSO SEAWELL. 1997: Sold to Natwest Leasing Facilities Ltd., (Coflexip Stena Offshore Ltd., managers), London. 2001: Managers restyled as Technip Offshore UK Ltd. 2003: Sold to Well Ops UK Ltd., Aberdeen, and renamed SEAWELL.

8600818

OFF.17. STENA MAYO (1987 - 1991)

4,294g. 1,288n. 2,706d. 91.12 x x 6.500 metres.

Four, 6-cyl. 4 S.C.S.A. (320 x 350mm) Wartsila 6R32 type oil engines (7,692 BHP) made by Oy., Wartsila Ab., Vaasa/Vasa, driving generators, powering two 2,719 SHP., electric motors, geared to two directional thrust propellers aft, and three thwartship thrust controllable pitch propellers forward.

Diving, maintenance support / fire fighting vessel, for offshore installations.

5.2.1986: Ordered from Dannebrog Vaerft AS, Aarhus (Yard No. 188), by Stena Offshore Ltd., (Northern Coasters Ltd., managers), London. 27.2.1986: Keel laid. 10.4.1986: Launched for KS., Difko XLV / Kodif XLV ApS., (same managers), Denmark. 17.6.1987: Completed for Nedifko XLV C.V., (Workships B.V., managers), Rotterdam. 1990: Owners restyled Difko 45 C.V., (Stena Offshore Ltd., managers). 1991: Sold to Difko Administration AS., (Workships Contractors B.V., managers), and renamed MAYO. 1993: Transferred to Nedifko XLV C.V., (Subsea Offshore Ltd., managers), Bahamas, and renamed SUBSEA MAYO. 1994: Sold to Sondenfjeldske Mayo Ks., (same managers). 1999: DSND Offshore AS appointed as managers. 2004: Sold to Petroleum Marine Services, Cairo, Egypt, (Subsea 7 Vessel Management AS, Grimstad, Norway, managers), and renamed PMS MAYO, under the Egyptian flag.

8302014

OFF.18. STENA VENTURER (1) (1987)

As built: 9,487g. 2,846n. 10,569d. 121.95 x 34.80 x 5.374 metres.

Post 1997:10,617g. 3,185n. 10,569d.

Five, 12-cyl. 4 S.C.S.A. (220 x 280mm) Daihatsu 6DV-22A vee type oil engines made by Daihatsu Diesel Manufacturing Company Ltd., Moriyama, powering five generators, each driving four 1,700 SHP., electric motors, geared to twin directional propellers aft., and two retractable propellers forward. 11,000 BHP. 10 kts.

Cable laying vessel.

15.6.1983: Keel laid as ITM VENTURER by Hyundai Mipo Dockyard Company Ltd., Ulsan (Yard No. 831), for I.T.M. (Offshore) Ltd., London. 16.10.1983: Launched. 1.12.1983: Completed. 1987: Purchased by Stena Ab, and renamed STENA VENTURER. 1987: Renamed NORTHERN VENTURER. 1989: Sold to Euroshipping S.p.A. di Navigazione, Italy, and renamed GIULIO VERNE. 1997: Sold to V-Ships Italy (Shipping Management S.A.M. (V-Ships), managers), Italy. 1999: Sold to Pirelli Cavi, Monte Carlo, Monaco, (same managers), retaining the Italian flag. 2002: V. Ships Monaco, Monte Carlo, appointed as managers.

OFF.19. NORTHERN VENTURER (1987 - 1989) see ship No. OFF.17, above.

STENA MARIANOS

(Stena)

8601513

OFF.20. STENA MARIANOS (1987 - 1995)

4,294g. 1,288n. 2,706d. 91.12 x x 6.50 metres.

Four, 6-cyl. 4 S.C.S.A. (320 x 350mm) Wartsila 6R32D type oil engines (7,692 BHP) made by Oy. Wartsila Ab, Vaasa / Vasa, driving generators, powering two 2,719 SHP., electric motors, geared to two directional thrust propellers aft, and three thwartship thrust controllable pitch propellers forward.
Diving, maintenance support / fire fighting vessel, for offshore installations.
5.3.1986: Ordered from Dannebrog Værft AS., Aarhus (Yard No. 189), by Stena Offshore Ltd., (Northern Coasters Ltd., managers), London. 31.10.1986: Keel laid. 28.4.1987: Launched for KS., Difko XLV / Kodif XLV Aps., (same managers), Denmark. 18.12.1987: Completed for Nedifko XLV C.V., (Workships B.V., managers), Rotterdam. 1990: Owners restyled Difko 45 C.V., (Stena Offshore Ltd., managers). 1994: COFLEXIP / Stena Offshore Ltd., appointed as managers. 1995: Renamed CSO MARIANOS. 1997: Sold to Coflexip Stena Offshore Ltd., Aberdeen, under the Bahamas flag. 2001: Sold to Technip Offshore UK Ltd., Aberdeen. 4.3.2005: Agreement reached to sell vessel to Mermaid Offshore Services Ltd., with delivery in 8.2005. 10.2005: Renamed MERMAID COMMANDER, under the Thailand flag.

STENA WELLSERVICER

(World Ship Society Ltd)

8324579

OFF.21. STENA SEAWELL II / STENA WELLSERVICER (1988 - 1995)

9,158g. 2,747n. 4,615d. 111.40 x 22.96 x 7.260 metres.
Six, 18-cyl. 4 S.C.S.A. (210 x 210mm) Hedamora V18B/12 vee type oil engines made by Hedemora Verkstader Ab, Hedemora, geared to 3 directional thrust controllable pitch propellers aft, and 3 thwartship thrust controllable pitch propellers forward. 17,220 BHP. 15 kts.
Diving, maintenance support / fire fighting vessel, for offshore installations.
1983: Ordered as STENA SEAWELL II from North Eastern Shipbuilders Ltd., Sunderland (Yard No. 25), by Northern Coasters Ltd., London. 20.3.1985: Keel laid. 30.1.1987: Launched for Fitzroy Finance Ltd., (Northern Coasters Ltd., managers), London. 1988: Completed. 1991: Stena Offshore Ltd., appointed as managers. 1995: Renamed CSO WELLSERVICER, Coflexip Stena Offshore Ltd., appointed as managers. 2001: Managers restyled as Technip Offshore UK Ltd., Aberdeen. 2005: Sold to BMBF No. 3 Ltd., (same managers)

OFF.22. MAERSK ATTENDER (1988) see ship No. OFF.13 above.

7723613

OFF.23. STENA APACHE (1989 - 1995)

As built: 5,563g. 2,116n. 9,000d. 122.92 x 21.37 x 5.500 metres.
Post 1994: 7,280g. 2,184n. 4,994d.
Two, 20-cyl 2 S.C.S.A. (230 x 254mm) 20-645-E7 vee type oil engines made by General Motors Corp. Electromotive Division, La Grange, U.S.A., reverse reduction geared to four thruster units, two forward and two aft. 7,200 BHP.
Pipelayer, diving support vessel with a 89 ton and 40 ton crane.
26.1.1978: Keel laid as APACHE by Todd Shipyards Corp., Galveston (Yard No. 56), for Santa Fe-Pomeroy Marine Services Corp. U.S.A. 12.12.1978: Launched. 16.6.1979: Completed. 1980: Sold to Marina Equipment & Shipping Corp., U.S.A. 1981: Sold to Apache Marine Services Inc., (Santa Fe Overseas Inc., managers), U.S.A. 1986: Sold to Santa Fe International Corp., U.S.A. 1987: Owners restyled as Santa Fe Offshore Constructions Corp. 1989: Purchased by Stena Ab, and renamed STENA APACHE. 1995:

Transferred to Coflexip Stena Offshore Ltd., Aberdeen, and renamed CSO APACHE. 2001: Sold to Technip Offshore UK Ltd., Aberdeen.

8208854

OFF.24. STENA ORELIA (1989 - 1995)

As built: 5,553g. 3,080n. 2,700d. 123.50 x 19.36 x 4.501 metres.
Post 1995: 6,368g. 1.910n. 2,700d.
Ten, Mirlees Blackstone ESL6M type oil engines, six connected to generators powering six Stone Vickers type thrusters.
Diving & Submersibles support vessel.
14.6.1982: Keel laid as ORELIA by Swan, Hunter Shipbuilders Ltd., Wallsend (Yard No. 120), for Houlder Offshore Ltd., (Houlder Comex Ltd., operators), London. 11.12.1982: Launched. 12.6.1984: Completed 1989: Purchased by Stena Ab, and renamed STENA ORELIA. 1991: Stena Offshore Ltd., appointed as managers. 1991: Transferred to Stena Offshore Ships Three Ltd. 1991: Transferred to Coflexip Stena Offshore Ships Three Ltd., and renamed CSO ORELIA. 2001: Sold to Technip Offshore UK Ltd., Aberdeen. 2004: Transferred to the Marshall Islands flag.

7529902

OFF.25. UNCLE JOHN (1989 - 2000)

5,581g. 3,298n. 3,639d.
Platform rectangular 77.03 x 52.63 x 6.0 metres.
Service draught; 15.511 metres with 9,692 tonnes displacement.
Transit draught; 5.791 metres with 6,957 tonnes displacement.
Five, 18-cyl. 4 S.C.S.A. Hedemora V18A12 vee type oil engines (11,000 BHP total) each driving a generator, powering four 1,500 SHP., electric motors driving two stern propellers at 12 kts. Also powering generators connected to six 1,000 SHP., electric motors for use in positioning.
Semi-submersible, self propelled fire-fighting and diving support platform.
1977: Completed by Nylands Verksted, Oslo, (Yard No. 727), for Houlder Offshore Ltd., Ellerman Lines Ltd., & Ugland (UK) Ltd., (Houlder Comex Ltd., operators). 1983: Ellerman Lines Ltd., transferred their shareholding to their subsidiary Domino Containerships Ltd. 1989: Stena Ab acquired the Houlder shareholding and created Stena Houlder Ltd., (Houlder Offshore Ltd., managers). Stena subsequently acquired the remaining shareholdings. 2000: Sold to Technip Offshore UK Ltd., Aberdeen. 2002: Sold to Cal Dive Offshore Inc., (Cal Dive International Inc., managers), Morgan City, USA, under the Bahamas flag.

8928480

OFF.26. HUNTER (1989 - 1997)

7,638g. 355'0"oa x 248'7" x 120'0" to main deck.
70' operating draught (Transit draught 16'0" minimum).
Four, 12-cyl. 4 S.C.S.A. Bergen KVGB-12 type oil engines (8,800 BHP) driving 4 generators powering 4 electric motors (1,734 SHP), driving twin screws. 9.5 kts.
Aker H-3 design semi-submersible drilling rig with rectangular platform.
15.12.1975: Completed as TREASURE HUNTER by Nylands Verksted, Oslo (Yard No. 722), as a semi-submersible drilling rig for Wilh Wilhelmsen. 10.1976: Converted by her builders into a construction support vessel. 1989: Sold to KS Hunter Drilling, Bahamas, and renamed HUNTER, and operated by Comex Houlder Ltd., London. 1989: Percentage control acquired by Stena Houlder Ltd., (Stena Offshore Ltd., managers). 1997: Sold to Agasoster Batservice Shipping, Norway, and renamed ORION II 2001: Sold to Hamour Shipping AS, and renamed HUNTER. 2002: Sold to Thor AS, Faeroe Islands, (Uksnoy AS, managers), and renamed THOR SUPPORTER. 2003: Removed from management.

8755742

OFF.27. YATZY (1989 - 1990)

14,230g. 4,269n.
Platform rectangular 79.0 x 60.0 x 32.5 metres.
Service draught 21.5 metres with 25,909 tonnes displacement.
Transit draught 10.5 metres with 17,549 tonnes displacement.
Four cylindrical support columns.
Nine, 16-cyl. 4 S.C.S.A. CMI type oil engines driving generators powering electric motors driving six rotatable controllable pitch propellers at 7 kts.
Self-propelled semi-submersible drilling rig.
1988: Completed by Boelwerf S. A., Temse (Yard No. 1521), for Exmar N. V., Belgium, for operation by Comex Houlder Ltd., London. 1989: Houlder Offshore Ltd., acquired by Stena Ab., together with operating

rights on rig. 1990: Sold to Exmar Lux S.A., (Arethusa Zapata Offshore Ltd., managers), Luxemburg. 2003: Sold to Yatzy Drilling SA, (Diamond Offshore Drilling Inc., Houston Texas, managers), and renamed OCEAN YATZY under Panamanian flag.

8751083

OFF.28. DUNDEE KINGSNORTH (1989 - 1990)

13,180 tons displacement. 108.2 x 67.46 metres. Transit depth 6.706 metres.
Four, 12-cyl. 4 S.C.S.A. Bergen KVGB-12 type oil engines (8,800 BHP) driving 4 generators powering 4 electric motors (1,734 SHP), driving twin screws. 9.5 kts.
Aker H-3 design semi-submersible drilling rig with rectangular platform.
1975: Completed by Rauma-Repola Oy, Mantyluoto (Yard No. RR3), for Kingsnorth Marine Drilling Ltd., Bahamas, for operation by Comex Houlder Ltd., London. 1989: Sold to Bluewater Shipping Ltd. 1989: Houlder Offshore Ltd., acquired by Stena Ab., together with operating rights on rig. 1990: Sold to KS Dundee Explorer, (Ross Offshore Ltd., managers), Bahamas, and renamed DUNDEE EXPLORER. 1995: Sold to Triton Holdings Ltd., (Sedco-Forex Drilling Services Ltd., operators), Liberia, and renamed SEDCO EXPLORER. 2004: Sold to Pride North Sea BV1, and renamed SEA EXPLORER.

8752192

OFF.29. KINGSNORTH UK (1989 - 1990)

13,180 tons displacement. 108.2 x 67.46 metres. Transit depth 6.706 metres.
Four, 12-cyl. 4 S.C.S.A. Bergen KVGB-12 type oil engines (8,800 BHP) driving 4 generators powering 4 electric motors (1,734 SHP), driving twin screws. 9.5 kts.
Aker H-3 design semi-submersible drilling rig with rectangular platform.
1975: Completed by Rauma-Repola Oy, Mantyluoto (Yard No. RR4), for Kingsnorth Marine Drilling Ltd., Bahamas, for operation by Comex Houlder Ltd., London. 1989: Sold to Sunrise Shipping Ltd. 1989: Houlder Offshore Ltd., acquired by Stena Ab., together with operating rights on rig. 1990: Sold to KS Kingsnorth Explorer, (Ross Offshore Ltd., managers), Bahamas, and renamed KINGSNORTH EXPLORER. 1995: Sold to Transocean ASA, and renamed TRANSOCEAN EXPLORER, under the Bahamas flag 2005: Transferred to Transocean Offshore UK Ltd., Aberdeen, retaining the Bahamas flag.

8755297

OFF.30. SHELF DRILLER (1989 - 1991)

5,421g. 4,751n. 73.15 x 86.26 x 7.49 metres rectangular platform.
Transit draught 3.987 metres at 10,668 tonnes displacement.
Three 438' lattice type legs.
Self-elevating cantilever type drilling rig, non-propelled.
1982: Completed by C.F.E.M. Cie.Francaise d'Enterprises Metalliques, France, (Yard No. T2005), for Cintra Inc., (Houlder Marine Drilling Ltd., operators), London, for operation by Comex Houlder Ltd., London. 1989: Houlder Offshore Ltd., acquired by Stena Ab., together with operating rights on rig. 1991: Sold to KS Shelf Explorer, (Ross Offshore Ltd., managers), Liberia, and renamed SHELF EXPLORER 1995: Sold to Transocean ASA, under the Liberian flag. 2005: Sold to Transocean International Offshore Ventures Inc., Houston, and renamed TRANSOCEAN SHELF EXPLORER, retaining the Liberian flag.

8751681

OFF.31. HIGHSEAS DRILLER (1989 - 2001)

9,996g. 7,181n. 79.25 x 67.06 metres.
Transit draught 7.315 metres at 16,256 tonnes displacement.
Service draught 19. 812 metres at 25,000 tonnes displacement.
Six cylindrical support columns.
Four, 12-cyl. 4 S.C.S.A. Bergen KVGB-12 type oil engines (8,800 BHP) driving 4 generators powering 4 electric motors (1,734 SHP), driving twin screws. 9.5 kts.
semi-submersible drilling rig with rectangular platform.
Friede & Goldman L 907 design semi-submersible drilling rig with rectangular platform.
1983: Completed by Daewoo SB and Heavy Machinery Ltd., Okpo (Yard No. 3007), for Houlder Offshore Ltd., London, for operation by Comex Houlder Ltd., London. 1989: Houlder Offshore Ltd., acquired by Stena Ab. 2001: Transferred to Stena HSD Ltd., (Stena Drilling Ltd., managers), Aberdeen, and renamed STENA SPEY.

8007171

OFF.32. DYNAMIC CONSTRUCTOR / ESSAR STENA I (1989 - 1995)

As built: 4,484g. 1,087n. 2,986d. 105.59 x 19.66 x 5.520 metres.
Post 1995: 8,300g. 2,490n. 2,100d. 129.10 x 24.72 x 6.014 metres.

Five, 8-cyl. 4 S.C.S.A. (240 x 330mm) MaK 8M332AK type oil engines made by Krupp MaK. Maschinenbau GmbH, Kiel, 9,000 BHP., driving five generators each connected to two 1,500 SHP., electric motors forward and two 2,200 SHP., electric motors aft, geared to screw shafts. Two directional propellers forward & aft. Thwartship thrust propeller forward and aft.
Fire-fighting, moonpool diving maintenance support vessel for offshore oil installations.
15.10.1980: Keel laid as SEABEX ONE by Werft Nobiskrug GmbH, Rendsburg (Yard No. 705), for Seabex Industrielle Tiefseetechnik GmbH i Bereiligungs K.G. 7.3.1981: Launched. 30.6.1981: Completed. 1986: Sold to Midland Montague Ltd., and Warburg Leasing Company (No.4) Ltd., (Single Buoy Moorings (U.K.) Ltd., managers), London, and renamed DYNAMIC CONSTRUCTOR. 1989: Purchased by Stena Shipping Line Ltd., (Stena Offshore Ltd., managers), London. 1989: Transferred to Essar Shipping Ltd., India, and renamed ESSAR STENA 1. 1995: Sold to Stena Offshore Ltd., Aberdeen, and renamed STENA VENTURER, under the Bahamas flag. 1995: Transferred to Coflexip Stena Offshore Ships One Ltd., (Coflexip Stena Offshore Ltd., managers), lengthened, widened, and renamed CSO VENTURER. 2001: Sold to Technip Ships One Ltd., Aberdeen, (Technip Offshore UK Ltd., Aberdeen, managers), retaining the Bahamas flag.

STENA WILCHIEF

(Author's collection)

8304799

OFF.33. STENA WILCHIEF (1992 - 1995)

3,700g. 1,110n. 1,959d. 78.31 x x 5.579 metres.
Two, 16-cyl. 4 S.C.S.A. (250 x 300mm) Normo KVGB-16 type oil engines (centre), 7,260 BHP. made by AS Bergens M.V.., Bergen, each driving two generators 2,715kW 660V a.c., each powering two electric motors, each of 2,600 SHP.
Two, 12-cyl. 4 S.C.S.A. (250 x 300mm) Normo KVGB-12 type oil engines (wings), 5,620 bhp. made by AS Bergens M.V.., Bergen, each driving two generators 2,020kW 660V a.c., each powering two electric motors, each of 2,600 SHP.
All motors above, connected to twin screw shafts with controllable pitch propellers; Three thwartship thrust controllable pitch propellers forward; Tunnel thruster unit, and a thwartship thrust controllable pitch propeller aft. 12 kts.
Fire-fighting diving support ship with two moonpools, for offshore installations.
11.4.1983: Keel laid as WILCHIEF by Trosvik Verksted AS, Trosvik (Yard No. 135), for KS North Sea Diving Support AS, (Anders Wilhelmsen and Company, managers), Norway. 10.12.1983: Launched. 9.3.1984: Completed. 1992: Stena Offshore Ltd., appointed as lease / managers, and renamed STENA WILCHIEF. 1993: Transferred to Stena Offshore Ltd. 1995: Transferred to Coflexip Stena Offshore Ltd., and renamed CSO ALLIANCE. 2000: Transferred to the Bahamas flag. 2001: Sold to Technip Offshore UK Ltd., Aberdeen.

OFF.34. CSO ALLIANCE **(1995 - 2001)** see ship No. OFF. 33 above.

OFF.35. STENA VENTURER (2) **(1995)** see ship No. OFF. 32 above.

OFF.36. CSO VENTURER **(1995 - 2001)** see ship No. OFF. 32 above.

CSO VENTURER

(Internet source / Ronald Englesmann)

OFF.37. CSO APACHE **(1995 - 2001)** see ship No. OFF. 23 above.

OFF.38. CSO SEAWELL **(1995 - 2001)** see ship No. OFF. 16 above.

OFF.39. CSO MARIANOS **(1995 - 2001)** see ship No. OFF. 20 above.

OFF.40. CSO WELLSERVICER **(1995 - 2001)** see ship No. OFF. 21 above.

OFF.41. CSO CONSTRUCTER **(1995 - 2001)** see ship No. OFF. 3 above.

CSO CONSTRUCTOR following lengthening and conversion into a pipelayer.

(Author's collection)

8110942

OFF.42. FLEX INSTALLER (1995 - 1998)

As built: 1,586g. 480n. 3,050d. 85.32 x 19.44 x 5.122 metres oa,
Post 1989: 4,416g. 1,324n. 6,200d. 102.70 x 19.42 x 6.700 metres
Two, 8-cyl. (320 x 350mm) Wartsila 8R32 type engines made by Oy Wartsila Ab., Vaasa/Vasa, reared to twin controllable pitch propellers. 7,400 BHP., 13.5 kts. 3 thwartship thrust controllable pitch propellers forward and aft.
Deck cargo diving support ship.
Post 1989: Cable laying additional to above.
25.5.1982: Keel laid as UGLAND COMEX I by FEAB Marstrandsverken, Marstrand (Yard No. 160), for John Menzies (Leasing) Ltd., (Ugland Brothers Ltd., managers), London. 16.8.1982: Launched. 130.4.983: Completed. 1985: Sold to Barclays Mercantile (No.3) Ltd., (same managers), London, and renamed ITM INSTALLER. 1986: Sold to Northern Installer Ltd., (Denholm Ship Management (I.O.M.) Ltd., managers),

Isle of Man, and renamed NORTHERN INSTALLER. 1989: Sold to Northern Contractors International Ltd., (Ugland Offshore AS, managers), Cayman Islands, lengthened and converted for additionally laying cable. 1995: Sold to Flex Installer Offshore Ltd., (Coflexip Stena Offshore Ltd., managers), and renamed FLEX INSTALLER. 1998: Renamed CSO INSTALLER. 2000: Sold to Technip Offshore UK Ltd., Aberdeen. 2000: Sold to Global Marine Systems Ltd., and renamed WAVE ALERT. 2003: Sold to Torch Offshore Inc, Gretna, Lousiana , and renamed MIDNIGHT WRANGLER, under the Vanuatu flag. 2005: Sold to Louisiana Pipelaying Inc, (Quay Marine Associates, Dartmouth NS, managers), and renamed SEA WRANGLER, retaining the Vanuatu flag.

8752996

OFF.43. STENA CLYDE (1996 -)

O.N. 376547. 8,397g. 4,710n. 355 x 221 x 120 feet.

Two engines made by Ruston Paxman Diesels Ltd., Lincoln, driving electric generators, powering 4 electric motors connected in pairs to twin screws. 10,560 BHP, total. 8 kts.

Self-propelled, semi-submersible oil rig.

1974: Ordered as ATLANTIC 3 from Rauma Repola Oy, Pori, Finland, for Atlantic Drilling Company, (Reardon Smith Exploration Ltd., managers), Cardiff. 1976: Completed as SEA CONQUEST for Celtic Drilling Company, (Reardon Smith Exploration Ltd., managers), for bare-boat charter to British Petroleum Company Ltd., London. 1.1979: Sold to BP Petroleum Development Ltd., London. 7.1982: Sold to Ben Line Group, Leith, and renamed OCEAN BENLOYAL 1996: Sold to Stenloyal Ltd., (Stena Drilling Ltd., operating managers), Leith, and renamed STENA CLYDE. 2005: Transferred to Stena International Ltd., Ashford, (same operating managers).

STENA CLYDE (Courtesy Stena Ab)

CSO INSTALLER

(Author's collection)

OFF.44. CSO INSTALLER (1998 - 2001) see ship No. OFF.42 above.

5290777

OFF.45. FLEXSERVICE 1 (1999 - 2000)

As built: 6,805g. 2,692n. 9,896d. 129.70 x 17.51 x 7,798 metres

Post 1976: 7,679g. 2,303n. 9,896d. 131.86 x 22.26 x 7.013 metres oa

3-cyl. 2 S.C.S.A. (600 x 2320mm) Doxford type engine made by North Eastern Marine Engineering Company Ltd., Wallsend. 2,600 BHP. 11.5 kts.

7.1976: Twin directional thrust propellers fitted forward of the engine room and twin directional thrust propellers fitted forward.

Pipelayer.

6.10.1960: Keel laid as RAVENSWORTH by Austin & Pickersgill Ltd., Southwick, Sunderland (Yard No. 365), an ore carrier, for Watergate Steamship Company Ltd., (R. S. Dalgliesh Ltd., managers), Newcastle.

12.12.1960: Completed. 1976: Sold Flexservice N. V., Netherlands Antilles, (Ugland Management Company AS, managers), converted into a cable layer, and renamed FLEXSERVICE 1. 1987: Transferred to Panamanian flag. 1989: Ugland Offshore AS, appointed managers. 1999: Sold to Deepsea Ltd., (Coflexip Stena Offshore Ltd., managers). 2000: Sold to unspecified Cambodia flag operators and renamed SERVICE, registered at Phnom Pen. 14.2.2001: Demolition commenced.

8764418

OFF.46. STENA DON (2001 -)

20,064g. 6,019n. 3,700d. 95.5 x 69.0 x 21.5 metres.
Non-propelled drilling-Platform.
10.12.1999: Keel laid by Kvaerner Warnow-Werft, Warnemunde (Yard No.NB400), for Stena Don Ltd., Aberdeen. 20.1.2001: Launched. 30.10.2001: Completed.

STENA DON

(Courtesy Stena Ab)

STENA SPEY

(Courtesy Stena Ab)

OFF.47. STENA SPEY (2001 -) see OFF.31. above

STENA DEE

(Courtesy Stena Ab)

OFF.48. STENA DEE (2001 -) see OFF.11. above

8758847

OFF.49. STENA TAY (2001 -)

19,813g. 5,943n. Rectangular platform 76.5 x 63.5 x 33.83 transit, metres

Five Wartsila F212; seven Wartsila 16V25 and one Wartsila 12V25 type engines driving generators providing power and driving electric motors powering 8 azimuthing thruster units.

1981: Completed as SAFE GOTHIA by Gotaverken Arendal Ab, Gothenburg (Yard No. 921), as an accommodation rig for Consafe Offshore Ab., Sweden. Subsequently converted into a drilling rig by Keppel FELS Ltd., Singapore. 2001: Sold to Stena Tay Ltd., (Stena Drilling Ltd., operators), and renamed STENA TAY under the Bermudan flag.

STENA DRILLMAX - Artist Impression

(Courtesy Stena Ab)

9364942

OFF.50. STENA DRILLMAX 1 / STENA FORTH (2007 -)

228.0 x 42.0 x 8.5 metres

On order from Samsung Heavy Industries, Koje, for Stena Forth Ltd., (Stena Drilling Ltd), under the Bermudan flag.

9364954

OFF.51. STENA DRILLMAX 2 (2008 -)

228.0 x 42.0 x 8.5 metres

On order from Samsung Heavy Industries, Koje, for Stena Drilling Ltd.

"Minority- Part" Owned Offshore Vessels

8216019

OFF.C.1. PEERLESS STENA I (1995 - 2001) Chartered / managed.

2,248g. 629n. 1,751d. 76.38 x x 5.071 metres.

Two, 10-cyl. 4 S.C.S.A. (300 x 450mm) Wichmann 10AXAG type oil engines made by AS Wichmann, Rubbestadneset, geared to twin controllable pitch propellers. 6,200 BHP. 14.5 kts. Twin thwartship thrust controllable pitch propellers forward and aft.

Ice strengthened deck cargo / fire-fighting support vessel for offshore instalations.

4.6.1982: Keel laid as TENDER TARTAN by AS Tangen Verft Kragero, Kragero (Yard No. 209), for Harstad Maritime II KS AS., (Wilh. Wilhelmsen, managers), Norway. 12.2.1983: Launched. 7.5.1983: Completed. 1986: Transferred to Harstad Maritime II Ltd., (Harstad Maritime Services KS AS, managers), Bermuda, and renamed BRITISH PROVIDENCE. 1988: Sold to Peerless Drive Ltd., India, and renamed DRIVE OCEAN. 1995: Transferred to Peerless Shipping & Oilfield Services Ltd., India and renamed PEERLESS STENA I. 2001: Sold to South East Asia Marine Engineering & Construction Ltd., Mumbai, India, and renamed SEAMEC I.

8109292

OFF.C.2. PEERLESS STENA II (1995 - 2001) Chartered / managed.

3,966g. 1,108n. 2,067d. 92.82 x 18.45 x 5.201 metres.

Four 9-cyl. 4 S.C.S.A. (250 x 300mm) MAN 9L25/30 type oil engines made by Brons Industri N.V., Appingedam, 9,244 BHP, total, each driving an electric generator connected to two electric motors each of

2,555 SHP., and single reduction geared to screw shafts with directional propellers. 12 kts. Two Thwartship thrust controllable pitch propellers forward .
Fire-fighting, diving maintenance support ship with two moonpools.
30.6.1981: Keel laid as SHEARWATER TOPAZ by Scheepswerf "De Hoop" B.V., Lobith, (Yard No.298), for Marbucon BV, Rotterdam. 1.5.1982: Launched. 17.8.1982: Completed 1985: Sold to Essar Shipping Ltd., India, and renamed NAND REWANT. 1994: Sold to Peerless Shipping & Oilfield Ltd., India. 1995: Transferred to Peerless Shipping & Oilfield Services Ltd., India and renamed PEERLESS STENA II. 2001: Sold to South East Asia Marine Engineering & Construction Ltd., Mumbai, India, and renamed SEAMEC II.

8128339
OFF.C.3. PEERLESS STENA III (1995 - 2001) Chartered / managed.
3,963g. 1,112n. 2,067d. 92.70 x 21.00 x 5.215 metres.
Four 9-cyl. 4 S.C.S.A. (250 x 300mm) MAN 9L25/30 type oil engines made by Brons Industri N.V., Appingedam, 9,244 BHP, total, each driving an electric generator connected to two electric motors each of 2,555 SHP., and single reduction geared to screw shafts with directional propellers. 12 kts. Two Thwartship thrust controllable pitch propellers forward .
Fire-fighting, diving maintenance support ship with two moonpools.
26.2.1982: Keel laid as SHEARWATER SAPPHIRE by Scheepswerf "De Hoop" B.V., Lobith, (Yard No.297), for Shearwater Pacific Pty Ltd. & Shearwater Marine Group Ltd, (Atlas Offshore, managers), under Australian flag. 18.12.1982: Launched. 9.4.1983: Completed. 1985: Sold to Essar Shipping Ltd., India, and renamed NAND SHAMID. 1994: Sold to Peerless Shipping & Oilfield Ltd., India. 1995: Transferred to Peerless Shipping & Oilfield Services Ltd., India and renamed PEERLESS STENA II. 2001: Sold to South East Asia Marine Engineering & Construction Ltd., Mumbai, India, and renamed SEAMEC III.

Cancelled Offshore Vessels

Four offshore support vessels, contracted to Gotaverken, Arendal in 1977 were subsequently cancelled when the yard became financially insolvent. Although technical details are no longer available, we know that they were allocated the following yard numbers / names:

936 - STENA PROVIDER (PROPOSED)

937 - STENA PRODUCER (PROPOSED)

938 - STENA PROSPECTOR (PROPOSED)

939 - STENA PATROLLER (PROPOSED)

This cancelled quartet were replaced by the Stena Seaspread class, subsequently ordered from Oresundsvarvet.

Bibliography.

Lloyd's Register of Shipping – Registers all for relevant years.

Lloyd's Register of Shipping – Casualty Returns.

Lloyd's Register of Shipping – Wreck Books.

Lloyd's Register of Shipping – Shipbuilding records.

Lloyd's Confidential Indicies – for all relevant years.

Lloyd's Register of International Shipowning Groups – for all relevant years.

Stena Group – Annual Reports and other documents held within their archives.

Stena 1939 – 1989.

Stena Line 1962 - 1992.

Acknowledgements.

Special thanks go to Sten Allan Olsson, Dan Sten Olsson – Stena Ab. for Company support and after fifteen years, once again for the pleasure of working with Maud Weidemann - Stena Ab, for her drive and enthusiasm for the project, for the supply of photographs and digging up answers to numerous questions in our strive for fullness and accuracy of content.

Barbara Jones, Anne Cowne, Pete Brazier, Les Spurling and Dick Pryde, all current or former members of staff at Lloyds Register of Shipping, London.

Photographs.

These are of varying degrees of quality having been obtained by scanning prints, transparencies and documents or from a supply of electronic digital images.

All are credited to the known source near each image. Unfortunately not all the images within the selection have an identifiable source although the following people have over the years, supplied photographs, either prints or electronically, for the authors collection, many having been supplied for the original book produced by Stena – The Company archives, Lennard Ramsvik, Donald McFie, Sweden, Gerhard Fiebiger, Germany, Alan Geddes, J. K. Byass, William Darlow, Trevor Kidd, Aubrey Dale, John Hendy, Miles Cowsill and William Mayes, UK, and Hans Mornhout, Holland.

Modern media methods such as the internet have also provided a source of images. Where these have been used and the original photographer identified that name is credited in the caption. (e.g. Internet source / A. N. Other) However, that said, many downloaded images were credited to the collection of one person or other, therefore I have captioned them as (Internet source) rather than allocate originality to that person, but if that decision is wrong, then I can only apologise.

Index

BOLD uppercase are the names carried during Company involvement. Non-bold, lower-case are names carried prior or subsequent to Company involvement. Both are followed by the relevant page number (s).

Colour Photograph Selection

The original funnel markings on the left gave way to those below in 1963 and lasted until 1996 when changed to the current red, white and blue colour scheme, as shown on the front cover.

The size of the funnel on the **STENA SCANDINAVICA** is seen to good advantage in comparison to the crew member engaged on painting duties

POSEIDON was one of the pioneer passenger vessels.

(Courtesy Stena Ab)

STENA SCANDINAVICA was one of the Yugoslavian built sisters

(Internet source)

STENA DANICA wearing the original colours and "Living Kattegat" logo on the hull

(Hans Mornhout collection)

STENA CONGRESS was one of the group of tankers acquired from Universe Tankships

(Courtesy Stena Ab)

STENA WELLSERVICER (right) (World Ship Society Ltd)

and

STENA SEAWELL (below) (Courtesy Stena Ab) were Stena's second generation offshore support craft to support seabed operations and had the ultimate versatility of their time

STENA ADRIATICA was one of the first large tankers operated by Stena Bulk

(Courtesy Fotoflite)

STENA CONDUCTOR

(Internet source)

STENA COMPATRIOT

(Internet source / Marcel Lopes)

STENA CONTENDER

(Internet source / Philippe Holtof)

STENA CONQUEROR

(Courtesy Stena Ab)

STENA VISION is seen to good advantage clearly showing her twin rudders and propellers

(Courtesy Stena Ab)

Stena have developed tanker designs that maximise safety by providing vessels with double skin hulls, two engine rooms, propellers and rudders to optimise manoeuvrability. So far we have seen the V-max (above), the C-max, P-max, B-max types enter service with E-max planned.

STENA ALEXITA is one of the numerous Stena Ugland partnership, bow-loading shuttle tanker designed for loading at offshore wellheads.

(Courtesy Fotoflite)

STENA SIRITA is one of the numerous Stena Teekay partnership, bow-loading shuttle tanker designed for loading at offshore wellheads.
(Courtesy Fotoflite)

The vessels above typify the modern high class tankers being operated by Stena Bulk either owned within the Stena Group or on charter.

STENA BRITANNICA II

(Internet source / Rob De Visser

STENA CARRIER Is one unit of the Italian built 4-runner class that was to suffer long delays following the financial collapse of the shipyard.

(Internet source / Dirk Jankowsky)

ELK after widening

(Internet source)

SVEALAND, seen whilst on charter to Scandlines, has since been purchased

(Hans Mornhout collection)

STENA SEARIDER is the oldest member of the roro cargo fleet and still gives sterling service on the North Sea route and will be replaced in 2006.

(Internet source)

COTE DE AZUR

(Internet source / Andreas Worteler)

SEAFRANCE MANET clearly shows the similarity in the SeaFrance colour scheme to that of Stena Line.

(Internet source)

STENA INVICTA was one of the large ferries deployed to the Dover Straits upon acquisition of SEALINK British Ferries. There was a binding clause in the contract of sale that the colour scheme should be retained although STENA LINE was placed where BRITISH FERRIES had been on the hull.

(Hans Mornhout collection)

STENA HIBERNIA in the modified Stena Sealink hull colours

(Hans Mornhout collection).

STENA NAUTICA, a sister of STENA INVICTA is seen in the colour scheme introduced in 1996.

(Hans Mornhout collection)

STENA NAUTICA as **LION KING**

(Hans Mornhout collection)

ISLE OF INISHFREE

(Hans Mornhout collection

STENA JUTLANDICA III being taken seaward from her Dutch shipbuilder's yard. She has the white hull colours because although looking like a freight ferry she carries a large number of passengers.

(Hans Mornhout collection).

STENA CALEDONIA showing her stern as modified to comply with SOLAS rules, departs Belfast whilst **STENA VOYAGER** arrives.

(Both courtesy of Alan Geddes)

STENA TRANSPORTER was one of a number of former Stena vessels returned to the fold when P&O sold several of their routes to Stena.

(Hans Mornhout collection)

STENA NORDICA left became **LION KING** below

(Hans Mornhout collection)

FINNCLIPPER was one of three sisters that passed from Stena to Finnlines shortly after completion

(Hans Mornhout collection)

STENA CAMBRIA seen in two different liveries

(Author's collection)

CSO APACHE

KONONGEN BEATRIX when purchased and operating under the Crown Line route.

(Hans Mornhout collection)

STENA BALTICA formerly KONINGEN BEATRIX when trading in the Baltic.

(Hans Mornhout collection)

CROWN PRINCESS VICTORIA arriving in Canada

KONINGEN BEATRIX outward at Hoek van Holland passes the inward **STENA BRITANNICA**

(Courtesy Stena Ab)

JOLLY GIALLO

(Internet source)

CONSTELLATION ENTERPRISE

(Internet source)

The eleven units of Korean built class of the 1970's have given many operators valiant service and during their life have undergone many types of conversion. Two units in their original format are depicted on the previous page.

BALTIC FERRY seen in this shot had undergone the first phase of work wherein the superstructure was extended aft and another upper deck added

(Internet source)

BALTIC FERRY after phase two when additional passenger accommodation was added to the upper deck. This was subsequently removed by P&O.

(Internet source)

GRAIP was the ultimate conversion for the class. Stena organised and co-ordinated the conversion on behalf of Nordstrom & Thulin who purchased the end product.. (Internet source)